Lecture Notes in Computer Science 8762

Commenced Publication in 1973
Founding and Former Series Editors:
Gerhard Goos, Juris Hartmanis, and Jan van Leeuwen

Editorial Board

David Hutchison
   Lancaster University, UK
Takeo Kanade
   Carnegie Mellon University, Pittsburgh, PA, U.
Josef Kittler
   University of Surrey, Guildford, UK
Jon M. Kleinberg
   Cornell University, Ithaca, NY, USA
Alfred Kobsa
   University of California, Irvine, CA, USA
Friedemann Mattern
   ETH Zurich, Switzerland
John C. Mitchell
   Stanford University, CA, USA
Moni Naor
   Weizmann Institute of Science, Rehovot, Israel
Oscar Nierstrasz
   University of Bern, Switzerland
C. Pandu Rangan
   Indian Institute of Technology, Madras, India
Bernhard Steffen
   TU Dortmund University, Germany
Demetri Terzopoulos
   University of California, Los Angeles, CA, USA
Doug Tygar
   University of California, Berkeley, CA, USA
Gerhard Weikum
   Max Planck Institute for Informatics, Saarbruecken, Germany

T0236194

Joël Ouaknine   Igor Potapov
James Worrell (Eds.)

Reachability Problems

8th International Workshop, RP 2014
Oxford, UK, September 22-24, 2014
Proceedings

 Springer

Volume Editors

Joël Ouaknine
University of Oxford
Department of Computer Science
Oxford, UK
E-mail: joel@cs.ox.ac.uk

Igor Potapov
University of Liverpool
Department of Computer Science
Liverpool, UK
E-mail: potapov@liverpool.ac.uk

James Worrell
University of Oxford
Department of Computer Science
Oxford, UK
E-mail: jbw@cs.ox.ac.uk

ISSN 0302-9743   e-ISSN 1611-3349
ISBN 978-3-319-11438-5   e-ISBN 978-3-319-11439-2
DOI 10.1007/978-3-319-11439-2
Springer Cham Heidelberg New York Dordrecht London

Library of Congress Control Number: 2014948071

LNCS Sublibrary: SL 1 – Theoretical Computer Science and General Issues

© Springer International Publishing Switzerland 2014
This work is subject to copyright. All rights are reserved by the Publisher, whether the whole or part of
the material is concerned, specifically the rights of translation, reprinting, reuse of illustrations, recitation,
broadcasting, reproduction on microfilms or in any other physical way, and transmission or information
storage and retrieval, electronic adaptation, computer software, or by similar or dissimilar methodology
now known or hereafter developed. Exempted from this legal reservation are brief excerpts in connection
with reviews or scholarly analysis or material supplied specifically for the purpose of being entered and
executed on a computer system, for exclusive use by the purchaser of the work. Duplication of this publication
or parts thereof is permitted only under the provisions of the Copyright Law of the Publisher's location,
in ist current version, and permission for use must always be obtained from Springer. Permissions for use
may be obtained through RightsLink at the Copyright Clearance Center. Violations are liable to prosecution
under the respective Copyright Law.
The use of general descriptive names, registered names, trademarks, service marks, etc. in this publication
does not imply, even in the absence of a specific statement, that such names are exempt from the relevant
protective laws and regulations and therefore free for general use.
While the advice and information in this book are believed to be true and accurate at the date of publication,
neither the authors nor the editors nor the publisher can accept any legal responsibility for any errors or
omissions that may be made. The publisher makes no warranty, express or implied, with respect to the
material contained herein.

Typesetting: Camera-ready by author, data conversion by Scientific Publishing Services, Chennai, India

Printed on acid-free paper

Springer is part of Springer Science+Business Media (www.springer.com)

Preface

This volume contains the papers presented at the 8th International Workshop on Reachability Problems (RP 2014) held during September 22–24, 2014, at the Department of Computer Science, University of Oxford, UK.

RP 2014 was the eighth in the series of workshops, following successful meetings at the Uppsala University, Sweden, in 2013, University of Bordeaux, France, in 2012, the University of Genoa, Italy, in 2011, Masaryk University of Brno, Czech Republic, in 2010, Ecole Polytechnique, France, in 2009, at the University of Liverpool, UK, in 2008, and at Turku University, Finland, in 2007.

The aim of the workshop is to bring together scholars from diverse fields with a shared interested in reachability problems. Reachability is a fundamental computational problem that appears in many different contexts: concurrent systems, computational models such as cellular automata and Petri nets, decision procedures for logical theories, program analysis, discrete and continuous systems, time-critical systems, hybrid systems, rewriting systems, algebraic structures (groups, semigroups and rings), deterministic or non-deterministic iterative maps, probabilistic and parametric systems, and open systems modelled as games.

Typically, for a fixed system description given in some form (rewriting rules, transformations by computable functions, systems of equations, logical formulas, etc.) a reachability problem consists in checking whether a given set of target states can be reached starting from a fixed set of initial states. The set of target states can be represented explicitly or via some implicit representation (e.g., a system of equations, a set of minimal elements with respect to some ordering on the states). Sophisticated quantitative and qualitative properties can often be reduced to basic reachability questions. Decidability and complexity boundaries, algorithmic solutions, and efficient heuristics are all important aspects to be considered in this context. Algorithmic solutions are often based on different combinations of exploration strategies, symbolic manipulations of sets of states, decomposition properties, reduction to optimisation problems and logical decision procedures. Such algorithms also benefit from approximations, abstractions, accelerations, and extrapolation heuristics. Ad hoc solutions as well as solutions based on general-purpose constraint solvers and deduction engines are often combined in order to balance efficiency and flexibility.

The purpose of the conference is to promote the exploration of new approaches for the modelling and analysis of computational processes by combining mathematical, algorithmic, and computational techniques. Topics of interest include (but are not limited to): reachability for infinite state systems; rewriting systems; reachability analysis in counter/timed/cellular/communicating automata; Petri- nets; computational aspects of semigroups, groups, and rings; reachability in dynamical and hybrid systems; frontiers between decidable and undecidable reachability problems; complexity and decidability aspects; predictability in iterative maps and new computational paradigms. All these aspects were discussed in the presentations of the eighth edition of the RP workshop. The proceedings of the previous editions of the workshop appeared in the following volumes:

Mika Hirvensalo, Vesa Halava, Igor Potapov, Jarkko Kari (Eds.): Proceedings of the Satellite Workshops of DLT 2007. TUCS General Publication No 45, June 2007. ISBN: 978-952-12-1921-4.

Vesa Halava and Igor Potapov (Eds.): Proceedings of the Second Workshop on Reachability Problems in Computational Models (RP 2008). Electronic Notes in Theoretical Computer Science. Volume 223, Pages 1-264 (26 December 2008).

Olivier Bournez and Igor Potapov (Eds.): Reachability Problems, Third International Workshop, RP 2009, Palaiseau, France, September 23–25, 2009, Lecture Notes in Computer Science, 5797, Springer 2009.

Antonin Kucera and Igor Potapov (Eds.): Reachability Problems, 4th International Workshop, RP 2010, Brno, Czech Republic, August 28–29, 2010, Lecture Notes in Computer Science, 6227, Springer 2010.

Giorgio Delzanno, Igor Potapov (Eds.): Reachability Problems, 5th International Workshop, RP 2011, Genoa, Italy, September 28–30, 2011, Lecture Notes in Computer Science, 6945, Springer 2011.

Alain Finkel, Jerome Leroux, Igor Potapov (Eds.): Reachability Problems, 6th International Workshop, RP 2012, Bordeaux, France, September 17-19, 2012. Lecture Notes in Computer Science 7550, Springer 2012.

Parosh Aziz Abdulla, Igor Potapov (Eds.): Reachability Problems, 7th International Workshop, RP 2013, Uppsala, Sweden, September 24-26, 2013. Lecture Notes in Computer Science 8169, Springer 2013.

The four keynote speakers at the 2014 conference were:

- **Byron Cook**, UCL and Microsoft Research, UK.
- **Kousha Etessami**, University of Edinburgh, UK.
- **Anca Muscholl**, LaBRI, University of Bordeaux, France.
- **Sylvain Schmitz**, LSV and ENS-Cachan, France.

There were 25 submissions. Each submission was reviewed by at least three Program Committee members. The full list of the members of the Program Committee and the list of external reviewers can be found on the next two pages. The Program Committee is grateful for the highly appreciated and high-quality work produced by these external reviewers. Based on these reviews, the Program

Committee decided to accept 17 papers, in addition to the four invited talks. The workshop also provided the opportunity to researchers to give informal presentations that are prepared very shortly before the event and inform the participants about current research and work in progress.

We gratefully acknowledge the organization team for their help. In particular we wish to thank Andrea Pilot, Renate Henison, Jordan Summers-Young and Elizabeth Walsh.

It is also a great pleasure to acknowledge the team of the EasyChair system, and the fine cooperation with the Lecture Notes in Computer Science team of Springer, which made the production of this volume possible in time for the conference. Finally, we thank all the authors for their high-quality contributions, and the participants for making this edition of RP 2014 a success.

September 2014   Joël Ouaknine
                                                           Igor Potapov
                                                           James Worrell

Organization

Program Committee

Marius Bozga	Verimag/CNRS, France
Thomas Brihaye	University of Mons, Belgium
Véronique Bruyère	University of Mons, Belgium
Laurent Doyen	LSV, ENS Cachan and CNRS, France
John Fearnley	University of Liverpool, UK
Gilles Geeraerts	Université Libre de Bruxelles, Belgium
Kim Guldstrand Larsen	Aalborg University, Denmark
Stefan Göller	University of Bremen, Germany
Martin Lange	University of Kassel, Germany
Ranko Lazic	University of Warwick, UK
Rupak Majumdar	MPI-SWS, Germany
Nicolas Markey	LSV, CNRS and ENS Cachan, France
Madhavan Mukund	Chennai Mathematical Institute, India
Andrzej Murawski	University of Warwick, UK
Joel Ouaknine	Oxford University, UK
Paritosh Pandya	TIFR, India
Igor Potapov	The University of Liverpool, UK
Alexander Rabinovich	Tel Aviv University, Israel
Tayssir Touili	LIAFA, CNRS and University Paris Diderot, France
Thomas Wahl	Northeastern University, USA
James Worrell	Oxford University, UK
Lijun Zhang	DTU, Denmark

Additional Reviewers

André, Étienne	Fribourg, Laurent
Bertrand, Nathalie	Hofman, Piotr
Blondin, Michael	Praveen, M.
Boigelot, Bernard	Reichert, Julien
Bonnet, Remi	Rezine, Ahmed
Chistikov, Dmitry	Song, Lei
Devillers, Raymond	Steffen, Martin
Donze, Alexandre	Turrini, Andrea
Forejt, Vojtech	Velner, Yaron

Abstracts of Invited Talks

Algorithms for
Branching Markov Decision Processes

Kousha Etessami

School of Informatics
University of Edinburgh
kousha@inf.ed.ac.uk

Multi-type branching processes (BPs) are classic stochastic processes with applications in many areas, including biology and physics. A BP models the stochastic evolution of a population of entities of distinct types. In each generation, every entity of each type, t, produces a set of entities of various types in the next generation according to a given probability distribution on offsprings for the type t. In a *Branching Markov Decision Process* (BMDP), there is also a controller who can take actions that affect the probability distribution of the offsprings for each entity of each type. For both BPs and BMDPs, the state space consists of all possible populations, given by the number of entities of each type, so there are infinitely many states.

In recent years there has been a body of research aimed at studying the computational complexity of key analysis problems associated with MDP extensions (and, more generally *stochastic game* extensions) of important classes of finitely-presented but (countably) infinite-state stochastic processes, including BMDPs, and closely related models, such as stochastic context-free grammars extended with a controller. A central analysis problem for all of these models, which forms the key to a number of other analyses, is the problem of computing their optimal termination (extinction) probability. In the setting of BMDPs, these are the maximum (minimum) probabilities, over all control strategies (or policies), starting from a single entity of a given type, that the process will eventually reach extinction (i.e., the state where no entities have survived). From these quantities, one can compute the optimum probability for any initial population, as well as other quantities of interest.

One can write Bellman optimality equations for the optimal extinction probabilities of BMDPs, and for a number of related important infinite-state MDP models. These Bellman equations are multivariate systems of monotone probabilistic max (or min) *polynomial* equations, which we call max/minPPSs. They have the form $x_i = P_i(x_1, \ldots, x_n)$, $i = 1, \ldots, n$, where each $P_i(x) \equiv \max_j q_{i,j}(x)$ (respectively $P_i(x) \equiv \min_j q_{i,j}(x)$) is the max (min) over a finite number of probabilistic polynomials, $q_{i,j}(x)$. A *probabilistic polynomial*, $q(x)$, is a multi-variate polynomial where the monomial coefficients and constant term of $q(x)$ are all non-negative and sum to ≤ 1. The *least fixed point* (LFP) solution of such Bellman equations, corresponding to a given BMDP, captures its vector of optimal extinction probabilities, starting with one object of each type.

This talk will survey algorithms for, and discuss the complexity of, some key analysis problems for BMDPs. In particular, I will discuss recent joint work with

Alistair Stewart and Mihalis Yannakakis ([2, 1]), which forms part of Alistair Stewart's Ph.D. thesis, in which we have obtained polynomial time algorithms for computing, to within arbitrary desired precision, the (optimal) extinction probability values for BPs and BMDPs, by computing the LFP solution of the corresponding max/min polynomial Bellman equations. Our algorithms combine generalizations of Newton's method with other techniques, including linear programming.

References

1. Etessami, K., Stewart, A., Yannakakis, M.: Polynomial time algorithms for branching Markov decision processes and probabilistic Min(Max) polynomial Bellman equations. In: Czumaj, A., Mehlhorn, K., Pitts, A., Wattenhofer, R. (eds.) ICALP 2012, Part I. LNCS, vol. 7391, pp. 314–326. Springer, Heidelberg (2012)
2. Etessami, K., Stewart, A., Yannakakis, M.: Polynomial-time algorithms for multitype branching processes and stochastic context-free grammars. In: Proc. 44th ACM Symposium on Theory of Computing (STOC), pp. 579–588 (2012), Full version available at ArXiv:1201.2374

Walking with Data - Where Does it Stop?

Anca Muscholl

LaBRI, University of Bordeaux, France

Data formalisms apply to numerous settings where the reasoning involves explicit comparisons of object identities. Such formalisms are usually based on automata or logics that have the ability to compare data from an unbounded domain. In the realm of databases, data may take the meaning of attribute values. In program verification, data may represent identities of processes, communication channels, pointers or any other resource that can be of interest in the analysis of programs with dynamic objects.

This talk will survey several models of logics and automata with data and analyse their limits in decidability regarding fundamental questions such as non-emptiness (satisfiability) and inclusion (containment). We will focuss on recently considered data formalisms such as data-walking automata and Datalog, that are promising models regarding the above problems.

References

1. Abiteboul, S., Bourhis, P., Muscholl, A., Wu, Z.: Recursive queries on trees and data trees. In: Proc. of ICDT 2013, pp. 93–104. ACM (2013)
2. Alur, R., Cerný, P., Weinstein, S.: Algorithmic analysis of array-accessing programs. ACM Trans. Comput. Log. 13(3), 27 (2012)
3. Björklund, H., Schwentick, T.: On notions of regularity for data languages. Theor. Comput. Sci. 411(4-5), 702–715 (2010)
4. Bojańczyk, M., David, C., Muscholl, A., Schwentick, T., Segoufin, L.: Two-variable logic on data words. ACM Trans. Comput. Log. 12(4), 27 (2011)
5. Bojańczyk, M., Lasota, S.: An extension of data automata that captures XPath. Logical Methods in Computer Science 8(1) (2012)
6. Bojańczyk, M., Muscholl, A., Schwentick, T., Segoufin, L.: Two-variable logic on data trees and XML reasoning. J. ACM 56(3) (2009)
7. David, C., Gheerbrant, A., Libkin, L., Martens, W.: Containment of pattern-based queries over data trees. In: Proc. of ICDT 2013, pp. 210–212. ACM (2013)
8. Figueira, D.: Alternating register automata on finite words and trees. Logical Methods in Computer Science 8(1) (2012)
9. Figueira, D., Segoufin, L.: Bottom-up automata on data trees and vertical XPath. In: Proc. of STACS 2011. LIPIcs, pp. 93–104. Schloss Dagstuhl - Leibniz-Zentrum fuer Informatik (2011)
10. Grumberg, O., Kupferman, O., Sheinvald, S.: An automata-theoretic approach to reasoning about parameterized systems and specifications. In: Van Hung, D., Ogawa, M. (eds.) ATVA 2013. LNCS, vol. 8172, pp. 397–411. Springer, Heidelberg (2013)
11. Kaminski, M., Francez, N.: Finite memory automata. Theor. Comput. Sci. 134(2), 329–363 (1994)

12. Kara, A., Schwentick, T., Tan, T.: Feasible automata for two-variable logic with successor on data words. In: Dediu, A.-H., Martín-Vide, C. (eds.) LATA 2012. LNCS, vol. 7183, pp. 351–362. Springer, Heidelberg (2012)
13. Manuel, A., Muscholl, A., Puppis, G.: Walking on data words. In: Bulatov, A.A., Shur, A.M. (eds.) CSR 2013. LNCS, vol. 7913, pp. 64–75. Springer, Heidelberg (2013)
14. Neven, F., Schwentick, T., Vianu, V.: Finite state machines for strings over infinite alphabets. ACM Trans. Comput. Log. 15(3), 403–435 (2004)
15. Segoufin, L.: Automata and logics for words and trees over an infinite alphabet. In: Ésik, Z. (ed.) CSL 2006. LNCS, vol. 4207, pp. 41–57. Springer, Heidelberg (2006)
16. Tan, T.: Extending two-variable logic on data trees with order on data values and its automata. ACM Trans. Comput. Log. 15(1), 39 (2014)
17. Tzevelekos, N.: Fresh-register automata. In: Proc. of ACM SIGPLAN-SIGACT Symp. on Principles of Programming Languages (POPL), pp. 295–306 (2011)

Complexity Bounds for Ordinal-Based Termination*

Sylvain Schmitz

LSV, ENS Cachan & CNRS & INRIA, France

Abstract. 'What more than its truth do we know if we have a proof of a theorem in a given formal system?' We examine Kreisel's question in the particular context of program termination proofs, with an eye to deriving complexity bounds on program running times.

Our main tool for this are *length function theorems*, which provide complexity bounds on the use of well quasi orders. We illustrate how to prove such theorems in the simple yet until now untreated case of ordinals. We show how to apply this new theorem to derive complexity bounds on programs when they are proven to terminate thanks to a ranking function into some ordinal.

---

* Work funded in part by the ANR grant 11-BS02-001-01 REACHARD.

On the Subtle Interaction Between Reachability and Liveness

Byron Cook

Microsoft Research, Cambridge, UK

Abstract. One of the key difficulties of proving program termination and liveness of systems is managing the subtle interplay between the finding of a termination argument and the finding of the arguments supporting invariant. In this talk I will discuss some mechanisms that we have used to facilitate better cooperation between these two types of reasoning in tools, both for software as well as biological models.

Table of Contents

Complexity Bounds
for Ordinal-Based Termination*
(Invited Talk)

Sylvain Schmitz

LSV, ENS Cachan & CNRS & INRIA, France

Abstract. 'What more than its truth do we know if we have a proof of a theorem in a given formal system?' We examine Kreisel's question in the particular context of program termination proofs, with an eye to deriving complexity bounds on program running times.

Our main tool for this are *length function theorems*, which provide complexity bounds on the use of well quasi orders. We illustrate how to prove such theorems in the simple yet until now untreated case of ordinals. We show how to apply this new theorem to derive complexity bounds on programs when they are proven to terminate thanks to a ranking function into some ordinal.

1998 ACM Subject Classification. F.2.0 Analysis of Algorithms and Problem Complexity; F.3.1 Logics and Meanings of Programs

Keywords: Fast-growing complexity, length function theorem, Ramsey-based termination, ranking function, well quasi order.

1 Introduction

Whenever we prove the termination of a program, we might also expect to gain some information on its complexity. The jump from termination to complexity analysis is however often involved. The question has already been studied for many termination techniques, e.g. termination orderings [21, 38, 39, 9, 25], polynomial interpretations [7], dependency pairs [20], size-change abstractions [5, 13], abstract interpretation [19], or ranking functions [2] to cite a few.

The purpose of this paper is to present the complexity bounds one can similarly derive from termination proofs relying on *well quasi orders* (wqo). There are already some accessible introductions to the subject [33, 34], with applications to algorithms for so-called 'well-structured systems.' Our emphasis here is however on the particular case of *well orders*, i.e. of ranking functions into ordinal numbers. Although this is arguably the oldest and best-understood termination proof technique, which can be tracked back for instance to works by Turing [36] or Floyd [18], deriving complexity bounds for well orders has only been considered in restricted cases in the wqo literature [1]. As we shall see, by

---

* Work funded in part by the ANR grant 11-BS02-001-01 ReacHard.

© Springer International Publishing Switzerland 2014

revisiting ideas by Buchholz, Cichoń, and Weiermann [10, 8] and the framework of [32], the case of well orders turns out to be fairly simple, and provides an introduction to the definitions and techniques employed for more complex wqos.

Contents. After setting the stage in Sec. 2 by recalling the definitions of well quasi orders, ranking functions, and order types, we work out the details of the proof of a *length function theorem* for ordinals below ε_0 in Sec. 3. Such combinatorial statements provide bounds on the length of so-called *bad sequences* of elements taken from a wqo—i.e. of descending sequences in the case of a well-order—, and thus on the running time of programs proved to terminate using the same wqos.

More precisely, we first recall in Sec. 3.1 the main notions employed in the proofs of such theorems in [32, 33], and apply them to the ordinal case in Sec. 3.3. This yields a new length function theorem, this time for ordinals (Thm. 3.3). As far as we know, this is an original contribution, which relies on ideas developed by Cichoń and others in the 1990's [10, 8] on the use of ordinal norms for substructural hierarchies (recalled in Sec. 3.2). Unlike the length function theorems for other wqos found in the literature [28, 12, 38, 11, 17, 32, 33, 1], Thm. 3.3 does not just provide an upper bound on the maximal length of bad sequences, but offers instead an *exact* explicit formulation for such lengths using Cichoń's hierarchy of functions.

Those bounds are often more precise than actually needed, and we show in Sec. 4 how to classify them into suitable *fast-growing* complexity classes [31]. We also zoom in on the bounds for lexicographic ranking functions in Sec. 5, and relate them to the bounds obtained in [17] for the Ramsey-based termination technique of Podelski and Rybalchenko [30].

2   Well Quasi Orders and Termination

In terms of operational semantics, a termination proof establishes that the relation between successive program configurations is well founded. Rather than proving well foundedness from first principles, it is much easier to rely on existing well founded relations, whether we are attempting to prove termination with pen and paper or using an automatic tool. Well quasi orders and well orders are in this regard very well studied and well behaved classes of well founded relations.

2.1   Well Quasi Orders

A *quasi order* (qo) $\langle A, \leq \rangle$ consists of a support set A along with a transitive reflexive relation $\leq \subseteq A \times A$. We call a finite or infinite sequence $x_0, x_1, x_2, \ldots$ over A *good* if there exist two indices $i < j$ such that $x_i \leq x_j$, and *bad* otherwise.

Definition 2.1. *A* well quasi order *(wqo) is a qo* $\langle A, \leq \rangle$ *such that any infinite sequence* $x_0, x_1, x_2, \ldots$ *of elements over A is good. Equivalently, any bad sequence over A is finite.*

There are many equivalent definitions for wqos [see e.g. 33, Chap. 1]. Notably, $\langle A, \leq \rangle$ is a wqo if and only if

1. $\leq$ is *well-founded*, i.e. there does not exist any infinite decreasing sequence $x_0 > x_1 > x_2 > \cdots$ of elements in A, where $< \overset{\text{def}}{=} \leq \setminus \geq$, and
2. there are *no infinite antichains* over A, i.e. infinite sets of mutually incomparable elements for $\leq$.

Well (Partial) Orders. A wqo where $\leq$ is antisymmetric is called a *well partial order* (wpo). Note that quotienting a wqo by the equivalence $\equiv \overset{\text{def}}{=} \leq \cap \geq$, i.e. equating elements x and y whenever $x \leq y$ and $y \leq x$, yields a wpo.

A wpo $\langle A, \leq \rangle$ where $\leq$ is linear (aka total), is a *well order* (wo). Because a wo has antichains of cardinal at most 1, this coincides with the usual definition as a well-founded linear order. Finally, any *linearisation* of a wpo $\langle A, \leq \rangle$, i.e. any linear order $\preceq \supseteq \leq$ defines a wo $\langle A, \preceq \rangle$. One can think of the linearisation process as one of 'orienting' pairs of incomparable elements; such a linearisation always exists thanks to the order-extension principle.

Examples. For a basic example, consider any finite set Q along with the equality relation, which is a wqo $\langle Q, = \rangle$ (even a wpo) by the pigeonhole principle. As explained above, any wo is a wqo, which provides us with another basic example: the set of natural numbers along with its natural ordering $\langle \mathbb{N}, \leq \rangle$.

Many more examples can be constructed using algebraic operations: for instance, if $\langle A, \leq_A \rangle$ and $\langle B, \leq_B \rangle$ are wqos (resp. wpos), then so is their *Cartesian product* $\langle A \times B, \leq_\times \rangle$, where $(x, y) \leq_\times (x', y')$ if and only if $x \leq_A x'$ and $y \leq_B y'$ is the *product ordering*; in the case of $\langle \mathbb{N}^d, \leq_\times \rangle$ this result is also known as Dickson's Lemma. Some further popular examples of operations that preserve wqos include the set of finite sequences over A with subword embedding $\langle A^*, \leq_* \rangle$ (a result better known as Higman's Lemma), finite trees labelled by A with the homeomorphic embedding $\langle T(A), \leq_T \rangle$ (aka Kruskal's Tree Theorem), and finite graphs labelled by A with the minor ordering $\langle G(A), \leq_{\text{minor}} \rangle$ (aka Robertson and Seymour's Graph Minor Theorem).

Turning to well orders, an operation that preserves wos is the *lexicographic product* $\langle A \times B, \leq_{\text{lex}} \rangle$ where $(x, y) \leq_{\text{lex}} (x', y')$ if and only if $x <_A x'$, or $x = x'$ and $y \leq_B y'$. This is typically employed in d-tuples of natural numbers ordered lexicographically $\langle \mathbb{N}^d, \leq_{\text{lex}} \rangle$: observe that this is a linearisation of $\langle \mathbb{N}^d, \leq_\times \rangle$. Another classical well order employed in termination proofs is the *multiset* order $\langle \mathbb{M}(A), \leq_{\text{mset}} \rangle$ of Dershowitz and Manna [15]. There, $\mathbb{M}(A)$ denotes the set of finite multisets over the wo $\langle A, \leq \rangle$, i.e. of functions $m \colon A \to \mathbb{N}$ with finitely many x in A such that $m(x) > 0$, and $m \leq_{\text{mset}} m'$ if and only if for all x in A, if $m(x) > m'(x)$, then there exists $y >_A x$ such that $m(y) < m'(y)$ [see also 23].

2.2   Termination

We illustrate the main ideas in this paper using a very simple program, given in pseudo-code in Fig. 1a. Formally, we see the operational semantics of a program

$\ell_0:$ **while** x >= 0 **and** y > 0 **do**
   if x > 0 **then**
     $a:$ x := x−1; n := 2n;
   else
     $b:$ x := n; y := y−1; n := 2n;
done

$a:$
assume(x>0);
assume(y>0);
x := x−1;
n := 2n;

$b:$
assume(x=0);
assume(y>0);
x := n;
y := y−1;
n := 2n;

ℓ_0

(a) A program over integer variables   **(b)** The associated control-flow graph

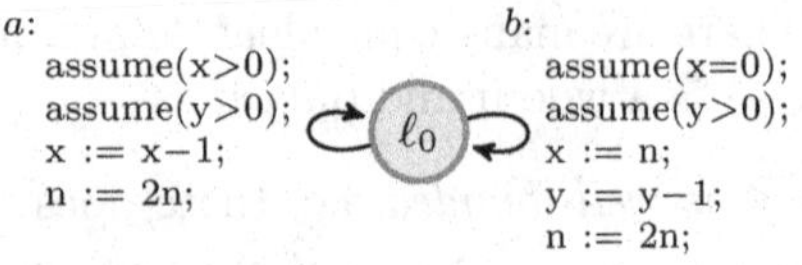

Fig. 1. A simple terminating program

as the one in Fig. 1a as a transition system $\mathcal{S} = \langle \mathit{Conf}, \to_\mathcal{S} \rangle$ where Conf denotes the set of program configurations and $\to_\mathcal{S} \subseteq \mathit{Conf} \times \mathit{Conf}$ a transition relation. In such a simple non-recursive program, the set of configurations is a variable valuation, including a program counter **pc** ranging over the finite set of program locations. For our simple program a single location suffices and we set

$$\mathit{Conf} = \{\ell_0\} \times \mathbb{Z} \times \mathbb{Z} \times \mathbb{Z} , \tag{1}$$

where the last three components provide the values of x, y, and n, and the first component the value of **pc**. The corresponding transition relation contains for instance

$$(\ell_0, 3, 1, 4) \to_\mathcal{S} (\ell_0, 2, 1, 8) \tag{2}$$

using transition a in Fig. 1b.

Proving Termination. We say that a transition system $\mathcal{S} = \langle \mathit{Conf}, \to_\mathcal{S} \rangle$ *terminates* if every execution $c_0 \to_\mathcal{S} c_1 \to_\mathcal{S} \cdots$ is finite. For instance, in order to prove the termination of the program of Fig. 1 by a wqo argument, consider some (possibly infinite) execution

$$(\ell_0, x_0, y_0, n_0) \to_\mathcal{S} (\ell_0, x_1, y_1, n_1) \to_\mathcal{S} (\ell_0, x_2, y_2, n_2) \to_\mathcal{S} \cdots \tag{3}$$

over Conf. Because a negative value for x or y would lead to immediate termination, the associated sequence of pairs

$$(x_0, y_0), (x_1, y_1), (x_2, y_2), \ldots \tag{4}$$

is actually over $\mathbb{N}^2$. Consider now two indices $i < j$:

- either b is never fired throughout the execution between steps i and j, and then $y_i = \cdots = y_j$ and $x_i > x_j$,
- or b is fired at least once, and $y_i > y_j$.

In both cases $(x_i, y_i) \not\leq_\times (x_j, y_j)$, i.e. the sequence (4) is bad for the product ordering. Since $\langle \mathbb{N}^2, \leq_\times \rangle$ is a wqo, this sequence is necessarily finite, and so is the original sequence (3): the program of Fig. 1 terminates on all inputs.

Quasi-Ranking Functions. The above termination argument for our example program easily generalises:

Definition 2.2. *Given a transition system* $\mathcal{S} = \langle Conf, \rightarrow_{\mathcal{S}} \rangle$, *a quasi-ranking function is a map* $f: Conf \rightarrow A$ *into a wqo* $\langle A, \leq \rangle$ *such that, whenever* $c \rightarrow_{\mathcal{S}}^+ c'$ *is a non-empty sequence of transitions of* $\mathcal{S}$, $f(c) \nleq f(c')$.

In our treatment of the program of Fig. 1 above, we picked $f(\ell_0, x, y, z) = (x, y)$ and $\langle A, \leq \rangle = \langle \mathbb{N}^2, \leq_\times \rangle$. The existence of a quasi-ranking function always yields termination:

Proposition 2.3. *Given a transition system* $\mathcal{S} = \langle Conf, \rightarrow_{\mathcal{S}} \rangle$, *if there exists a quasi-ranking function for* $\mathcal{S}$, *then* $\mathcal{S}$ *terminates.*

Proof. Let f be a quasi-ranking function of $\mathcal{S}$ into a wqo $\langle A, \leq \rangle$. Any sequence of configurations $c_0 \rightarrow_{\mathcal{S}} c_1 \rightarrow_{\mathcal{S}} \cdots$ of $\mathcal{S}$ is associated by f to a bad sequence $f(c_0), f(c_1), \ldots$ over A and is therefore finite. □

Note that the converse statement also holds; see Remark 2.4 below.

Ranking Functions. The most typical method in order to prove that a program terminates for all inputs is to exhibit a *ranking function* f into some well-order, such that $\rightarrow_{\mathcal{S}}$-related configurations have decreasing rank [36, 18]. Note that this is a particular instance of quasi-ranking functions: a ranking function can be seen as a quasi-ranking function into a wo $\langle A, \leq \rangle$. Indeed, if $c \rightarrow_{\mathcal{S}} c'$, then the condition $f(c) \nleq f(c')$ of Def. 2.2 over a wo is equivalent to requiring $f(c) > f(c')$, and then implies by transitivity $f(c) > f(c')$ whenever $c \rightarrow_{\mathcal{S}}^+ c'$.

The program of Fig. 1 can easily be given a ranking function: define for this $f(\ell_0, x, y, n) = (y, x)$ ranging over the wo $\langle \mathbb{N}^2, \leq_{\text{lex}} \rangle$. Cook, See, and Zuleger [14] and Ben-Amram and Genaim [4] consider for instance the automatic synthesis of such lexicographic linear ranking functions for integer loops like Fig. 1a. Such ranking functions into $\langle \mathbb{N}^d, \leq_{\text{lex}} \rangle$ are described there by d functions $f_1, f_2, \ldots, f_d$: $Conf \rightarrow \mathbb{N}$ such that, whenever $c \rightarrow_{\mathcal{S}} c'$, then $(f_1(c), f_2(c), \ldots, f_d(c)) >_{\text{lex}} (f_1(c'), f_2(c'), \ldots, f_d(c'))$; in our example $f_1(c) = y$ and $f_2(c) = x$. Linearity means that each function f_i is a linear affine function of the values of the program variables.

Remark 2.4. Observe that any *deterministic* terminating program can be associated to a (quasi-)ranking function into $\mathbb{N}$, which maps each configuration to the number of steps before termination. We leave it as an exercise to the reader to figure out such a ranking function for Fig. 1—the answer can be found in Sec. 3. There are at least two motivations for considering other wqos:

- Programs can be nondeterministic, for instance due to interactions with an environment. Then the supremum of the number of steps along all the possible paths can be used as the range for a ranking function; this is a countable well-order.

– Whether by automated means or by manual means, such monolithic ranking functions are often too hard to synthesise and to check once found or guessed—note that the canonical 'number of steps' function is not recursive in general. This motivates employing more complex well (quasi-)orders in exchange for simpler ranking functions.

2.3 Ordinals

Write $\langle [d], \leq \rangle$ for the initial segment of the naturals $[d] = \{0, \ldots, d-1\}$; this is a finite linear order for each d. We can then replace our previous lexicographic ranking function for Fig. 1 with a multiset ranking function into $\langle \mathbb{M}([2]), \leq_{\text{mset}} \rangle$: $f(\ell_0, x, y, m) = \{1^y, 0^x\}$ is a ranking function that associates a multiset containing y copies of the element '1' and x copies of '0' to the configuration (ℓ_0, x, y, n).

This might seem like a rather artificial example of a multiset ranking function, and indeed more generally $\langle \mathbb{N}^d, \leq_{\text{lex}} \rangle$ and $\langle \mathbb{M}([d]), \leq_{\text{mset}} \rangle$ are *order-isomorphic* for every dimension d: indeed, $r(n_1, \ldots, n_d) = \{(d-1)^{n_1}, \ldots, 0^{n_d}\}$ is a bijection satisfying $(n_1, \ldots, n_d) \leq_{\text{lex}} (n'_1, \ldots, n'_d)$ if and only if $r(n_1, \ldots, n_d) \leq_{\text{mset}} r(n'_1, \ldots, n'_d)$.

In order to pick a unique representative for each isomorphism class of (simple enough) well orders, we are going to employ their *order types*, presented as *ordinal terms* in Cantor normal form. For instance ω^d is the order type of both $\langle \mathbb{N}^d, \leq_{\text{lex}} \rangle$ and $\langle \mathbb{M}([d]), \leq_{\text{mset}} \rangle$.

Ordinals in ε_0 can be canonically represented as *ordinal terms* α in Cantor normal form

$$\alpha = \omega^{\alpha_1} + \cdots + \omega^{\alpha_p} \tag{CNF}$$

with *exponents* $\alpha > \alpha_1 \geq \cdots \geq \alpha_p$. We write as usual 1 for the term ω^0 and ω for the term ω^1. Grouping equal exponents yields the strict form

$$\alpha = \omega^{\alpha_1} \cdot c_1 + \cdots + \omega^{\alpha_p} \cdot c_p$$

with $\alpha > \alpha_1 > \cdots > \alpha_p$ and *coefficients* $0 < c_1, \ldots, c_p < \omega$. The ordinal ε_0, i.e. the least solution of $\omega^x = x$, is the supremum of the ordinals presentable in this manner.

Computing Order Types. The order types $o(A, \leq_A)$ of the well orders $\langle A, \leq_A \rangle$ we already mentioned in this paper are well-known: $o([d], \leq) = d$, $o(\mathbb{N}, \leq) = \omega$, $o(A \times B, \leq_{\text{lex}}) = o(A, \leq_A) \cdot o(B, \leq_B)$, and $o(\mathbb{M}(A), \leq_{\text{mset}}) = \omega^{o(A, \leq_A)}$. The ranking function for the program in Fig. 1 can now be written as $f(\ell_0, x, y, n) = \omega \cdot y + x$ and ranges over the set of ordinal terms below ω^2. Note that we will identify the latter set with ω^2 itself as in the usual set-theoretic definition of ordinals; thus $\beta < \alpha$ if and only if $\beta \in \alpha$.

By extension, we also write $o(x)$ for the ordinal term in $o(A)$ associated to an element x in A; for instance in $\langle \mathbb{N}^d, \leq_{\text{lex}} \rangle$, $o(n_1, \ldots, n_d) = \omega^{d-1} \cdot n_1 + \cdots + n_d$.

3   Complexity Bounds

We aim to provide complexity upper bounds for programs proven to terminate thanks to some (quasi-)ranking function. There are several results of this kind in the literature [28, 12, 38, 11, 17, 32, 1], which are well-suited for algorithms manipulating complex data structures—for which we can employ the rich wqo toolkit.

A major drawback of all these complexity bounds is that they are *very* high— i.e., non-elementary except in trivial cases—, whereas practitioners are mostly interested in polynomial bounds. Such high complexities are however unavoidable, because the class of programs terminating thanks to a quasi-ranking function encompasses programs with matching complexities. For instance, even integer loops can be deceivingly simple: recall that the program of Fig. 1 terminated using a straightforward ranking function into ω^2. Although this is just one notch above a ranking function into ω, we can already witness fairly complex computations. Observe indeed that the following are some execution steps of our program:

$$(\ell_0, x, y, 1) \xrightarrow{a^x b}_S (\ell_0, 2^x, y-1, 2^{x+1})$$
$$\xrightarrow{a^{2^x} b}_S (\ell_0, 2^{2^x + x + 1}, y-2, 2^{2^x + x + 2})$$
$$\xrightarrow{a^{2^{2^x + x + 1}} b}_S (\ell_0, 2^{2^{2^x + x + 1} + 2^x + x + 2}, y-3, 2^{2^{2^x + x + 1} + 2^x + x + 3}) .$$

Continuing this execution, we see that our simple program exhibits executions of length greater than a tower of exponentials in y, i.e. it is non elementary.

3.1   Controlled Ranking Functions

By Def. 2.1, bad sequences in a wqo are always finite—which in turn yields the termination of programs with quasi-ranking functions—, but no statement is made regarding *how long* they can be. This is for a very good reason: they can be arbitrarily long.

For instance, over the wo $\langle \mathbb{N}, \leq \rangle$,

$$n, n-1, \ldots, 1, 0 \tag{5}$$

is a bad sequence of length $n+1$ for every n. Arguably, this is not so much of an issue, since what we are really interested in is the length *as a function* of the initial configuration—which includes the inputs to the program. Thus (5) is the maximal bad sequence over $\langle \mathbb{N}, \leq \rangle$ with initial element of 'size n.'

However, as soon as we move to more complex wqos, we can exhibit arbitrary bad sequence lengths even with fixed initial configurations. For instance, over $\langle \mathbb{N}^2, \leq_{\text{lex}} \rangle$,

$$(1,0), (0,n), (0,n-1), \ldots, (0,1), (0,0) \tag{6}$$

is a bad sequence of length $n+2$ for every n starting from the fixed $(1,0)$. Nonetheless, the behaviour of a program exhibiting such a sequence of ranks is rather unusual: such a sudden 'jump' from $(1,0)$ to an arbitrary $(0,n)$ is not possible in a deterministic program once the user inputs have been provided.

Controlled Sequences. In the following, we will assume that no such arbitrary jump can occur. This comes at the price of some loss of generality in the context of termination analysis, where nondeterministic assignments of arbitrary values are typically employed to model values provided by the environment—for instance interactive user inputs or concurrently running programs—, or because of abstracted operations. Thankfully, in most cases it is easy to *control* how large the program variables can grow during the course of an execution.

Formally, given a wqo $\langle A, \leq_A \rangle$, we posit a *norm* function $|.|_A : A \to \mathbb{N}$ on the elements of A. In order to be able to derive combinatorial statements, we require

$$A_{\leq n} \overset{\text{def}}{=} \{x \in A \mid |x|_A \leq n\} \tag{7}$$

to be finite for every n. We will use the following norms on the wqos defined earlier: in a finite Q, all the elements have the same norm 0; in $\mathbb{N}$ or $[d]$, n has norm $|n|_{\mathbb{N}} = n$; for Cartesian or lexicographic products with support $A \times B$, (x, y) has the infinite norm $\max(|x|_A, |y|_B)$; finally, for multisets $\mathbb{M}(A)$, m has norm $\max_{x \in A, m(x) > 0}(m(x), |x|_A)$.

Let $g: \mathbb{N} \to \mathbb{N}$ be a monotone and expansive function: for all x, x', $x \leq x'$ implies $g(x) \leq g(x')$ and $x \leq g(x)$. We say that a sequence $x_0, x_1, x_2, \ldots$ of elements in A is (g, n_0)-*controlled* for some n_0 in $\mathbb{N}$ if

$$|x_i|_A \leq g^i(n_0) \tag{8}$$

for all i, where g^i denotes the ith iterate of g. In particular $|x_0|_A \leq g^0(n_0) = n_0$, which prompts the name of *initial norm* for n_0, and amortised steps cannot grow faster than g the *control function*.

By extension, a quasi-ranking function $f: Conf \to A$ for a transition system $\mathcal{S} = \langle Conf, \to_\mathcal{S} \rangle$ and a normed wqo $\langle A, \leq_A, |.|_A \rangle$ is g-*controlled* if, whenever $c \to_\mathcal{S} c'$ is a transition in $\mathcal{S}$,

$$|f(c')|_A \leq g(|f(c)|_A) . \tag{9}$$

This ensures that any sequence $f(c_0), f(c_1), \ldots$ of ranks associated to an execution $c_0 \to_\mathcal{S} c_1 \to_\mathcal{S} \cdots$ of $\mathcal{S}$ is $(g, |f(c_0)|_A)$-controlled. For instance, our ranking function $f(\ell_0, x, y, n) = (y, x)$ for the program of Fig. 1 into $\langle \mathbb{N}^2, \leq_{\text{lex}} \rangle$ is g-controlled for $g(x) = 2x$.

Length Functions. The motivation for controlled sequences is that their length can be bounded. Consider for this the tree one obtains by sharing common prefixes of all the (g, n_0)-controlled bad sequences over a normed wqo $(A, \leq_A, |.|_A)$. This tree has

– finite branching by (7) and (8), more precisely branching degree bounded by the cardinal of $A_{\leq g^i(n_0)}$ for a node at depth i, and
– no infinite branches thanks to the wqo property.

By Kőnig's Lemma, this tree of bad sequences is therefore finite, of some height $L_{g,n_0,A}$ representing the length of the maximal (g, n_0)-controlled bad sequence(s) over A. In the following, since we are mostly interested in this length as a function of the initial norm n_0, we will see this as a *length function* $L_{g,A}(n_0)$.

Length Function Theorems. Observe that $L_{g,A}$ also bounds the asymptotic execution length in a program endowed with a g-controlled quasi-ranking function into $\langle A, \leq_A, |.|_A \rangle$. Our purpose will thus be to obtain explicit complexity bounds on $L_{g,A}$ depending on g and A. We call such combinatorial statements *length function theorems*; see [28, 12, 38, 11, 17, 32, 1] for some examples.

For applications to termination analysis, we are especially interested in the case of well orders. Somewhat oddly, this particular case has seldom been considered; to our knowledge the only instance is due to Abriola, Figueira, and Senno [1] who derive upper bounds for multisets of tuples of naturals ordered lexicographically, i.e. for $L_{g,M(\mathbb{N}^d)}$ (beware that their notion of control is defined slightly differently).

3.2   Hardy and Cichoń Hierarchies

As we saw with the example of Fig. 1, even simple terminating programs can have a very high complexity. In order to express such high bounds, a convenient tool is found in *subrecursive hierarchies*, which employ recursion over ordinal indices to define faster and faster growing functions. We define in this section two such hierarchies.

Fundamental Sequences and Predecessors. Let us first introduce some additional notions on ordinal terms. Consider an ordinal term α in Cantor normal form $\omega^{\alpha_1} + \cdots + \omega^{\alpha_p}$. In this representation, $\alpha = 0$ if and only if $p = 0$. An ordinal α of the form $\alpha' + 1$ (i.e. with $p > 0$ and $\alpha_p = 0$) is called a *successor* ordinal, and otherwise if $\alpha > 0$ it is called a *limit* ordinal, and can be written as $\gamma + \omega^\beta$ by setting $\gamma = \omega^{\alpha_1} + \cdots + \omega^{\alpha_{p-1}}$ and $\beta = \alpha_p$. We usually write 'λ' to denote a limit ordinal.

A *fundamental sequence* for a limit ordinal λ is a sequence $(\lambda(x))_{x<\omega}$ of ordinal terms with supremum λ. We use the standard assignment of fundamental sequences to limit ordinals defined inductively by

$$(\gamma + \omega^{\beta+1})(x) \stackrel{\text{def}}{=} \gamma + \omega^\beta \cdot (x+1), \qquad (\gamma + \omega^\lambda)(x) \stackrel{\text{def}}{=} \gamma + \omega^{\lambda(x)}. \qquad (10)$$

This particular assignment satisfies e.g. $0 < \lambda(x) < \lambda(y)$ for all $x < y$. For instance, $\omega(x) = x + 1$, $(\omega^{\omega^4} + \omega^{\omega^3 + \omega^2})(x) = \omega^{\omega^4} + \omega^{\omega^3 + \omega \cdot (x+1)}$.

The *predecessor* $P_x(\alpha)$ of an ordinal term $\alpha > 0$ at a value x in $\mathbb{N}$ is defined inductively by

$$P_x(\alpha + 1) \stackrel{\text{def}}{=} \alpha, \qquad P_x(\lambda) \stackrel{\text{def}}{=} P_x(\lambda(x)). \qquad (11)$$

In essence, the predecessor of an ordinal is obtained by repeatedly taking the xth element in the fundamental sequence of limit ordinals, until we finally reach a successor ordinal and remove 1. For instance, $P_x(\omega^2) = P_x(\omega \cdot (x+1)) = P_x(\omega \cdot x + x + 1) = \omega \cdot x + x$.

Subrecursive Hierarchies. In the context of controlled sequences, the hierarchies of Hardy and Cichoń turn out to be especially well-suited [11]. Let $h \colon \mathbb{N} \to \mathbb{N}$ be a function. The *Hardy hierarchy* $(h^\alpha)_{\alpha \in \varepsilon_0}$ is defined for all $0 < \alpha < \varepsilon_0$ by[1]

$$h^0(x) \stackrel{\text{def}}{=} x , \qquad\qquad h^\alpha(x) \stackrel{\text{def}}{=} h^{P_x(\alpha)}(h(x)) , \qquad\qquad (12)$$

and the *Cichoń hierarchy* $(h_\alpha)_{\alpha \in \varepsilon_0}$ is similarly defined for all $0 < \alpha < \varepsilon_0$ by

$$h_0(x) \stackrel{\text{def}}{=} 0 , \qquad\qquad h_\alpha(x) \stackrel{\text{def}}{=} 1 + h_{P_x(\alpha)}(h(x)) . \qquad\qquad (13)$$

Observe that h^k for some finite k is the kth iterate of h. This intuition carries over: h^α is a transfinite iteration of the function h, using diagonalisation in the fundamental sequences to handle limit ordinals.

For instance, starting with the successor function $H(x) \stackrel{\text{def}}{=} x + 1$, we see that a first diagonalisation yields $H^\omega(x) = H^x(x+1) = 2x+1$. The next diagonalisation occurs at $H^{\omega \cdot 2}(x) = H^{\omega + x}(x + 1) = H^\omega(2x + 1) = 4x + 3$. Fast-forwarding a bit, we get for instance a function of exponential growth $H^{\omega^2}(x) = 2^{x+1}(x + 1) - 1$, and later a non-elementary function H^{ω^3}, an 'Ackermannian' non primitive-recursive function H^{ω^ω}, and a 'hyper-Ackermannian' non multiply recursive-function $H^{\omega^{\omega^\omega}}$. Regarding the Cichoń functions, an easy induction on α shows that $H^\alpha(x) = H_\alpha(x) + x$.

On the one hand, Hardy functions are well-suited for expressing large iterates of a control function, and therefore for bounding the norms of elements in a controlled sequence. For instance, the program in Fig. 1 computes $g^{\omega \cdot y + x}(n)$ for the function $g(x) = 2x$ when run on non-negative inputs x, y, n. On the other hand, Cichoń functions are well-suited for expressing the length of controlled sequences. For instance, $g_{\omega \cdot y + x}(n)$ is the length of the execution of the program. This relation is a general one: we can compute how many times we should iterate h in order to compute $h^\alpha(x)$ using the corresponding Cichoń function:

$$h^\alpha(x) = h^{h_\alpha(x)}(x) . \qquad\qquad (14)$$

Monotonicity Properties. Assume h is monotone and expansive. Then both h^α and h_α are monotone and expansive [see 11, 33, 35]. However, those hierarchies are not monotone in the ordinal indices: for instance, $H^\omega(x) = 2x+1 < 2x+2 = H^{x+2}(x)$ although $\omega > x + 2$.

Some refinement of the ordinal ordering is needed in order to obtain monotonicity of the hierarchies. Define for this the *pointwise ordering* $\prec_x$ at some x in $\mathbb{N}$ as the smallest transitive relation such that

$$\alpha \prec_x \alpha + 1 , \qquad\qquad \lambda(x) \prec_x \lambda . \qquad\qquad (15)$$

The relation '$\beta \prec_x \alpha$' is also noted '$\beta \in \alpha[x]$' in [35, pp. 158–163]. The $\prec_x$ relations form a strict hierarchy of refinements of the ordinal ordering $<$:

$$\prec_0 \subsetneq \prec_1 \subsetneq \cdots \subsetneq \prec_x \subsetneq \cdots \subsetneq < . \qquad\qquad (16)$$

---

[1] Note that this is equivalent to defining $h^{\alpha+1}(x) \stackrel{\text{def}}{=} h^\alpha(h(x))$ and $h^\lambda(x) \stackrel{\text{def}}{=} h^{\lambda(x)}(x)$.

As desired, our hierarchies are monotone for the pointwise ordering [11, 33, 35]:

$$\beta \prec_x \alpha \qquad \text{implies} \qquad h_\beta(x) \leq h_\alpha(x) . \qquad (17)$$

Ordinal Norms. As a first application of the pointwise ordering, define the *norm* of an ordinal as the maximal coefficient that appears in its associated CNF: if $\alpha = \omega^{\alpha_1} \cdot c_1 + \cdots + \omega^{\alpha_p} \cdot c_p$ with $\alpha_1 > \cdots > \alpha_p$ and $c_1, \ldots, c_p > 0$, then

$$N\alpha \overset{\text{def}}{=} \max\{c_1, \ldots, c_p, N\alpha_1, \ldots, N\alpha_p\} . \qquad (18)$$

Observe that this definition essentially matches the previously defined norms over multisets and tuples of vectors: e.g. in $\langle \mathbb{N}^d, \leq_{\text{lex}} \rangle$, the ordinal norm satisfies $No(n_1, \ldots, n_d) = \max(d, |(n_1, \ldots, n_d)|_{\mathbb{N}^d})$, and in $\langle \mathbb{M}(\mathbb{N}^d), \leq_{\text{mset}} \rangle$, $No(m) = \max(d, |m|_{\mathbb{M}(\mathbb{N}^d)})$. The relation between ordinal norms and the pointwise ordering is that [33, 35, p. 158]

$$\beta < \alpha \qquad \text{implies} \qquad \beta \prec_{N\beta} \alpha . \qquad (19)$$

Together with (16) and (17), this entails that for all $x \geq N\beta$, $h_\beta(x) \leq h_\alpha(x)$.

3.3   A Length Function Theorem for ε_0

We are now equipped to prove a length function theorem for all ordinals α below ε_0, i.e. an explicit expression for $L_{g,\alpha}$ for the wo $\langle \alpha, \leq, N \rangle$. This proof relies on two main ingredients: a *descent equation* established in [32] for all normed wqos, and an alternative characterisation of the Cichoń hierarchy in terms of maximisations inspired by [10, 8].

Residuals and a Descent Equation. Let $\langle A, \leq, |.| \rangle$ be a normed wqo and x be an element of A. We write

$$A/x \overset{\text{def}}{=} \{y \in A \mid x \not\leq y\} \qquad (20)$$

for the *residual* of A in x. Observe that by the wqo property, there cannot be infinite sequences of residuations $A/x_0/x_1/x_2/\cdots$ since $x_i \not\leq x_j$ for all $i < j$.

Consider now a (g, n_0)-controlled bad sequence $x_0, x_1, x_2, \ldots$ over $\langle A, \leq, |.|_A \rangle$. Assuming the sequence is not empty, then because this is a bad sequence we see that for all $i > 0$, $x_0 \not\leq x_i$, i.e. that the suffix $x_1, x_2, \ldots$ is actually a bad sequence over A/x_0. This suffix is now $(g(n), n_0)$-controlled, and thus of length bounded by $L_{g,A/x_0}(g(n_0))$. This yields the following *descent equation* when considering all the possible (g, n)-controlled bad sequences:

$$L_{g,A}(n) = \max_{x \in A_{\leq n}} 1 + L_{g,A/x}(g(n)) . \qquad (21)$$

In the case of a wo $\langle \alpha, \leq, N \rangle$, residuals can be expressed more simply for $\beta \in \alpha$ as

$$\alpha/\beta = \{\gamma \in \alpha \mid \beta > \gamma\} = \beta . \qquad (22)$$

Thus the descent equation simplifies into

$$L_{g,\alpha}(n) = \max_{\beta < \alpha, N\beta \leq n} 1 + L_{g,\beta}(g(n)) . \qquad (23)$$

Norm Maximisation. The reader might have noticed a slight resemblance between the ordinal descent equation (23) and the definition of the Cichoń hierarchy (13). It turns out that they are essentially the same functions: indeed, we are going to show in Prop. 3.2 that if $N\alpha \leq x$, then choosing $\beta = P_x(\alpha)$ maximises $h_\beta(h(x))$ among those $\beta < \alpha$ with $N\beta \leq x$; we follow in this [10, 8]. This is a somewhat technical proof, so the reader might want to skip the details and jump directly to Thm. 3.3.

Lemma 3.1. *Let $\alpha < \varepsilon_0$ and $x \geq N\alpha$. Then $P_x(\alpha) = \max_{\beta<\alpha,N\beta\leq x} \beta$.*

Proof. We prove the lemma through a sequence of claims.

Claim 3.1.1. $P_x(\alpha) < \alpha$.

We show for this first claim that, by transfinite induction over $\alpha > 0$, for all x

$$P_x(\alpha) \prec_x \alpha \qquad (24)$$

Indeed, $P_x(\alpha+1) = \alpha \prec_x \alpha+1$ for the successor case, and $P_x(\lambda) = P_x(\lambda(x)) \prec_x \lambda(x) \prec_x$ by induction hypothesis on $\lambda(x) < \lambda$ for the limit case. Then (16) allows to conclude.

Let us introduce a variant of the ordinal norm. Let $\alpha = \omega^{\alpha_1} \cdot c_1 + \cdots + \omega^{\alpha_p} \cdot c_p$ be an ordinal in CNF with $\alpha > \alpha_1 > \cdots > \alpha_p$ and $\omega > c_1, \ldots, c_p > 0$. We say that α is *almost x-lean* if either (i) $c_p = x + 1$ and both $N\sum_{i<p} \omega^{\alpha_i} \leq x$ and $N\alpha_p \leq x$, or (ii) $c_p \leq x$, $N\sum_{i<m} \omega^{\alpha_i} \leq x$, and α_p is almost x-lean. Note that an almost x-lean ordinal α has *not* norm x; it has however norm $x + 1$. Here are several properties of note for almost x-lean ordinals:

Claim 3.1.2. If $N\lambda \leq x$, then $\lambda(x)$ is almost x-lean.

We prove this claim by induction on λ, letting $\lambda = \omega^{\lambda_1} \cdot c_1 + \cdots + \omega^{\lambda_p} \cdot c_p$ as above, where necessarily $N\lambda_p \leq x$. If λ_p is a successor ordinal $\beta + 1$ (and thus $N\beta \leq x$), $\lambda(x) = \omega^{\lambda_1} \cdot c_1 + \cdots + \omega^{\lambda_p} \cdot (c_p - 1) + \omega^\beta \cdot (x+1)$ is almost x-lean by case (i). If λ_p is a limit ordinal, $\lambda(x) = \omega^{\lambda_1} \cdot c_1 + \cdots + \omega^{\lambda_p} \cdot (c_p - 1) + \omega^{\lambda_p(x)}$ is x-lean by case (ii) and the induction hypothesis on $\lambda_p < \lambda$.

Claim 3.1.3. If $\alpha + 1$ is almost x-lean, then $N\alpha \leq x$.

Let $\alpha+1 = \omega^{\alpha_1} \cdot c_1 + \cdots + \omega^{\alpha_p} \cdot c_p$ with $\alpha_p = 0$. We must be in case (i) since $\alpha_p = 0$ cannot be x-lean, thus $c_p = x + 1$ and $N\alpha = N\omega^{\alpha_1} \cdot c_1 + \cdots + \omega^{\alpha_p} \cdot (c_p - 1) \leq x$.

Claim 3.1.4. If λ is almost x-lean, then $\lambda(x)$ is almost x-lean.

We prove the claim by induction on λ, letting $\lambda = \omega^{\lambda_1} \cdot c_1 + \cdots + \omega^{\lambda_p} \cdot c_p$:

If λ_p is a successor ordinal $\beta + 1$, $\lambda(x) = \omega^{\lambda_1} \cdot c_1 + \cdots + \omega^{\lambda_p} \cdot (c_p - 1) + \omega^\beta \cdot (x + 1)$, and either (i) $c_p = x + 1$ and $N\lambda_p \leq x$, and then $\lambda(x)$ also verifies (i), or (ii) $c_p \leq x$ and $\beta + 1$ is almost x-lean and thus $N\beta \leq x$ by Claim 3.1.3, and $\lambda(x)$ is again almost x-lean verifying condition (i).

If λ_p is a limit ordinal, then $\lambda(x) = \omega^{\lambda_1} \cdot c_1 + \cdots + \omega^{\lambda_p} \cdot (c_p - 1) + \omega^{\lambda_p(x)}$. Either (i) $c_p = x + 1$ and $N\lambda_p \leq x$, and by Claim 3.1.2 $\lambda_p(x)$ is almost x-lean and thus $\lambda(x)$ is almost x-lean by condition (ii), or (ii) $c_p \leq x$ and λ_p is almost x-lean, and by induction hypothesis $\lambda_p(x)$ is almost x-lean, and therefore $\lambda(x)$ is again almost x-lean by condition (ii).

Claim 3.1.5. If α is almost x-lean, then $NP_x(\alpha) \leq x$.

By induction over $\alpha > 0$: we see for the successor case that $NP_x(\alpha+1) = N\alpha \leq x$ by Claim 3.1.3, and for the limit case that $\lambda(x)$ is almost x-lean by Claim 3.1.4 and thus $P_x(\lambda(x)) \leq x$ by induction hypothesis.

Claim 3.1.6. If $N\alpha \leq x$, then $NP_x(\alpha) \leq x$.

Indeed, either α is a successor and this is immediate, or it is a limit λ and then $\lambda(x)$ is almost x-lean by Claim 3.1.2 and therefore $NP_x(\lambda) = NP_x(\lambda(x)) \leq x$ by Claim 3.1.5.

Claim 3.1.7. If $\beta < \alpha$ and $N\beta \leq x$, then $\beta \preceq_x P_x(\alpha)$.

Because the hypotheses entail $\beta \prec_x \alpha$ by (19), we can consider a sequence of atomic steps according to (15) for the pointwise ordering: $\beta = \beta_n \prec_x \cdots \prec_x \beta_1 \prec_x \alpha$. If α is a successor, then $\beta \preceq_x \beta_1 = P_x(\alpha)$. Otherwise β_1 is almost x-lean by Claim 3.1.2. Because $N\beta \leq x$, β is not almost x-lean, and by Claim 3.1.3 and Claim 3.1.4 there must be a greatest index $1 \leq i < n$ such that all the β_j's for $1 \leq j < i$ are almost x-lean limit ordinals and β_i is a successor almost x-lean ordinal. Thus $\beta \preceq_x \beta_{i+1} = P_x(\alpha)$.

To conclude the proof, $P_x(\alpha) < \alpha$ by Claim 3.1.1, $NP_x(\alpha) \leq x$ by Claim 3.1.6, and if $\beta < \alpha$ is such that $N\beta \leq x$, then $\beta \leq P_x(\alpha)$ by Claim 3.1.7 and (16), which together prove the lemma. $\qquad\square$

Proposition 3.2. *Let $\alpha < \varepsilon_0$ and $x \geq N\alpha$. Then $h_\alpha(x) = \max_{\beta<\alpha, N\beta \leq x} 1 + h_\beta(h(x))$.*

Proof. If $\alpha = 0$ then there are no $\beta < \alpha$ and $\max_{\beta<\alpha, N\beta \leq x} 1 + h_\beta(h(x)) = 0 = h_0(x)$.

Otherwise by Lem. 3.1, since $P_x(\alpha) < \alpha$ and $NP_x(\alpha) \leq x$, $h_\alpha(x) = 1 + h_{P_x(\alpha)}(h(x)) \leq \max_{\beta<\alpha, N\beta \leq x} 1 + h_\beta(h(x))$. Conversely, let $\beta < \alpha$ with $N\beta \leq x$ be such that $\max_{\beta<\alpha, N\beta \leq x} 1 + h_\beta(h(x)) = 1 + h_\beta(h(x))$. By Lem. 3.1, $\beta \leq P_x(\alpha)$ and therefore by (19) $\beta \preceq_x P_x(\alpha)$. Since h is expansive, by (16), $\beta \preceq_{h(x)} P_x(\alpha)$. Therefore by (17), $1 + h_\beta(h(x)) \leq 1 + h_{P_x(\alpha)}(h(x)) = h_\alpha(x)$. $\qquad\square$

Theorem 3.3 (Length Function Theorem for Ordinals). *Let $\alpha < \varepsilon_0$ and $x \geq N\alpha$. Then $L_{g,\alpha}(x) = g_\alpha(x)$.*

Proof. We use the ordinal descent equation (23) and Prop. 3.2. $\qquad\square$

As an immediate corollary, we can bound the asymptotic complexity of programs proven to terminate through a g-controlled ranking function:

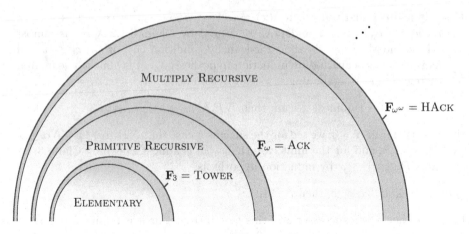

Fig. 2. Some complexity classes beyond Elementary

Corollary 3.4. *Given a transition system $\mathcal{S} = \langle Conf, \rightarrow_{\mathcal{S}} \rangle$, if there exists a g-controlled ranking function into $\alpha < \varepsilon_0$, then $\mathcal{S}$ runs in time $O(g_\alpha(n))$.*

As an illustration, a program proven to terminate thanks to a g-controlled ranking function into $\langle \mathbb{N}^d, \leq_{\text{lex}}, |\cdot|_{\mathbb{N}^d} \rangle$ has therefore an $O(g_{\omega^d}(n))$ bound on its worst-case asymptotic complexity. In the case of the program of Fig. 1, this yields an upper bound of $g_{\omega^2}(m) = 1 + g_{\omega \cdot m + m}(m)$ on its complexity for $g(x) \stackrel{\text{def}}{=} 2x$ and $m \stackrel{\text{def}}{=} \max(x, y, n)$. This matches its actual complexity.

4   Complexity Classification

As already mentioned, the complexity bounds provided by Thm. 3.3 are so high that they are only of interest for algorithms of very high complexity. Rather than obtaining precise complexity statements as in Thm. 3.3, the purpose is then to classify the complexity in rather broad terms: e.g., is the algorithm elementary? primitive-recursive? multiply-recursive?

4.1   Fast-Growing Classes

In order to tackle the complexities derived from Thm. 3.3, we need to employ complexity classes for very high complexity problems. For $\alpha > 2$, we define respectively the *fast-growing function* classes $(\mathscr{F}_\alpha)_\alpha$ of Löb and Wainer [27] and the *fast-growing complexity* classes $(\mathbf{F}_\alpha)_\alpha$ of [31] by

$$\mathscr{F}_{<\alpha} \stackrel{\text{def}}{=} \bigcup_{\beta < \omega^\alpha} \text{FDTime}\big(H^\beta(n)\big), \quad \mathbf{F}_\alpha \stackrel{\text{def}}{=} \bigcup_{p \in \mathscr{F}_{<\alpha}} \text{DTime}\big(H^{\omega^\alpha}(p(n))\big). \quad (25)$$

Recall that H^α denotes the αth function in the Hardy hierarchy with generative function $H(x) \stackrel{\text{def}}{=} x + 1$, and that $\text{FDTime}(t(n))$ (resp. $\text{DTime}(t(n))$) denotes the set of functions computable (resp. problems decidable) in deterministic time $O(t(n))$.

Some important complexity milestones can be characterised through these classes. Regarding the function classes, $\mathscr{F}_{<3}$ is the class of elementary functions, $\mathscr{F}_{<\omega}$ the class of primitive-recursive functions, $\mathscr{F}_{<\omega^\omega}$ the class of multiply-recursive functions, and $\mathscr{F}_{<\varepsilon_0}$ the class of ordinal-recursive functions. Turning to the complexity classes, $\mathbf{F}_3 = \text{TOWER}$ is the class of problems with complexity bounded by a tower of exponentials of height bounded by an elementary function of the input, $\mathbf{F}_\omega = \text{ACK}$ the class of problems with complexity bounded by the Ackermann function of some primitive-recursive function of the input, and $\mathbf{F}_\omega^\omega = \text{HACK}$ of problems with complexity bounded by the hyper-Ackermann function $H^{\omega^{\omega^\omega}}$ composed with some multiply-recursive function. In other words, $\mathbf{F}_3$ (resp. $\mathbf{F}_\omega$ and $\mathbf{F}_{\omega^\omega}$) is the smallest complexity class $\mathbf{F}_\alpha$ which contains non elementary problems (resp. non primitive recursive and non multiply recursive problems); see Fig. 2.

4.2 Classification

The explicit formulation for the length function provided by Thm. 3.3 yields upper bounds in the $(\mathbf{F}_\alpha)_\alpha$ complexity classes. Assume that g belongs to the function class $\mathscr{F}_{<\gamma}$ for some γ. Then, by [31, Thm. 4.2], an algorithm with a g_{ω^α} complexity yields an upper bound in $\mathbf{F}_{\gamma+\alpha}$. In particular, a decision procedure terminating thanks to a lexicographic ranking function into $\langle \mathbb{N}^d, \leq_{\text{lex}}, |.|_{\mathbb{N}^d} \rangle$ with a linear control yields an $\mathbf{F}_{d+1}$ complexity upper bound. At greater complexities, if g is primitive recursive—i.e. is in $\mathscr{F}_{<\omega}$—and $\alpha \geq \omega$, then we obtain an upper bound in $\mathbf{F}_\alpha$ [31, Cor. 4.3].

5   Product vs. Lexicographic Orderings

Although we focus in this paper on ranking functions, automated termination provers employ many different techniques. While lexicographic ranking functions are fairly common [e.g. 14, 4, 37, for recent references], *disjunctive termination arguments* (aka Ramsey-based termination proofs) [30] are also a popular alternative.

5.1   Disjunctive Termination Arguments

In order to prove a program transition relation $\rightarrow_S$ to be well-founded, Podelski and Rybalchenko [30] show that it suffices to exhibit a finite set of well-founded relations $T_1, \ldots, T_d \subseteq Conf \times Conf$ and prove that the transitive closure $\rightarrow_S^+$ is included in the union $T_1 \cup \cdots \cup T_d$. In practice, we can assume each of the T_j for $1 \leq j \leq d$ to be proved well-founded through a quasi-ranking function f_j into a wqo $\langle A_j, \leq_j \rangle$. In the case of the program in Fig. 1, choosing

$$T_1 = \{((\ell_0, x, y, n), (\ell_0, x', y', n')) \mid x > 0 \land x' < x\} \tag{26}$$
$$T_2 = \{((\ell_0, x, y, n), (\ell_0, x', y', n')) \mid y > 0 \land y' < y\} \tag{27}$$

yields such a disjunctive termination argument, with $A_1 = A_2 = \mathbb{N}$.

Another way of understanding disjunctive termination arguments is that they define a quasi-ranking function f into the product wqo $\langle A_1 \times \cdots \times A_d, \leq_\times \rangle$, which maps a configuration c to the tuple $\langle f_1(c), \ldots, f_d(c) \rangle$, c.f. [17, Sec. 7.1].

5.2   A Comparison

Let us consider disjunctive termination arguments where each of the d relations T_j has a ranking function into $\mathbb{N}$, i.e. defining a quasi-ranking function into $\langle \mathbb{N}^d, \leq_\times \rangle$. A natural question at this point is how does it compare with a ranking function into $\langle \mathbb{N}^d, \leq_{\text{lex}} \rangle$, which seems fairly similar? Which programs can be shown to terminate with either method?

We might attempt to differentiate them through their *maximal order types* [22, 6]. In general, this is the supremum of the order types of all the linearisations of a wqo:

$$o(A, \leq) \overset{\text{def}}{=} \sup\{o(A, \preceq) \mid \preceq \text{ is a linearisation of } \leq\} . \tag{28}$$

However, in the case of $\langle \mathbb{N}^d, \leq_\times \rangle$, this maximal order type is ω^d, matching the order type of $\langle \mathbb{N}^d, \leq_{\text{lex}} \rangle$.

We can consider instead the maximal length of their controlled bad sequences. Those are different: the following example taken from [17, Remark 6.2] is a $(g, 1)$-controlled bad sequence over $\langle \mathbb{N}^2, \leq_\times \rangle$, which is good for $\langle \mathbb{N}^2, \leq_{\text{lex}} \rangle$, where $g(x) \overset{\text{def}}{=} x + 2$:

$$(1,1), (3,0), (2,0), (1,0), (0,9), (0,8), \ldots, (0,1), (0,0) \tag{29}$$

This sequence has length 14 whereas the maximal $(g, 1)$-controlled bad sequence for $\langle \mathbb{N}^2, \leq_{\text{lex}} \rangle$ is of length $g_{\omega^2}(1) = 8$:

$$(1,1), (1,0), (0,5), (0,4), \ldots, (0,1), (0,0) . \tag{30}$$

5.3   Length Functions for the Product Ordering

More generally, the length function theorems for $\langle \mathbb{N}^d, \leq_\times \rangle$ provide larger upper bounds than the g_{ω^d} bound provided by Thm. 3.3 [28, 12, 17, 33, 1]. The following version from [33, Chap. 2] is easy to compare with Thm. 3.3:

Fact 5.1 ([33]). *Let $d \geq 0$ and $h(x) \overset{\text{def}}{=} d \cdot g(x)$. Then $L_{g, \mathbb{N}^d}(x) \leq h_{\omega^d}(dx)$.*

Fact 5.1 allows to bound the running time of programs proven to terminate with d transition invariants T_j, each shown well-founded through some g-controlled ranking function into $\mathbb{N}$. In particular, for linearly controlled ranking functions, d-dimensional transition invariants entail again upper bounds in $\mathbf{F}_{d+1}$, just like linearly controlled ranking functions into $\langle \mathbb{N}^d, \leq_{\text{lex}} \rangle$ do. Thus, at the coarse-grained level of the fast-growing complexity classes, the differences between Thm. 3.3 and Fact. 5.1 disappear.

5.4   Controlling Abstractions

The previous classifications into primitive recursive complexity classes $\mathbf{F}_{d+1}$ might be taken to imply that non-primitive recursive programs are beyond the reach of the current automated termination methods, which usually rely on the synthesis of affine ranking functions. This is not the case, as we can better see with the example of *size-change termination* proofs: Lee, Jones, and Ben-Amram [24] consider as their Example 3 the two-arguments Ackermann function:

$$a(m,\ n)\ =\ \textbf{if}\ m = 0\ \textbf{then}\ n + 1\ \textbf{else}$$
$$\textbf{if}\ n = 0\ \textbf{then}\ a(m{-}1,\ 1)$$
$$\textbf{else}\ a(m{-}1,\ a(m,\ n{-}1))$$

They construct a size-change graph on two variables to prove its termination. The longest decreasing sequence in such a graph is of length $O(n^2)$.[2] Here we witness an even larger gap between the actual program complexity and the complexity derived from its termination argument: the Ackermann function vs. an $O(n^2)$ bound.

The source of this apparent paradox is abstraction: the size-change graph for a(m, n) terminates if and only if the original program does, but its complexity is 'lost' during this abstraction. In the example of the Ackermann function, the call stack is abstracted away, whereas we should include it for Thm. 3.3 to apply. This is done by Dershowitz and Manna [15, Example 3], who prove the termination of the Ackermann function by exhibiting a H-controlled ranking function into $\langle \mathbb{M}(\mathbb{N}^2), \leq_{\text{mset}}\rangle$, for which Thm. 3.3 yields an $O(H_{\omega^{\omega^2}}(n))$ complexity upper bound—this is pretty much optimal.

The question at this point is how to deal with abstractions. For size-change abstractions, Ben-Amram [3] shows for instance that the programs provable to terminate are always multiply recursive, but this type of analysis is missing for other abstraction techniques, e.g. for abstract interpretation ones [37].

6   Concluding Remarks

Length function theorems often seem to relate the length function $L_{g,A}$ for (g, n)-controlled bad sequences over a wqo $\langle A, \leq \rangle$ with a Cichoń function $h_{o(A, \leq)}$ indexed by the maximal order type $o(A, \leq)$ (recall Eq. (28)) for some 'reasonable' generative function h. This is certainly the case of e.g. Thm. 3.3, where $h(x) = g(x)$, but also of Fact. 5.1 where $h(x) = d \cdot g(x)$, and of the corresponding theorem in [32] for Higman's Lemma, where $h(x) = x \cdot g(x)$.

This is a relaxation of *Cichoń's Principle* [10], who observed that rewriting systems with a termination ordering of order type α [16] often had a complexity bounded by the slow-growing function G_α (defined by choosing $G(x) \overset{\text{def}}{=} x$ as generative function in Cichoń's hierarchy). A counter-example to the principle was given by Lepper [26] using the Knuth-Bendix order; however it did not

---

[2] Colcombet, Daviaud, and Zuleger [13] recently showed that the asymptotic worst-case complexity of a size-change graph is $\Theta(n^r)$ for a computable rational r.

disprove the relaxed version of Cichoń's Principle, where the generative function h can be chosen more freely. A recent analysis of generalised Knuth-Bendix orders by Moser [29] exhibits a counter-example to the relaxed version. An open question at the moment is therefore to find general conditions which ensure that this relaxed Cichoń Principle holds.

Acknowledgements. The author thanks Christoph Haase, Georg Moser, and Philippe Schnoebelen for helpful discussions.

References

1. Abriola, S., Figueira, S., Senno, G.: Linearizing bad sequences: Upper bounds for the product and majoring well quasi-orders. In: Ong, L., de Queiroz, R. (eds.) WoLLIC 2012. LNCS, vol. 7456, pp. 110–126. Springer, Heidelberg (2012)
2. Alias, C., Darte, A., Feautrier, P., Gonnord, L.: Multi-dimensional rankings, program termination, and complexity bounds of flowchart programs. In: Cousot, R., Martel, M. (eds.) SAS 2010. LNCS, vol. 6337, pp. 117–133. Springer, Heidelberg (2010)
3. Ben-Amram, A.M.: General size-change termination and lexicographic descent. The Essence of Computation, pp. 3–17. Springer (2002)
4. Ben-Amram, A.M., Genaim, S.: Ranking functions for linear-constraint loops (2013), http://arxiv.org/abs/1208.4041
5. Ben-Amram, A.M., Vainer, M.: Bounded termination of monotonicity-constraint transition systems (preprint, 2014), http://arxiv.org/abs/1202.4281
6. Blass, A., Gurevich, Y.: Program termination and well partial orderings. ACM Trans. Comput. Logic 9(3) (2008)
7. Bonfante, G., Cichoń, A.E., Marion, J.Y., Touzet, H.: Algorithms with polynomial interpretation termination proof. J. Funct. Programming 11, 33–53 (2001)
8. Buchholz, W., Cichoń, E.A., Weiermann, A.: A uniform approach to fundamental sequences and hierarchies. Math. Logic Quart. 40(2), 273–286 (1994)
9. Bucholz, W.: Proof-theoretic analysis of termination proofs. Ann. Pure App. Logic 75(1–2), 57–65 (1995)
10. Cichoń, E.A.: Termination orderings and complexity characterisations. Proof Theory, pp. 171–194. Cambridge University Press (1993)
11. Cichoń, E.A., Tahhan Bittar, E.: Ordinal recursive bounds for Higman's Theorem. Theor. Comput. Sci. 201(1-2), 63–84 (1998)
12. Clote, P.: On the finite containment problem for Petri nets. Theor. Comput. Sci. 43, 99–105 (1986)
13. Colcombet, T., Daviaud, L., Zuleger, F.: Size-change abstraction and max-plus automata. In: Csuhaj-Varjú, E., Dietzfelbinger, M., Ésik, Z. (eds.) MFCS 2014, Part I. LNCS, vol. 8634, pp. 208–219. Springer, Heidelberg (2014)
14. Cook, B., See, A., Zuleger, F.: Ramsey vs. Lexicographic termination proving. In: Piterman, N., Smolka, S.A. (eds.) TACAS 2013 (ETAPS 2013). LNCS, vol. 7795, pp. 47–61. Springer, Heidelberg (2013)
15. Dershowitz, N., Manna, Z.: Proving termination with multiset orderings. Commun. ACM 22(8), 465–476 (1979)
16. Dershowitz, N., Okada, M.: Proof-theoretic techniques for term rewriting theory. In: LICS 1988, pp. 104–111 (1988)
17. Figueira, D., Figueira, S., Schmitz, S., Schnoebelen, P.: Ackermannian and primitive-recursive bounds with Dickson's Lemma. In: LICS 2011., pp. 269–278. IEEE (2011)

18. Floyd, R.W.: Assigning meaning to programs. Mathematical Aspects of Computer Science. In: Proceedings of Symposia in Applied Mathematics, vol. 19, pp. 19–32. AMS (1967)
19. Gulwani, S.: SPEED: Symbolic complexity bound analysis. In: Bouajjani, A., Maler, O. (eds.) CAV 2009. LNCS, vol. 5643, pp. 51–62. Springer, Heidelberg (2009)
20. Hirokawa, N., Moser, G.: Automated complexity analysis based on the dependency pair method. In: Armando, A., Baumgartner, P., Dowek, G. (eds.) IJCAR 2008. LNCS (LNAI), vol. 5195, pp. 364–379. Springer, Heidelberg (2008)
21. Hofbauer, D.: Termination proofs by multiset path orderings imply primitive recursive derivation lengths. Theor. Comput. Sci. 105(1), 129–140 (1992)
22. de Jongh, D.H.J., Parikh, R.: Well-partial orderings and hierarchies. Indag. Math. 39(3), 195–207 (1977)
23. Jouannaud, J.P., Lescanne, P.: On multiset orderings. Inf. Process. Lett. 15(2), 57–63 (1982)
24. Lee, C.S., Jones, N.D., Ben-Amram, A.M.: The size-change principle for program termination. In: POPL 2001, pp. 81–92. ACM (2001)
25. Lepper, I.: Derivation lengths and order types of Knuth-Bendix orders. Theor. Comput. Sci. 269(1-2), 433–450 (2001)
26. Lepper, I.: Simply terminating rewrite systems with long derivations. Arch. Math. Logic 43(1), 1–18 (2004)
27. Löb, M.H., Wainer, S.S.: Hierarchies of number theoretic functions, I. Arch. Math. Logic 13, 39–51 (1970)
28. McAloon, K.: Petri nets and large finite sets. Theor. Comput. Sci. 32(1-2), 173–183 (1984)
29. Moser, G.: KBOs, ordinals, subrecursive hierarchies and all that. J. Logic Comput. (to appear, 2014)
30. Podelski, A., Rybalchenko, A.: Transition invariants. In: LICS 2004. pp. 32–41. IEEE (2004)
31. Schmitz, S.: Complexity hierarchies beyond Elementary (2013), http://arxiv.org/abs/1312.5686 (preprint)
32. Schmitz, S., Schnoebelen, P.: Multiply-recursive upper bounds with higman's lemma. In: Aceto, L., Henzinger, M., Sgall, J. (eds.) ICALP 2011, Part II. LNCS, vol. 6756, pp. 441–452. Springer, Heidelberg (2011)
33. Schmitz, S., Schnoebelen, P.: Algorithmic aspects of wqo theory. Lecture notes (2012), http://cel.archives-ouvertes.fr/cel-00727025
34. Schmitz, S., Schnoebelen, P.: The power of well-structured systems. In: D'Argenio, P.R., Melgratti, H. (eds.) CONCUR 2013 – Concurrency Theory. LNCS, vol. 8052, pp. 5–24. Springer, Heidelberg (2013), http://arxiv.org/abs/1402.2908
35. Schwichtenberg, H., Wainer, S.S.: Proofs and Computation. Perspectives in Logic. Cambridge University Press (2012)
36. Turing, A.M.: Checking a large routine. In: EDSAC 1949, pp. 67–69 (1949)
37. Urban, C., Miné, A.: An abstract domain to infer ordinal-valued ranking functions. In: Shao, Z. (ed.) ESOP 2014 (ETAPS). LNCS, vol. 8410, pp. 412–431. Springer, Heidelberg (2014)
38. Weiermann, A.: Complexity bounds for some finite forms of Kruskal's Theorem. J. Symb. Comput. 18(5), 463–488 (1994)
39. Weiermann, A.: Termination proofs for term rewriting systems by lexicographic path orderings imply multiply recursive derivation lengths. Theor. Comput. Sci. 139(1-2), 355–362 (1995)

On The Complexity of Bounded Time Reachability for Piecewise Affine Systems*

Hugo Bazille[3], Olivier Bournez[1], Walid Gomaa[2,4], and Amaury Pouly[1]

[1] École Polytechnique, LIX, 91128 Palaiseau Cedex, France
[2] Egypt Japan University of Science and Technology, CSE, Alexandria, Egypt
[3] ENS Cachan/Bretagne et Université Rennes 1, France
[4] Faculty of Engineering, Alexandria University, Alexandria, Egypt

Abstract. Reachability for piecewise affine systems is known to be un-decidable, starting from dimension 2. In this paper we investigate the exact complexity of several decidable variants of reachability and con-trol questions for piecewise affine systems. We show in particular that the region to region bounded time versions leads to NP-complete or co-NP-complete problems, starting from dimension 2.

1 Introduction

A (discrete time) dynamical system $\mathcal{H}$ is given by some space X and a function $f : X \to X$. A trajectory of the system starting from x_0 is a sequence $x_0, x_1, x_2, \ldots$ etc., with $x_{i+1} = f(x_i) = f^{[i+1]}(x_0)$ where $f^{[i]}$ stands for i^{th} iterate of f. A crucial problem in such systems is the *reachability question*: given a system $\mathcal{H}$ and $R_0, R \subseteq X$, determine if there is a trajectory starting from a point of R_0 that falls in R. Reachabilty is known to be *undecidable* for very simple functions f. Indeed, it is well-known that various types of dynamical systems, such as hybrid systems, piecewise affine systems, or saturated linear systems, can simulate Turing machines, see e.g., [1,2,3,4].

This question is at the heart of *verification* of systems. Indeed, a safety prop-erty corresponds to the determination if there is a trajectory starting from some set R_0 of possible initial states to the set R of bad states. The industrial and economical impact of having efficient computer tools, that are able to guaran-tee that a given system does satisfy its specification, have indeed generated very important literature. Particularly, many undecidability and complexity-theoretic results about the hardness of verification of safety properties have been obtained in the model checking community. However, as far as we know, the exact com-plexity of *natural restrictions* of the reachability question for systems as simple as piecewise affine maps are not known, despite their practical interest.

Indeed, existing results mainly focus on the frontier between decidability and undecidability. For example, it is known that reachability is undecidable for piecewise constant derivative systems of dimension 3, whereas it is decidable for dimension 2 [5]. It is known that piecewise affine maps of dimension 2 can

---

* This work was partially supported by DGA Project CALCULS.

J. Ouaknine, I. Potapov, and J. Worrell (Eds.): RP 2014, LNCS 8762, pp. 20–31, 2014.
© Springer International Publishing Switzerland 2014

simulate Turing machines [6], whereas the question for dimension 1 is still open and can be related to other natural problems [7,8,9]. Variations of such problems over the integers have recently been investigated [10].

Some complexity facts follow immediately from these (un)computability results: for example, point to point bounded time reachability for piecewise affine maps is P-complete as it corresponds to configuration to configuration reachability for Turing machines.

However, their remain many natural variants of reachability questions which complexity have not yet been established.

For example, in the context of verification, point to point reachability is often not sufficient. On the contrary, region to region reachability is a more general question, which complexity do not follow from existing results.

In this paper we choose to restrict to the case of piecewise affine maps and we consider the following natural variant of the problem.

Continuous Bounded Time. we want to know if region R is reached in less than some prescribed time T, with f assumed to be continuous

Remark 1. We consider piecewise affine maps over the domain $[0, 1]^d$, that is to say we do not restrict to the integers as in [10]. That would make the problem rather different. We also assume f to be continuous which makes the hardness result more natural.

In an orthogonal way, control of systems or constructions of controllers for systems often yield to dual questions. Instead of asking if some trajectory reaches region R, one wants to know if all trajectories reach R. The questions of stability, mortality, or nilpotence for piecewise affine maps and saturated linear systems have been established in [11]. Still in this context, the complexity of the problem when restricting to bounded time or fixed precision is not known.

This paper provides an exact characterization of the *algorithmic complexity* of those two types of reachability for discrete time dynamical systems. Let PAF_d denote the set of piecewise-affine *continuous* functions over $[0, 1]^d$. At the end we get the following picture.

Problem: REACH-REGION
Inputs: a continuous PAF_d f and two regions R_0 and R in $\mathrm{dom}(f)$
Question: $\exists x_0 \in R_0, t \in \mathbb{N}, f^{[t]}(x_0) \in R$?

Theorem 2 ([6]). *Problem* REACH-REGION *is undecidable (and recursively enumerable-complete).*

Problem: CONTROL-REGION
Inputs: a continuous PAF_d f and two regions R_0 and R in $\mathrm{dom}(f)$
Question: $\forall x_0 \in R_0, \exists t \in \mathbb{N}, f^{[t]}(x_0) \in R$?

Theorem 3 ([11]). *Problem* CONTROL-REGION *is undecidable (and co-recursively enumerable complete) for $d \geqslant 2$.*

Problem: REACH-REGION-TIME
Inputs: a time $T \in \mathbb{N}$ in unary, a continuous PAF_d f and two regions R_0 and R in $\mathrm{dom}(f)$
Question: $\exists x_0 \in R_0, \exists t \leqslant T, f^{[t]}(x_0) \in R$?

Theorem 4. *Problem REACH-REGION-TIME is NP-complete for $d \geqslant 2$.*

Problem: CONTROL-REGION-TIME
Inputs: a time $T \in \mathbb{N}$ in unary, a continuous PAF_d f and two regions R_0 and R in $\mathrm{dom}(f)$
Question: $\forall x_0 \in R_0, \exists t \leqslant T, f^{[t]}(x_0) \in R$?

Theorem 5. *Problem CONTROL-REGION-TIME is $coNP$-complete for $d \geqslant 2$.*

All our problems are region to region reachability questions, which requires new proof techniques.

Indeed, classical tricks to simulate a Turing machine using a piecewise affine maps encode a Turing machine configuration by a point, and assume that all the points of the trajectories encode (possibly ultimately) valid Turing machines configurations.

This is not a problem in the context of point to point reachability, but this can not be extended to region to region reachability. Indeed, a (non-trivial) region consists mostly in invalid points: mostly all points do not correspond to encoding of Turing machines for all the considered encodings in above references.

In order to establish hardness results, the trajectories of all (valid and invalid) points must be carefully controlled. This turns out not to be easily possible using the classical encodings.

Let us insist on the fact that we restrict to continuous dynamics. In this context, this is an additional source of difficulties. Indeed, such a system must necessarily have a sub-region which dynamics cannot be easily interpreted in terms of configurations.

In other words, the difficulty is in dealing with points and trajectories not corresponding to valid configurations or evolutions.

2   Preliminaries

2.1   Notations

The set of non-negative integers is denoted $\mathbb{N}$ and the set of the first n naturals is denoted $\mathbb{N}_n = \{0, 1, \ldots, n-1\}$. For any finite set Σ, let Σ^* denote the set of finite words over Σ. For any word $w \in \Sigma^*$, let $|w|$ denote the length of w. Finally, let λ denote the empty word. If w is a word, let w_1 denote its first character, w_2 the second one and so on. For any $i, j \in \mathbb{N}$, let $w_{i \ldots j}$ denote the subword $w_i w_{i+1} \ldots w_j$. For any $\sigma \in \Sigma$, and $k \in \mathbb{N}$, let σ^k denote the word of length k where all symbols are σ. For any function f, let $f \restriction E$ denote the restriction of f to E and let $\mathrm{dom}(f)$ denote the domain of definition of f. For any set $S \in \mathbb{R}^d$, $\mathring{S}$ denotes the interior of S.

2.2   Piecewise Affine Functions

Let I denote the unit interval $[0, 1]$. Let $d \in \mathbb{N}$. A convex closed polyhedron in the space I^d is the solution set of some linear system of inequalities:

$$A\mathbf{x} \leq \mathbf{b} \tag{1}$$

with coefficient matrix A and offset vector $\mathbf{b}$. Let PAF_d denote the set of piecewise-affine continuous functions over I^d. For any $f \colon I^d \to I^d$ in PAF_d, f satisfies:

- f is continuous,
- there exists a sequence $(P_i)_{1 \leq i \leq p}$ of convex closed polyhedron with nonempty interior such that $f_i = f \upharpoonright P_i$ is affine, $I^d = \bigcup_{i=1}^{p} P_i$ and $\mathring{P}_i \cap \mathring{P}_j = \emptyset$ for $i \neq j$.

In the following discussion we will always assume that any polyhedron P can be defined by a finite set of linear inequalities, where all the elements of A and $\mathbf{b}$ in (1) are all rationals. A polyhedron over which f is affine we also be called a region.

2.3   Decision Problems

In this paper, we will show hardness results by reduction to known hard problems. We give the statement of these latter problems in the following.

Problem: SUBSET-SUM
Inputs: a goal $B \in \mathbb{N}$ and integers $A_1, \ldots, A_n \in \mathbb{N}$.
Question: $\exists I \subseteq \{1, \ldots, n\}, \sum_{i \in I} A_i = B$?

Theorem 6 ([12]). *SUBSET-SUM is NP-complete.*

Problem: NOSUBSET-SUM
Inputs: a witness $B \in \mathbb{N}$ and integers $A_1, \ldots, A_n \in \mathbb{N}$.
Question: $\forall I \subseteq \{1, \ldots, n\}, \sum_{i \in I} A_i \neq B$?

Theorem 7. *NOSUBSET-SUM is coNP-complete.*

Proof. Basically the same proof as Theorem 6

3   Hardness of Bounded Time Reachability

In this section, we will show that REACH-REGION-TIME is an NP-hard problem by reducing it to SUBSET-SUM.

3.1   Solving SUBSET-SUM by Iteration

We will now show how to solve the SUBSET-SUM problem with a simple iterated function. Consider an instance $\mathcal{I} = (B, A_1, \ldots, A_n)$ of SUBSET-SUM. We will need to introduce some notions before defining our piecewise affine function. Our first notion is that of configurations, which represent partial summation of the number for a given choice of I.

Remark 8. Without loss of generality, we will only consider instances where $A_i \leqslant B$, for all i. Indeed, if $A_i > B$, it will never be part of a subset sum and so we can simply remove this variable from the problem. This ensures that $A_i < B+1$ in everything that follows.

Definition 9 (Configuration). *A configuration of $\mathcal{I}$ is a tuple $(i, \sigma, \varepsilon_i, \ldots, \varepsilon_n)$ where $i \in \{1, \ldots, n+1\}$, $\sigma \in \{0, \ldots, B+1\}$, $\varepsilon_i \in \{0, 1\}$ for all i. Let $\mathcal{C}_\mathcal{I}$ be the set of all configurations of $\mathcal{I}$.*

The intuitive understanding of a configuration, made formal in the next definition, is the following: $(i, \sigma, \varepsilon_i, \ldots, \varepsilon_n)$ represents a situation where after having summed a subset of $\{A_1, \ldots, A_{i-1}\}$, we got a sum σ and ε_j is 1 if and only if we are to pick A_j in the future.

Definition 10 (Transition function). *The transition function $T_\mathcal{I} : \mathcal{C}_\mathcal{I} \to \mathcal{C}_\mathcal{I}$, is defined as follows:*

$$T_\mathcal{I}(i, \sigma, \varepsilon_i, \ldots, \varepsilon_n) = \begin{cases} (i, \sigma) & \text{if } i = n+1 \\ (i+1, \min\left(B+1, \sigma + \varepsilon_i A_i\right), \varepsilon_{i+1}, \ldots, \varepsilon_n) & \text{otherwise} \end{cases}$$

It should be clear, by definition of a subset sum that we have the following simulation result.

Lemma 11. *For any configuration $c = (i, \sigma, \varepsilon_i, \ldots, \varepsilon_n)$ and $k \in \{0, \ldots, n+1-i\}$,*

$$T_\mathcal{I}^{[k]}(c) = (i+k, \min\left(B+1, \sigma + \Sigma_{j=i}^{i+k-1}\varepsilon_j A_j\right), \varepsilon_{i+k}, \ldots, \varepsilon_n)$$

Proof. By induction.

A consequence of this simulation by iterated function, is that we can reformulate satisfiability in terms of reachability.

Lemma 12. *$\mathcal{I}$ is a satisfiable instance (i.e., admits a subset sum) if and only if there exists a configuration $c = (1, 0, \varepsilon_1, \ldots, \varepsilon_n) \in \mathcal{C}_\mathcal{I}$ such that $T_\mathcal{I}^{[n]}(c) = (n+1, B)$.*

3.2   Solving a SUBSET-SUM Problem with a Piecewise Affine Function

In this section, we explain how to simulate the function $T_\mathcal{I}$ using a piecewise affine function and some encoding of the configurations for a given $\mathcal{I} = (B, A_1, \ldots, A_n)$.

Definition 13 (Encoding). *Define* $p = \lceil \log_2(n+2) \rceil$, $\omega = \lceil \log_2(B+2) \rceil$, $q = p + \omega + 1$ *and* $\beta = 5$. *Also define* $0^* = 1$ *and* $1^* = 4$. *For any configuration* $c = (i, \sigma, \varepsilon_i, \ldots, \varepsilon_n)$, *define the encoding of* c *as follows:*

$$\langle c \rangle = \left(i2^{-p} + \sigma 2^{-q}, 0^* \beta^{-n-1} + \sum_{j=i}^{n} \varepsilon_i^* \beta^{-i} \right)$$

Also define the following regions for any $i \in \{1, \ldots, n+1\}$ *and* $\alpha \in \{0, \ldots, \beta-1\}$:

$$R_0 = [0, 2^{-p-1}] \times [0, 1] \qquad R_i = [i2^{-p}, i2^{-p} + 2^{-p-1}] \times [0, \beta^{-i+1}] \quad (i \geqslant 1)$$

$$R_{i,\alpha} = [i2^{-p}, i2^{-p} + 2^{-p-1}] \times [\alpha\beta^{-i}, (\alpha+1)\beta^{-i}] \qquad R_i = \cup_{\alpha \in \mathbb{N}_\beta} R_{i,\alpha}$$

$$R_{i,1^*}^{lin} = [i2^{-p}, i2^{-p} + (B+1-A_i)2^{-q}] \times [1^*\beta^{-i}, 5\beta^{-i}] \qquad R_{i,1^*}^{sat} = R_{i,1^*} \setminus R_{i,1^*}^{lin}$$

The rationale behind this encoding is the following. On the first coordinate we put the current number i, "shifted" by as many bits as necessary to be between 0 and 1. Following i, we put σ, also shifted by as many bits as necessary. Notice that there is one padding bit between i and σ; this is necessary to make the regions R_i disjoint from each other. On the second component, we put the description of the variables ε_j, written in basis β to get some "space" between consecutive encodings. The choice of the value 1 and 4 for the encoding of 0 and 1, although not crucial, has been made to simplify the proof as much as possible.

The region R_0 is for initialization purposes and is defined differently for the other R_i. The regions R_i correspond to the different values of i in the configuration (the current number). Each R_i is further divided into the $R_{i,\alpha}$ which correspond to all the possible values of the next ε variable (recall that it is encoded in basis β). In the special case of $\varepsilon = 1$, we cut the region $R_{i,1^*}$ into a linear part and a saturated part. This is needed to emulate the $\max(\sigma + A_i, B+1)$ in Definition 10: the linear part corresponds to $\sigma + A_i$ and the saturated part to $B + 1$.

Figure 1 and Figure 2 give a graphical representation of the regions.

Lemma 14. *For any configuration* $c = (i, \sigma, \varepsilon_i, \ldots, \varepsilon_n)$, *if* $i = n + 1$ *then* $\langle c \rangle \in R_{n+1,0^*}$, *otherwise* $\langle c \rangle \in R_{i,\varepsilon_i^*}$. *Furthermore if* $\varepsilon_i = 1$ *and* $\sigma + A_i \leqslant B + 1$, *then* $\langle c \rangle \in R_{i,1^*}^{lin}$, *otherwise* $\langle c \rangle \in R_{i,1^*}^{sat}$.

We can now define a piecewise affine function which will mimic the behavior of $T_\mathcal{I}$. The region R_0 is here to ensure that we start from a "clean" value on the first coordinate.

Definition 15 (Piecewise affine simulation).

$$f_\mathcal{I}(a,b) = \begin{cases} (2^{-p}, b) & \text{if } (a,b) \in R_0 \\ (a, b) & \text{if } (a,b) \in R_{n+1} \\ (a + 2^{-p}, b - 0^*\beta^{-i}) & \text{if } (a,b) \in R_{i,0^*} \\ (a + 2^{-p} + A_i 2^{-q}, b - 1^*\beta^{-i}) & \text{if } (a,b) \in R_{i,1^*}^{lin} \\ ((i+1)2^{-p} + (B+1)2^{-q}, b - 1^*\beta^{-i}) & \text{if } (a,b) \in R_{i,1^*}^{sat} \end{cases}$$

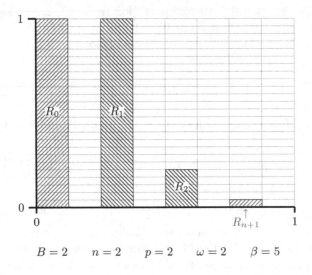

$$B = 2 \qquad n = 2 \qquad p = 2 \qquad \omega = 2 \qquad \beta = 5$$

Fig. 1. Graphical representation of the regions

Lemma 16 (Simulation is correct). *For any configuration $c \in \mathcal{C}_{\mathcal{I}}$, $\langle T_{\mathcal{I}}(c) \rangle = f_{\mathcal{I}}(\langle c \rangle)$.*

Notice that we have defined f over a subset of the entire space and it is clear that this subspace is not stable in any way[1]. In order to match the definition of a piecewise affine function, we need to define f over the entire space or a stable subspace (which contains the initial region). We follow this second approach and extend the definition of f on some more regions. More precisely, we need to define f over $R_i = R_{i,0} \cup R_{i,1} \cup R_{i,2} \cup R_{i,3} \cup R_{i,4}$ and at the moment we have only defined f over $R_{i,1} = R_{i,0*}$ and $R_{i,4} = R_{i,1*}$. Also note that $R_{i,4} = R_{i,4}^{lin} \cup R_{i,4}^{sat}$ and we define f separately on those two subregions.

In order to correctly and continuously extend f, we will need to further split the region $R_{i,3}$ into linear and saturated parts $R_{i,3}^{slo}$ and $R_{i,3}^{shi}$: see Figure 2.

Definition 17 (Extended region splitting). *For $i \in \{1, \dots, n\}$ and $\alpha \in \{0, \dots, \beta - 1\}$, define:*

$$R_{i,3}^{lin} = R_{i,3} \cap \left\{ (a,b) \,\Big|\, b\beta^i - 3 \leqslant \frac{2^{-p-1} + i2^{-p} - a}{2^{-p-1} - (B + 1 - A_i)2^{-q}} \right\} \qquad R_{i,3}^{sat} = R_{i,3} \setminus R_{i,3}^{lin}$$

It should be clear by definition that $R_{i,3}^{sat} = R_{i,3}^{slo} \cup R_{i,3}^{shi}$ and that the two subregions are disjoint except on the border.

---

[1] For example $R_{1,1} \subseteq f(R_0)$ but f is not defined over $R_{1,1}$.

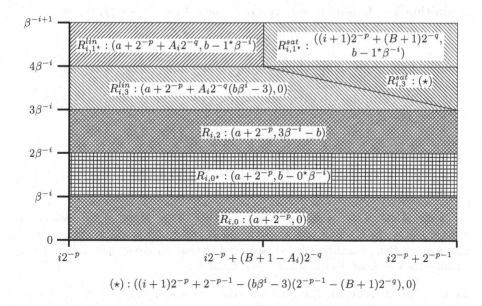

$$(\star) : ((i+1)2^{-p} + 2^{-p-1} - (b\beta^i - 3)(2^{-p-1} - (B+1)2^{-q}), 0)$$

Fig. 2. Zoom on one R_i with the subregions and formulas

Definition 18 (Extended piecewise affine simulation).

$$f_{\mathcal{I}}(a,b) = \begin{cases} (a+2^{-p}, 0) & \text{if } (a,b) \in R_{i,0} \\ (a+2^{-p}, 3\beta^{-i} - b) & \text{if } (a,b) \in R_{i,2} \\ (a+2^{-p} + A_i 2^{-q}(b\beta^i - 3), 0) & \text{if } (a,b) \in R_{i,3}^{lin} \\ ((i+\frac{3}{2})2^{-p} - (b\beta^i - 3)(2^{-p-1} - (B+1)2^{-q}), 0) & \text{if } (a,b) \in R_{i,3}^{sat} \end{cases}$$

This extension was carefully chosen for its properties. In particular, we will see that f is still continuous, which is a requirement of the piecewise affine functions we consider. Also, the domain of definition of f is f-stable (i.e. $f(\text{dom } f) \subseteq \text{dom } f$). And finally, we will see that f is somehow "reversible".

Lemma 19 (Simulation is continuous). *For any $i \in \{1, \ldots, n\}$, $f_{\mathcal{I}}(R_i)$ is well-defined and continuous over R_i.*

Lemma 20 (Simulation is stable). *For any $i \in \{1, \ldots, n\}$, $f_{\mathcal{I}}(R_i) \subseteq R_{i+1}$. Furthermore, $f(R_0) \subseteq R_1$ and $f(R_{n+1}) \subseteq R_{n+1}$.*

We now get to the core lemma of the simulation. Up to this point, we were only interested in forward simulation: that is given a point, what are the iterates of x. In order to prove the NP-hardness result, we need a backward result: given a point, what are the possible preimages of it. To this end, we introduce new subregions of the R_i which we call *unsaturated*. Intuitively, R_i^{unsat} corresponds to the encodings where $\sigma \leqslant B$, that is the sum did not saturate at $B+1$. We also introduce the R_{fin} region which will be the region to reach. We will be interested in the preimages of R_{fin}.

Definition 21 (Unsaturated regions). *For $i \in \{1, \ldots, n+1\}$, define*

$$R_i^{unsat} = [i2^{-p}, i2^{-p} + B2^{-q}] \times [\beta^{-n-1}, \beta^{-i+1} - \beta^{-n-1}]$$

$$R_{fin} = [(n+1)2^{-p} + B2^{-q} - 2^{-q-1}, (n+1)2^{-p} + B2^{-q}] \times [\beta^{-n-1}, 2\beta^{-n-1}]$$

Lemma 22 (Simulation is reversible). *Let $i \in \{2, \ldots, n\}$ and $(a, b) \in R_i^{unsat}$ Then the only points $\mathbf{x}$ such that $f_{\mathcal{I}}(\mathbf{x}) = (a', b')$ are:*

- $\mathbf{x} = (a - 2^{-p}, b' + 0^\star\beta^{-i+1}) \in R_{i-1,0^\star} \cap R_{i-1}^{unsat}$
- $\mathbf{x} = (a - 2^{-p}, \beta^i - b' + 0^\star\beta^{-i+1}) \in R_{i-1,2} \cap R_{i-1}^{unsat}$
- $\mathbf{x} = (a - 2^{-p} - A_i 2^{-q}, b' + 1^\star\beta^{-i+1}) \in R_{i-1,1^\star}^{lin} \cap R_{i-1}^{unsat}$ *(only if $a \geqslant 2^{-p} + A_i 2^{-q}$)*

The goal of those results in to show if there is a point in R_{fin} which is reachable from R_0 then we can extract, from its trajectory, a configuration which also reaches R_{fin}. Furthermore, we arranged so that R_{fin} contains the encoding of only one configuration:$(n+1, B)$ (see Lemma 12).

Lemma 23 (Backward-forward identity). *For any point $\mathbf{x} \in R_{fin}$, if there exists a point $\mathbf{y} \in R_0$ and an integer k such that $f_{\mathcal{I}}^{[k]}(\mathbf{y}) = \mathbf{x}$ then there exists a configuration $c = (1, 0, \varepsilon_1, \ldots, \varepsilon_n)$ such that $f_{\mathcal{I}}^{[k]}(\langle c \rangle) \in R_{fin}$.*

Lemma 24 (Final region is accepting). *For any configuration c, if $\langle c \rangle \in R_{fin}$ then $c = (n+1, B)$.*

3.3 Complexity Result

We now have all the tools to show that REACH-REGION-TIME is an NP-hard problem.

Theorem 25. *REACH-REGION-TIME is NP-hard for $d \geqslant 2$.*

Proof. Let $\mathcal{I} = (B, A_1, \ldots, A_n)$ be a instance of SUBSET-SUM. We consider the instance $\mathcal{J}$ of REACH-REGION-TIME defined in the previous section with maximum number of iterations set to n (the number of A_i), the initial region set to R_0 and the final region set to R_{fin}. One easily checks that this instance has polynomial size in the size of $\mathcal{I}$. The two directions of the proofs are:

- If $\mathcal{I}$ is satisfiable then use Lemma 11 and Lemma 16 to conclude that there is a point $x \in R_0$ in the initial region such that $f_{\mathcal{I}}^{[n]}(x) \in R_{fin}$ so $\mathcal{J}$ is satisfiable.
- If $\mathcal{J}$ is satisfiable then there exists $x \in R_0$ and $k \leqslant n$ such that $f_{\mathcal{I}}^{[k]}(x) \in R_{fin}$. Use Lemma 23 and Lemma 16 to conclude that there exists a configuration $c = (1, 0, \varepsilon_1, \ldots, \varepsilon_n)$ such that $\langle T_{\mathcal{I}}^{[k]}(c) \rangle = f_{\mathcal{I}}^{[k]}(\langle c \rangle) \in R_{fin}$. Apply Lemma 24 and use the injectivity of the encoding to conclude that $T_{\mathcal{I}}^{[k]}(c) = (n+1, B)$ and Lemma 12 to get that $\mathcal{I}$ is satisfiable.

4 Solving of Bounded Time Reachability

In the previous section we focused on what we can do with a reachability problem, and specifically how to solve a NP-hard problem with it. In this section, we take any such reachability problem and focus on how to actually solve it. More precisely we are interested in the complexity of solving the `REACH-REGION-TIME` problem.

4.1 Notations and Definitions

For any $i = 1, \ldots, d$, let $\pi_i^d \colon I^d \to I$ denote the ith projection function, that is, $\pi(x_1, \ldots, x_d) = x_i$. Let $g_d \colon I^{d+1} \to I^d$ be defined by $g_d(x_1, \ldots, x_{d+1}) = (x_1, \ldots, x_d)$. For a square matrix A of size $(d+1) \times (d+1)$ define the following pair of projection functions. The first function $h_{1,d}$ takes as input a square matrix A of size $(d+1) \times (d+1)$ and returns a square matrix of size $d \times d$ which is the upper-left block of A. The second function $h_{2,d}$ takes as input a square matrix A of size $(d+1) \times (d+1)$ and returns the vector of size d given by $[a_{1,d+1} \cdots a_{d,d+1}]^T$ (the last column of A minus the last element).

Let s denote the size function, its domain of objects will be overloaded and understood from the context. For $x \in \mathbb{Z}$, $s(x)$ is the length of the encoding of x in base 2. For $x \in \mathbb{Q}$ with $x = \frac{p}{q}$ we have $s(x) = \max(s(p), s(q))$. For an affine function f we define the size of $f(\mathbf{x}) = A\mathbf{x} + \mathbf{b}$ (where all entries of A and $\mathbf{b}$ are rationals) as: $s(f) = \max(\max_{i,j}(s(a_{i,j})), \max(s(b_i)))$. We define the size of a polyhedron r defined by $A\mathbf{x} \leqslant \mathbf{b}$ as: $s(r) = \max(s(A), s(\mathbf{b}))$.

We define the size of a piecewise affine function f as: $s(f) = \max_i(s(f_i), s(r_i))$ where f_i denotes the restriction of f to r_i the ith region.

We define the *signature* of a point $\mathbf{x}$ as the sequence of indices of the regions traversed by the iterates of f on $\mathbf{x}$ (that is, the region trajectory).

4.2 Results

In order to solve a reachability problem, we will formulate it with linear algebra. However a crucial issue here is that of the size of the numbers, especially when computing powers of matrices. Indeed, if taking the nth power of A yields a representation of exponential size, no matter how fast our algorithm is, it will run on exponentially large instances and thus be slow.

First off, we show how to move to homogenous coordinates so that f becomes piecewise linear instead of piecewise affine.

Lemma 26. *Assume that* $f(\mathbf{x}) = A\mathbf{x} + \mathbf{b}$ *with* $A = (a_{i,j})_{1 \leqslant i,j \leqslant d}$ *and let* $y = A'(\mathbf{x}, 1)^T$ *where* A' *is the block matrix* $\begin{pmatrix} A & \mathbf{b} \\ 0 & 1 \end{pmatrix}$. *Then* $f(x) = g_d(A'(\mathbf{x}, 1)^T)$.

Remark 27. Notice that this lemma extends nicely to the composition of affine functions: if $f(\mathbf{x}) = A\mathbf{x} + \mathbf{b}$ and $h(\mathbf{x}) = C\mathbf{x} + \mathbf{d}$ then $h(f(x)) = g_d(C'A'(\mathbf{x}, 1)^T)$.

We can now state the main lemma, namely that the size of the iterates of f vary linearly in the number of iterates, assuming that f is piecewise affine.

Lemma 28. *Let $d \geqslant 2$ and $f \in PAF_d$. Assume that all the coefficients of f on all regions are rationals. Then for all $t \in \mathbb{N}$, $s(f^{[t]}) \leqslant (d+1)^2 s(f)pt + (t - 1)\lceil \log_2(d+1)\rceil$ where p is the number of regions of f. This inequality holds even if all rationals are taken to have the same denominator.*

Finally, we need some result about the size of solutions to systems of linear inequalities. Indeed, if we are going to quantify over the existence of a solution of polynomial size, we must ensure that the size constraints does not change the satisfiability of the system.

Lemma 29 ([13]). *Let A be a $N \times d$ integer matrix and $\mathbf{b}$ an integer vector. If the $A\mathbf{x} \leqslant \mathbf{b}$ system admits a solution, then there exists a rational solution x_s such that $s(x_s) \leqslant (d+1)L + (2d+1)\log_2(2d+1)$ where $L = \max(s(A), s(b))$.*

Proof. See Theorem 5 of [13]: $s(x_s) \leqslant s\left((2d+1)!2^{L(2d+1)}\right)$.

Putting everything together, we obtain a fast nondeterministic algorithm to solve REACH-REGION-TIME. The nondeterministism allows use to choose a signature for the solution. Once the signature is fixed, we can write it as a linear program of reasonable size using Lemma 28 and solve it. The remaining issue is the one of the size of solution but fortunately Lemma 29 ensures us that there is a small solution which can be found quickly.

Theorem 30. *REACH-REGION-TIME is in NP.*

5 Other Results

In this section, we give succint proofs of the other result mentioned in the introduction about CONTROL-REGION-TIME. The proof is based on the same arguments as before.

Theorem 31. *Problem CONTROL-REGION-TIME is coNP-hard for $d \geqslant 2$.*

Proof. The proof is exactly the same except for two details:

- we modify f over R_{n+1} as follows: divide R_{n+1} in three regions: R_{low} which is below R_{fin}, R_{fin} and R_{high} which is above R_{fin}. Then build f such that $f(R_{low}) \subseteq R_{low}$, $f(R_{fin}) \subseteq R_{fin}$ and $f(R_{high}) \subseteq R_{low}$.
- we choose a new final region $R'_{fin} = R_{low}$.

Let $\mathcal{I} = (B, A_1, \ldots, A_n)$ be an instance of NOSUBSET-SUM, let $\mathcal{J}$ be the corresponding instance of CONTROL-REGION-TIME we just built. We have to show that $\mathcal{I}$ has no subset sum if and only if $\mathcal{J}$ is "controlled". This is the same as showing that $\mathcal{I}$ has a subset sum if and only if $\mathcal{J}$ has points never reaching R'_{fin}.

Now assume for a moment that the instance is in SUBSET-SUM (as opposed to NOSUBSET-SUM), then by the same reasoning as the previous proof, there will be a point which reaches the old R_{fin} region (which is disjoint from R'_{fin}). And since R_{fin} is a f-stable region, this point will never reach R'_{fin}.

And conversely, if the control problem is not satisfied, necessarily there is a point which trajectory went through the old R_{fin} (otherwise if would have reached either $R_{low} = R'_{fin}$ or R_{high} but $f(R_{high}) \subseteq R_{low}$). Now we proceed as in the proof of Theorem 25 to conclude that there is a subset which sums to B, and thus $\mathcal{I}$ is satisfiable.

Theorem 32. *Problem* CONTROL-REGION-TIME *is in coNP.*

Proof. Again the proof is very similar to that of Theorem 30: we have to build a non-deterministic machine which accepts the "no" instances. The algorithm is exactly the same except that we only choose signatures which avoid the final region (as opposed to end by the final region) and are of maximum length (that is $t = T$ as opposed to $t \leqslant T$). Indeed, if there is a such a trajectory, the problem is not satisfied. And for the same reasons as Theorem 30, it runs in non-deterministic polynomial time.

References

1. Koiran, P., Cosnard, M., Garzon, M.: Computability with low-dimensional dynamical systems. Theoretical Computer Science 132, 113–128 (1994)
2. Henzinger, T.A., Kopke, P.W., Puri, A., Varaiya, P.: What's decidable about hybrid automata? Journal of Computer and System Sciences 57, 94–124 (1998)
3. Moore, C.: Generalized shifts: unpredictability and undecidability in dynamical systems. Nonlinearity 4, 199–230 (1991)
4. Siegelmann, H.T., Sontag, E.D.: On the computational power of neural nets. Journal of Computer and System Sciences 50, 132–150 (1995)
5. Asarin, E., Maler, O., Pnueli, A.: Reachability analysis of dynamical systems having piecewise-constant derivatives. Theoretical Computer Science 138, 35–65 (1995)
6. Koiran, P., Cosnard, M., Garzon, M.: Computability with Low-Dimensional Dynamical Systems. Theoretical Computer Science 132, 113–128 (1994)
7. Asarin, E., Schneider, G.: Widening the boundary between decidable and undecidable hybrid systems. In: Brim, L., Jančar, P., Křetínský, M., Kučera, A. (eds.) CONCUR 2002. LNCS, vol. 2421, pp. 193–208. Springer, Heidelberg (2002)
8. Asarin, E., Schneider, G., Yovine, S.: On the decidability of the reachability problem for planar differential inclusions. In: Di Benedetto, M.D., Sangiovanni-Vincentelli, A.L. (eds.) HSCC 2001. LNCS, vol. 2034, pp. 89–104. Springer, Heidelberg (2001)
9. Bell, P., Chen, S.: Reachability problems for hierarchical piecewise constant derivative systems. In: Abdulla, P.A., Potapov, I. (eds.) RP 2013. LNCS, vol. 8169, pp. 46–58. Springer, Heidelberg (2013)
10. Ben-Amram, A.M.: Mortality of iterated piecewise affine functions over the integers: Decidability and complexity. In: STACS, pp. 514–525 (2013)
11. Blondel, V.D., Bournez, O., Koiran, P., Tsitsiklis, J.: The stability of saturated linear dynamical systems is undecidable. Journal of Computer and System Science 62, 442–462 (2001)
12. Garey, M.R., Johnson, D.S.: Computers and Intractability. W. H. Freeman and Co. (1979)
13. Koiran, P.: Computing over the reals with addition and order. Theor. Comput. Sci. 133, 35–47 (1994)

Reachability and Mortality Problems for Restricted Hierarchical Piecewise Constant Derivatives

Paul C. Bell[1], Shang Chen[1], and Lisa Jackson[2]

[1] Department of Computer Science, Loughborough University
[2] Department of Aeronautical and Automotive Engineering,
Loughborough University
{P.Bell,S.Chen3,L.M.Jackson}@lboro.ac.uk

Abstract. We show the NP-hardness of the reachability and mortality problems for a three dimensional variant of Piecewise Constant Derivative (PCD) system called a bounded 3-dimensional Restricted Hierarchical PCD (3-RHPCD). Both problems are shown to be in PSPACE, even for n-dimensional RHPCD. This is a restricted model with similarities to other models in the literature such as stopwatch automata, rectangular automata and PCDs. We also show that for an unbounded 3-RHPCD, both problems become undecidable via a simulation of a Minsky machine.

1 Introduction

The model of *Piecewise Constant Derivative* (PCD) system is a natural and intuitive hybrid system model. An n-dimensional PCD is a finite set of non-overlapping bounded or unbounded convex n-dimensional regions, for which each region is assigned a constant derivative. This derivative defines the direction of flow of points within that region, with the derivative changing when the trajectory passes from one region to the next. See Section 2 for formal definitions.

Among the possible problems one may consider for PCDs is the *reachability* problem. The reachability problem asks, given a PCD and two points x and y, does the trajectory starting at point x ever reach point y after some finite amount of time? It was shown in [11] that the reachability problem for 2-PCDs is *decidable*. In contrast, it was shown in [2] that reachability for 3-PCDs is actually *undecidable*.

In [4], a related model, called a *Hierarchical Piecewise Constant Derivative* (HPCD) system was introduced. An HPCD is a two-dimensional hybrid automaton where the dynamics in each discrete location is given by a 2-PCD (formal details are given in Section 2). Certain edges in the HPCD are called (transition) guards and cause the HPCD to change location if ever the trajectory reaches such an edge. When transitioning between locations, an affine reset rule may be applied. If all regions of the underlying PCDs are bounded, then the HPCD is called bounded. This model can thus be seen as an extension of a 2-PCD. Indeed, the reachability problem for a one-dimensional Piecewise Affine Map

J. Ouaknine, I. Potapov, and J. Worrell (Eds.): RP 2014, LNCS 8762, pp. 32–44, 2014.
© Springer International Publishing Switzerland 2014

(1-PAM), which is a longstanding open problem, was shown to be equivalent to that of reachability for a bounded HPCD with either: i) comparative guards, identity resets and elementary flows in Proposition 3.20 of [3] or else ii) affine resets, non-comparative guards and elementary flows in Lemma 3.4 of [3] (See Section 2 for definitions).

Further results for HPCDs were shown in [5]. The model of *Restricted HPCD* (RHPCD) was defined, which is an HPCD with restricted components. We aimed to study which restrictions of an HPCD lead to decidable reachability results. Essentially, the HPCD must have identity resets, elementary flows (derivatives of all continuous variables come from $\{0, \pm 1\}$) and non-comparative guards (all guards aligned with the x and y axes). These restrictions on the resets, derivatives and guards seem natural ones to consider. For example, restricting to identity resets means the trajectory will not have discontinuities in the continuous component, which is similar to a PCD trajectory. Restricting the derivatives to elementary flows ($\{0, \pm 1\}$) has similarities to a *stopwatch automaton*, for which all derivatives are from $\{0, 1\}$. Restricting the guards to be non-comparative gives strong similarities to the guards of a *rectangular automaton* [9], as well as the diagonal-free clock constraints of an *updatable timed automaton* [7].

Reachability for 2-RHPCDs was shown to be decidable. Together with the results in [3] mentioned above, the reachability problem for HPCDs was shown to be equivalent to that of 1-PAMs when the HPCD only has one of the following: comparative guards, linear resets or arbitrary constant flows. Furthermore, if the model is endowed with a non-deterministic transition function between locations, then the reachability problem becomes NP-hard.

Related to the reachability problem is the *mortality problem*. The mortality problem is the problem of determining if *all* valid initial points eventually reach some particular fixed point configuration (the mortal configuration). There is potentially more than one way to define the mortality problem for HPCDs. In this paper, we define the mortality problem to mean that from any valid initial configuration, the trajectory will reach some fixed point $(0, 0, 0)$ in a finite amount of time, after which the point never changes. Thus the trajectory can be said to halt at this stage.

In this paper, we consider an n-dimensional analogue of RHPCDs, which we denote n-RHPCD. In an analogous way to [3], our aim is to study the following question: "What is the simplest class of hybrid systems for which reachability is intractable or undecidable?" We show a lower bound that the reachability and mortality problems for bounded 3-RHPCDs are NP-hard by an encoding of the simultaneous incongruences problem. We then show that the reachability problem for unbounded 3-RHPCDs is actually undecidable by an encoding of a Minsky machine. Note that the reachability problem for a 3-dimensional HPCD is undecidable, even with only one location, since HPCDs are a superclass of 3-dimensional PCDs for which reachability is undecidable [2]. Finally, we give an upper bound by showing that the reachability and mortality problems for bounded n-RHPCD are in PSPACE.

Note that the systems we construct in this paper deal with trajectories of 'tubes' instead of single lines, which means tiny perturbations will not affect our results. This seems to coincide with the definition of *tube languages* introduced in [10] and implies that our models are *robust* in the properties considered in this paper, but we do not give full details in this conference version of the paper.

2 Preliminaries

Intervals of the form $(s,t), [s,t), (s,t], [s,t]$ are called open, half-open or closed bounded rational intervals (respectively), where $s,t \in \mathbb{Q}$. Let $S \in \mathbb{R}^n$ be a set in the n-dimensional Euclidean space. We define the *closure* of S to be the smallest closed set containing S, denoted $\overline{S}$. We use similar definitions as [3] for the following.

Definition 1. (HA) *An n-dimensional Hybrid Automaton (HA) [1] is a tuple $\mathcal{H} = (\mathcal{X}, Q, f, l_0, Inv, \delta)$ consisting of the following components:*

(1) A continuous state space $\mathcal{X} \subseteq \mathbb{R}^n$. Each $\boldsymbol{x} \in \mathcal{X}$ can be written $\boldsymbol{x} = (x_1, \ldots, x_n)$, and we use variables $x_1, \ldots, x_n$ to denote components of the state vector.

(2) A finite set of discrete locations Q.

(3) A function $f : Q \to (\mathcal{X} \to \mathbb{R}^n)$, which assigns a continuous vector field on $\mathcal{X}$ to each location. In location $l \in Q$, the evolution of the continuous variables is governed by the differential equation $\dot{\boldsymbol{x}} = f_l(\boldsymbol{x})$. The differential equation is called the dynamics of location l.

(4) An initial condition $I_0 : Q \to 2^{\mathcal{X}}$ assigning initial values to variables in each location.

(5) An invariant Inv: $Q \to 2^{\mathcal{X}}$. For each $l \in Q$, the continuous variables must satisfy the condition Inv(l) in order to remain in location l, otherwise it must make a discrete transition.

(6) A set of transitions δ. Every $tr \in \delta$ is of the form $tr = (l, g, \gamma, l')$, where $l, l' \in Q$, $g \subset \mathcal{X}$ is called the guard, defining when the discrete transition can occur, $\gamma \subset \mathcal{X} \times \mathcal{X}$ is called the reset relation applied after the transition from l to l'.

An HA is *deterministic* if it has exactly one solution for its differential equation in each location and the guards for the outgoing edges of locations are mutually exclusive. A configuration of an HA is a pair from $Q \times \mathcal{X}$. A *trajectory* of a hybrid automaton $\mathcal{H}$ starting from configuration $(l_0, \mathbf{x_0})$ where $l_0 \in Q, \mathbf{x_0} \in \mathcal{X}$ is a pair of functions $\pi_{l_0, \mathbf{x_0}} = (\lambda_{l_0, \mathbf{x_0}}(t), \xi_{l_0, \mathbf{x_0}}(t))$ such that

(1) $\lambda_{l_0, \mathbf{x_0}}(t) : [0, +\infty) \to Q$ is a piecewise function constant on every interval $[t_i, t_{i+1})$.

(2) $\xi_{l_0, \mathbf{x_0}}(t) : [0, +\infty) \to \mathbb{R}^n$ is a piecewise differentiable function and in each piece $\xi_{l_0, \mathbf{x_0}}$ is càdlàg (right continuous with left limits everywhere).

(3) On any interval $[t_i, t_{i+1})$ where $\lambda_{l_0, \mathbf{x_0}}$ is constant and $\xi_{l_0, \mathbf{x_0}}$ is continuous,

$$\xi_{l_0, \mathbf{x_0}}(t) = \xi_{l_0, \mathbf{x_0}}(t_i) + \int_{t_i}^{t} f_{\lambda_{l_0, \mathbf{x_0}}(t_i)}(\xi_{l_0, \mathbf{x_0}}(\tau)) d\tau$$

for all $\tau \in [t_i, t_{i+1})$.

(4) For any t_i, there exists a transition $(l, g, \gamma, l') \in \delta$ such that
  (i) $\lambda_{l_0, \mathbf{x_0}}(t_i) = l$ and $\lambda_{l_0, \mathbf{x_0}}(t_{i+1}) = l'$;
  (ii) $\xi_{l_0, \mathbf{x_0}}^{-}(t_{i+1}) \in g(l, l')$ where $\xi_{l_0, \mathbf{x_0}}^{-}(t)$ means the left limit of $\xi_{l_0, \mathbf{x_0}}$ at t;
  (iii) $(\xi_{l_0, \mathbf{x_0}}^{-}(t_{i+1}), \xi_{l_0, \mathbf{x_0}}(t_{i+1})) \in \gamma$.

Definition 2. (n-PCD) *An n-dimensional Piecewise Constant Derivative (n-PCD) system [2] is a pair $\mathcal{H} = (\mathbb{P}, \mathbb{F})$ such that:*

(1) $\mathbb{P} = \{P_s\}_{1 \leq s \leq k}$ is a finite family in $\mathbb{R}^n$, where $P_s \subseteq \mathbb{R}^n$ are non-overlapping convex polygonal sets.

(2) $\mathbb{F} = \{\mathbf{c}_s\}_{1 \leq s \leq k}$ is a family of vectors in $\mathbb{R}$.

(3) The dynamics are given by $\dot{\mathbf{x}} = \mathbf{c}_s$ for $\mathbf{x} \in P_s$.

An n-PCD is called bounded if for its regions $\mathbb{P} = \{P_s\}_{1 \leq s \leq k}$, there exists $r \in \mathbb{Q}^+$, such that for all P_s, we have that $P_s \subseteq B_\mathbf{0}(r)$, where $B_\mathbf{0}(r)$ is an origin-centered open ball of radius r and appropriate dimension. We define the *support set* of a PCD $\mathcal{H}$ as $\text{Supp}_{\text{PCD}}(\mathcal{H}) = \bigcup_{1 \leq s \leq k} P_s$.

For full definitions of Hybrid Automata and their trajectories, see [5]. In the following we slightly modify the definition of HPCD [3] to allow different dimensions to be studied.

Definition 3. (n-HPCD) *A n-dimensional Hierarchical Piecewise Constant Derivative (n-HPCD) system is a hybrid automaton $\mathcal{H} = (\mathcal{X}, Q, f, l_0, Inv, \delta)$ such that Q and l_0 are defined as in Definition 1, with the dynamics at each $l \in Q$ given by an n-PCD and each transition $tr = (l, g, \gamma, l')$ is such that: (1) Its guard g is a convex region such that $g \subseteq \mathbb{R}^{n-1}$; and (2) The reset relation γ is an affine function of the form: $\mathbf{x}' = \gamma(\mathbf{x}) = A\mathbf{x} + \mathbf{b}$, where $A \in \mathbb{R}^{n \times n}$ and $\mathbf{b} \in \mathbb{R}^n$. We denote the* internal guards *of an HPCD location to be the guards of the underlying PCD regions which cause a change of region when they are reached. The* transition guards *are the guards used in transitions between locations. The Invariant (Inv) for a location l is defined to be $\text{Supp}_{\text{PCD}}(\mathcal{H}) \setminus \mathcal{G}_l$, where $\text{Supp}_{\text{PCD}}(\mathcal{H})$ is the support set of the underlying PCDs of the HPCD and $\mathcal{G}_l$ is the set of transition guards in location l. If all the PCDs are bounded, then the n-HPCD is said to be bounded.*

In this paper, we are interested in a *restricted* form of n-HPCD.

(I) Under the HPCD model, when transitioning between locations, we may apply an affine reset to non-continuously modify the current point. An n-HPCD has identity (or no) resets if for every transition $tr = (l, g, \gamma, l')$, $\gamma(x) = x$ for all points $x \in \mathbb{R}^n$. This means that starting from any initial configuration $(l_0, \mathbf{x_0})$, for the trajectory $\pi_{l_0, \mathbf{x_0}} = (\lambda_{l_0, \mathbf{x_0}}(t), \xi_{l_0, \mathbf{x_0}}(t))$ we have that $\xi_{l_0, \mathbf{x_0}}(t)$ is a continuous function of t. Note that the trajectory for a PCD is also continuous, and thus this seems to be a natural restriction.

(II) An n-HPCD system has *elementary flows* if the derivatives of all variables in each location are from $\{0, \pm 1\}$, otherwise it has *arbitrary constant flows*.

(III) Guards are used to change the derivative being applied within a location (internal guards), or to change which location we are in (transition guards). They can be described by Boolean combinations of atomic formulae (linear inequalities). If each atomic formula contains only one variable, then the guard is called non-comparative (meaning the guard is aligned with ones of the axes). An n-HPCD has *non-comparative guards* if all guards (both internal and transition) are non-comparative, e.g., for a 3-RHPCD, $\frac{3}{2} \leq x \leq 7 \wedge y = -1 \wedge 2 \leq z \leq 7$ is a non-comparative guard, but $0 \leq x \leq 1 \wedge 0 \leq y \leq \frac{1}{2} \wedge z = 5 \wedge x = 2y$ is a comparative guard (due to the term $x = 2y$).

Definition 4. (n-RHPCD) *An n-dimensional Restricted Hierarchical Constant Derivative System (RHPCD) is a bounded n-HPCD with identity resets, non-comparative guards, elementary flows and a finite number of PCD regions. See Fig. 2a and Fig. 2b for an example of a 3-RHPCD.*

Finally, we will also require the following *simultaneous incongruences problem*, which is known to be NP-complete [8].

Problem 1. (Simultaneous incongruences) *Given a set $\{(a_1, b_1), \ldots, (a_n, b_n)\}$ of ordered pairs of positive integers with $a_i \leq b_i$ for $1 \leq i \leq n$. Does there exist an integer k such that $k \not\equiv a_i \pmod{b_i}$ for every $1 \leq i \leq n$?*

3   Reachability and Mortality for n-RHPCDs

The following lemma shows that if an instance of the simultaneous incongruences problem has a solution, then there must be a solution less than a particular bound.

Lemma 1. *There exist solutions for the simultaneous incongruences problem with a collection $\{(a_1, b_1), \ldots, (a_n, b_n)\}$ if and only if there exists a solution k such that $0 < k \leq \rho$, where*

$$\rho = lcm(b_1, \ldots, b_n)$$

and $lcm(b_1, \ldots, b_n)$ is the least common multiple of $b_1, \ldots, b_n$.

Proof. The sufficient part is trivial. We show the necessary part. Given an instance $\{(a_1, b_1), \ldots, (a_n, b_n)\}$, let $\rho = lcm(b_1, \ldots, b_n)$. Then for every $1 \leq i \leq n$, $\rho \equiv 0 \pmod{b_i}$.

For every integer $k > \rho$, we can rewrite k as $k = k_0 + m\rho$, where $0 < k_0 \leq \rho$ and $m \in \mathbb{N}$. Suppose there exists a solution $k_s > \rho$. According to the simultaneous incongruences problem, we know that $k_s \not\equiv a_i \pmod{b_i}$ for all i, where $1 \leq i \leq n$. So we can find a k_0, where $0 < k_0 \leq \rho$, and a positive integer m such that

$$k_s \equiv k_0 + m\rho \not\equiv a_i \pmod{b_i},$$

for every i, where $1 \leq i \leq n$. But $\rho \equiv 0 \pmod{b_i}$ for all $1 \leq i \leq n$, which implies that

$$k_0 \not\equiv a_i \pmod{b_i}$$

for all $1 \leq i \leq n$, thus k_0 is the solution we want. $\square$

Theorem 1. *The reachability problem for bounded 3-RHPCD systems is NP-hard.*

Proof. Consider an instance of the simultaneous incongruences problem with n pairs. We will encode the instance into a reachability problem for a 3-RHPCD. Starting from $k = 1$, we test whether $k \bmod b_i \neq a_i$ holds for each pair (a_i, b_i). If it does hold for every i, then the current value of k is the solution. If for some i we find $k \bmod b_i = a_i$, then the current value of k is not a potential solution. We increase the value of k by 1 and start the testing all over again. By Lemma 1 there are at most ρ integers to test.

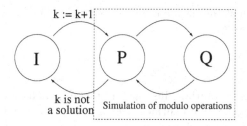

Fig. 1. Reachability problem for 3-RHPCD (Location I actually represents 3 locations I_1, I_2 and I_3)

We construct the corresponding 3-RHPCD in the following way. We define 5 locations P, Q, I_1, I_2 and I_3. Locations P and Q together can simulate the modulo operation test for a certain value of k and every pair of (a_i, b_i). Locations I_1, I_2 and I_3 can increase the value of k by 1 when we find the current k is not a potential solution. See Fig. 1. Define regions A_i and B_i in locations P and Q :

$$A_i = (s_{i-1}, s_i) \times (0, \rho) \times (0, \rho);$$
$$B_i = (s_{i-1}, s_i) \times (0, \rho) \times (-\rho, 0),$$

where $i \in \{1, 2, ..., n\}$, $s_0 = 0$, $s_i = \sum_1^i b_i$ for $1 \leq i \leq n$, and $\rho = \mathrm{lcm}(b_1, \ldots, b_n)$. We call a region *odd* (resp. *even*) A_i or B_i if i is odd (resp. even). We also define surface O :

$$O = [0, s_n] \times [0, \rho] \times \{0\}.$$

To simulate the modulo operation for a certain pair (a_i, b_i), we use the regions odd $\overline{A}_i$ and even $\overline{B}_i$ in both locations P and Q. Define the derivative to be $(1, 1, -1)$ in odd $\overline{A}_i$ in P $((1,1,1)$ in even $\overline{B}_i$ in $P)$ and $(-1, 0, 0)$ in both odd $\overline{A}_i$ and even $\overline{B}_i$ in Q. See Fig. 2. Intuitively, we arrange the regions alternately

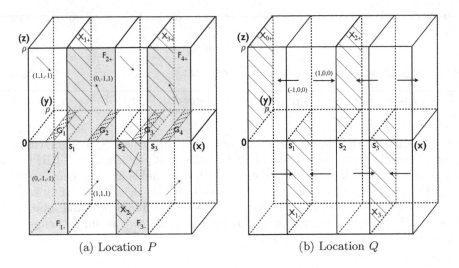

(a) Location P (b) Location Q

Fig. 2. 3-RHPCD simulating simultaneous incongruences problem (only location P and location Q are shown)

above and below the O surface instead of stacking them together. This is to avoid them sharing a common surface, which may cause nondeterminism when we define a (transition) guard on that surface.

For a point (x, y, z), we use the z coordinate to represent the current value of k and the y coordinate as a memory. Assuming i is odd (see Table. 1 for full details of both odd and even cases), we start at point $\boldsymbol{x_0} = (s_{i-1}, 0, k)$ in P and move according to the flow $\dot{\boldsymbol{x}} = (1, 1, -1)$. While $|z| > 0$, every time when $x = b_i + s_{i-1} = s_i$, we jump to Q. In Q we keep variables y and z unchanged, simply reset x to 0 by the flow $\dot{\boldsymbol{x}} = (-1, 0, 0)$ and jump back to P. Each time the trajectory goes from P to Q and jumps back to P, the absolute value of variable z will be subtracted by b_i. So when the trajectory hits the O surface (i.e., $z = 0$), the value of x will be equal to $s_{i-1} + (k \bmod b_i)$. Since y and z in P change at the same rate, when the absolute value of z drops from k to 0, the value of y will increase from 0 to k.

If $k \bmod b_i \neq a_i$, we reset y to 0 and $|z|$ to k by switching the value of these two variables, and enter region $\overline{B}_{(i+1)}$ to test whether $k \bmod b_{i+1} \neq a_{i+1}$. To do this, we use the regions odd $\overline{B}_i$ and even $\overline{A}_i$ in both locations P and Q. Define the derivative to be $(0, -1, -1)$ in odd $\overline{B}_i$ in P ($(0, -1, 1)$ in even $\overline{A}_i$ in P) and $(1, 0, 0)$ in both odd $\overline{B}_i$ and even $\overline{A}_i$ in Q. By the flows in P the value of y and $|z|$ are switched. When $y = 0$ we jump to Q and reset x to s_i, and then jump back to P to start testing the case of pair (a_{i+1}, b_{i+1}).

If $k \bmod b_i = a_i$, which means that the current value of k is not a potential solution, we jump to locations I_1, and then I_2 and I_3, (defined in Table 1) which moves the trajectory to point $(0, 0, k + 1)$ and 'restarts' in location P to test whether the new value $k + 1$ is a correct solution [1]. A correct solution k should satisfy that the trajectory starts from point $(0, 0, k)$ in location P and can finally reach some point (in location P) on the surface $(s_{n-1}, s_n) \times (0, \rho) \times \{0\}$ with $x \notin (s_{n-1} + a_n - \frac{\varepsilon}{2}, s_{n-1} + a_n + \frac{\varepsilon}{2})$.

Table 1. Reachability problem for 3-RHPCD

Location	Region	Flows	Guards
P	$\overline{A} \cup \overline{B}$	$\overline{A}_i$ (i is odd): $(1, 1, -1)$ $\overline{A}_i$ (i is even): $(0, -1, 1)$ $\overline{B}_i$ (i is odd): $(0, -1, -1)$ $\overline{B}_i$ (i is even): $(1, 1, 1)$	$\overline{X}_{i+}$ ($i = 1, 3, ..., n-1$), $\overline{X}_{i-}$ ($i = 2, 4, ...n$), $\overline{F}_{i+}$ ($i = 2, 4, ..., n$), $\overline{F}_{i-}$ ($i = 1, 3, ..., n-1$) : jump to Q G_i : jump to I_1
Q	$(\overline{A} \cup \overline{B}) \setminus C$	$\overline{A}_i$ (i is odd): $(-1, 0, 0)$ $\overline{A}_i$ (i is even): $(1, 0, 0)$ $\overline{B}_i$ (i is odd): $(1, 0, 0)$ $\overline{B}_i$ (i is even): $(-1, 0, 0)$	$\overline{X}_{i+}$ ($i = 0, 2, ..., n-2$), $\overline{X}_{i-}$ ($i = 1, 3, ..., n-1$) : jump to P
I_1	$\overline{A}$	$(-1, 0, 0)$	$x = 0$ jump to I_2
I_2	$\overline{A}$	$(0, 0, 1)$	$z = 1$ jump to I_3
I_3	$\overline{A}$	$(0, -1, 1)$	$y = 0$ jump to P

We now give the formal details of this construction. Without loss of generality, we assume n is even. Define 2 regions A and B :

$$A = \cup_1^n A_i;$$
$$B = \cup_1^n B_i.$$

Also define four types of surfaces F_{i+}, F_{i-}, X_{i+} and X_{i-} :

$$
\begin{aligned}
F_{i+} &= (s_{i-1}, s_i) \times \{0\} \times (0, \rho), & i = 1, 2, ..., n; \\
F_{i-} &= (s_{i-1}, s_i) \times \{0\} \times (-\rho, 0), & i = 1, 2, ..., n; \\
X_{i+} &= \{s_i\} \times (0, \rho) \times (0, \rho), & i = 0, 1, 2, ..., n; \\
X_{i-} &= \{s_i\} \times (0, \rho) \times (-\rho, 0), & i = 0, 1, 2, ..., n.
\end{aligned}
$$

---

[1] Note that here in the guards we do not require exactly $x = a_i + s_{i-1}$, but allow some error ε, so tiny perturbations will not affect our result. The same analysis can be applied to Theorem 2. This seems to imply that our system has robust reachability and mortality problems, but we do not expand on the details in this paper. See more details about robustness in [10]

Finally, we define a set of ε-width strips G_i and a set of ε-width cubes C :

$$G_i = (s_{i-1} + a_i - \tfrac{\varepsilon}{2}, s_{i-1} + a_i + \tfrac{\varepsilon}{2}) \times [0, \rho] \times \{0\}, \qquad i = 1, 2, ..., n;$$
$$C = \cup_1^{n-1} C_i,$$

where

$$C_i = \begin{cases} (s_i, s_i + \varepsilon) \times (0, \rho) \times (0, \rho), & \text{if} \quad i = 1, 3, ..., n - 1; \\ (s_i, s_i + \varepsilon) \times (0, \rho) \times (-\rho, 0), & \text{if} \quad i = 2, 4, ..., n - 2. \end{cases}$$

The set C is to prevent nondeterminism in location Q. With the help of these notations, we construct the 3-RHPCD in Table. 1.

The number of regions and guards in the constructed 3-RHPCD is clearly polynomial in the number of pairs of the simultaneous incongruences problem. Furthermore, the points defining each such region can be represented in binary and are therefore polynomial in the description size of the simultaneous incongruences problem. Therefore the constructed 3-RHPCD has a polynomial description size.   □

Theorem 2. *The mortality problem for a bounded 3-RHPCD system is NP-hard.*

Proof. We simulate a simultaneous incongruences problem by a bounded 3-RPHCD. The mortality problem asks whether for a certain system, starting from every initial configuration, the trajectory will eventually reach some fixed-point configuration, which we call the mortal configuration (in this case, the system is called mortal). Once we reach the mortal configuration, since it is a fixed point of the system, we assume the simulation halts since the point itself never changes. We construct our 3-RHPCD in such a way that the system is mortal if and only if there is no solution for the corresponding simultaneous incongruences problem, otherwise the system is immortal (i.e., starting from some configurations the system never reaches the mortal configuration).

For a pair (a_i, b_i) in the simultaneous incongruences problem, the derivatives of the associated regions $\overline{A}_i$ and $\overline{B}_i$ in locations P and Q are defined the same as in the proof of Theorem 1. In contrast to Theorem 1, in the mortality problem, we are not only concerned about some trajectories starting from certain points $(0, 0, k), 0 < k \leq \rho$, but want to know whether *all* the trajectories reach the mortal configuration.

In the following part we assume i is odd, similar analysis can be applied to the case when i is even. According to the flow $\dot{x} = (1, 1, -1)$ of an odd region $\overline{A}_i$ in location P, there are 2 boundaries the trajectories will eventually reach: the O surface and the $y = \rho$ surface (some trajectories may also reach the $\overline{X}_{i+}$ or $\overline{X}_{i-}$ surface, but they will jump to location Q and jump back, then reach either one of the above two surfaces at the end). In odd $\overline{A}_i$ in P, all the trajectories which reach the $y = \rho$ surface or reach the strip G_i on the O surface are considered as mortal trajectories and will jump to location M_1, in which all the trajectories will eventually reach the mortal configuration of point $(0, 0, 0)$ in locations $\{M_1, M_2, M_3\}$. The trajectories which reach the O surfaces but do not reach the strip G_i are considered as the potential solution trajectories and move on by following the flows for a further check.

In contrast to the proof of Theorem 1, in region $\overline{A}_n$ (or $\overline{B}_n$ depending on if i is odd or even) if any trajectory reaches the surface O but does not reach the strip G_n, we do not conclude that we find a solution k. Instead, we keep moving in P until we hit the guard, jump to location T, reset the trajectory to the point $(0, 0, k)$ and go to location P to start the test again. If k indeed is a correct solution to the corresponding simultaneous incongruences problem, the system will loop forever; otherwise the trajectory will go to location M_1 at some region odd $\overline{A}_i$ or even $\overline{B}_i$ in location P. Full details are shown in Table. 2.   □

Table 2. Mortality problem for 3RHPCD

Location	Region	Flows	Guards
P	$\overline{A} \cup \overline{B}$	$\overline{A}_i$ (i is odd): $(1, 1, -1)$ $\overline{A}_i$ (i is even): $(0, -1, 1)$ $\overline{B}_i$ (i is odd): $(0, -1, -1)$ $\overline{B}_i$ (i is even): $(1, 1, 1)$	$\overline{X}_{i+}$ ($i = 1, 3, ..., n-1$), $\overline{X}_{i-}$ ($i = 2, 4, ...n$), $\overline{F}_{i+}$ ($i = 2, 4, ..., n$), $\overline{F}_{i-}$ ($i = 1, 3, ..., n-1$) : jump to Q --- $(y = \rho), G_i$: jump to M_1
Q	$(\overline{A} \cup \overline{B}) \setminus C$	$\overline{A}_i$ (i is odd): $(-1, 0, 0)$ $\overline{A}_i$ (i is even): $(1, 0, 0)$ $\overline{B}_i$ (i is odd): $(1, 0, 0)$ $\overline{B}_i$ (i is even): $(-1, 0, 0)$	$\overline{X}_{i+}$ ($i = 0, 2, ..., n-2$), $\overline{X}_{i-}$ ($i = 1, 3, ..., n-1$) : jump to P --- $\overline{X}_{n+}$: jump to T
T	$\overline{A} \cup \overline{B}$	$(-1, 0, 0)$	$x = 0$: jump to P
M_1	$\overline{A} \cup \overline{B}$	$\overline{A} : (0, 0, -1)$ $\overline{B} : (0, 0, 1)$	z=0: jump to M_2
M_2	$\overline{A} \cup \overline{B}$	$(-1, 0, 0)$	x=0: jump to M_3
M_3	$\overline{A} \cup \overline{B}$	$(0, -1, 0)$	y=0: jump to M_1

Theorem 3. *Reachability and mortality are undecidable for unbounded 3-RHPCD systems.*

Proof. Both problems can be shown to be undecidable via a simulation of a two counter (Minsky) machine which represents a universal model of computation [12]. However we omit the details here due to page limit.   □

The following proposition gives an upper bound of the complexity for both the reachability and mortality problems for bounded n-RHPCDs.

Proposition 1. *The reachability and mortality problems for bounded n-RHPCDs are in PSPACE.*

Proof. The proof is similar to that used to show that reachability for a 2-RHPCD is decidable, as was shown in [5]. Given an n-RHPCD $\mathcal{H}$, an initial configuration $(q_0, \boldsymbol{x}_0)$ and a target configuration $(q_f, \boldsymbol{x}_f)$, we show that starting from $(q_0, \boldsymbol{x}_0)$, the trajectory will hit the internal and transition guards finitely many times before either reaching $(q_f, \boldsymbol{x}_f)$, or detecting a cycle, or hitting some endpoints (at which the calculation halts), thus 'convergence' to a point is possible.

By the definition of n-RHPCD, the guards of $\mathcal{H}$ are of the form

$$\left(\bigwedge_{1 \leq i \leq n \wedge i \neq j} (a_i \prec x_i \prec' b_i) \right) \wedge (x_j = c_j)$$

where $j \in \{1, \ldots, n\}, x_i, x_j, a_i, b_i, c_i \in \mathbb{Q}$, and $\prec, \prec' \in \{<, \leq\}$.

By definition, the components of $\boldsymbol{x}_0 = (x_{0_1}, \ldots, x_{0_n})$ and $\boldsymbol{x}_f = (x_{f_1}, \ldots, x_{f_n})$ are rational numbers, i.e., $\boldsymbol{x}_0, \boldsymbol{x}_f \in \mathbb{Q}^n$. Define

$$\gamma = \operatorname{lcd}(a_1, \ldots, a_n, b_1, \ldots, b_n, c_j, x_{0_1}, \ldots, x_{0_n}, x_{f_1}, \ldots, x_{f_n}),$$

where lcd denotes the *least common denominator*, and define

$$A_i = \gamma a_i, B_i = \gamma b_i, C_j = \gamma c_j, X_0 = \gamma \boldsymbol{x}_0, X_f = \gamma \boldsymbol{x}_f.$$

Thus, $A_i, B_i, C_j \in \mathbb{Z}$ and $\boldsymbol{X}_0, \boldsymbol{X}_f \in \mathbb{Z}^n$. Define a new n-RHPCD $\mathcal{H}'$ with initial configuration $(q_0, \boldsymbol{X}_0)$ and target configuration $(q_f, \boldsymbol{X}_f)$ by replacing $a_i, b_i, c_j, \boldsymbol{x}_0, \boldsymbol{x}_f$ by $A_i, B_i, C_j, \boldsymbol{X}_0, \boldsymbol{X}_f$. Clearly, $\mathcal{H}$ reaches $\boldsymbol{x}_f$ iff $\mathcal{H}'$ reaches $\boldsymbol{X}_f$.

Because all the flows of $\mathcal{H}'$ are chosen from the set $\{0, 1, -1\}$, when one variable x_i changes its value from one integer to another integer, any other variable x_j remains an integer. As the trajectory starts at integer point X_0, and the guards of $\mathcal{H}'$ are defined by integers, every time the trajectory hits a guard, it will have integer components.

We now prove that the problem can be solved in PSPACE. Note that the representation size of γ is clearly polynomial in the representation size of $\mathcal{H}$, thus so is the size of $\mathcal{H}'$. We now show that the representation size of the number of possible transition configurations (the configuration when the trajectory hits the guard and takes transition) of $\mathcal{H}'$ is also polynomial in the size of $\mathcal{H}$.

Let $k > 0$ be the number of locations of $\mathcal{H}'$. Since $\mathcal{H}$ is bounded, we can calculate $\tau \in \mathbb{N}$ to be the maximal absolute value of the endpoint of any invariant of $\mathcal{H}$ over all locations. Thus the range of variables of $\mathcal{H}'$ is contained within $[-\gamma\tau, \gamma\tau]$. Since we have n variables, the maximal number of transition configurations of $\mathcal{H}'$, starting at initial configuration $(q_0, \boldsymbol{X}_0)$ is thus $k(2\gamma\tau)^n$, which can be represented in size polynomial in the size of $\mathcal{H}$, since it requires at least $k \log(\gamma\tau)^n = nk \log(\gamma\tau)$ space to store $\mathcal{H}$ and

$$\frac{\log(k(2\gamma\tau)^n)}{nk \log(\gamma\tau)} = \frac{\log(k) + n \log(2\gamma\tau)}{nk \log(\gamma\tau)} < c$$

for some computable constant $c > 0$. We can use a counter to keep track of the number of transitions the trajectory of $\mathcal{H}'$ makes, starting from $(q_0, \boldsymbol{X}_0)$. As each transition is taken, we can determine if the final configuration was reached since the last transition. Otherwise, we increment the counter and proceed. If the counter reaches $k(2\gamma\tau)^n$, then the configurations must be periodic and we can halt. Using a similar approach, we can also show that the mortality problem for n-RHPCDs is also in PSPACE, however we omit the details here.   □

4   Conclusions

We showed that for bounded three-dimensional Restricted Hierarchical Piece-wise Constant Derivative systems (3-RHPCDs), the reachability and mortality problems are NP-hard (using the simultaneous incongruences problem) but also in PSPACE, even in the n-dimensional case. For unbounded 3-RHPCDs, we showed that both problems are undecidable by an encoding of a Minsky machine. Clearly there is still a gap left for the complexity of the reachability and mortality problems for bounded n-RHPCDs. To close the gap we need to answer some interesting open problems:

- Is there a large n for which both problems for n-RHPCD are PSPACE-hard?
- Can both problems be solved in NP in dimension three?
- Can both problems be solved in P in dimension two?

The model of RHPCD restricts various components of the hybrid automaton in ways which have parallels to other models, such as stopwatch automata, rect-angular automata and PCDs. RHPCDs have decidable reachability problems for them but endowing them with small additional powers renders them much more powerful. Therefore they seem a useful tool in studying the frontier of undecid-ability and tractability, in a similar way to the model of HPCD which inspired them.

Acknowledgements: We would like to thank the anonymous referees for their very useful suggestions and comments.

References

1. Alur, R., Courcoubetis, C., Halbwachs, N., Henzinger, T.A., Ho, P.H., Nicollin, X., Olivero, A., Sifakis, J., Yovine, S.: The algorithmic analysis of hybrid systems. Theoretical Computer Science 138(1), 3–34 (1995)
2. Asarin, E., Maler, O., Pnueli, A.: Reachability analysis of dynamical systems having piecewise constant derivatives. Theoretical Computer Science 138, 35–65 (1995)
3. Asarin, E., Mysore, V., Pnueli, A., Schneider, G.: Low dimensional hybrid systems - decidable, undecidable, don't know. Information and Computation 211, 138–159 (2012)
4. Asarin, E., Schneider, G.: Widening the boundary between decidable and unde-cidable hybrid systems. In: Brim, L., Jančar, P., Křetínský, M., Kučera, A. (eds.) CONCUR 2002. LNCS, vol. 2421, pp. 193–208. Springer, Heidelberg (2002)
5. Bell, P.C., Chen, S.: Reachability problems for hierarchical piecewise constant derivative systems. In: Abdulla, P.A., Potapov, I. (eds.) RP 2013. LNCS, vol. 8169, pp. 46–58. Springer, Heidelberg (2013)

6. Blondel, V.D., Bournez, O., Koiran, P., Papadimitriou, C., Tsitsiklis, J.N.: Deciding stability and mortality of piecewise affine dynamical systems. Theoretical Computer Science 255(1-2), 687–696 (2001)
7. Bouyer, P., Dufourd, C., Fleury, E., Petit, A.: Updatable timed automata. Theoretical Computer Science 321(2), 291–345 (2004)
8. Garey, M.R., Johnson, D.S.: Computers and Intractability: A Guide to the Theory of NP-Completeness. W. H. Freeman and Co., New York (1979)
9. Henzinger, T., Kopka, P., Puri, A., Varaiya, P.: What's decidable about hybrid automata? In: 27th ACM STOC, pp. 373–382. ACM Press (1995)
10. Henzinger, T.A., Raskin, J.-F.: Robust undecidability of timed and hybrid systems. In: Lynch, N.A., Krogh, B.H. (eds.) HSCC 2000. LNCS, vol. 1790, pp. 145–159. Springer, Heidelberg (2000)
11. Maler, O., Pnueli, A.: Reachability analysis of planar multi-linear systems. In: Courcoubetis, C. (ed.) CAV 1993. LNCS, vol. 697, pp. 194–209. Springer, Heidelberg (1993)
12. Minsky, M.: Computation: Finite and Infinite Machines. Prentice-Hall International, Englewood Cliffs (1967)

Parameterized Verification of Communicating Automata under Context Bounds

Benedikt Bollig[1], Paul Gastin[1], and Jana Schubert[2]

[1] LSV, ENS Cachan & CNRS
{bollig,gastin}@lsv.ens-cachan.fr
[2] Fakultät für Informatik, TU Dresden
jana.schubert@tu-dresden.de

Abstract. We study the verification problem for parameterized communicating automata (PCA), in which processes synchronize via message passing. A given PCA can be run on any topology of bounded degree (such as pipelines, rings, or ranked trees), and communication may take place between any two processes that are adjacent in the topology. Parameterized verification asks if there is a topology from a given topology class that allows for an accepting run of the given PCA. In general, this problem is undecidable even for synchronous communication and simple pipeline topologies. We therefore consider context-bounded verification, which restricts the behavior of each single process. For several variants of context bounds, we show that parameterized verification over pipelines, rings, and ranked trees is decidable. More precisely, it is PSPACE-complete for pipelines and rings, and EXPTIME-complete for ranked trees. Our approach is automata-theoretic. We build a finite (tree, respectively) automaton that identifies those topologies that allow for an accepting run of the given PCA. The verification problem then reduces to checking nonemptiness of that automaton.

1 Introduction

Communicating automata (CA) are a fundamental and well-studied model of parallel systems [7]. They consist of finite-state machines that exchange messages over channels determined by a fixed and known communication topology. CA are known to be Turing equivalent so that even basic problems of formal verification such as reachability are undecidable. Therefore, modifications and restrictions have been considered which bring back decidability. Reachability is decidable, for example, when the analysis is restricted to executions with a fixed maximum number of pending messages, or when channels are lossy [2].

In some contexts such as ad-hoc networks, multi-core programming, or communication-protocol verification, assuming a fixed and known communication topology is not appropriate. Lately, there has been a lot of (ongoing) research in the area of *parameterized* verification [1,3,9,13,14], which aims to validate a given system independently of the number of processes and the communication topology. A lot of different models of such systems have been proposed (cf. [12]

J. Ouaknine, I. Potapov, and J. Worrell (Eds.): RP 2014, LNCS 8762, pp. 45–57, 2014.
© Springer International Publishing Switzerland 2014

for a recent survey). In this paper, we investigate the reachability problem for parameterized communicating automata (PCAs). A PCA is a collection of finite automata that can be plugged into *any* communication topology of bounded degree. PCAs have recently been introduced to initiate a logical study of parameterized systems [5]. Their verification problem has not been considered. Roughly, it can be stated as follows: Given a PCA $\mathcal{A}$ and a regular set $\mathfrak{T}$ of pipeline, ring, or tree topologies, is there a topology $\mathcal{T} \in \mathfrak{T}$ such that $\mathcal{A}$ has an accepting run on $\mathcal{T}$? Here, "regular" means given by some finite automaton (for pipelines and rings) or tree automaton (for tree topologies), which is part of the input. Note that there is also a universal variant of that problem, and our decision procedures will take care of that case as well.

We actually consider a restriction of PCAs with rendez-vous synchronization, albeit distinguishing between send and receive events. This considerably simplifies the presentation, but the overall approach can be extended to systems with asynchronous bounded channels. Note that rendez-vous communication can also be seen as an underapproximation of the latter.

While bounding the channel capacity or imposing rendez-vous communication bring back decidability of reachability for CA with fixed communication topology, this is no longer true in the case of PCAs. For various other (undecidable) models of concurrent systems, decidability is achieved by introducing a context (or "phase") bound, limiting the part of the model simulating synchronization or communication of concurrent processes [6,15,16,18,19]. We adopt the general approach, but introduce new natural definitions of contexts that are suitable for our setting. An *interface-context* restricts communication of a process to one neighbor in the topology (e.g., the left neighbor in the pipeline). Another context type separates send from receive events while restricting reception to one interface. Imposing such bounds is justified, as many distributed algorithms use a bounded number of contexts, such as certain leader-election protocols, P2P protocols, etc.

We show that context-bounded parameterized verification is decidable: it is PSPACE-complete for pipelines and rings, and EXPTIME-complete for ranked trees. Our decidability proof is automata-theoretic and uniform. We transform a given PCA $\mathcal{A}$, in several steps, into a topology acceptor (a finite automaton or a tree automaton) that recognizes the set of pipeline and, respectively, tree topologies allowing for an accepting run of $\mathcal{A}$. For rings, an additional adjustment is needed, which rules out cyclic behaviors that the topology acceptor is not able to detect on its own.

Related Work. Parameterized verification can be classified into verification of multithreaded programs running on a single core, and protocol verification. Context-bounded verification for systems consisting of an unbounded number of threads has already been considered [4, 17]. In [4], a model with process creation is presented, in which a context switch is observed whenever an active thread is interrupted and resumed. In [17], an unbounded number of threads are scheduled in several rounds. In both cases, the context bound does not impose a bound on the number of threads. However, every thread will be resumed and become active a bounded number of times. For protocol verification, which is based on the concept of independent (finite-state) processes communicating over a network-like structure, this does not seem to be suitable. For example, take four processes, $P_1, \ldots, P_4$. Suppose P_1 synchronizes unboundedly often with P_2, and P_3 synchronizes unboundedly often with P_4. In particular, no communication takes place between $\{P_1, P_2\}$ and $\{P_3, P_4\}$. Due to the absence of a global scheduler, there should be no bound on the number of switches between P_2 and P_3 (or P_1 and P_3, etc.). This issue is particularly important when a system is compared to a partial global specification that is not necessarily closed under permutation of independent events. Our *local* context definition does not impose any a priori bound on the number of switches between *independent* processes.

A versatile framework for parameterized verification, capturing rendez-vous communication in pipelines, rings, and trees, is presented in [1]. The verification problem is phrased in terms of minimal bad configurations, which does not necessitate context bounds. Motivated by ad-hoc networks, [9] considers systems modeled by finite automata that communicate in a broadcast or unicast manner. In the case of unicast communication, the recipient is chosen nondeterministically from the set of neighbors, which is incomparable with the unicast communication of PCAs. Direction-aware token-passing systems [3, 10, 11] can be modeled in our framework as far as bounded-degree structures such as rings are concerned. To the best of our knowledge, neither context bounds nor the PCA model have been considered yet for protocol verification.

Outline. Section 2 recapitulates basic notions such as words and finite (tree) automata. In Section 3, we introduce topologies, PCAs, and several context-bounded verification problems. Section 4 presents our main results and illustrates the crucial proof ideas. Missing details can be found in the full version of the paper: http://hal.archives-ouvertes.fr/hal-00984421/

2   Preliminaries

For $n \in \mathbb{N}$, we set $[n] := \{1, \ldots, n\}$. Let $\mathbb{A}$ be an alphabet, i.e., a nonempty finite set. The set of finite words over $\mathbb{A}$ is denoted by $\mathbb{A}^*$, which includes the empty word ε. The concatenation of words $w_1, w_2 \in \mathbb{A}^*$ is denoted by $w_1 \cdot w_2$ or $w_1.w_2$. Given an index set I and a tuple $a = (a_i)_{i \in I} \in \mathbb{A}^I$, we write $a|_i$ to denote a_i.

A *finite automaton* over $\mathbb{A}$ is a tuple $\mathcal{B} = (S, \Longrightarrow, \iota, F)$ where S is the finite set of states, $\iota \in S$ is the initial state, $F \subseteq S$ is the set of final states, and $\Longrightarrow \subseteq S \times \mathbb{A} \times S$ is the transition relation. We write $s \overset{a}{\Longrightarrow} s'$ instead of $(s, a, s') \in \Longrightarrow$. A run of $\mathcal{B}$ on a word $w = a_1 \ldots a_n \in \mathbb{A}^*$ is a sequence $s_0 s_1 \ldots s_n \in S^*$ of states such that $s_0 = \iota$ and $s_{i-1} \overset{a_i}{\Longrightarrow} s_i$ for all $i \in [n]$. The run is accepting if $s_n \in F$. Finally, the language of $\mathcal{B}$ is defined as $L(\mathcal{B}) := \{w \in \mathbb{A}^* \mid$ there is an accepting run of $\mathcal{B}$ on $w\}$.

For trees, we fix a (maximal) *rank* $r \in \mathbb{N}$ with $r \geq 2$. An *r-tree* over $\mathbb{A}$ is a pair (V, π) where V is a nonempty finite prefix-closed subset of $\{1, \ldots, r\}^*$, and $\pi : V \to \mathbb{A}$ is a labeling function. The set V is the set of nodes of the tree, and ε is its root. For $u \in V$ and $l \in [r]$ with $u.l \in V$, we say that $u.l$ is the l-th child

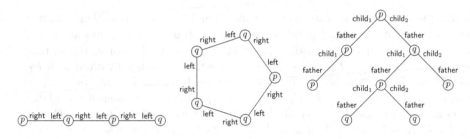

Fig. 1. Pipeline   **Fig. 2.** Ring   **Fig. 3.** Tree

of u. An r-*tree automaton* over $\mathbb{A}$ is a tuple $\mathcal{B} = (S, \Delta, F)$ where S is the finite set of states, $F \subseteq S$ is the set of final states, and $\Delta \subseteq S \times \mathbb{A} \times (S \uplus \{\bot\})^r$ is the transition relation. A run of $\mathcal{B}$ on an r-tree (V, π) is a mapping $\rho : V \to S$ such that, for all $u \in V$, $(\rho(u), \pi(u), (s_l)_{l \in [r]}) \in \Delta$ where $s_l = \rho(u.l)$ if $u.l \in V$, and $s_l = \bot$ if $u.l \notin V$. The run is accepting if $\rho(\varepsilon) \in F$. By $L(\mathcal{B})$, we denote the set of r-trees accepted by $\mathcal{B}$.

3   Parameterized Communicating Automata

In this section, we introduce our model of a communicating system that can be run on arbitrary topologies of bounded degree.

Topologies. A topology is a graph, whose nodes are connected via interfaces. The idea is that each node runs a finite-state process (of type $p, q, \ldots$). Some topologies are depicted in Figures 1–3. In Figure 1, for example, nodes are arranged in a pipeline, which allows a process to communicate with a left and a right neighbor (if they exist). When a node u emits a message m via its interface right, then m can be received by the neighbor on the right of u, using interface left. Let $\mathcal{N} = \{a, b, c, \ldots\}$ and $\mathcal{P} = \{p, q, \ldots\}$ be nonempty finite sets of *interface names* (or, simply, interfaces) and *process types*, respectively.

Definition 1. *A topology over $\mathcal{N}$ and $\mathcal{P}$ is a tuple $\mathcal{T} = (V, \nu, \pi)$ where V is the nonempty finite set of* nodes *(or processes), $\pi : V \to \mathcal{P}$ associates with every node a process type, and $\nu : V \times \mathcal{N} \rightharpoonup V$ is a partial mapping. Intuitively, $\nu(u, a) = v$ means that the interface a of u points to v. We suppose that, for all $u \in V$, there is at last one $a \in \mathcal{N}$ such that $\nu(u, a)$ is defined. Moreover, we require that $\nu(u, a) = v$ implies*

- *$u \ne v$ (there are no self-loops),*
- *$\nu(v, b) = u$ for some $b \in \mathcal{N}$ (adjacent processes are mutually connected), and*
- *$\nu(u, a') = v'$ implies $[a = a'$ iff $v = v']$, for all $a' \in \mathcal{N}$ and $v' \in V$ (an interface points to at most one process, and two distinct interfaces point to distinct processes).*

We write $u \xmapsto{a\ b} v$ if $\nu(u, a) = v$ and $\nu(v, b) = u$, and we write $u \longmapsto v$ if $u \xmapsto{a\ b} v$ for some $a, b \in \mathcal{N}$. This paper will focus on three topology classes:

Pipelines. A *pipeline* over a nonempty finite set $\mathcal{P}$ of process types is a topology over $\mathcal{N} = \{\text{left}, \text{right}\}$ and $\mathcal{P}$. It is of the form $\mathcal{T} = (\{1, \ldots, n\}, \nu, \pi)$, with $n \geq 2$, such that $\nu(i, \text{right}) = i + 1$ and $\nu(i + 1, \text{left}) = i$ for all $i \in [n - 1]$, and $\nu(1, \text{left})$ and $\nu(n, \text{right})$ are both undefined. A finite automaton $\mathcal{B}$ over $\mathcal{P}$ can be seen as a pipeline recognizer. Indeed, a pipeline is uniquely given by the sequence $\pi(1) \ldots \pi(n) \in \mathcal{P}^*$. So, we let $L_{pipe}(\mathcal{B})$ denote the set of pipelines $(\{1, \ldots, n\}, \nu, \pi)$ over $\mathcal{P}$ such that $\pi(1) \ldots \pi(n) \in L(\mathcal{B})$. Instead of $\mathcal{B}$, we may use a classical regular expression. An example pipeline is depicted in Figure 1. It is uniquely given by the word $pqpq$.

Rings. A *ring* over $\mathcal{P}$ is a topology over $\mathcal{N} = \{\text{left}, \text{right}\}$ and $\mathcal{P}$ of the form $\mathcal{T} = (\{1, \ldots, n\}, \nu, \pi)$, with $n \geq 3$, where $\nu(i, \text{right}) = (i \bmod n) + 1$ and $\nu((i \bmod n) + 1, \text{left}) = i$ for all $i \in [n]$. Similarly to pipelines, a finite automaton $\mathcal{B}$ over $\mathcal{P}$ can be used as a *ring* recognizer: we let $L_{ring}(\mathcal{B})$ denote the set of rings $(\{1, \ldots, n\}, \nu, \pi)$ over $\mathcal{P}$ such that there is $i \in [n]$ satisfying $\pi(i) \ldots \pi(n)\pi(1) \ldots \pi(i - 1) \in L(\mathcal{B})$. This takes into account that, a priori, rings do not have an "initial" node. Figure 2 depicts a ring with five nodes.

Trees. For $r \geq 2$, an *r-tree topology* over $\mathcal{P}$ is a topology $\mathcal{T} = (V, \nu, \pi)$ over $\{\text{father}, \text{child}_1, \ldots, \text{child}_r\}$ and $\mathcal{P}$ such that (V, π) is an r-tree over $\mathcal{P}$, $\nu(\varepsilon, \text{father})$ is undefined, and for all $u \in V$ and $l \in [r]$, we have (1) $u.l \in V$ implies $\nu(u, \text{child}_l) = u.l$ and $\nu(u.l, \text{father}) = u$, and (2) $u.l \notin V$ implies that $\nu(u, \text{child}_l)$ is undefined. An r-tree automaton $\mathcal{B}$ over $\mathcal{P}$ can be seen as a recognizer for tree topologies: we write $L_{tree}(\mathcal{B})$ for the set of r-tree topologies (V, ν, π) such that $(V, \pi) \in L(\mathcal{B})$. A sample 2-tree topology is depicted in Figure 3.

The Automata Model. Next, we introduce our system model. As suggested above, a parameterized communicating automaton is a collection of finite-state processes whose actions refer to an interface. Unless stated otherwise, we assume that $\mathcal{N}$ is a *fixed* nonempty finite set of interface names.

Definition 2. *A* parameterized communicating automaton *(PCA) over $\mathcal{N}$ is a tuple $\mathcal{A} = (\mathcal{P}, Msg, (\mathcal{A}_p)_{p \in \mathcal{P}})$ where*
 - $\mathcal{P}$ *is a nonempty finite set of process types,*
 - *Msg is a nonempty finite set of messages, and*
 - $\mathcal{A}_p$ *is a finite automaton over $\Sigma_{\mathcal{A}} := \{a!m, a?m \mid a \in \mathcal{N} \text{ and } m \in Msg\}$, for every $p \in \mathcal{P}$.*

We call the elements of $\Sigma_{\mathcal{A}}$ actions.

A *pipeline PCA* or *ring PCA* is a PCA over $\{\text{left}, \text{right}\}$. Moreover, for $r \geq 2$, an *r-tree PCA* is a PCA over $\{\text{father}, \text{child}_1, \ldots, \text{child}_r\}$.

The idea is the following: When $\mathcal{A}$ is run on a topology (V, ν, π) with adjacent processes $u \xrightarrow{a \ b} v$, then u runs a copy of $\mathcal{A}_{\pi(u)}$ and can emit a message m through interface a by executing $a!m$. Process v receives the message if it is ready to execute $b?m$. We assume that communication is by rendez-vous, i.e., messages are received instantaneously.

For convenience, we write Σ instead of $\Sigma_{\mathcal{A}}$. Sometimes, we will even mention Σ without any reference to $\mathcal{A}$. However, notice that the alphabet depends on a

PCA (more precisely, on $\mathcal{N}$ and a set of messages). Let $\Sigma_! := \{a!m \mid a \in \mathcal{N}$ and $m \in Msg\}$ and let $\Sigma_?$ be defined accordingly. These sets are further refined to $\Sigma_{a!}$ and $\Sigma_{a?}$, containing only those actions that refer to interface $a \in \mathcal{N}$.

Semantics of PCAs. Let $\mathcal{A} = (\mathcal{P}, Msg, (\mathcal{A}_p)_{p \in \mathcal{P}})$ be a PCA over $\mathcal{N}$, with $\mathcal{A}_p = (S_p, \Longrightarrow_p, \iota_p, F_p)$ for all $p \in \mathcal{P}$. The PCA $\mathcal{A}$ can be run on any topology $\mathcal{T} = (V, \nu, \pi)$ over $\mathcal{N}$ and $\mathcal{P}$. Its semantics wrt. $\mathcal{T}$ is a finite automaton $[\![\mathcal{A}]\!]^{\mathcal{T}} = (S, \Longrightarrow, \iota, F)$ over $\Sigma^{\mathcal{T}} \subseteq (\Sigma \cup \{\varepsilon\})^V$. The alphabet $\Sigma^{\mathcal{T}}$ contains, for all $v \xmapsto{a\ b} v'$ and $m \in Msg$, the tuple $\langle v, m, v' \rangle := (\sigma_u)_{u \in V}$ where $\sigma_v = a!m$, $\sigma_{v'} = b?m$, and $\sigma_u = \varepsilon$ for all $u \in V \setminus \{v, v'\}$. For $W = \gamma_1 \ldots \gamma_n \in (\Sigma^{\mathcal{T}})^*$ and $u \in V$, we define the projection of W to u as $W|_u := (\gamma_1|_u) \cdot \ldots \cdot (\gamma_n|_u) \in \Sigma^*$.

Given a process $u \in V$, we write $\mathcal{A}_u, S_u, \Longrightarrow_u, \iota_u, F_u$ as abbreviations for $\mathcal{A}_{\pi(u)}, S_{\pi(u)}, \Longrightarrow_{\pi(u)}, \iota_{\pi(u)}, F_{\pi(u)}$, respectively. The set of states of $[\![\mathcal{A}]\!]^{\mathcal{T}}$ is $S = \prod_{u \in V} S_u$, keeping track of the local state of every process in the topology. Accordingly, the initial state is $\iota = (\iota_u)_{u \in V}$, and the set of final states is $F = \prod_{u \in V} F_u$. The transition relation $\Longrightarrow \subseteq S \times \Sigma^{\mathcal{T}} \times S$ is defined as follows. Let $s = (s_u)_{u \in V} \in S$, $s' = (s'_u)_{u \in V} \in S$, and $\sigma = (\sigma_u)_{u \in V} \in \Sigma^{\mathcal{T}}$. Then, $s \xRightarrow{\sigma} s'$ if, for all $u \in V$, we have that $\sigma_u \neq \varepsilon$ implies $s_u \xRightarrow{\sigma_u}_u s'_u$, and $\sigma_u = \varepsilon$ implies $s_u = s'_u$. The language of $\mathcal{A}$ wrt. $\mathcal{T}$ is defined as $L(\mathcal{A}, \mathcal{T}) := L([\![\mathcal{A}]\!]^{\mathcal{T}})$.

Example 1. We consider a simplified version of the IEEE 802.5 token-ring protocol, in which a binary token (carrying a value in $\{0, 1\}$) circulates in a ring. At any time of an execution, there is exactly one process that has the token. When a process executes an action of the form right!m, it sets the token value to $m \in \{0, 1\}$ and passes it to its right neighbor. The latter executes left?m to receive the token. Since we discard actions of the form left!m and right?m, we actually deal with a unidirectional ring.

In our protocol, a process of type p emits a message, which will circulate on the given ring until it is received. The fact that the message is currently in transit is indicated by token value 1 (the concrete message contents is abstracted away). Processes of type q will just pass on the token without changing its value. When the token reaches a process of type $\bar{p}$, the message is received. The receiving process sets the token to 0 and passes it to its right neighbor. From there, it is again forwarded by processes of type q until it reaches the "initial" process, which thus gets the confirmation that its message has been received.

Our protocol is modeled by the ring PCA $\mathcal{A} = (\mathcal{P}, Msg, (\mathcal{A}_p, \mathcal{A}_{\bar{p}}, \mathcal{A}_q))$, over the set of interfaces $\mathcal{N} = \{\text{left}, \text{right}\}$, where $\mathcal{P} = \{p, \bar{p}, q\}$, $Msg = \{0, 1\}$, and the local languages are given as follows:

- $L(\mathcal{A}_p) = \{(\text{right}!1)(\text{left}?0)\}$
- $L(\mathcal{A}_{\bar{p}}) = \{(\text{left}?1)(\text{right}!0)\}$
- $L(\mathcal{A}_q) = \{(\text{left}?1)(\text{right}!1), (\text{left}?0)(\text{right}!0)\}$

Note that $L(\mathcal{A}, \mathcal{T}) = \emptyset$ for all $\mathcal{T} \in L_{ring}(q^*)$. Even though two successive processes qq match locally, in the sense that the letter right!m in the execution of the first q matches the letter left?m in the second occurrence of q, closing a sequence q^n towards a ring is not possible due to the causal dependencies that are

Table 1. Context-bounded nonemptiness problems and summary of results

PIPELINE-NONEMPTINESS(t)	RING-NONEMPTINESS(t)

I: pipeline PCA $\mathcal{A} = (\mathcal{P}, Msg, (\mathcal{A}_p)_{p \in \mathcal{P}})$
  $k \geq 1$; finite automaton $\mathcal{B}$ over $\mathcal{P}$
Q: $L_{(k,t)}(\mathcal{A}, \mathcal{T}) \neq \emptyset$ for some $\mathcal{T} \in L_{pipe}(\mathcal{B})$?
	I: ring PCA $\mathcal{A} = (\mathcal{P}, Msg, (\mathcal{A}_p)_{p \in \mathcal{P}})$
	  $k \geq 1$; finite automaton $\mathcal{B}$ over $\mathcal{P}$
	Q: $L_{(k,t)}(\mathcal{A}, \mathcal{T}) \neq \emptyset$ for some $\mathcal{T} \in L_{ring}(\mathcal{B})$?

TREE$_r$-NONEMPTINESS(t)		s⊕r1	intf
I: r-tree PCA $\mathcal{A} = (\mathcal{P}, Msg, (\mathcal{A}_p)_{p \in \mathcal{P}})$ $k \geq 1$; r-tree automaton $\mathcal{B}$ over $\mathcal{P}$ Q: $L_{(k,t)}(\mathcal{A}, \mathcal{T}) \neq \emptyset$ for some $\mathcal{T} \in L_{tree}(\mathcal{B})$?	pipelines	PSPACE-c	PSPACE-c
	rings	PSPACE-c	PSPACE-c
	trees	EXPTIME-c	EXPTIME-c

created. The receive that remains open on the first q is always scheduled before the remaining open send in the last q. Thus, matching both will create a cyclic dependency and not lead to a valid run of $\mathcal{A}$. We actually have, for all rings $\mathcal{T}$ over $\mathcal{P}$, that $L(\mathcal{A}, \mathcal{T}) \neq \emptyset$ iff $\mathcal{T} \in L_{ring}((pq^*\bar{p}q^*)^*)$. Detecting cyclic dependencies will be one challenge when we tackle the verification problem for rings.

As we aim at modeling a token-ring protocol, we shall only consider rings that contain exactly one process of type p (only one process can have the token). In our decision problems, the input will contain a finite (tree, respectively) automaton that may serve as a corresponding filter.   ◊

Note that reachability in token-ring protocols is undecidable when the token is binary [11]. Our approach to get decidability is orthogonal to that from [3,11]. Though the latter assume that a process knows whether it has the token or not, the token itself is unary and does not carry extra information. In our setting, simulating a unary token corresponds to letting Msg be a singleton set. In this paper, we do not restrict the amount of (finite) information that a token can carry (i.e., Msg can be an arbitrary nonempty finite set), but the local process behavior. This allows us to verify protocols like in Example 1.

Context-Bounded Parameterized Nonemptiness. Next, we define several natural variants of contexts, which restrict the behavior of each process of a PCA. A word $w \in \Sigma^*$ is called an

- (s⊕r)-context if $w \in \Sigma_!^* \cup \Sigma_?^*$,
- (s1+r1)-context if $w \in (\Sigma_{a!} \cup \Sigma_{b?})^*$ for some $a, b \in \mathcal{N}$,
- (s⊕r1)-context if $w \in \Sigma_!^* \cup \Sigma_{a?}^*$ for some $a \in \mathcal{N}$, and
- intf-context if $w \in (\Sigma_{a!} \cup \Sigma_{a?})^*$ for some $a \in \mathcal{N}$.

The case s1⊕r ($w \in \Sigma_{a!}^* \cup \Sigma_?^*$ for some $a \in \mathcal{N}$) is symmetric to s⊕r1, and we only consider the latter. All results hold verbatim when we replace s⊕r1 with s1⊕r.

Let $k \geq 1$ and $t \in \{$s⊕r, s1+r1, s⊕r1, intf$\}$ be a context type. We say that $w \in \Sigma^*$ is (k, t)-bounded if there are $w_1, \ldots, w_k \in \Sigma^*$ such that $w = w_1 \cdot \ldots \cdot w_k$ and w_i is a t-context, for all $i \in [k]$. The set of all (k, t)-bounded words (over

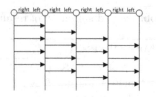   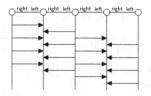

Fig. 4. Undecidability for s1+r1   **Fig. 5.** Undecidability for s⊕r

a fixed Σ) is denoted by $\mathbb{W}_{(k,t)}$. For a PCA $\mathcal{A} = (\mathcal{P}, Msg, (\mathcal{A}_p)_{p \in \mathcal{P}})$ and a topology $\mathcal{T} = (V, \nu, \pi)$, we define $L_{(k,t)}(\mathcal{A}, \mathcal{T}) := \{W \in L(\mathcal{A}, \mathcal{T}) \mid W|_u \in \mathbb{W}_{(k,t)}$ for all $u \in V\}$. Note that $\mathbb{W}_{(k,t)}$ is a regular word language that is recognized by a finite automaton $\mathcal{B}_{(k,t)}$ whose number of states is linear in k and at most quadratic in $|\mathcal{N}|$ (but linear for the decidable cases of t). Let $\mathcal{A}'$ be the PCA $(\mathcal{P}, Msg, (\mathcal{A}_p \times \mathcal{B}_{(k,t)})_{p \in \mathcal{P}})$ where $\mathcal{A}_p \times \mathcal{B}_{(k,t)}$ is the classical product of two finite automata. It is easy to see that $L_{(k,t)}(\mathcal{A}, \mathcal{T}) = L(\mathcal{A}', \mathcal{T})$. This means that the context-bound restriction can be built into the PCA.

Applying the definitions to the PCA $\mathcal{A}$ from Example 1, we have $L(\mathcal{A}, \mathcal{T}) = L_{(2,s \oplus r1)}(\mathcal{A}, \mathcal{T}) = L_{(2,\text{intf})}(\mathcal{A}, \mathcal{T})$ for all topologies over $\{\text{left}, \text{right}\}$ and $\{p, \bar{p}, q\}$.

Note that many distributed algorithms use a bounded number of contexts (or even a bounded number of actions) per process. Prominent examples are some leader-election protocols and P2P protocols. Even when the number of contexts is unbounded, there is often an exponential trade-off between the number of contexts and the (larger) number of processes (e.g., for leader election). Thus, context-bounded verification may sometimes be more appropriate than cut-off techniques, which bound the number of processes.

For $t \in \{s \oplus r, s1+r1, s \oplus r1, \text{intf}\}$, we consider the problems listed in Table 1. Note that the context bound k is part of the input. We assume that k is encoded in unary. Table 1 also contains a summary of the positive results of the paper. For some context types, however, all problems are undecidable.

Theorem 1. *All problems listed in Table 1 are undecidable for $t \in \{s \oplus r, s1+r1\}$, even when we restrict to one context for each process.*

Proof (sketch). Figures 4 and 5 demonstrate how to generate grid-like structures of arbitrary height i and width j, using only one context on each single process. Figure 4, for example, visualizes an execution of the form

$$(\langle 1, m_{(1,1)}, 2 \rangle \langle 2, m_{(1,2)}, 3 \rangle \dots \langle j, m_{(1,j)}, j + 1 \rangle) \dots (\langle 1, m_{(i,1)}, 2 \rangle \langle 2, m_{(i,2)}, 3 \rangle \dots \langle j, m_{(i,j)}, j + 1 \rangle).$$

The idea is now to simulate a Turing machine, using the (unbounded) vertical dimension to encode its tape, which changes along the (unbounded) horizontal line. More precisely, the leftmost process generates a sequence of messages $(m_{(1,1)}, \dots, m_{(i,1)})$ that corresponds to the initial configuration with arbitrarily many cells. Each further process may locally change that configuration while passing it to its right neighbor, and so on. In the case of s⊕r, the transfer of

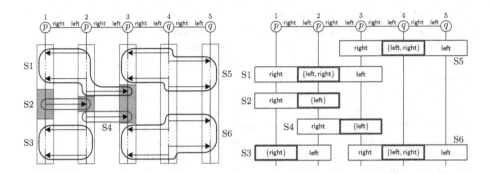

Fig. 6. Cell transitions wrt. s⊕r1   **Fig. 7.** Run of finite automaton

a configuration is sometimes accomplished by a receive context. Obviously, the encoding also works for rings and for trees.   □

4   Context-Bounded Parameterized Verification

We now present our main results: decidability of all our context-bounded parameterized verification problems, as far as context types s⊕r1 and intf are concerned.

Theorem 2. *For all* $t \in \{$s⊕r1, intf$\}$*, the following hold:*

- PIPELINE-NONEMPTINESS(t) *is* PSPACE-*complete,*
- RING-NONEMPTINESS(t) *is* PSPACE-*complete, and*
- TREE$_r$-NONEMPTINESS(t) *is* EXPTIME-*complete, for all* $r \geq 2$.

In the remainder of this section, we develop the main proof ideas.

General Proof Idea for Upper Bounds. We illustrate the proof by means of pipelines and context type s⊕r1, which is slightly more difficult than the case of intf. Given a pipeline PCA $\mathcal{A} = (\mathcal{P}, Msg, (\mathcal{A}_p)_{p \in \mathcal{P}})$ and $k \geq 1$, we will construct a finite automaton $\mathcal{B}_{\mathcal{A}}$ that recognizes exactly those pipelines $\mathcal{T}$ such that $L_{(k, \text{s⊕r1})}(\mathcal{A}, \mathcal{T}) \neq \emptyset$. While reading a pipeline (i.e., a word over $\mathcal{P}$), the finite automaton will guess an accepting run of $\mathcal{A}$. When every local language $L(\mathcal{A}_p)$ is finite, this can be done as follows: A state of $\mathcal{B}_{\mathcal{A}}$ is a string from some local language. When reading p, the automaton guesses an element of $L(\mathcal{A}_p)$ and checks if its projection to left-actions matches the current state. A state is final if it does not communicate through interface right. However, though we can restrict to $(k, \text{s⊕r1})$-bounded words, the local language $L(\mathcal{A}_p)$ of a process type p is in general infinite so that the naive construction is not applicable.

The trick is to find a bounded abstraction of the infinitely many (local) runs. This is illustrated in Figure 6, which depicts a $(3, \text{s⊕r1})$-bounded execution (in fact, a set of "order"-equivalent executions). Processes 1, 2, and 3 use three contexts, while 4 and 5 can do with a single one. The dotted areas on a process line suggest that we actually consider an arbitrary number of actions. Our aim is to aggregate these unboundedly many actions in a bounded number of summaries Si so that a finite automaton can read the pipeline (i.e., the word $pppqq$) from left to right, while verifying that the summaries can be glued together towards an accepting run of the given PCA.

As process 4 alternates between sending to 3 and sending to 5, its summaries have to include the behavior of processes 3 and 5. A summary is then given by a *cell transition* of the form s $\xrightarrow{pqq}$ s'. Here, *cell* refers to pqq, which represents an isomorphism type of a pipeline of length three. Moreover, s, s' $\in S_p \times S_q \times S_q$ denote how states evolve in that particular fragment within a bigger pipeline, for example when executing all actions gathered in S5. Cells have bounded size so that the set of cell transitions can be effectively computed and represented.

Now, the behavior of process 4 can only be captured when we use at least two cell transitions (for S5 and S6). The reason is that receives of process 3 from 4 are interrupted by receives from process 2. Similarly, the receive context in the middle of process 3 will belong to two different summaries, as it is interrupted by a context switch on process 2. The splitting is not unique, as we could have merged S3 and S4. However, the total number of splits can be bounded: a send (receive) context is split whenever the complementary receives (sends, respectively) belong to distinct contexts. Thus, it is divided into at most $k \cdot |\mathcal{N}|$ summaries. Using this, one can show that any $(k, \mathsf{s} \oplus \mathsf{r}1)$-bounded execution of a PCA is captured by a sequence of cell transitions such that each process is involved at most $k \cdot (|\mathcal{N}|^2 + 2|\mathcal{N}| + 1)$ times. This gives us a bounded abstraction of a priori unbounded behaviors so that we can build a finite automaton that guesses such an abstraction and, simultaneously, checks if it corresponds to an accepting run of the PCA. A run of the finite automaton is depicted in Figure 7 (where we omit local states). On a process, we only keep "blocks" indicating both the interfaces that are employed and whether we deal with a sending phase (*set* of interfaces) or a receiving phase (*single* interface).

Note that the size of $\mathcal{B}_\mathcal{A}$ is exponential in k. However, nonemptiness can be checked "on-the-fly", which takes only polynomial space. The construction works similarly for trees; we then come up with a tree automaton, which gives us an EXPTIME procedure. However, the idea is not directly applicable to rings. Consider the PCA from Example 1. Figure 8 illustrates a possible run of the finite automaton $\mathcal{B}_\mathcal{A}$ over $qqqq$. Since the final state and the state taken after reading the first position match locally, we are tempted to say that $\mathcal{B}_\mathcal{A}$ should accept the *ring* $\mathcal{T}$ induced by $qqqq$. However, we have $L(\mathcal{A}, \mathcal{T}) = \emptyset$. The trick is now to retrieve cyclic dependencies that violate the run conditions of PCAs. In the example, we have to record that the gray-shaded left-block (which arose from a receive action) is scheduled *before* the gray-shaded {right}-block (which arose from a send action). Those blocks cannot be matched, i.e., the run of the finite automaton $\mathcal{B}_\mathcal{A}$ does not reflect a run of $\mathcal{A}$. We will, therefore, enrich the previous construction to obtain a decision procedure for rings.

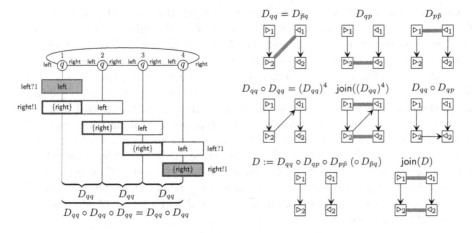

Fig. 8. Finite automaton on a ring   **Fig. 9.** Dependence graphs

Dependence Graphs. The idea is to add *dependence graphs*, which keep track of the causal dependencies between cell transitions. They arise naturally when we combine the behavior of two processes in terms of states of $\mathcal{B}_A$. For processes 1 and 2 in Figure 8, we obtain the dependence graph D_{qq} depicted in Figure 9. There are two kinds of constraints, an undirected (i.e., symmetric) one representing synchronizations (the thick gray lines), and a directed one for strict causality (depicted by arrows $\rightarrow$). In D_{qq}, for example, the nodes $\triangleright_1$ and $\triangleright_2$ on the left represent the two strictly causally ordered blocks of the first process, while the nodes $\triangleleft_1$ and $\triangleleft_2$ on the right represent the two blocks of the second process. Moreover, $\triangleright_2$ and $\triangleleft_1$ are synchronized, i.e., they happen instantaneously.

The effect of appending a further process of type q can be computed as a composition $D_{qq} \circ D_{qq}$, which we obtain as follows:

1. Merge every node $\triangleleft_i$ of the first graph with the corresponding node $\triangleright_i$ of the second graph.
2. A path containing at least one $\rightarrow$-constraint and synchronization constraints in either direction becomes a new $\rightarrow$-constraint.
3. The new synchronization constraints are given by the transitive closure of the (union of the) old ones.
4. Remove the merge nodes.

Note that, in the figure, we represent the composition by a minimal set of constraints.

Now, "closing" the pipeline $qqqq$ towards a ring corresponds to joining the left and right hand side of $(D_{qq})^4 = (D_{qq})^2$. Technically, we add synchronization constraints between $\triangleright_i$ and $\triangleleft_i$. The result is depicted as $\mathrm{join}((D_{qq})^4)$ in Figure 9. However, the join contains a cycle using at least one constraint of type $\rightarrow$ (recall that synchronization edges can be taken in either direction), which has to be interpreted as a violation of the run condition of PCAs.

Consider, on the other hand, the "pipeline" $qqp\bar{p}$. It induces the graph $D_{qq} \circ D_{qp} \circ D_{p\bar{p}}$ (depicted at the bottom left of the figure), which resolves any dependency between the leftmost and the rightmost process. To check whether the pipeline can be closed towards a ring, we apply the join operation to $D_{qq} \circ D_{qp} \circ D_{p\bar{p}} \circ D_{\bar{p}q}$. The result is depicted at the bottom right of Figure 9. The join is harmless, since it does not create any cycle containing at least one $\rightarrow$-edge. Thus, the ring given by $qqp\bar{p}$ allows for an accepting run of the given PCA.

Note that, in the ring case (and for context type s⊕r1), summaries are defined in a slightly different way to make sure that dependencies are reflected correctly. A summary then either involves only two processes, or it has at least two alternations between sending to the left and sending to the right. This guarantees that the induced synchronization constraints in dependence graphs are indeed symmetric. The new definition of summaries results in a linear blow up of the number of blocks on each process.

Lower Bounds. To illustrate the lower-bound proofs, we consider trees. For $t \in$ {s⊕r1, intf} and $r \geq 2$, EXPTIME-hardness of TREE$_r$-NONEMPTINESS(t) is established by a reduction from the intersection problem for binary-tree automata, which is EXPTIME-complete [20] (similarly, the lower bounds for pipelines and rings use the intersection problem for finite automata). Without loss of generality, we assume here that (1) tree automata accept only trees where the root and every internal node have exactly two children and (2) the node labeling tells us whether we deal with the root, a leaf, or an internal node. Given $k \geq 1$ and binary-tree automata $\mathcal{B}_1, \ldots, \mathcal{B}_k$, we can construct, in polynomial time, a PCA $\mathcal{A}$ such that, for all 2-tree topologies $\mathcal{T}$, we have $L_{(2k,\text{s}\oplus\text{r1})}(\mathcal{A}, \mathcal{T}) \neq \emptyset$ iff $L_{(3k,\text{intf})}(\mathcal{A}, \mathcal{T}) \neq \emptyset$ iff $\mathcal{T} \in L_{tree}(\mathcal{B}_1) \cap \ldots \cap L_{tree}(\mathcal{B}_k)$. The idea is that each process u with two children chooses transitions $\delta_1, \ldots, \delta_k$ of $\mathcal{B}_1, \ldots, \mathcal{B}_k$, respectively, that are applied at u. These transitions are sent to the children $u.1$ and $u.2$ of u. When $u.1$ (or $u.2$) receives a transition δ_i, it immediately sends a corresponding transition δ_i' to its own children. This is why the PCA works with $2k$ and $3k$ contexts.

5 Conclusion

We showed that verification of PCAs running on pipelines, rings, and trees is decidable under certain context bounds. Using automata complementation, we also obtain decidability of the *universal* variants of our verification problem: Do *all* topologies accepted by a finite (tree) automaton allow for an accepting run of the given PCA?

It would be worthwhile to study if there are other natural, maybe more general classes of graphs that come with a decidable context-bounded nonemptiness problem. Moreover, one may consider model checking against temporal logics, and automata models that run over topologies of unbounded degree such as star topologies and unranked trees. These models may include registers so that a process can remember some of its neighbors [8].

Acknowledgment. We thank the anonymous reviewers for comments that helped to improve the presentation of the paper.

References

1. Abdulla, P.A., Haziza, F., Holík, L.: All for the price of few. In: Giacobazzi, R., Berdine, J., Mastroeni, I. (eds.) VMCAI 2013. LNCS, vol. 7737, pp. 476–495. Springer, Heidelberg (2013)
2. Abdulla, P.A., Jonsson, B.: Verifying programs with unreliable channels. In: LICS 1993, pp. 160–170 (1993)
3. Aminof, B., Jacobs, S., Khalimov, A., Rubin, S.: Parameterized model checking of token-passing systems. In: McMillan, K.L., Rival, X. (eds.) VMCAI 2014. LNCS, vol. 8318, pp. 262–281. Springer, Heidelberg (2014)
4. Atig, M.F., Bouajjani, A., Qadeer, S.: Context-bounded analysis for concurrent programs with dynamic creation of threads. Log. Methods Comput. Sci. 7(4) (2011)
5. Bollig, B.: Logic for communicating automata with parameterized topology. In: CSL-LICS 2014. ACM (2014)
6. Bouajjani, A., Emmi, M.: Bounded phase analysis of message-passing programs. In: Flanagan, C., König, B. (eds.) TACAS 2012. LNCS, vol. 7214, pp. 451–465. Springer, Heidelberg (2012)
7. Brand, D., Zafiropulo, P.: On communicating finite-state machines. Journal of the ACM 30(2) (1983)
8. Delzanno, G., Sangnier, A., Traverso, R.: Parameterized verification of broadcast networks of register automata. In: Abdulla, P.A., Potapov, I. (eds.) RP 2013. LNCS, vol. 8169, pp. 109–121. Springer, Heidelberg (2013)
9. Delzanno, G., Sangnier, A., Zavattaro, G.: On the power of cliques in the parameterized verification of ad hoc networks. In: Hofmann, M. (ed.) FOSSACS 2011. LNCS, vol. 6604, pp. 441–455. Springer, Heidelberg (2011)
10. Emerson, E.A., Kahlon, V.: Parameterized model checking of ring-based message passing systems. In: Marcinkowski, J., Tarlecki, A. (eds.) CSL 2004. LNCS, vol. 3210, pp. 325–339. Springer, Heidelberg (2004)
11. Emerson, E.A., Namjoshi, K.S.: On reasoning about rings. Int. J. Found. Comput. Sci. 14(4), 527–550 (2003)
12. Esparza, J.: Keeping a crowd safe: On the complexity of parameterized verification. In: STACS 2014. LIPIcs, vol. 25, pp. 1–10 (2014)
13. Esparza, J., Finkel, A., Mayr, R.: On the verification of broadcast protocols. In: LICS 1999, pp. 352–359. IEEE Computer Society Press (1999)
14. Esparza, J., Ganty, P., Majumdar, R.: Parameterized Verification of Asynchronous Shared-Memory Systems. In: Sharygina, N., Veith, H. (eds.) CAV 2013. LNCS, vol. 8044, pp. 124–140. Springer, Heidelberg (2013)
15. Heußner, A., Leroux, J., Muscholl, A., Sutre, G.: Reachability analysis of communicating pushdown systems. Log. Methods Comput. Sci. 8(3:23), 1–20 (2012)
16. La Torre, S., Madhusudan, P., Parlato, G.: Context-bounded analysis of concurrent queue systems. In: Ramakrishnan, C.R., Rehof, J. (eds.) TACAS 2008. LNCS, vol. 4963, pp. 299–314. Springer, Heidelberg (2008)
17. La Torre, S., Madhusudan, P., Parlato, G.: Model-checking parameterized concurrent programs using linear interfaces. In: Touili, T., Cook, B., Jackson, P. (eds.) CAV 2010. LNCS, vol. 6174, pp. 629–644. Springer, Heidelberg (2010)
18. Madhusudan, P., Parlato, G.: The tree width of auxiliary storage. In: POPL 2011, pp. 283–294. ACM (2011)
19. Qadeer, S., Rehof, J.: Context-bounded model checking of concurrent software. In: Halbwachs, N., Zuck, L.D. (eds.) TACAS 2005. LNCS, vol. 3440, pp. 93–107. Springer, Heidelberg (2005)
20. Seidl, H.: Haskell overloading is DEXPTIME-complete. Information Processing Letters 52(2), 57–60 (1994)

Regular Strategies in Pushdown Reachability Games

A. Carayol and M. Hague

LIGM, Université Paris-Est & CNRS and Royal Holloway University of London

Abstract. We show that positional winning strategies in pushdown reachability games can be implemented by deterministic finite state automata of exponential size. Such automata read the stack and control state of a given pushdown configuration and output the set of winning moves playable from that position.

This result can originally be attributed to Kupferman, Piterman and Vardi using an approach based on two-way tree automata. We present a more direct approach that builds upon the popular saturation technique. Saturation for analysing pushdown systems has been successfully implemented by Moped and WALi. Thus, our approach has the potential for practical applications to controller-synthesis problems.

1   Introduction

Pushdown systems are well-studied in the software verification community. Their stack mirrors the call stack of a first-order recursive program, and, as such, the control flow of such programs (for instance C and Java programs) can be accurately modelled [10]. These models have been a major part of the automata-theoretic approach to software model checking and considerable progress has been made in the implementation of scalable model checkers of pushdown systems. These tools (e.g. Bebop [2] and Moped [7,13,17,18,16]) are an essential back-end components of high-profile model checkers such as SLAM [1].

Verification instances are often simple reachability properties. That is, is there a path in the system leading to some designated "error" state? A richer model is that of *games* where two players (Éloise and Abelard) compete to meet a certain goal. Often these players model the system (Éloise) running in an antagonistic environment (Abelard). In a reachability game, one might ask whether it's possible for the system to eventually reach a desired state, regardless of the environmental input. More complex winning conditions, such as Büchi or parity conditions, allow games equivalent to verification against expressive temporal logics such as μLTL or the modal μ-calculus (e.g. [6]).

In a seminal paper [20], Walukiewicz showed that determining the winner of a pushdown parity game is EXPTIME-complete. Cachat [5] and Serre [14] have independently generalised Walukiewicz's algorithm to compute the winning regions of these games. That is, the set of all positions in the game where a given player can force a win. They use Walukiewicz's algorithm as an oracle

J. Ouaknine, I. Potapov, and J. Worrell (Eds.): RP 2014, LNCS 8762, pp. 58–71, 2014.
© Springer International Publishing Switzerland 2014

to guide the construction of a finite-state automaton recognising the winning region. Another approach, introduced by Piterman and Vardi [12], uses two-way alternating tree automata to navigate a tree representing all possible stacks: after several reductions, including the complementation of Büchi automata, an automaton accepting the winning region can be constructed.

An alternative approach, *saturation*, was popularised as a model-checking algorithm for pushdown systems by Bouajjani *et al.* [3] and independently by Finkel *et al.* [8]. The algorithm was extended to constructing the winning regions of pushdown reachability games by Bouajjani *et al.* [3], Büchi games by Cachat [4], and parity games by Hague and Ong [9].

As well as constructing the winning region, one may also wish to construct a representation of a player's *winning strategy*. A winning strategy monitors the progression of the play of a game and, when a state is in the player's winning region, advises which of a range of possible moves should be played in order to win the game. When the players are the system and the environment, a winning strategy describes *how* to control the system to ensure correctness. This is the *controller-synthesis* problem: given a system and a specification, construct a *controller* of the system that behaves according to the specification.

In the case of pushdown reachability, Büchi, or parity games, it is known that the players have *positional* winning strategies. That is, in order to prescribe the next winning move, a strategy needs only to have access to the current state of the game (as opposed to the entire history of play) [21].

Cachat has given two realisations of Éloise's winning strategy in a pushdown reachability game [4]. The first is a positional strategy, constructed via the saturation technique, that requires space linear in the size of the stack to compute the possible next moves. Alternatively, Cachat presents a strategy implemented by a pushdown automaton that tracks the moves of Abelard and recommends moves to Éloise. Since the automaton tracks the game, the strategy is not positional. However, prescribing the next move requires only constant time. Cachat also argues that similar strategies can be computed for Abelard for positions in his winning region [5].

In the case of Büchi games Cachat also showed that it is possible to construct a linear space positional strategy and a constant time (though not positional) pushdown strategy for Éloise. However, Cachat also observes that adopting his techniques for computing strategies for Abelard is not clear [5]. However, it is known that, even for the full case of parity games, a pushdown strategy exists using different techniques due to Walukiewicz [20] and Serre [15].

The above results use relatively complex systems to define winning strategies. One of the simplest representations of a positional winning strategy over a pushdown game is a regular strategy. In this case, the stack and control state of the current position in the game are read by a finite-state automaton which then outputs the next possible winning moves.

It can be shown that a positional strategy for pushdown parity games can be defined as a regular automaton, exponential in size. Kupferman *et al.* [11] obtain this result from Piterman and Vardi [12]. Essentially, the two-way tree automaton can be reduced to a one-way tree automaton of exponential size, and from this a deterministic automaton reading each branch of the tree (where each branch represents a stack) and recommending next moves can be derived.

However, as mentioned above, this tree automaton approach requires several involved reductions and it is unclear how such a technique may be implemented in practice. The saturation algorithm, however, lends itself readily to implementations computing the winning regions (e.g. Moped [7,13,17] and WALi [19] for single-player and Moped for two-player [18] reachability games).

In this work we show how regular positional strategies can be constructed for Éloise in a pushdown reachability game. In Cachat's technique, weights are assigned to runs of the winning region automaton. Éloise's strategy is to take the minimal accepting run of the current configuration and play the move associated to its first transition. Following this strategy the reachability goal will eventually be satisfied. However, this does not provide a regular positional strategy because the weights require space linear in the size of the run to compute. We show that a more subtle method of assigning weights allows different runs to be compared with constant space requirements. Thus, we construct a deterministic regular automaton implementing a positional winning strategy.

Like Piterman and Vardi's technique, our automaton is also exponential in size. However, we believe our construction to be more direct and more likely to be practicable. Indeed, the first step of the algorithm (the construction of the winning region) has already been successfully implemented, whereas Piterman and Vardi's has not.

2 Preliminaries

2.1 Pushdown Games

A *pushdown reachability game* $\mathcal{G}$ is a given by a tuple $(\mathcal{P}, \Sigma, \mathcal{R}, \mathcal{C}_F)$ where $\mathcal{P} = \mathcal{P}_A \uplus \mathcal{P}_E$ is a finite set of control states partitioned into Abelard and Éloise states respectively, Σ is the finite stack alphabet, $\mathcal{R} \subseteq (\mathcal{P} \times \Sigma) \times (\mathcal{P} \times \Sigma^{\leq 2})$ is the set of transitions and $\mathcal{C}_F$ is a set of target configurations, where a *configuration* is a tuple (p, w) with p being a control state in $\mathcal{P}$ and w a stack in Σ^*.

We write $(p, a) \hookrightarrow (p', w)$ for the transition $((p, a), (p', w))$. In the configuration $\alpha = (p, aw)$, the pushdown system can apply the transition $(p, a) \hookrightarrow (p', u)$ to go to the configuration $\alpha' = (p', uw)$.

In the following, for technical convenience, we will assume for each $p \in \mathcal{P}$ and $a \in \Sigma$ there exists some $(p, a) \hookrightarrow (p', w) \in \mathcal{R}$. Furthermore, we will assume a bottom-of-stack symbol $\perp$ that is neither pushed onto nor popped from the stack. These two conditions together ensure that from a configuration $(p, w\perp)$ it is not possible for the system to become stuck; that is, reach a configuration with no successor.

A *play* of a pushdown game is a sequence $(p_0, w_0), (p_1, w_1), \ldots$ where (p_0, w_0) is some starting configuration and (p_{i+1}, w_{i+1}) is obtained from (p_i, w_i) via some $(p_i, a) \hookrightarrow (p_{i+1}, w) \in \mathcal{R}$. In the case where $p_i \in \mathcal{P}_E$ it is Éloise who chooses the transition to apply, otherwise Abelard chooses the transition.

The *winner* of a play $(p_0, w_0), (p_1, w_1), \ldots$ is Éloise if there exists some i such that $(p_i, w_i) \in \mathcal{C}_F$; otherwise, Abelard wins the play. The *winning region* $\mathcal{W}$ of a pushdown game is the set of all configurations from which Éloise can always win all plays, regardless of the transitions chosen by Abelard.

2.2 Alternating $\mathcal{P}$-Automata

To recognise sets of configurations, we use *alternating $\mathcal{P}$-automata*. These were first used by Bouajjani *et al.* [3].

An alternating $\mathcal{P}$ automaton is a tuple $\mathcal{A} = (\mathcal{Q}, \Sigma, \mathcal{F}, \delta)$ where $\mathcal{Q}$ is a finite set of states such that $\mathcal{P} \subseteq \mathcal{Q}$, Σ is a finite alphabet, $\mathcal{F} \subseteq \mathcal{Q}$ is the set of accepting states, and $\delta \subseteq \mathcal{Q} \times \Sigma \times 2^{\mathcal{Q}}$ is a transition relation. We denote a transition (q, a, Q) as $q \xrightarrow{a} Q$.

A *run over a word* $a_1 \ldots a_n \in \Sigma^*$ from a state q_0 is a sequence

$$Q_1 \xrightarrow{a_1} \cdots \xrightarrow{a_n} Q_{n+1}$$

where each Q_i is a set of states such that $Q_1 = \{q_0\}$, and for each $1 \leq i \leq n$ we have

$$Q_i = \{q_1, \ldots, q_m\} \quad \text{and} \quad Q_{i+1} = \bigcup_{1 \leq j \leq m} P_j$$

where for each $1 \leq j \leq m$ we have $q_j \xrightarrow{w} P_j$. The run is accepting if $Q_{n+1} \subseteq \mathcal{F}$. Thus, for a given state q, we define $\mathcal{L}_q(\mathcal{A})$ to be the set of words over which there is an accepting run of $\mathcal{A}$ from $\{q\}$. Finally, we define

$$\mathcal{L}(\mathcal{A}) = \{(p, w) \mid p \in \mathcal{P} \text{ and } w \in \mathcal{L}_p(\mathcal{A})\} .$$

When Q_i is a singleton set, we will often omit the set notation. For example, the run above could be written $q_0 \xrightarrow{a_1} \cdots \xrightarrow{a_n} Q_{n+1}$. Furthermore, when $w = a_1 \ldots a_n$ we will write $q \xrightarrow{w} Q$ as shorthand for a run from q to Q. In particular, we always have $q \xrightarrow{\varepsilon} q$ for any $q \in \mathcal{Q}$.

2.3 Constructing the Winning Region

We recall the saturation technique for computing Éloise's winning region of a pushdown reachability game. The algorithm was introduced by Bouajjani *et al.* [3] and is essentially an accelerated backwards fixpoint computation beginning with the target set of configurations and then computing all configurations that may reach it. We adapt the algorithm slightly by annotating each added transition with the number of iterations of the algorithm required to add the transition to the automaton. A similar, though more complex annotation scheme was used by Cachat to give a positional (though non-regular) winning strategy for Éloise [4].

Fix a pushdown reachability game $\mathcal{G} = (\mathcal{P}, \Sigma, \mathcal{R}, \mathcal{C}_F)$ such that $\mathcal{C}_F$ is represented by an alternating $\mathcal{P}$-automata $\mathcal{A}$ with $\mathcal{L}(\mathcal{A}) = \mathcal{C}_F$. We will show how to construct an automaton $\mathcal{B}$ such that $\mathcal{L}(\mathcal{B}) = \mathcal{W}$, where $\mathcal{W}$ is Éloise's winning region of $\mathcal{G}$.

Without loss of generality, we assume that there are no incoming transitions to any state $p \in \mathcal{P}$ of $\mathcal{A}$. The saturation algorithm constructs the automaton $\mathcal{B}$ that is the least fixed point of the sequence of automata $\mathcal{A}_0, \mathcal{A}_1, \ldots$ defined below. We simultaneously construct the sequence $\mathcal{A}_0, \mathcal{A}_1, \ldots$ and two annotation functions I and R that annotate each transition $t \in \mathcal{Q} \times \Sigma \times 2^{\mathcal{Q}}$. The I function assigns to each rule its *birthdate* : a natural number which is intuitively the number of iterations of the saturation algorithm required to add the transition to $\mathcal{B}$. Since the algorithm is a backwards reachability algorithm, the birthdate broadly gives the number of transitions required to either remove the corresponding stack character or rewrite it to part of a stack in the set of target configurations. The R partial function assigns to each transition starting with a state of Éloise and whose birthdate is not 0 the rule of the pushdown game responsible for the addition of the transition to the automaton. All transitions in $\mathcal{A}_0$ will have the birthdate 0 assigned by I.

Initially, let $I(t) = 0$ for each $t \in \delta_0$ and define $\mathcal{A}_0 = \mathcal{A} = (\mathcal{Q}, \Sigma, \delta_0, \mathcal{F})$. Then we define $\mathcal{A}_{i+1} = (\mathcal{Q}, \Sigma, \delta_{i+1}, \mathcal{F})$ where δ_{i+1} is the smallest set of transitions such that

1. $\delta_i \subseteq \delta_{i+1}$, and
2. for each $p \in \mathcal{P}_E$, if $r = (p, a) \hookrightarrow (p', w) \in \mathcal{R}$ and $p' \xrightarrow{w} Q$ is a run of $\mathcal{A}_i$, then

$$t = p \xrightarrow{a} Q \in \delta_{i+1}$$

   and if $t \notin \delta_i$ then set $I(t) = i + 1$ and $R(t) = r$, and
3. for each $p \in \mathcal{P}_A$ and $a \in \Sigma$ we have

$$t = p \xrightarrow{a} Q \in \delta_{i+1}$$

where, letting

$$\{(p_1, w_1), \ldots, (p_m, w_m)\} = \{(p', w) \mid (p, a) \hookrightarrow (p', w) \in \mathcal{R}\}$$

we have $Q = \bigcup_{1 \leq j \leq m} Q_j$ where for each $1 \leq j \leq m$, $p_j \xrightarrow{w_j} Q_j$ is a run of $\mathcal{A}_i$.
Furthermore, if $t \notin \delta_i$ then set $I(t) = i + 1$.

One can prove that $\mathcal{L}(\mathcal{B}) = \mathcal{W}$. Since the maximum number of transitions of an alternating automaton is exponential in the number of states (and we do not add any new states), we have that $\mathcal{B}$ is constructible in exponential time.

Theorem 1 ([3]). *The winning region of a pushdown reachability game is regular and constructible in exponential time.*

Before proceeding with the construction of the strategy, we briefly discuss why $\mathcal{L}(\mathcal{B}) = \mathcal{W}$. It is well known that the winning region for Éloise is the smallest set $\mathcal{W}$ such that $\mathcal{L}(\mathcal{A}_0) \subseteq \mathcal{W}$ and $\mathcal{W} = \mathrm{Pre}(\mathcal{W})$ where for any set of configuration C,

$$\mathrm{Pre}(C) = \{c' \text{ of Éloise} \mid \exists c \in C, c' \to c\}$$
$$\cup \{c' \text{ of Abelard} \mid \forall c \in C, c' \to c \Rightarrow c \in C\}$$

The key property of the algorithm is that it ensures that $\mathcal{L}(\mathcal{B})$ is closed under the Pre operation (*i.e.*, $\mathrm{Pre}(\mathcal{L}(\mathcal{B})) = \mathcal{L}(\mathcal{B})$). More precisely, it ensures that for all $i \geq 0$, $\mathrm{Pre}(\mathcal{L}(\mathcal{A}_i)) \subseteq \mathcal{L}(\mathcal{A}_{i+1})$. Hence as $\mathcal{B}$ is by definition equal to $\mathcal{A}_N = \mathcal{A}_{N+1}$, we have that $\mathrm{Pre}(\mathcal{L}(\mathcal{B})) = \mathcal{L}(\mathcal{B})$. As $\mathcal{L}(\mathcal{B})$ contains $\mathcal{L}(\mathcal{A}_0)$, it follows that $\mathcal{L}(\mathcal{B})$ contains the winning region of Éloise.

For the converse inclusion, it is necessary to show that every configuration accepted by $\mathcal{B}$ belongs to the winning region of Éloise. For this we need to fix a strategy for Éloise that is winning from every configuration in $\mathcal{L}(\mathcal{B})$.

The strategies of Éloise considered in this article consist of associating to every run ρ a weight $\Omega(\rho)$ and a well-founded ordering $<$ on weights. The strategy consists in picking the successor of a configuration of Éloise in $\mathcal{L}(\mathcal{B}) \backslash \mathcal{A}_0$ accepted by a run of $\mathcal{B}$ with the smallest possible weight. The weight is defined such that along any play following this strategy the weight of the smallest accepting run strictly decreases. As the ordering is assumed to be well-founded this ensures that a configuration in $\mathcal{L}(\mathcal{A})$ is eventually reached.

The key property here is that the algorithm ensures that for every configuration c of Éloise accepted by a run ρ of $\mathcal{B}$ which does not belong to $\mathcal{L}(\mathcal{A}_0)$, there exists a configuration c' accepted by a run ρ' of $\mathcal{B}$ such that $c \to c'$. Moreover ρ' is obtained by replacing the topmost transition of ρ by several transitions which are *younger*. Similarly for a configuration c of Abelard accepted by some run ρ of $\mathcal{B}$, we have that any configuration c' such that $c \to c'$ is accepted by a run ρ' of $\mathcal{B}$ which is obtained by replacing the topmost transition of ρ by several transitions which are *younger*.

A possible weight for a run ρ is hence a tuple $(n_N, \ldots, n_0) \in \mathbb{N}$ where N is the maximum birthdate of a transition appearing in the automaton $\mathcal{B}$ and, for all $i \geq 0$, n_i is the number of transitions of birthdate i. The ordering is here the lexicographic ordering. Sadly this notion of weight cannot be handled by a finite state automaton which is the goal of this article. In the following section, we define a notion of weight that is compatible with finite state automata.

3   Regular Strategies

3.1   Runs as Trees

A run of $\mathcal{B}$ over a word $a_1 \ldots a_n \in \Sigma^*$ from a state q_0 can be represented by an unordered, unranked tree of depth n such that,

1. the root node is labelled q_0.
2. for each node η at depth $0 \leq i < n$ of the tree labelled q there is a transition $t = q \xrightarrow{t} \{q_1, \ldots, q_m\}$ such that η has children $\eta_1, \ldots, \eta_m$ labelled $q_1, \ldots, q_m$ respectively and each edge (η, η_j) for all $1 \leq j \leq m$ is labelled by t.

A run, represented as a tree, gives rise to a set of sequences of transitions $t_1, \ldots, t_n$ that are the labellings of the edges of each complete branch of the tree (that is, running from the root node to some leaf node). Given a run ρ, let Branches(ρ) be the set of sequences of labels on the branches of ρ.

3.2 Ordering on Runs

To define strategies, we first introduce an ordering between runs of the saturated automaton. To do so, we assign to each branch of the run a weight and take the weight of the run to be the maximum weight of all of its branches. The runs are then (pre-)ordered by comparing their weights.

Weights. Let N be the number of iterations required for the saturation to reach a fixed point. That is N is the smallest number such that for all t we have $I(t) \leq N$. Note that N is fixed for a given $\mathcal{B}$. The weights are tuples in $\mathbb{N}^{N+1}$ where $\mathbb{N}$ denotes the set of natural numbers. The weights are compared using the reverse lexicographic-ordering

$$(i_0, \ldots, i_N) \prec (i'_0, \ldots, i'_N)$$

whenever there exists $N \geq j \geq 0$ such that $i_j < i'_j$ and for all $N \geq k > j$ we have $i_k = i'_k$. Similarly, we write $\preceq$ to denote $\prec \cup =$. Moreover we write

$$(i_0, \ldots, i_N) \prec_j (i'_0, \ldots, i'_N)$$

whenever $i_j < i'_j$ and for all $N \geq k > j$ we have $i_k = i'_k$.

Weight of a branch. Fix a branch $\beta = t_n, \ldots, t_1$ of the run which reads the stack from top to bottom (thus t_n reads the topmost character and t_1 the bottommost character). For all $0 \leq j \leq N$, we take lft_j to be the position from the bottom of stack of the left-most transition of birthdate j and 0 if no such transition exists, *i.e.* $\mathrm{lft}_j = \max\{i \mid I(t_i) = j\}$ (with $\max \emptyset = 0$). Intuitively we first take into account the position (from the bottom) of the transition of birthdate N that is the furthest from the bottom. The greater this position is the greater the weight. Then we look at the position of the transition of age $N - 1$ that is the furthest from the bottom. We only take it into account if it is after the previous position. This restriction is only here to ensure that the order can be implemented by an automaton with an exponential number of states. And so on....

The weight of the branch β is defined to be

$$\Omega(\beta) := (i_0, \ldots, i_N)$$

where $i_j = \mathrm{lft}_j$ if $\mathrm{lft}_j > \max\{\mathrm{lft}_{j+1}, \ldots, \mathrm{lft}_N\}$ and 0 otherwise.

For example, consider a branch $t_1, t_2, t_3, t_4, t_5, t_6$ with a corresponding sequence of birthdates $1, 4, 2, 2, 5, 1$ and assume that $N = 5$. We have $\mathrm{lft}_5 = 2$, $\mathrm{lft}_4 = 5$, $\mathrm{lft}_3 = 0$, $\mathrm{lft}_2 = 4$, $\mathrm{lft}_1 = 6$ and $\mathrm{lft}_0 = 0$. The weight of this branch is hence $(0, 6, 0, 0, 5, 2)$.

Weight of a run and of a configuration. The weight of a run ρ is the maximum weight (for $\prec$) of one of its branches.

$$\Omega(\rho) := \max\{\Omega(\beta) \mid \beta \in \mathrm{Branches}(\rho)\}$$

Finally we assign to any configuration (p, w) accepted by the automaton $\mathcal{B}$ the weight $\Omega((p, w)) = \min \{\Omega(\rho) \mid \rho \text{ accepts } (p, w)\}$ of its smallest accepting run.

The ordering $\prec$ is naturally extended to a total pre-ordering on runs by taking for any two runs ρ and ρ', $\rho \prec \rho'$ if $\Omega(\rho) \prec \Omega(\rho')$. Similarly $\prec$ is extended to configurations accepted by $\mathcal{B}$.

3.3   Éloise's Winning Strategy

Given the ordering defined above, we can define a winning strategy for Éloise. Her strategy is a simple one. At any configuration (p, aw) in her winning region, let ρ be a smallest accepting run of $\mathcal{B}$ with respect to $\prec$. Furthermore, let $t = p \xrightarrow{a} Q$ be the first transition of ρ. To win the game, Éloise can play the rule $R(t)$. For any configuration (p, w) with $p \in \mathcal{P}_E$, let $\text{Play}_E((p, w))$ be the set of rules r that annotate the first transition of a $\prec$-smallest run of $\mathcal{B}$ over (p, w) whenever $(p, w) \in \mathcal{W} \setminus \mathcal{C}_F$. Otherwise, let $\text{Play}_E((p, w)) = \emptyset$.

Lemma 1. *For a given pushdown reachability game* $\mathcal{G} = (\mathcal{P}, \Sigma, \mathcal{R}, \mathcal{C}_F)$ *with* $\mathcal{W}$, $\mathcal{B}$ *and* $\prec$ *being Éloise's winning region, the automaton constructed by saturation and its associated ordering respectively, it is the case that, for all configurations* $(p, aw) \in \mathcal{W}$, *we have either*

1. $(p, aw) \in \mathcal{C}_F$, *or*
2. $p \in \mathcal{P}_E$ *and for all* $(p, a) \hookrightarrow (p', u) \in \text{Play}_E((p, w))$ *we have*

$$(p', uw) \prec (p, aw) \quad \text{with} (p', uw) \in \mathcal{W},$$

3. $p \in \mathcal{P}_A$ *and for all* $(p, a) \hookrightarrow (p', u) \in \mathcal{R}$ *we have*

$$(p', uw) \prec (p, aw) \quad \text{with} (p', uw) \in \mathcal{W}.$$

Proof. We only consider Éloise's case as Abelard's case is similar. Let $(p, aw) \in \mathcal{W}$ be a configuration of Éloise. Let ρ be a minimal run accepting for (p, aw) and let $t = p \xrightarrow{a} Q$ be the first transition of ρ. Furthermore for all $q \in Q$, let ρ_q be the subrun of ρ accepting w from q Finally assume that $R(t) = (p, a) \hookrightarrow (p', u)$.

By definition of the saturation algorithm, there exists a run ρ_u of the form $p' \xrightarrow{u} Q$ where every transition t' labelling ρ_u is such that $I(t') < I(t)$. Let ρ' be the run obtained by plugging into ρ_u the run ρ_q at each leaf labelled by $q \in Q$. This runs accepts (p', uw) and hence (p', uw) belongs to $\mathcal{W}$.

Furthermore every branch β' of ρ' is obtained from some branch β of ρ by replacing the first transition t by a sequence of transitions $t_1, \ldots, t_{|u|}$ where for all $1 \leq j \leq |u|$, $I(t_j) < I(t)$. By definition of the order $\prec$, $\Omega(\beta') \prec_{I(t)} \Omega(\beta)$. Hence $\Omega((p', uw)) \preceq \Omega(\rho') \prec \Omega(\rho) = \Omega((p, aw))$. $\qquad\square$

Theorem 2. *The positional strategy* Play_E *is winning for Éloise from every configuration of her winning region.*

Proof. Assume towards a contradiction that there exists an infinite play $c_0, c_1 \ldots$ which starts in the winning region of Éloise and that does not reach a configuration in $\mathcal{C}_F$. From Lemma 1, we immediately obtain that $\Omega(c_0) \succ \Omega(c_1) \succ \cdots$. Being a (reverse) lexicographic ordering built upon well-founded orderings, $\prec$ is a well-founded total ordering on weights which brings the contradiction. $\qquad\square$

3.4   Regular Winning Strategies

We show that the above strategy can be implemented by a regular automaton. That is, we define a finite deterministic automaton which processes a configuration (p, w) and outputs the set of rules $\text{Play}_E((p, w))$ whenever $p \in \mathcal{P}_E$ and $(p, w) \in \mathcal{W} \setminus \mathcal{C}_F$, and $\emptyset$ otherwise. The automaton reads the stack content w from the bottom of the stack and reaches some state s. The output is obtained by applying a mapping Out_p to s. We first formally define strategy automata.

Definition 1. *Given a pushdown game* $(\mathcal{P}, \Sigma, \mathcal{R}, \mathcal{C}_F)$, *a* strategy automaton S *is a tuple* $(S, \Sigma, s_0, \delta, (\text{Out}_p)_{p \in \mathcal{P}_E})$ *where S is a finite set of states, Σ is an input alphabet, s_0 is an initial state and $\delta : S \times \Sigma \mapsto S$ is a transition function and for all $p \in \mathcal{P}_E$, $\text{Out}_p : S \mapsto 2^{\mathcal{R}}$ is an output mapping for the control state p.*

As usual, we extend the transition function δ to words over the input alphabet Σ. Writing $\tilde{w}$ to denote the mirror of the word w, the output $\text{Play}_S((p, w))$ of a strategy automaton S over a given configuration (p, w) is defined to be

$$\text{Play}_S((p, w)) := \text{Out}_p(\delta(s_0, \tilde{w}))$$

Given a pushdown game $\mathcal{G} = (\mathcal{P}, \Sigma, \mathcal{R}, \mathcal{C}_F)$ as well as an automaton $\mathcal{B} = (\mathcal{Q}, \Sigma, \delta, \mathcal{F})$ representing Éloise's winning region, obtained by saturation, along with its associated ordering $\prec$. We define a strategy automaton $S_\mathcal{B}$ such that for all (p, w) we have

$$\text{Play}_{S_\mathcal{B}}((p, w)) = \text{Play}_E((p, w)) \ .$$

3.5   The Automaton $S_\mathcal{B}$

The State-Set. The automaton $S_\mathcal{B}$ will run $\mathcal{B}$ in reverse, starting from the bottom of the stack. Assuming that the automaton has read the word $\tilde{w}$, the state of $S_\mathcal{B}$ will have as a component a mapping $\text{Moves}_w : \mathcal{P}_E \mapsto 2^{\mathcal{R}}$ such that for all state $p \in \mathcal{P}_E$, $\text{Moves}_w(p) = \text{Play}_E((p, w))$. Note that this mapping is only defined for states belonging to Éloise as those are the only states for which she is required to make a decision. Clearly if the automaton can maintain this information, we have constructed a strategy automaton. In order to update this component while keeping the state set at most exponential, the automaton will maintain two additional pieces of information.

- the set of states $\text{Acc}_w \in 2^{\mathcal{Q}}$ from which $\mathcal{B}$ admits an accepting run on w,
- a partial mapping in $f_w : \mathcal{Q} \times \mathcal{Q} \to \{\prec_\iota, \text{EQ}, \succ_\iota \mid 0 \leq \iota \leq N\}$ which when applied to two states q_1 and $q_2 \in \text{Acc}_w$ compares the minimal runs of $\mathcal{B}$ starting in state q_1 and q_2 respectively.

Intuitively, for the automaton to update Moves_{wa}, it is only necessary to know the transitions that can start a minimal accepting run for any state of Éloise. We will see below that this information can be computed only using the comparison provided by f_w.

More formally, let w be a stack content. The set $\mathrm{Acc}_w \subseteq \mathcal{Q}$ is the set of states $\mathcal{B}$ from which $\mathcal{B}$ has an accepting run, that is

$$\mathrm{Acc}_w := \left\{ q \in \mathcal{Q} \ \middle| \ q \xrightarrow{w} F \subseteq \mathcal{F} \right\} .$$

The partial mapping $f_w : \mathcal{Q} \times \mathcal{Q} \to \{\prec_\iota, \mathrm{EQ}, \succ_\iota \mid 0 \leq \iota \leq N\}$ is defined for all states q_1 and $q_2 \in \mathrm{Acc}_w$ by taking

$$f_w(q_1, q_2) := \begin{cases} \prec_\iota & \text{if } \Omega(\rho_1) \prec_\iota \Omega(\rho_2) \\ \succ_\iota & \text{if } \Omega(\rho_1) \succ_\iota \Omega(\rho_2) \\ \mathrm{EQ} & \text{if } \Omega(\rho_1) = \Omega(\rho_2) \end{cases}$$

where ρ_1 and ρ_2 are $\prec$-minimal runs accepting w from q_1 and q_2 respectively.

The Transition Function. To define the transition function of the strategy automaton, it remains to show how to compute Acc_{aw}, f_{aw} and Moves_{aw} using only a, Acc_w and f_w. To do this we will define three functions $\mathrm{Up}_{\mathrm{Acc}}$, Up_f, and $\mathrm{Up}_{\mathrm{Moves}}$ that perform the updates for their respective components.

We define $\mathrm{Up}_{\mathrm{Acc}}$ following the standard membership algorithm for alternating automata, and obtain the following lemma.

Definition 2 ($\mathrm{Up}_{\mathrm{Acc}}$). *We define*

$$\mathrm{Up}_{\mathrm{Acc}}(a, \mathrm{Acc}_w) := \left\{ q \ \middle| \ q \xrightarrow{a} Q \in \delta \wedge Q \subseteq \mathrm{Acc}_w \right\} .$$

Lemma 2. *For all $w \in \Sigma^*$ and all $a \in \Sigma$ we have $\mathrm{Acc}_{aw} = \mathrm{Up}_{\mathrm{Acc}}(a, \mathrm{Acc}_w)$.*

Computing f_{aw} is more involved and requires some preliminary notations.

First observe that the mapping f_w induces a total pre-ordering on the set Acc_w. For all subsets $Q \subseteq \mathrm{Acc}_w$, we denote by $\max(Q)$ the set of all maximal elements for this ordering. We write $f_w(\max(Q_1), \max(Q_2))$ for the value $f_w(q, q')$ for any $q \in \max(Q_1)$ and $q' \in \max(Q_1)$. As all the elements of $\max(Q_1)$ (resp. $\max(Q_2)$) are equal for the ordering, the choice of q and q' is irrelevant.

As a first step, we use the information of f_w to compare the weights of minimal runs on aw starting with two given transitions t_1 and t_2. Take any two transitions $t_1 = q_1 \xrightarrow{a} Q_1$ and $t_2 = q_2 \xrightarrow{a} Q_2$ with $Q_1 \subseteq \mathrm{Acc}_w$ and $Q_2 \subseteq \mathrm{Acc}_w$ and $I(t_1) = \gamma_1$ and $I(t_2) = \gamma_2$. There are two cases to comparing runs starting with t_1 and t_2. In the first case, the minimal runs from Q_1 and Q_2 differ on some weight $\iota > \gamma_1, \gamma_2$. In this case the ordering is dominated by ι and remains unchanged. If, however, $\gamma_1 \geq \iota$ or $\gamma_2 \geq \iota$, then the relative ordering of the runs is decided by t_1 and t_2. More formally, we write

$$t_1 \prec_\iota t_2$$

if either

1. the ordering between the minimal runs is not decided by t_1 and t_2, that is
   (a) $f_w(\max(Q_1), \max(Q_2)) = \prec_\iota$, and
   (b) $\iota > \gamma_1, \gamma_2$.

2. the ordering is decided by t_1 and t_2, that is
   (a) $\gamma_1 < \gamma_2$ and $\iota = \gamma_2$ and
   (b) $f_w(\max(Q_1), \max(Q_2)) \notin \{\prec_{\iota'}, \succ_{\iota'} \mid \gamma_2 < \iota' \leq N\}$, or

In addition, we write $t_1 \succ_\iota t_2$ when $t_2 \prec_\iota t_1$. We also write $t_1 \operatorname{EQ} t_2$ when

1. $\gamma_1 = \gamma_2$, and
2. $f_w(\max(Q_1), \max(Q_2))$ belongs to $\{\operatorname{EQ}, \prec_\iota, \succ_\iota \mid 0 \leq \iota \leq \gamma_1 = \gamma_2\}$.

Lemma 3. *For any two transitions $t_1 = q_1 \xrightarrow{a} Q_1$ and $t_2 = q_2 \xrightarrow{a} Q_2$ with $Q_1 \subseteq \operatorname{Acc}_w$ and $Q_2 \subseteq \operatorname{Acc}_w$, $t_1 \prec_\iota t_2$ (resp. $t_1 \succ_\iota t_2$, resp. $t_1 \operatorname{EQ} t_2$) if and only if $\Omega(\rho_1) \prec_\iota \Omega(\rho_2)$ (resp. $\Omega(\rho_1) \succ_\iota \Omega(\rho_2)$, resp. $\Omega(\rho_1) = \Omega(\rho_2)$) where ρ_1 and ρ_2 are the minimal runs accepting aw and starting with t_1 and t_2 respectively.*

Proof. Let $I(t_1) = \gamma_1$ and $I(t_2) = \gamma_2$. We first argue that a minimal run beginning with t_1 (resp. t_2) can be constructed from t_1 and a minimal run from Q_1 (resp. Q_2). Let ρ_1' be a minimal run from Q_1. Let $\rho_1 = t_1 \rho_1'' \prec_\iota t_1 \rho_1'$. If $\gamma_1 \geq \iota$, then $\Omega(t_1 \rho_1'') = \Omega(t_1 \rho_1')$ and thus $t_1 \rho_1'$ is also a minimal run. Otherwise $\gamma_1 < \iota$ and $\rho_1 = t_1 \rho_1'' \prec_\iota t_1 \rho_1'$ implies $\rho_1'' \prec_\iota \rho_1'$, contradicting the minimality of ρ_1'.

Now, let $\rho_1 = t_1 \rho_1'$ and $\rho_2 = t_2 \rho_2'$. Suppose $t_1 \prec_\iota t_2$. There are two cases. When $f_w(\max(Q_1), \max(Q_2)) = \prec_\iota$ (implying $\rho_1' \prec_\iota \rho_2'$) and $\iota > \gamma_1, \gamma_2$ then we conclude $t_1 \rho_1' \prec_\iota t_2 \rho_2'$. Otherwise $\gamma_1 < \gamma_2 = \iota$ and $f_w(\max(Q_1), \max(Q_2))$ is not $\prec_{\iota'}$ or $\succ_{\iota'}$ for some $\iota' > \gamma_2$. From the last condition, we know ρ_1' and ρ_2' are equal or differ only on some weight $\iota' \leq \gamma_2$. Thus we know $t_1 \rho_1' \prec_{\gamma_2 = \iota} t_2 \rho_2'$.

In the other direction, suppose $t_1 \rho_1' \prec_\iota t_2 \rho_2'$. If $\iota > \gamma_1, \gamma_2$, then we have $\rho_1' \prec_\iota \rho_2'$ and thus $f_w(\max(Q_1), \max(Q_2)) = \prec_\iota$. We then have $t_1 \prec_\iota t_2$ as required. If $\gamma_1 \geq \iota$ or $\gamma_2 \geq \iota$, then for $t_1 \rho_1'$ to be smaller than $t_2 \rho_2'$ we must have $\gamma_1 < \gamma_2 = \iota$ and moreover ρ_1' and ρ_2' must have the same weight, or differ on some $\iota' \leq \iota$. Thus, $f_w(\max(Q_1), \max(Q_2)) \notin \{\prec_{\iota'}, \succ_{\iota'} \mid \gamma_2 < \iota' \leq N\}$ and $t_1 \prec_\iota t_2$.

The case for $\succ_\iota$ is symmetric, hence it only remains to consider EQ. We have $t_1 \operatorname{EQ} t_2$ if and only if $\gamma_1 = \gamma_2$ and $f_w(\max(Q_1), \max(Q_2))$ belongs to $\{\operatorname{EQ}, \prec_\iota, \succ_\iota \mid 0 \leq \iota \leq \gamma_1 = \gamma_2\}$. We have this iff ρ_1' and ρ_2' have equal weights or differ only on some $\iota \leq \gamma_1, \gamma_2$ and, thus, iff $\Omega(t_1 \rho_1') = \Omega(t_2 \rho_2')$.   □

As a consequence of the above lemma, we have defined a total pre-order on the set of a-transitions. For any set of a-transitions T, we denote by $\min(T)$ the set of minimal elements for this order. We are now ready to define Up_f.

Definition 3 (Up_f). *We define $\operatorname{Up}_f(a, \operatorname{Acc}_w, f_w)$ as the mapping g defined for all states q_1 and $q_2 \in \operatorname{Acc}_{aw}$ by*

$$g(q_1, q_2) := f_w(\min(T_{q_1}), \min(T_{q_2}))$$

where $T_{q_1} = \{q_1 \xrightarrow{a} Q_1 \mid Q_1 \subseteq \operatorname{Acc}_w\}$ and $T_{q_2} = \{q_2 \xrightarrow{a} Q_2 \mid Q_2 \subseteq \operatorname{Acc}_w\}$.

It directly follows from Lemma 3 that:

Lemma 4. *For all $w \in \Sigma^*$ and all $a \in \Sigma$, we have $f_{aw} = \operatorname{Up}_f(a, \operatorname{Acc}_w, f_w)$.*

Finally, we define $\operatorname{Up}_{\operatorname{Moves}}$.

Definition 4 ($\mathrm{Up}_{\mathrm{Moves}}$). *We define* $\mathrm{Up}_{\mathrm{Moves}}(a, \mathrm{Acc}_w, f_w)$ *to be the mapping associating to any control state* $p \in \mathcal{P}_E$ *the set* $\{R(t) \mid t \in \min(T_p)\}$ *where* $T_p = \left\{ p \xrightarrow{a} Q \mid Q \subseteq \mathrm{Acc}_w \right\}$.

Lemma 5. *For all* $w \in \Sigma^*$ *and all* $a \in \Sigma$, *we have*

$$\mathrm{Moves}_{aw} = \mathrm{Up}_{\mathrm{Moves}}(a, \mathrm{Acc}_w, f_w) \ .$$

The Definition of $\mathcal{S}_\mathcal{B}$ We bring together the above discussion and define $\mathcal{S}_\mathcal{B}$.

Definition 5. *Given a pushdown game* $\mathcal{G} = (\mathcal{P}, \Sigma, \mathcal{R}, \mathcal{C}_F)$ *as well as an anno-tated automaton* $\mathcal{B} = (\mathcal{Q}, \Sigma, \delta, \mathcal{F})$ *constructed by saturation in* N *steps, we define* $\mathcal{S}_\mathcal{B}$ *to be the strategy automaton* $(S, \Sigma, s_0, \delta, (\mathrm{Out}_p)_{p \in \mathcal{P}_E})$ *where*

$$S = 2^{\mathcal{Q}} \times (\mathcal{Q} \times \mathcal{Q} \to \{\prec_\iota, \mathrm{EQ}, \succ_\iota \mid 0 \leq \iota \leq N\}) \times (\mathcal{P}_E \mapsto 2^{\mathcal{R}})$$

and $s_0 = (\mathcal{F}, f_0, \mathrm{Moves}_0)$ *where we have* $f_0(q_1, q_2) = \mathrm{EQ}$ *for all* $q_1, q_2 \in \mathcal{F}$ *and* $\mathrm{Moves}_0(p) = \emptyset$ *for all* $p \in \mathcal{P}_E$, *and*

$$\delta(a, (\mathrm{Acc}, f, \mathrm{Moves})) = \left(\mathrm{Up}_{\mathrm{Acc}}(a, \mathrm{Acc}), \mathrm{Up}_f(a, \mathrm{Acc}, f), \mathrm{Up}_{\mathrm{Moves}}(a, \mathrm{Acc}, f)\right)$$

and finally, for all $p \in \mathcal{P}_E$, $\mathrm{Out}_p(\mathrm{Acc}, f, \mathrm{Moves}) = \mathrm{Moves}(p)$.

The size of the automaton $\mathcal{S}_\mathcal{B}$ is exponential in the size of pushdown game.

Theorem 3. *Given a* $\mathcal{P}$-*automaton* $\mathcal{B} = (\mathcal{Q}, \Sigma, \delta, \mathcal{F})$ *constructed by saturation and a strategy automaton* $\mathcal{S}_\mathcal{B}$ *constructed as above, we have*

$$\mathrm{Play}_{\mathcal{S}_\mathcal{B}}((p, w)) = \mathrm{Play}_E((p, w)) \ .$$

Proof. Take a configuration (p, w). By induction on the length of w, we show that upon reading $\tilde{w}$ the automaton $\mathcal{S}_\mathcal{B}$ reaches the state $(\mathrm{Acc}_w, f_w, \mathrm{Moves}_w)$.

In the base case, the initial state s_0 is by definition $(\mathrm{Acc}_\varepsilon, f_\varepsilon, \mathrm{Moves}_\varepsilon)$. The induction step immediately follows from Lemma 2, 4 and 5. The output is there-fore $\mathrm{Moves}_w(p)$ which is by definition equal to $\mathrm{Play}_E((p, w))$. □

4   Conclusion

We gave the construction of a regular postional strategy for Éloise in a push-down reachability game. The strategy automaton is a deterministic automaton of exponential size in the size of the pushdown game.

To define a similar strategy for Abelard, observe that any strategy of Abelard consisting in picking a move that stays outside of the winning region of Éloise is winning. A deterministic strategy automaton implementing such a strategy has states in $\Sigma \times 2^{\mathcal{Q}}$. After reading a stack content $a\tilde{w}$, the automaton reaches the state (a, Acc_w). For all $p \in \mathcal{P}_A$, the output mapping Out_p associates to a state

(a, Acc_w) the set of rules $(p, a) \hookrightarrow (p', u) \in \mathcal{R}$ such there are no runs of $\mathcal{B}$ of the form $p' \xrightarrow{u} Q' \subseteq \text{Acc}_w$.

If we consider pushdown Büchi reachability games, computing a regular positional strategy for Éloise can be reduced to the reachability case. Let $\mathcal{W}$ be the winning region of Éloise in the Büchi game and $\mathcal{C}_F$ be a regular set of final configurations. Consider the positional strategy consisting of playing any move that stays in $\mathcal{W}$ for configurations in $\mathcal{W} \cap \mathcal{C}_F$ and for configurations in $\mathcal{W} \setminus \mathcal{C}_F$ plays the regular positional strategy for the reachability game to $\mathcal{W} \cap \mathcal{C}_F$. As $\mathcal{W}$ is regular, the resulting strategy is regular and can be implemented by strategy automaton of exponential size.

Abelard's strategy is more complex and leads to the open problem of extending our approach to pushdown parity games. The saturation method underlying our approach was extended to these settings in [9]. The challenge is to define an ordering on runs of the saturated automaton that can be implemented by a finite state automaton of size at most exponential in that of the pushdown game.

Acknowledgments. This work was supported by the Engineering and Physical Sciences Research Council [EP/K009907/1] and the Labex Bézout as part of the program "Investissements d'Avenir" (ANR-10-LABX-58).

References

1. Ball, T., Levin, V., Rajamani, S.K.: A decade of software model checking with slam. Commun. ACM 54(7), 68–76 (2011)
2. Ball, T., Rajamani, S.K.: Bebop: A symbolic model checker for boolean programs. In: SPIN, pp. 113–130 (2000)
3. Bouajjani, A., Esparza, J., Maler, O.: Reachability analysis of pushdown automata: Application to model-checking. In: Mazurkiewicz, A., Winkowski, J. (eds.) CONCUR 1997. LNCS, vol. 1243, pp. 135–150. Springer, Heidelberg (1997)
4. Cachat, T.: Symbolic strategy synthesis for games on pushdown graphs. In: Widmayer, P., Triguero, F., Morales, R., Hennessy, M., Eidenbenz, S., Conejo, R. (eds.) ICALP 2002. LNCS, vol. 2380, pp. 704–715. Springer, Heidelberg (2002)
5. Cachat, T.: Games on Pushdown Graphs and Extensions. PhD thesis, RWTH Aachen (2003)
6. Emerson, E.A., Jutla, C.S.: Tree automata, mu-calculus and determinacy (extended abstract). In: FOCS, pp. 368–377 (1991)
7. Esparza, J., Schwoon, S.: A BDD-based model checker for recursive programs. In: Berry, G., Comon, H., Finkel, A. (eds.) CAV 2001. LNCS, vol. 2102, pp. 324–336. Springer, Heidelberg (2001)
8. Finkel, A., Willems, B., Wolper, P.: A direct symbolic approach to model checking pushdown systems. In: INFINITY, vol. 9, pp. 27–37 (1997)
9. Hague, M., Ong, C.-H.L.: Winning regions of pushdown parity games: A saturation method. In: Bravetti, M., Zavattaro, G. (eds.) CONCUR 2009. LNCS, vol. 5710, pp. 384–398. Springer, Heidelberg (2009)
10. Jones, N.D., Muchnick, S.S.: Even simple programs are hard to analyze. J. ACM 24, 338–350 (1977)

11. Kupferman, O., Piterman, N., Vardi, M.Y.: An automata-theoretic approach to infinite-state systems. In: Manna, Z., Peled, D.A. (eds.) Time for Verification. LNCS, vol. 6200, pp. 202–259. Springer, Heidelberg (2010)
12. Piterman, N., Vardi, M.Y.: Global model-checking of infinite-state systems. In: Alur, R., Peled, D.A. (eds.) CAV 2004. LNCS, vol. 3114, pp. 387–400. Springer, Heidelberg (2004)
13. Schwoon, S.: Model-checking Pushdown Systems. PhD thesis, Technical University of Munich (2002)
14. Serre, O.: Note on winning positions on pushdown games with [omega]-regular conditions. Inf. Process. Lett. 85(6), 285–291 (2003)
15. Serre, O.: Contribution à létude des jeux sur des graphes de processus á pile. PhD thesis, Université Paris 7 – Denis Diderot, UFR dinformatique (2004)
16. Suwimonteerabuth, D., Berger, F., Schwoon, S., Esparza, J.: jMoped: A test environment for java programs. In: Damm, W., Hermanns, H. (eds.) CAV 2007. LNCS, vol. 4590, pp. 164–167. Springer, Heidelberg (2007)
17. Suwimonteerabuth, D., Schwoon, S., Esparza, J.: jMoped: A java bytecode checker based on moped. In: Halbwachs, N., Zuck, L.D. (eds.) TACAS 2005. LNCS, vol. 3440, pp. 541–545. Springer, Heidelberg (2005)
18. Suwimonteerabuth, D., Schwoon, S., Esparza, J.: Efficient algorithms for alternating pushdown systems with an application to the computation of certificate chains. In: Graf, S., Zhang, W. (eds.) ATVA 2006. LNCS, vol. 4218, pp. 141–153. Springer, Heidelberg (2006)
19. WALi, https://research.cs.wisc.edu/wpis/wpds/download.php
20. Walukiewicz, I.: Pushdown processes: Games and model-checking. Inf. Comput. 164(2), 234–263 (2001)
21. Zielonka, W.: Infinite games on finitely coloured graphs with applications to automata on infinite trees. Theor. Comput. Sci. 200(1-2), 135–183 (1998)

Parameterized Verification of Graph Transformation Systems with Whole Neighbourhood Operations*

Giorgio Delzanno[1] and Jan Stückrath[2]

[1] Università di Genova, Italy
giorgio.delzanno@unige.it

[2] Universität Duisburg-Essen, Germany
jan.stueckrath@uni-due.de

Abstract. We introduce a new class of graph transformation systems in which rewrite rules can be guarded by universally quantified conditions on the neighbourhood of nodes. These conditions are defined via special graph patterns which may be transformed by the rule as well. For the new class for graph rewrite rules, we provide a symbolic procedure working on minimal representations of upward closed sets of configurations. We prove correctness and effectiveness of the procedure by a categorical presentation of rewrite rules as well as the involved order, and using results for well-structured transition systems. We apply the resulting procedure to the analysis of the Distributed Dining Philosophers protocol on an arbitrary network structure.

1 Introduction

Parameterized verification of distributed algorithms is a very challenging task. Distributed algorithms are often sensible to the network topology and they are based on communication patterns like broadcast messages and conditions on channels that can easily generate undecidable verification instances or finite-state problems of high combinatorial complexity. In order to naturally model interaction rules of topology-sensitive protocols it seems natural to consider languages based on graph rewriting and transformations as proposed in [21]. However, in this formalism rules can only match fixed subgraph in the graph they are applied to. Since we need to specify rules where the entire neighbourhood of a node is matched by the rule, we extend the standard approach by universally quantified patterns attached to nodes. With these patterns the matching of a left side of a rule can be increased until the entire neighbourhood of a node is covered. If the matching cannot be extended in this way the rule is not applicable, e.g. we could formalize a rule which only matches a node when every incident edge is incoming. Additionally the matched occurrences of the patterns can also be changed by the rule. A similar approach are adaptive star grammars [20], the difference being that we do not restrict our left rule sides to be stars.

The resulting formal language can be applied to specify distributed versions of concurrent algorithms like Dining Philosophers in which neighbour processes use channels to request and grant access to a given shared resource. The protocol we use has been

---

* Research partially supported by DFG project GaReV.

J. Ouaknine, I. Potapov, and J. Worrell (Eds.): RP 2014, LNCS 8762, pp. 72–84, 2014.
© Springer International Publishing Switzerland 2014

proposed by Namjoshi and Trefler in [25]. There requests are specified using process identifiers attached to edges representing point-to-point communication channels. Universally quantified guards are used to ensure mutual exclusive access to a resource. In this paper we formulate the protocol without need of introducing identifiers. We instead use our extended notion of graph transformation systems to specify ownership of a given communication link. Universally quantified patterns attached to a requesting node are used then as guards to ensure exclusive access. Erroneous or undesirable configurations in the algorithm can be presented by a set of minimal error configurations. We then use a backward procedure to check if a configuration containing one of the error configurations is reachable. If none is reachable, the algorithm is proven to be correct.

Following the approach proposed in [7,24], we use basic ingredients of graph transformation and category theory (e.g. pushouts) to formally specify the operational semantics of our model. Parameterized verification for the resulting model is undecidable in general, even without universally quantified patterns [7]. To overcome this problem, we provide an approximated symbolic backward procedure using result for well-structured transition systems [6,22] to guarantee correctness and termination.

Although the over-approximation is based on the monotonic abstraction approach proposed in [3,5], its application to the considered class of infinite-state systems is highly non trivial. In fact, our universal quantification approach is not restricted to process states only, but it can specify complex graph patterns as shown on the right. There the node marked with the X-edge represents a group where every node attached with a G-edge is a member of.

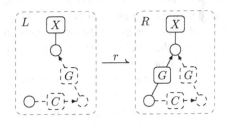

The rule can be applied if every edge attached to the two solid nodes is matched and has the form of the dashed part (the quantification). Effectively the rule adds a node to a group if all other connected nodes (via a C-edge) are already members of the group.

We have implemented a prototype version of the algorithms in the tool UNCOVER and tested on some case-studies. For instance, our prototype can verify the Distributed Dining Philosophers example without need of additional invariants as in [25]. Due to space limitations, the proofs can be found in an extended version of this paper [17].

2 Preliminaries

In this paper we use hypergraphs, a generalization of directed graphs, where an edge can connect an arbitrary large but finite set of nodes. Furthermore we use graph morphisms to define rewriting rules.

Hypergraph Let Λ be a finite sets of edge labels and $ar: \Lambda \to \mathbb{N}$ a function that assigns an arity to each label (including the arity zero). A *(Λ-)hypergraph* (or simply graph) is a tuple (V_G, E_G, c_G, l_G) where V_G is a finite set of nodes, E_G is a finite set of edges,

$c_G : E_G \to V_G^*$ is a connection function and $l_G : E_G \to \Lambda$ is an edge labelling function. We require that $|c_G(e)| = ar(l_G(e))$ for each edge $e \in E_G$. An edge e is called *incident* to a node v if v occurs in $c_G(e)$. An *undirected path* of length n in a hypergraph is an alternating sequence $v_0, e_1, v_1, \ldots, v_{n-1}, e_n, v_n$ of nodes and edges such that for every index $1 \leq i \leq n$ both nodes v_{i-1} and v_i are incident to e_i and the undirected path contains all nodes and edges at most once.

Let G, G' be (Λ-)hypergraphs. A *partial hypergraph morphism* (or simply *morphism*) $\varphi : G \rightharpoonup G'$ consists of a pair of partial functions ($\varphi_V : V_G \rightharpoonup V_{G'}, \varphi_E : E_G \rightharpoonup E_{G'}$) such that for every $e \in E_G$ it holds that $l_G(e) = l_{G'}(\varphi_E(e))$ and $\varphi_V(c_G(e)) = c_{G'}(\varphi_E(e))$ whenever $\varphi_E(e)$ is defined. Furthermore if a morphism is defined on an edge, it must be defined on all nodes incident to it. We denote *total morphisms* by an arrow of the form $\to$ and write $\rightarrowtail$ if the total morphism is known to be injective.

Pushout Our rewriting formalism is the so-called *single-pushout approach* (SPO) based on the categorical notion of pushouts in the category of graphs and partial graph morphisms [21]. Given two morphisms $\varphi : G_0 \rightharpoonup G_1$ and $\psi : G_0 \rightharpoonup G_2$, the *pushout* of φ, ψ consists of the graph G_3 and two morphisms $\varphi' : G_2 \rightharpoonup G_3$ and $\psi' : G_1 \rightharpoonup G_3$. It corresponds to a merge of G_1 and G_2 along a common interface G_0 while at the same time deleting every element of one of the graphs if it has a preimage in G_0 which is not mapped to an element in the other graph. It is known that in our category the pushout of two morphisms always exists and is unique (up to isomorphism). It can be computed in the following way.

Let $\equiv_V$ and $\equiv_E$ be the smallest equivalences on $V_{G_1} \cup V_{G_2}$ and $E_{G_1} \cup E_{G_2}$ satisfying $\varphi(v) \equiv_V \psi(v)$ for all $v \in V_{G_0}$ and $\varphi(e) \equiv_E \psi(e)$ for all $e \in E_{G_0}$. The nodes and edges of the pushout object G_3 are then all *valid* equivalence classes of $\equiv_V$ and $\equiv_E$. An equivalence class is *valid* if it does not contain the image of some $x \in G_0$ for which $\varphi(x)$ or $\psi(x)$ is undefined. The equivalence class of an edge is also considered invalid if it is incident to a node with an invalid equivalence class. The morphisms φ' and ψ' map each element to its equivalence class if this class is valid and are undefined otherwise.

For a backward step in our procedure we also need the notion of a *pushout complement* which is, given $\varphi : G_0 \rightharpoonup G_1$ and $\psi' : G_1 \rightharpoonup G_3$, a graph G_2 and morphisms $\psi : G_0 \rightharpoonup G_2$, $\varphi' : G_2 \rightharpoonup G_3$ such that G_3 is the pushout of φ, ψ. For graphs pushout complements not necessarily exist and if they exist there may be infinitely many. See [23] for a detailed description on how pushout complements can be computed.

GTS A *rewriting rule* is a partial morphism $r : L \rightharpoonup R$, where L is called left-hand and R right-hand side. A *match* (of r) is a total and injective morphism $m : L \rightarrowtail G$. Given a rule and a match, a *rewriting step* or rule application is given by a pushout diagram as shown on the right, resulting in the graph H. Note that injective matchings are not a restriction since non-injective matchings can be simulated, but are necessary for universally the quantified rules defined later.

$$
\begin{array}{ccc}
L & \xrightarrow{\ r\ } & R \\
\downarrow{\scriptstyle m} & & \downarrow{\scriptstyle m'} \\
G & \longrightarrow & H
\end{array}
$$

A *graph transformation system (GTS)* is a finite set of rules $\mathcal{R}$. Given a fixed set of graphs $\mathcal{G}$, a *graph transition system* on $\mathcal{G}$ generated by a graph transformation system $\mathcal{R}$ is represented by a tuple $(\mathcal{G}, \Rightarrow)$ where $\mathcal{G}$ is the set of states and $G \Rightarrow G'$ if and only if $G, G' \in \mathcal{G}$ and G can be rewritten to G' using a rule of $\mathcal{R}$.

A computation is a sequence of graphs $G_0, G_1, \ldots$ s.t. $G_i \Rightarrow G_{i+1}$ for $i \geq 0$. G_0 can reach G_1 if there exists a computation from G_0 to G_1.

3   Graph Transformations with Universally Quantified Conditions

To clarify the ideas and illustrate the usefulness of universally quantified conditions on the neighbourhood of nodes, let us consider the following example.

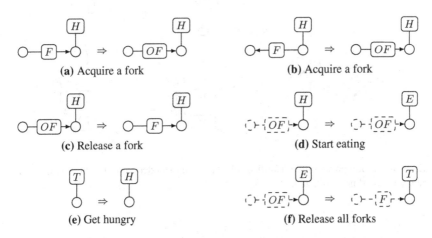

(a) Acquire a fork

(b) Acquire a fork

(c) Release a fork

(d) Start eating

(e) Get hungry

(f) Release all forks

Fig. 1. Modelling of the dining philosophers problem on an arbitrary net

Example 1. Figure 1 shows a set of rules describing the Dining Philosophers Problem on an arbitrary graph structure. Each node represents a philosopher who can be in one of three different states: hungry (H), eating (E) or thinking (T). Each state is indicated by a unary edge attached to the philosopher. Between two philosophers there may be a free fork (an F-edge) or a fork owned by one of the philosophers (an OF-edge pointing to its owner). Note that our directed edges are in fact hyperedges of arity two, where the first node is the source and the second node is the target.

Philosophers can take unowned forks (Figure 1a and 1b) and also release control (Figure 1c). If a philosopher owns all connected forks, he can start to eat (Figure 1d). The dashed part of the rule indicates a universal quantification, meaning that the rule can only be applied if all edges attached to the philosopher are part of the matching and in fact forks owned by him. At some point the philosopher finished eating, releasing all forks (Figure 1f) and may become hungry in the future (Figure 1e). When releasing all forks, all forks owned by the philosopher are converted to unowned forks.

Rules matching the entire neighbourhood of a node (in the following called *quantified node*), such as the rules in Figure 1d and 1f cannot be described by normal rewriting rules. Therefore we extend normal rules to so-called universally quantified rules consisting of a normal rule and a set of universal quantifications. The idea is to first find a matching for the rule and then extend the rule as well as the matching until the entire neighbourhood of quantified nodes is part of the matching.

We apply the rule in Figure 1f to the graph G shown in Figure 2. There exists a match $m : L \rightarrowtail G$ where $r : L \rightharpoonup R$ is the rule without any use of the quantification. However, this matching does not match the entire neighbourhood of the quantified node (marked grey). Before applying the rule we have to add multiple copies of the quantification to r generating a so-called instantiation η where the extended match $\overline{m}$ contains the entire neighbourhood of the quantified node.

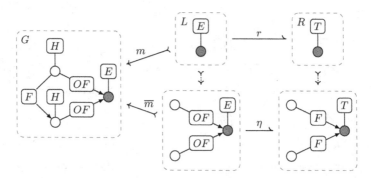

Fig. 2. A match of a universally quantified rule has to be extended until the entire neighbourhood of each quantified node is matched

In the following we formalize the notion of universally quantified rules as an extension of normal rules and introduce instantiations via a sequence of recursive instantiation steps.

Definition 1 (Universally quantified rules). *A* universally quantified rule *is a pair* $\rho = (r, U)$, *where* $r : L \rightharpoonup R$ *is a partial morphism and* U *is a finite set of universal quantifications. A* universal quantification *is a pair* $(p_u, q_u) = u \in U$ *where* $p_u : L \rightarrowtail L_u$ *is a total injective morphism and* $q_u : L_u \rightharpoonup R_u$ *is a partial morphism satisfying the restriction that* $q_u(p_u(x))$ *is defined and has exactly one preimage in* L_u *for every* $x \in L$.

With $qn(u)$ *we denote the set of* quantified nodes of u, *which is the set of all* $v \in V_L$ *such that there is an edge incident to* $p_u(v)$ *which has no preimage in* L. *We denote the quantified nodes of a rule the same way, i.e.* $qn(\rho) = \bigcup_{u \in U} qn(u)$. *We require that* $qn(u) \neq \emptyset$ *for all* $u \in U$.

In the rest of the paper we will use UGTS to denote the extension of GTS with universally quantified rules.

Definition 2 (Instantiation of a universally quantified rule). *An instantiation of a universally quantified rule* $\rho = (r, U)$ *consists of a total injective morphism* $\pi : L \rightarrowtail \overline{L}$ *and a partial morphism* $\gamma : \overline{L} \rightharpoonup \overline{R}$ *and is recursively defined as follows:*

- *The pair* $(id_L : L \rightarrowtail L, r)$, *where* id_L *is the identity on* L, *is an instantiation of* ρ.
- *Let* $(\pi : L \rightarrowtail \overline{L}, \gamma : \overline{L} \rightharpoonup \overline{R})$ *be an instantiation of* ρ *and let* $(p_u : L \rightarrowtail L_u, q_u : L_u \rightharpoonup R_u) = u \in U$. *Furthermore, let* $\overline{L}_u$ *be the pushout of* π, p_u *and let* $\overline{R}_u$ *be the pushout of* $\gamma \circ \pi$, $q_u \circ p_u$, *as shown in the diagram to the right. Then* $p'_u \circ \pi$ *and the (unique) mediating morphism* η *are also an instantiation of* ρ. *We write* $(p'_u \circ \pi, \eta) = (\pi, \gamma) \diamond u$ *to indicate that the instantiation* (π, γ) *was extended by* u.

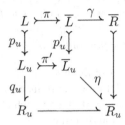

We say that the length of an instantiation is the number of steps performed to generate the instantiation, where (id_L, r) *has a length of* 0.

Example 2. Figure 3 shows a possible instantiation of the rule in Figure 1f. There is only one universal quantification u and this quantification is used once to generate the instantiation $(p'_u \circ id_L, \eta)$. Any further instantiation will add an additional node and OF-edge to L_u and an additional node and F-edge to $\overline{R}_u$. The universally quantified node (i.e. $qn(u)$) is marked grey. This means that η is only applicable if the grey node is matched to a node with degree (exactly) two. The rule application is performed by calculating the pushout of η (not r) and a valid matching m. The matching is only valid if all edges incident to the grey node have a preimage in $\overline{L}_u$, such that an application will always result in all incident OF-edges to be replaced by F-edges. Although the number of affected edges can be arbitrary large, the quantification it bounded to the neighbourhood of the grey node and therefore the change is still local.

The order in which universal quantifications are used to generate instantiations can be neglected, since different sequences will still yield the same instantiation (up to isomorphism). Therefore we can uniquely specify instantiations by the number each universal quantification in its sequence.

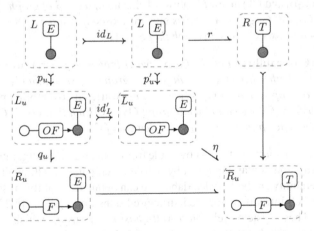

Fig. 3. A possible instantiation of the rule in Figure 1f

Definition 3 (Rule application). *Let ρ be a universally quantified rule. We say that ρ is applicable to a graph G, if there is an instantiation (π, γ) of ρ and a total injective match $m : \overline{L} \rightarrowtail G$, such that for every $x \in qn(\rho)$, there is no $e \in E_G$ incident to $m(\pi(x))$ without a preimage in $\overline{L}$. The application of ρ to G via m results in the graph H, the pushout of m and γ.*

We reuse the notation $G \Rightarrow G'$ to denote a rewriting step from G to G'. The previous definition introduces a restricted form of negative application condition since the existence of an edge, which cannot be mapped by a quantification, may block the application of a rule.

4   A Procedure for Coverability in UGTS

In this paper we focus our attention on verification problems that can be formulated as reachability and coverability decision problems. Given an initial configuration G_0 and a target configuration G_1 reachability consists in checking whether there exists a computation from G_0 to G_1. The coverability problem is similar to the reachability problem, but additionally relies on an ordering. In this paper we use the subgraph ordering, but there are other suitable orders such as the minor ordering or the induced subgraph ordering [24].

Definition 4 (Subgraph Ordering). *A graph G_1 is a subgraph of G_2, written $G_1 \subseteq G_2$, if there exists a partial, injective and surjective morphism from G_2 to G_1, written $\mu : G_2 \rightarrowtail G_1$. Such morphisms are called subgraph morphisms.*

Given a G, a subgraph can always be obtained by a sequence of node and edge deletions. Note that due to the morphism property every edge attached to a deleted node must be deleted as well. Using the subgraph ordering we can represent sets of configurations by minimal graphs and define two variants of the coverability problem.

Definition 5 (Upward Closure). *The* upward closure *of a set S of graphs is defined as $\uparrow S = \{G' \mid G \subseteq G', G \in S\}$. A set S is* upward-closed *if it satisfies $S = \uparrow S$. A* basis *of an upward-closed set S is a set B such that $S = \uparrow B$.*

Definition 6 (Coverability). *Let G_0, G_1 be two graphs. The* general coverability problem *is to decide whether from G_0 we can reach a graph G_2 such that $G_1 \subseteq G_2$.*

Let G a set of graphs and let $G_0, G_1 \in G$. The restricted coverability problem *is to decide whether from G_0 we can reach a graph $G_2 \in G$ such that $G_1 \subseteq G_2$ and every graph on the sequence from G_0 to G_2 is an element of G.*

In other words, a configuration is coverable from some initial configuration if we can reach a configuration containing (as subgraph) a given pattern. Although general and restricted coverability are both undecidable, we can obtain decidability results by using a backward search introduced for well-structured transition systems [6,22] as already shown in [7]. These systems rely on a *well-quasi-order (wqo)*, which is a transitive reflexive order $\leq$ such that there is no infinite, strictly decreasing sequence of elements and no infinite antichain, a sequence of pairwise incomparable elements, wrt. $\leq$. A direct consequence of this property is that every upward-closed set wrt. some wqo has a finite basis. It has been shown that the subgraph ordering is a well-quasi-order on $\mathcal{G}_k$, the class of graphs in which every undirected path has at most the length k [19]. We remark that the property does not hold if only directed paths are restricted.

The backward search presented in this paper is a version of the general backward search presented in [24] adapted to be compatible with UGTS. We denote the set of *predecessors* for a set of graphs S by $Pred(S) = \{G' \mid \exists G \in S \colon G' \Rightarrow G\}$. Furthermore we denote the predecessors reachable within multiple step by $Pred^*(S)$ and the *restricted predecessors* by $Pred_{\mathcal{G}}(S) = Pred(S) \cap \mathcal{G}$. We will present a procedure for UGTS to compute so-called effective pred-basis and effective $\mathcal{G}_k$-pred-basis. An *effective pred-basis* for a graph G is a finite basis $pb(G)$ of $\uparrow Pred(\uparrow\{G\})$ and an *effective $\mathcal{G}_k$-pred-basis* is a finite basis $pb_k(G)$ of $\uparrow Pred_{\mathcal{G}_k}(\uparrow\{G\})$. Using the effective $\mathcal{G}_k$-pred-basis the backward search will terminate and compute a finite basis $\mathcal{B}$. If $G \in \uparrow\mathcal{B}$, then G covers a configuration of S in $\Rightarrow$ (general coverability). If $G \notin \uparrow\mathcal{B}$, then G does not cover a configuration of S in $\Rightarrow_{\mathcal{G}_k}$ (no restricted coverability), where $\Rightarrow_{\mathcal{G}_k}$ is the restriction $\Rightarrow \cap (\mathcal{G}_k \times \mathcal{G}_k)$. By using the effective pred-basis the backward search computes a finite basis for $Pred^*(S)$, but is not guaranteed to terminate.

The computation of a $\mathcal{G}_k$-pred-basis is performed by Procedure 1. We assume that for a graph G and a rule ρ there is an upper bound on the length of instantiations necessary to compute a backward step and write $bound_\rho(G)$ to denote such an upper bound. The existence of this upper bound is shown later on in Proposition 1. The result of a backward step is a finite set S of graphs such that $Pred(\uparrow\{G\}) \subseteq \uparrow S$.

Procedure 1 (Backward Step).
Input: A rule ρ and a graph G.
Procedure:
1. First compute all instantiations $(\pi : L \rightarrowtail \overline{L}, \gamma : \overline{L} \rightharpoonup \overline{R})$ of ρ up to the length $bound_\rho(G)$.
2. For each γ compute all subgraph morphisms $\mu : \overline{R} \rightarrowtail R'$. Note that it is sufficient to take a representative R' for each of the finitely many isomorphism classes.
3. For each $\mu \circ \gamma$ compute all total injective morphisms $m' : R' \rightarrow G$ (co-matches of R' in G).
4. For each such morphism m' calculate all minimal pushout complements $G', m : \overline{L} \rightarrowtail G'$ of m' and $\mu \circ \gamma$ where m is injective and G' is an element of $\mathcal{G}_k$. Drop all G' where m does not satisfy the application condition of Definition 3, i.e. there is an edge incident to a quantified node which is not in the matching.

Result: The set of all graphs not dropped in Step 4, written $pb_k(G)$.

The motivation behind Step 2 is that G represents not just itself but also its upward closure. Therefore, the rule must also be applied to every graph larger than G. Instead of using partial co-matches we concatenate with subgraph morphisms to simulate this behaviour.

The procedure for a single backward step can be used to define a backward search procedure for the coverability problem for UGTS. The procedure exploits the property that, even if compatibility is not satisfied, $Pred(\uparrow S) \subseteq \uparrow Pred(\uparrow S)$ still holds for every set of graphs S. We can iteratively compute backward steps for all minimal graphs G of $\uparrow S$ and check that no initial state is reached backwards.

Procedure 2 (Backward Search).

Input: A natural number k, a set $\mathcal{R}$ of graph transformation rules and a finite set of final graphs $\mathcal{F}$. Start with the working set $\mathcal{W} = \mathcal{F}$.

Backward Step: For each $G \in \mathcal{W}$ add all graphs of $pb_k(G)$ to $\mathcal{W}$ and minimize $\mathcal{W}$ by removing all graphs H' for which there is a graph $H'' \in \mathcal{W}$ with $H' \neq H''$ and $H'' \subseteq H'$. Repeat this backward steps until the sequence of working sets $\mathcal{W}$ becomes stationary, i.e. for every $G \in \mathcal{W}$ the computation of the backward step using G results in no change of $\mathcal{W}$.

Result: The resulting set $\mathcal{W}$ contains minimal representatives of graphs from which a final state is coverable. This set may be an over-approximation, even without quantified rules.

To show the termination of Procedure 1 and 2 it is important to show the existence of a bounding function $bound_\rho()$. By the following proposition this function exists for every rule ρ, but as we will show later this bound can be tightened in most cases.

Proposition 1. *Let ι be an instantiation of length k of some rule ρ. If k is larger than the number of nodes and edges of G, then every graph computed by the backward application of ι is already represented by the backward application of an instantiation of lower length.*

The following two lemmas prove that Procedure 1 computes a finite basis of an over-approximation of the restricted predecessors.

Lemma 1. *The set $pb_k(G)$ is a finite subset of $Pred(\uparrow\{G\})$ and $pb_k(G) \subseteq \mathcal{G}_k$.*

Lemma 2. *It holds that $\uparrow pb_k(G) \supseteq \uparrow Pred_{\mathcal{G}_k}(\uparrow\{G\})$.*

We recapitulate our main result in the following proposition.

Proposition 2. *For each graph G, $pb_k(G)$ is an effective $\mathcal{G}_k$-pred-basis. Furthermore, Procedure 2 terminates and computes an over-approximation of all configurations in $\mathcal{G}_k$ from which a final configuration is coverable.*

Proof. By Lemma 1 and 2 we know that $\uparrow pb_k(G) = \uparrow Pred_{\mathcal{G}_k}(\uparrow\{G\})$ and thus $pb_k(G)$ is a $\mathcal{G}_k$-pred-basis. According to Proposition 1 for every $\rho \in \mathcal{R}$ the number of necessary instantiation steps is bounded by $bound_\rho(G)$, thus, the number of instantiations is fine. For each instantiation the minimal pushout complements restricted to $\mathcal{G}_k$ are finite and computable. Since the subgraph ordering is decidable the minimization is computable and $pb_k(G)$ is effective.

Since the subgraph ordering is a wqo on $\mathcal{G}_k$, every infinite increasing sequence of upward-closed set becomes stationary. The upward-closures of the working sets $\mathcal{W}$ form such an infinite increasing sequence, thus the termination criteria of Procedure 2 will be satisfied at some point. □

A Variant of $pb_k()$ Without Path Bound

In Step 4 of Procedure 1 every graph which is not an element of $\mathcal{G}_k$ is dropped. This is needed to guarantee that the working set of Procedure 2 becomes stationary and the search terminates. However, this restriction can be dropped to obtain a backward search which solves the general coverability problem. Termination is not guaranteed, but correctness can be proven analogously to the restricted variant, as already shown in [24]. Let $pb()$ be Procedure 1 without the restriction to $\mathcal{G}_k$. We summarize the decidability of this second variant in the following proposition.

Proposition 3. *For each graph G, $pb(G)$ is an effective pred-basis. Furthermore, when using $pb()$ instead of $pb_k()$, Procedure 2 computes an over-approximation of all configurations from which a final configuration is coverable.*

Experimental Results

We added support for universally quantified rules to the UNCOVER tool. This tool can perform the backward search for the subgraph ordering and the minor ordering (a coarser order compared to subgraphs). Both variants of the backward search are implemented, but a timeout might occur when using the unrestricted variant. However, given the rules in Figure 1 and the error graphs in Figure 4 the unrestricted variant terminates after 12 seconds and results in a set of 12 minimal graphs. Two of these graphs are the initial error graphs and two other computed graph are shown in Figure 5. Every minimal graph contains a node in the state E. Since initially no philosopher is eating, the initial configuration is not represented and none of the initial error graphs is reachable. This proves that two adjacent philosophers cannot be eating at the same time.

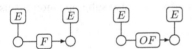

Fig. 4. Two error configurations in the Dining Philosophers Problem

Fig. 5. Two other error graphs computed by the backward search

5   Optimizations

In this section we discuss and formalize some optimizations that can be applied to the basic backward procedure described in the previous section.

Lifting the Application Condition to a Post Conditions. In Procedure 1 the application condition is checked in Step 4 for each pushout complement. However, by lifting the application condition over the instantiation we can check beforehand whether the backward step yields new graphs. We show the lifting in the following lemma.

Lemma 3. *Let ρ be a rule, $(\pi : L \rightarrowtail \overline{L}, \gamma : \overline{L} \rightharpoonup \overline{R})$ an instantiation of ρ and $m : \overline{R} \rightarrowtail G$ a co-match of the instantiation to some graph G. If there is a node $x \in qn(\rho)$ where $m(\gamma(\pi(x))$ is defined and attached to an edge e without preimage in $\overline{R}$, then there is no pushout complement H of γ, m satisfying the condition of Definition 3.*

Tightening the Upper Bound of Instantiations. The bound on the length of instantiations proven to exist in Proposition 1 can be improved depending on the rule used. Let $\rho = (r : L \rightharpoonup R, U)$ be a rule. Obviously $bound_\rho(G) = 0$ if $U = \emptyset$. The same holds if instantiations only increase the left side of the rule, i.e. for every $u \in U$ given the instantiation $(id_L, r) \diamond u = (\pi : L \rightarrowtail \overline{L}_u, \gamma : \overline{L}_u \rightharpoonup \overline{R}_u)$, the graphs $\overline{R}_u$ and R are isomorphic.

A more common situation is that quantifications do not add edges to the right side of the instantiations which are solely incident to nodes of the original rule r. This is case for all rules used in Example 1. The bound can be reduced as shown below.

Lemma 4. *Let $\rho = (r : L \rightharpoonup R, U)$ and let $(id_L, r) \diamond u = (\pi : L \rightarrowtail \overline{L}_u, \gamma : \overline{L}_u \rightharpoonup \overline{R}_u)$. If for every $u \in U$ every edge $e \in \overline{R}_u$ without preimage in R is connected to a node $v \in \overline{R}_u$ without preimage in R, then $bound_\rho(G) = |V_G|$.*

Optimization by Preparation. The general framework in [24] uses a preparation step in the backward search to compute the concatenation of rules and subgraph morphisms performed in Step 2 of Procedure 1. This is not fully possible with universally quantified rules since the instantiations are generated within the backward steps. However, the preparation step can be performed for rules without universal quantifications. For rules with quantification the inner rule morphism can be concatenated with subgraph morphisms to partially prepare the rule. It can also be show that any concatenation of an instantiation and a subgraph morphism which is also a subgraph morphism, will not yield new graph in the backward step and thus can be dropped. This also holds for rules with universal quantification if all possible instantiations are also subgraph morphisms.

6   Conclusions and Related Work

In this paper we introduced a categorical formalization for an extension of graph transformation systems with universally quantified rules built on the single pushout approach. These rules are powerful enough to model distributed algorithms which use broadcast communication. A similar concept are adaptive star grammars [20] where the left-hand side of a rule is a star, i.e. a designated center node connected to a set of other nodes. Arbitrary large graphs can be matched by cloning parts of the star, which is – apart of the restriction to stars – one of the main differences to our approach. Technically our instantiations are a special form of amalgamated graph transformations [9], a technique to merge rules.

The backward search procedure presented in this paper is an extension of [24] with universally quantified rules and can be used for the verification of distributed algorithms, similar to [14]. There the induced subgraph ordering was used, which was also shown to be compatible with the framework in [24]. However, our quantifications differ as we have a stronger negative application condition such that the induced subgraph ordering is not enough to cause our UGTS to satisfy the compatibility condition. This also causes the approached to differ in expressiveness. In general our approach should be compatible with the induced subgraph ordering and the minor ordering, but we did not yet investigated this.

Parameterized verification of combinations of automata- and graph-based models of distributed systems has been studied, e.g. in [10,4,15,16,13,12]. In [5] we applied graph-based transformations to model intermediate evaluations of non-atomic mutual exclusion protocols with universally quantified conditions. The conditions are not defined however in terms of graph rewrite rules. Semi-decision procedures can be defined by resorting to upward closed abstractions during backward search (monotonic abstraction as in [11]). In [10] we studied decidability of reachability and coverability for a graph-based specification used to model biological systems. Among other results, we proved undecidability for coverability for graph rewrite systems that can only increase the size of a configuration. Reachability problems for graph-based representations of protocols have also been considered in [4] where symbolic representations combining a special graph ordering and constraint-based representation of relations between local data of different nodes have been used to verify parameterized consistency protocols. Coverability for GTS is studied in [8] where it was proved that it is decidable for bounded path graphs ordered via subgraph inclusion. A model with topologies represented as acyclic directed graphs has been presented in [1]. Coverability for automata-based models of broadcast communication has recently been studied in [15,16,13,18,12]. In the context of program analysis approximated backward search working on graphs representing data structures with pointers have been considered in [2]. In this setting approximations are defined via edges or node deletion.

References

1. Abdulla, P.A., Atig, M.F., Rezine, O.: Verification of directed acyclic ad hoc networks. In: Beyer, D., Boreale, M. (eds.) FORTE 2013 and FMOODS 2013. LNCS, vol. 7892, pp. 193–208. Springer, Heidelberg (2013)
2. Abdulla, P.A., Cederberg, J., Vojnar, T.: Monotonic abstraction for programs with multiply-linked structures. Int. J. Found. Comput. Sci. 24(2), 187–210 (2013)
3. Abdulla, P.A., Delzanno, G., Rezine, A.: Approximated parameterized verification of infinite-state processes with global conditions. Formal Methods in System Design 34(2), 126–156 (2009)
4. Abdulla, P.A., Delzanno, G., Rezine, A.: Automatic verification of directory-based consistency protocols with graph constraints. Int. J. Found. Comput. Sci. 22(4) (2011)
5. Abdulla, P.A., Ben Henda, N., Delzanno, G., Rezine, A.: Handling parameterized systems with non-atomic global conditions. In: Logozzo, F., Peled, D.A., Zuck, L.D. (eds.) VMCAI 2008. LNCS, vol. 4905, pp. 22–36. Springer, Heidelberg (2008)
6. Abdulla, P.A., Čerāns, K., Jonsson, B., Tsay, Y.: General decidability theorems for infinite-state systems. In: Proc. of LICS 1996, pp. 313–321. IEEE (1996)
7. Bertrand, N., Delzanno, G., König, B., Sangnier, A., Stückrath, J.: On the decidability status of reachability and coverability in graph transformation systems. In: RTA 2012. LIPIcs, vol. 15, pp. 101–116. Schloss Dagstuhl - Leibniz-Zentrum fuer Informatik (2012)
8. Bertrand, N., Delzanno, G., König, B., Sangnier, A., Stückrath, J.: On the decidability status of reachability and coverability in graph transformation systems. In: RTA, pp. 101–116 (2012)
9. Boehm, P., Fonio, H., Habel, A.: Amalgamation of graph transformations: A synchronization mechanism. Journal of Computer and System Sciences 34, 377–408 (1987)

10. Delzanno, G., Di Giusto, C., Gabbrielli, M., Laneve, C., Zavattaro, G.: The κ-lattice: Decidability boundaries for qualitative analysis in biological languages. In: Degano, P., Gorrieri, R. (eds.) CMSB 2009. LNCS, vol. 5688, pp. 158–172. Springer, Heidelberg (2009)

11. Delzanno, G., Rezine, A.: A lightweight regular model checking approach for parameterized systems. STTT 14(2), 207–222 (2012)

12. Delzanno, G., Sangnier, A., Traverso, R.: Parameterized verification of broadcast networks of register automata. In: Abdulla, P.A., Potapov, I. (eds.) RP 2013. LNCS, vol. 8169, pp. 109–121. Springer, Heidelberg (2013)

13. Delzanno, G., Sangnier, A., Traverso, R., Zavattaro, G.: On the complexity of parameterized reachability in reconfigurable broadcast networks. In: FSTTCS 2012. LIPIcs, vol. 18, pp. 289–300. Schloss Dagstuhl - Leibniz-Zentrum fuer Informatik (2012)

14. Delzanno, G., Sangnier, A., Zavattaro, G.: Parameterized verification of ad hoc networks. In: Gastin, P., Laroussinie, F. (eds.) CONCUR 2010. LNCS, vol. 6269, pp. 313–327. Springer, Heidelberg (2010)

15. Delzanno, G., Sangnier, A., Zavattaro, G.: Parameterized verification of ad hoc networks. In: Gastin, P., Laroussinie, F. (eds.) CONCUR 2010. LNCS, vol. 6269, pp. 313–327. Springer, Heidelberg (2010)

16. Delzanno, G., Sangnier, A., Zavattaro, G.: On the power of cliques in the parameterized verification of ad hoc networks. In: Hofmann, M. (ed.) FOSSACS 2011. LNCS, vol. 6604, pp. 441–455. Springer, Heidelberg (2011)

17. Delzanno, G., Stückrath, J.: Parameterized verification of graph transformation systems with whole neighbourhood operations, arXiv:1407.4394 (2014)

18. Delzanno, G., Traverso, R.: Decidability and complexity results for verification of asynchronous broadcast networks. In: Dediu, A.-H., Martín-Vide, C., Truthe, B. (eds.) LATA 2013. LNCS, vol. 7810, pp. 238–249. Springer, Heidelberg (2013)

19. Ding, G.: Subgraphs and well-quasi-ordering. Jornal of Graph Theory 16, 489–502 (1992)

20. Drewes, F., Hoffmann, B., Janssens, D., Minas, M., Van Eetvelde, N.: Adaptive star grammars. In: Corradini, A., Ehrig, H., Montanari, U., Ribeiro, L., Rozenberg, G. (eds.) ICGT 2006. LNCS, vol. 4178, pp. 77–91. Springer, Heidelberg (2006)

21. Ehrig, H., Heckel, R., Korff, M., Löwe, M., Ribeiro, L., Wagner, A., Corradini, A.: Algebraic approaches to graph transformation—part II: Single pushout approach and comparison with double pushout approach. In: Rozenberg, G. (ed.) Handbook of Graph Grammars and Computing by Graph Transformation: Foundations. ch. 4, vol. 1, World Scientific (1997)

22. Finkel, A., Schnoebelen, P.: Well-structured transition systems everywhere? Theoretical Computer Science 256(1-2), 63–92 (2001)

23. Heumüller, M., Joshi, S., König, B., Stückrath, J.: Construction of pushout complements in the category of hypergraphs. In: Proc. of GCM 2010 (Workshop on Graph Computation Models) (2010)

24. König, B., Stückrath, J.: A general framework for well-structured graph transformation systems. In: Baldan, P. (ed.) CONCUR 2014. LNCS, vol. 8704, pp. 467–481. Springer, Heidelberg (2014)

25. Namjoshi, K.S., Trefler, R.J.: Uncovering symmetries in irregular process networks. In: Giacobbazzi, R., Berdine, J., Mastroeni, I. (eds.) VMCAI 2013. LNCS, vol. 7737, pp. 496–514. Springer, Heidelberg (2013)

Equivalence Between Model-Checking Flat Counter Systems and Presburger Arithmetic[*]

Stéphane Demri[2], Amit Kumar Dhar[1], and Arnaud Sangnier[1]

[1] LIAFA, Univ Paris Diderot, Sorbonne Paris Cité, CNRS, France
[2] NYU – CNRS

Abstract. We show that model-checking flat counter systems over CTL* (with arithmetical constraints on counter values) has the same complexity as the satisfiability problem for Presburger arithmetic. The lower bound already holds with the temporal operator EF only, no arithmetical constraints in the logical language and with guards on transitions made of simple linear constraints. This complements our understanding of model-checking flat counter systems with linear-time temporal logics, such as LTL for which the problem is already known to be (only) NP-complete with guards restricted to the linear fragment.

1 Introduction

Branching-time temporal logics for counter systems. At first glance, model-checking counter systems with temporal logics seems a hopeless enterprise since control-state reachability problem for Minsky machines is already known to be undecidable [23]. Fortunately, many subclasses of counter systems admit a decidable reachability problem and more importantly, sometime the reachability sets are even definable in Presburger arithmetic (PA) [24]. That is why, model-checking problems with temporal logics for one-counter automata [15,16], Petri nets [17], reversal-bounded counter systems [2], flat counter systems [14] have been considered. The previous list is certainly not exhaustive and a general question is how to take advantage of the decidability of the reachability problem to conclude the decidability of model-checking problems with temporal logics. This can lead to endless studies, since the variety of subclasses of counter systems and temporal logics is extremely rich. By way of example, reachability sets of flat counter systems are known to be definable in (PA), see e.g. [3,6,14,4], but it is unclear how this can be extended to model-checking problems with temporal logics, which indeed, is done in [10] for flat counter systems. A complexity characterization for model-checking linear-time properties is provided in [9]. In the present paper, we study flat counter systems and branching-time temporal logics, more specifically with a variant of CTL* [12], already known to be difficult to mechanize in the propositional case with labelled transition systems.

[*] Work partially supported by the EU Seventh Framework Programme under grant agreement No. PIOF-GA-2011-301166 (DATAVERIF).

Our motivations We have seen that reachability problems and the verification of linear-time properties for flat counter systems are nowadays well-studied (see e.g. [9,4]) and in this paper we wish to understand the computational complexity for branching-time temporal logics such as CTL or CTL* (see e.g. [12]). Branching-time extensions often lead to undecidability, see e.g. the case with Petri nets for which CTL is undecidable (with propositional variables only) whereas the reachability problem and model-checking for several LTL variants are known to be decidable [17]. For flat counter systems, we are on the safe side since decidability of model-checking CTL* formulae is established in [10] but no lower bound is provided in [10] and the translation into (PA) gives an exponential size formula, which is rather unsatisfactory. Our main motivation is therefore to understand the complexity of model-checking flat counter systems with branching-time logics so that optimal algorithms for model-checking can be eventually designed.

Our contribution. We show that the model-checking problem for flat counter systems over a version of CTL* with arithmetical constraints on counter values is equivalent to satisfiability for (PA), modulo logarithmic-space reductions.

- For the complexity lower bound, we show that the satisfiability problem for (PA) can be reduced to the model-checking problem but there is no need for arithmetical constraints and for temporal operators other than EF.
- For the complexity upper bound, we reduce the model-checking problem to satisfiability problem in (PA) by using the fact that runs in flat counter systems can be encoded by tuples of natural numbers and then the semantics for CTL* can be internalized in (PA). This very fact has been already observed in [10] but herein, we provide a logarithmic-space reduction which makes a substantial difference with [10]. Indeed, we are also able to quantify over path schemas (symbolic representation of potential infinite sets of runs), but concisely. This witnesses once more, that verification problems can be encoded efficiently to (PA), see e.g. [5].
- As a consequence, we are able to get the equivalence with (PA) to known branching-time temporal logics stronger than CTL_{EF} (such as CTL) and our proof technique can be applied to extensions with past-time operators with a minimal amount of change.

As far as proofs are concerned, for the lower bound, we take advantage of the observation that a quantification in (PA) over a variable z can be simulated by a loop that increments a corresponding counter and there is a correspondence between first-order quantifier $\exists$ [resp. $\forall$] and temporal connective EF [resp. AG]. For the upper bound, quantification over path schemas is done, directly followed by a quantification over the number of times loops are visited. However, we provide a new way to encode runs in flat counter systems, which is rewarding complexity-wise. Not only we provide a much better complexity characterization than [10] but also our reduction into (PA) is much simpler, and therefore this leaves some hope to use then some solvers for (PA), see e.g. [7,20].
Due to lack of space, omitted proofs can be found in [11].

2 Branching-Time Temporal Logics on Flat Counter Systems

Presburger arithmetic. (PA), i.e. the first-order theory of natural numbers with addition, is introduced by M. Presburger who has shown decidability by quantifier elimination. Let VAR $= \{z_1, z_2, z_3, \ldots\}$ be a countably infinite set of *variables. Terms* are expressions of the form $a_1 z_1 + \cdots + a_n z_n + k$ where a_1, $\ldots$, a_n, k are in $\mathbb{N}$. A *valuation* f is a map VAR $\rightarrow \mathbb{N}$ and it can be extended to the set of all terms as follows: $f(k) = k$, $f(az) = a \times f(z)$ and $f(t + t') = f(t) + f(t')$ for all terms t and t'. *Formulae* are defined by the grammar $\phi ::= t \leq t' \mid \neg \phi \mid \phi \wedge \phi \mid \exists z \, \phi$ where t and t' are terms and $z \in$ VAR. A formula ϕ is in the *linear fragment* $\overset{\text{def}}{\Leftrightarrow}$ ϕ is a Boolean combination of atomic formulae of the form $t \leq t'$. The semantics for formulae in (PA) is defined with the satisfaction relation $\models$: for instance $f \models t \leq t' \overset{\text{def}}{\Leftrightarrow} f(t) \leq f(t')$ and $f \models \exists z \, \phi \overset{\text{def}}{\Leftrightarrow}$ there is $n \in \mathbb{N}$ such that $f[z \mapsto n] \models \phi$. Any formula $\phi(z_1, \ldots, z_n)$ whose free variables are among $z_1, \ldots, z_n$, with $n \geq 1$, defines a set of n-tuples $[\![\phi(z_1, \ldots, z_n)]\!] \overset{\text{def}}{=} \{\langle f(z_1), \ldots, f(z_n) \rangle \in \mathbb{N}^n : f \models \phi\}$, in that case for a vector $\mathbf{v} \in \mathbb{N}^n$, we will also write $\mathbf{v} \models \phi$ for $\mathbf{v} \in [\![\phi(z_1, \ldots, z_n)]\!]$. For a given PA formula ϕ, the set of free variables of ϕ is denoted by free(ϕ). The *satisfiability problem* for (PA) is a decision problem that takes as input a formula ϕ and asks whether there is a valuation f such that $f \models \phi$. If such a valuation exists, we say that ϕ is *satisfiable*. Decidability of Presburger arithmetic has been shown in [24]. An exact complexity characterization is provided in [1].

Counter systems. Let $C = \{x_1, x_2, \ldots\}$ be a countably infinite set of *counters* with the finite subset $\{x_1, \ldots, x_n\}$ denoted as C_n and AT $= \{p_1, p_2, \ldots\}$ be a countably infinite set of atomic propositional variables. A *counter system* is a tuple $\langle Q, C_n, \Delta, \ell \rangle$ where Q is a finite set of *control states*, $\ell : Q \rightarrow 2^{\text{AT}}$ is a *labelling function*, $\Delta \subseteq Q \times G_n \times \mathbb{Z}^n \times Q$ is a finite set of edges labelled by *guards* and *updates* of the counter values *(transitions)* where G_n is a finite set of Presburger formulae ϕ with free$(\phi) \subseteq \{x_1, \ldots, x_n\}$. Guards are quite general and we basically only need them in the linear fragment. However, since we provide a translation into (PA), we can be a bit more general, as in Presburger counter machines [10,19].

For each transition $\delta = \langle q, \mathbf{g}, \mathbf{u}, q' \rangle$ in Δ, we use the following notations: *source*$(\delta) = q$, *target*$(\delta) = q'$, *guard*$(\delta) = \mathbf{g}$ and *update*$(\delta) = \mathbf{u}$. As usual, to a counter system $S = \langle Q, C_n, \Delta, \ell \rangle$, we associate a labelled transition system $\mathfrak{T}(S) = \langle C, \rightarrow \rangle$ where $C = Q \times \mathbb{N}^n$ is the set of *configurations* and $\rightarrow \subseteq C \times \Delta \times C$ is the *transition relation* defined by: $\langle \langle q, \mathbf{v} \rangle, \delta, \langle q', \mathbf{v}' \rangle \rangle \in \rightarrow$ (also written $\langle q, \mathbf{v} \rangle \overset{\delta}{\rightarrow} \langle q', \mathbf{v}' \rangle$) iff $q = $ *source*(δ), $q' = $ *target*(δ), $\mathbf{v} \models$ *guard*(δ) and $\mathbf{v}' = \mathbf{v} + $ *update*(δ). We write $c \rightarrow c'$ iff there exists some edge δ, such that $c \overset{\delta}{\rightarrow} c'$.

Given $c_0 \in Q \times \mathbb{N}^n$, a *run* ρ starting from c_0 in S is a (possibly infinite) path in the associated transition system $\mathfrak{T}(S)$ denoted as $\rho := c_0 \overset{\delta_0}{\rightarrow} \cdots \overset{\delta_{m-1}}{\rightarrow} c_m \overset{\delta_m}{\rightarrow}$ $\cdots$, where $c_i \in Q \times \mathbb{N}^n$ and $\delta_i \in \Delta$, for all $i \in \mathbb{N}$.

Let $trans(\rho)$ be the ω-word $\delta_0\delta_1 \ldots$ of the sequence of transitions appearing in the run ρ. For every $i \geq 0$, we define $\rho(i) = c_i$ and $\rho_{\leq i} = c_0 \xrightarrow{\delta_0} c_1 \cdots \xrightarrow{\delta_{i-1}} c_i$. Also, we say $c \rightarrow^* c'$ iff there exist a run ρ and $i \in \mathbb{N}$ such that $\rho(0) = c$ and $\rho(i) = c'$. Note that a run in a counter system S is either finite or infinite. A run ρ is *maximal* iff either it is infinite, or it is finite and the last configuration is a deadlock (i.e. with no successor configurations). For a finite maximal run $\rho := c_0 \xrightarrow{\delta_0} \cdots \xrightarrow{\delta_{m-1}} c_m \xrightarrow{\delta_m} c_{m+1}$, we write $|\rho| = m$, otherwise for an infinite maximal run ρ, $|\rho| = \omega$.

A counter system is *flat* if every node in the underlying graph belongs to at most one simple cycle (a cycle being simple if no edge is repeated twice in it) [6,22]. In a flat counter system, simple cycles can be organized as a DAG where two simple cycles are in the relation whenever there is path between a node of the first cycle and a node of the second cycle. We denote by FlatCS the class of flat counter systems.

Logical specifications. The formulae for CTL* are defined as follows: $\phi ::= \mathsf{p} \mid \psi(\mathsf{x}_1, \ldots, \mathsf{x}_n) \mid \phi \wedge \phi \mid \neg\phi \mid \mathsf{X}\phi \mid \phi\mathsf{U}\phi \mid \mathsf{E}\phi$ where $\mathsf{p} \in \mathrm{AT}$ and $\psi(\mathsf{x}_1, \ldots, \mathsf{x}_n)$ is a Presburger formula. We write CTL$_{\mathrm{EF}}$ to denote the fragment of CTL* in which the only (unary) temporal operator is EF (EF$\phi \overset{\mathrm{def}}{=} \mathsf{E} (\top \mathsf{U} \phi)$ and $\top \overset{\mathrm{def}}{=} (\mathsf{x}_1 = \mathsf{x}_1)$). Our version of CTL* is defined as the standard version, see e.g. [12], except that the Kripke structures are replaced by transition systems from counter systems and at the atomic level, arithmetical constraints are allowed. Let $S = \langle Q, \mathsf{C}_n, \Delta, \ell \rangle$ be a counter system with transition system $\mathfrak{T}(S) = \langle \mathcal{C}, \rightarrow \rangle$. The satisfaction relation $\models$ is defined as follows (CTL* formula ϕ, maximal run ρ in $\mathfrak{T}(S)$, position $i < |\rho|$):

$\rho, i \models \mathsf{p}$ $\overset{\mathrm{def}}{\Leftrightarrow}$ $\mathsf{p} \in \ell(q)$, where $\rho(i) = \langle q, \mathbf{v} \rangle$

$\rho, i \models \psi(\mathsf{x}_1, \ldots, \mathsf{x}_n)$ $\overset{\mathrm{def}}{\Leftrightarrow}$ $\mathbf{v} \models \psi(\mathsf{x}_1, \ldots, \mathsf{x}_n)$, where $\rho(i) = \langle q, \mathbf{v} \rangle$

$\rho, i \models \mathsf{X}\psi$ $\overset{\mathrm{def}}{\Leftrightarrow}$ $\rho, i+1 \models \psi$ and $i+1 < |\rho|$

$\rho, i \models \psi_1\mathsf{U}\psi_2$ $\overset{\mathrm{def}}{\Leftrightarrow}$ $\rho, j \models \psi_2$ for some $i \leq j$
                                such that $j < |\rho|$ and $\rho, k \models \psi_1$ for all $i \leq k < j$

$\rho, i \models \mathsf{E}\phi$ $\overset{\mathrm{def}}{\Leftrightarrow}$ there is a maximal run ρ' s.t. $\rho'(0) = \rho(i)$ and $\rho', 0 \models \phi$

Given a CTL* formula ϕ, a counter system S and a configuration c from S, we say that $S, c \models \phi$ iff there exists a maximal run ρ in the configuration graph $\mathfrak{T}(S)$ with $\rho(0) = c$ such that $\rho, 0 \models \phi$ (note that there is an overload for $\models$ in $S, c \models \phi$). A flat counter system S is called *non-blocking* if every maximal run ρ in S is infinite. Otherwise it is called a *blocking* flat counter system.

Lemma 1. *Let* L *be either* CTL* *or* CTL$_{\mathrm{EF}}$. *Given a flat counter system* S, *a configuration* c *and a formula* ϕ *in* L, *there exist a non-blocking flat counter system* S', *a configuration* c' *and a formula* ϕ' *in* L *such that* $S, c \models \phi$ *iff* $S', c' \models \phi'$. *Such a reduction can be performed in logarithmic space.*

It is easy to see that we can add some dummy state to a blocking flat counter system to obtain a non-blocking one preserving the satisfiability of formulae.

The formula is also transformed by using a standard relativization method (a new propositional variable is introduced that holds true only on configurations that were not reachable in the original counter system). Due to Lemma 1, henceforth we consider only non-blocking flat counter systems. Since the reachability relation is definable in (PA) for flat counter systems [10], it is even possible to decide whether all maximal runs from a given configuration are infinite.

The model-checking problem for flat counter systems over CTL* is defined as follows (let us call it MC(CTL*, FlatCS)): given a flat counter system S, a configuration c and a formula ϕ in CTL*, determine whether $S, c \models \phi$. We know that MC(CTL*, FlatCS) is decidable [10] but its exact complexity is not fully characterized (actually, this is the purpose of the present paper). The restriction to LTL formulae is known to be NP-complete [8] when guards are restricted to the linear fragment. In Section 3, we show that the satisfiability problem for (PA) can be reduced to MC(CTL*, FlatCS) restricted to CTL$_{EF}$ without arithmetical constraints and to flat counter systems such that the guards are restricted to simple linear constraints. By contrast, model-checking flat finite Kripke structures over CTL* is Δ_2^P-complete [13,18].

3   Reducing (PA) to a Subproblem of MC(CTL*, FlatCS)

In a flat counter system with n counters, the guards on transitions are Presburger formulae with free variables in $\{x_1, \ldots, x_n\}$. That is why, it is easy to show that the satisfiability problem for (PA) can be reduced (in logarithmic space) to MC(CTL*, FlatCS). Clearly, this is not interesting and the generality of the guards in the paper is only considered because, when establishing the complexity upper bound, we can be quite liberal with the set of guards. However, a more reasonable set of guards is the linear fragment (i.e., without any first-order quantification). Below, we show that a very restricted fragment of MC(CTL*, FlatCS), simply called MC$^-$(CTL*, FlatCS), is already as hard as the satisfiability problem for (PA) and our reduction is based on a simple and nice correspondence between quantifiers in (PA) and the temporal operators EF and AG in CTL*. First, let us define MC$^-$(CTL*, FlatCS) as the subproblem of MC(CTL*, FlatCS) with the following restrictions: (a) atomic formulae are restricted to propositional variables and the only temporal connective is EF (and its dual AG, by closure under negation) and (b) the guards on the transitions are linear constraints $t \leq t'$ or their negations.

Theorem 2. *There is a logarithmic-space reduction from the satisfiability problem for (PA) to MC$^-$(CTL*, FlatCS).*

Proof. (sketch) Let ϕ be a formula in (PA). Without any loss of generality, we can assume that ϕ has the form $Q_1 z_1 Q_2 z_2 \cdots Q_n z_n \phi'(z_1, z_2, \ldots, z_n)$ with $Q_1, Q_2, \ldots, Q_n \in \{\exists, \forall\}$ and ϕ' is a quantifier-free formula. Note that given any formula in (PA), we can reduce it to an equisatisfiable formula of that form in logarithmic space (which is then fine for our main result since logarithmic-space reductions are closed under composition). This is essentially based on the construction of formulae in prenex normal form in first-order logic.

Let us consider S_ϕ defined below where $\mathbf{e}_i \in \mathbb{N}^n$ is the ith unit vector.

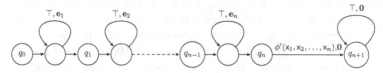

Observe that $\phi'(\mathsf{x}_1, \mathsf{x}_2, \ldots, \mathsf{x}_n)$ may contain Boolean connectives but we explain below how to get rid of them in S_ϕ. Below, we define ψ in $\mathtt{CTL_{EF}}$ whose atomic formulae are among $q_1, \ldots, q_{n+1}$ (also abusively understood as control states) such that (†) $S_\phi, \langle q_0, \mathbf{0} \rangle \models \psi$ iff ϕ is satisfiable in (PA). Intuitively, the possible value associated to each variable z_i from ϕ is taken care of by the ith loop (that can only increment the ith counter). This is not enough, and additionally, the quantifications from ϕ are simulated in the formula ψ by using EF or AG, depending whether the first-order quantification is either existential or universal. Let us define below the formulae ψ_i with $i \in [1, n+1]$ so that $\psi \stackrel{\text{def}}{=} \psi_1$, $\psi_{n+1} \stackrel{\text{def}}{=}$ EF q_{n+1}, and for every $i \in [1, n]$, if $\mathcal{Q}_i = \exists$ then $\psi_i \stackrel{\text{def}}{=}$ EF$(q_i \wedge \psi_{i+1})$, otherwise $\psi_i \stackrel{\text{def}}{=}$ AG$(q_i \Rightarrow \psi_{i+1})$. In order to establish (†) it is sufficient to show the property (††) below. Given a valuation $f : \mathrm{VAR} \to \mathbb{N}$, we write $\mathbf{v}_f \in \mathbb{N}^n$ to denote the vector such that $\mathbf{v}_f[i] \stackrel{\text{def}}{=} f(z_i)$ for every $i \in [1, n]$. One can show that (††) for all f, we have $f \models \phi'(z_1, z_2, \ldots, z_n)$ iff $\langle q_n, \mathbf{v}_f \rangle \models \psi_{n+1}$ and for all $i \in [1, n]$ and for all valuations f such that $f(z_i) = \cdots = f(z_n) = 0$, we have $f \models \mathcal{Q}_i z_i \cdots \mathcal{Q}_n z_n \phi'(z_1, z_2, \ldots, z_n)$ iff $\langle q_{i-1}, \mathbf{v}_f \rangle \models \psi_i$. We get the property (†) by applying (††) with $i = 1$.

To eliminate the Boolean connectives in the guard of the transition between q_n and q_{n+1}, we follow two simple rules, while preserving flatness (easy to check since that transition does not belong to a loop). W.l.o.g., we can assume that negations are only in front of linear constraints. A transition $q \xrightarrow{\psi_1 \wedge \psi_2, \mathbf{0}} q'$ is replaced by $q \xrightarrow{\psi_1, \mathbf{0}} q'' \xrightarrow{\psi_2, \mathbf{0}} q'$ where q'' is new. Similarly, a transition $q \xrightarrow{\psi_1 \vee \psi_2, \mathbf{0}} q'$ is replaced by $q \xrightarrow{\psi_1, \mathbf{0}} q'$ and $q \xrightarrow{\psi_2, \mathbf{0}} q'$, assuming that q does not belong to a loop. It is easy to show that S_ϕ can be transformed into a flat counter system S_ϕ' by applying the two rules above as much as possible so that eventually, S_ϕ' is a proper counter system for MC$^-$(CTL*, FlatCS). □

4 From MC(CTL*, FlatCS) to (PA)

In this section, we present a logarithmic-space reduction from MC(CTL*, FlatCS) to the satisfiability problem for (PA). In [10], a reduction is already presented to get decidability of MC(CTL*, FlatCS). Unfortunately, it requires exponential space and is quite difficult to parse. Following a similar idea, we propose here a simpler reduction that has the great advantage to be optimal complexity-wise. The idea of this reduction is based on the two following points:

1. encoding the runs in flat counter systems by tuples of natural numbers thanks to a symbolic representation for potential infinite sets of runs, see path schemas in [8],

2. internalizing CTL* semantics into (PA) by using the encoding of runs.

Below, we consider a fixed flat counter system $S = \langle Q, \mathsf{C}_n, \Delta, \ell \rangle$ and w.l.o.g, $Q = \{1, \ldots, \alpha\}$ for some $\alpha \geq 1$ and $\Delta = \{\delta_1, \ldots, \delta_\beta\}$. Since $Q \subseteq \mathbb{N}$, configurations of S are vectors in $\mathbb{N}^{n+1}$ where the first component represents the control state.

4.1   Minimal Path Schemas

In [8], following an idea from [21], *minimal path schemas* are introduced as a mean to symbolically represent all runs in flat counter systems. Path schemas can be defined as finite sequences made of transitions or simple loops (conditions apply). Formal definition is recalled below. A *simple loop* l of S is a non-empty finite sequence of transitions $\delta_1, \ldots, \delta_m$ such that $source(\delta_1) = target(\delta_m)$, $source(\delta_j) = target(\delta_{j+1})$ for all $j \in [1, m-1]$, and, for all $j, k \in [1, m]$, if $j \neq k$ then $\delta_j \neq \delta_k$. The length of l, written $length(l)$, is the value m and we denote by $source(l) = target(l)$ the control state $source(\delta_1)$. The number of simple loops is necessarily finite and we assume that the set of loops of S is $L = \{l_1, l_2, \ldots, l_\gamma\}$. Since S is flat, we have $\gamma \leq \alpha$. A *minimal path schema* P is a non-empty sequence $u_1, \ldots, u_N$ s.t. each $u_i \in \Delta \cup L$ and the following conditions are verified.

1. u_N is a loop,
2. $i \neq j$ implies $u_i \neq u_j$,
3. for all $i \in [1, N-1]$, we have $target(u_i) = source(u_{i+1})$.

The second condition guarantees minimality whereas the third condition ensures that P respects the control graph of S. The *size* of P, denoted by $size(P)$, is equal to N. For all $j \in [1, N]$, we write $P[j]$ to denote u_j. Here is an obvious result.

Lemma 3. *The size of a minimal path schema is bounded by $\beta + \gamma \leq \beta + \alpha$.*

In order to obtain concrete paths from a path schema P, we augment P with a vector specifying how many times each internal loop is visited. By definition, a loop in P is *internal* if it is not the last one. An *iterated path schema* is a pair $\langle P, \mathbf{m} \rangle$ where P is a minimal path schema and $\mathbf{m} \in \mathbb{N}^{size(P)}$ such that $\mathbf{m}[1] = size(P)$ and for all $i \in [1, size(P)-1]$, $\mathbf{m}[i+1] > 0$ and if $P[i] \in \Delta$, then $\mathbf{m}[i+1] = 1$. From $\langle P, \mathbf{m} \rangle$, we define the ω-word

$$trans(P, \mathbf{m}) \stackrel{\text{def}}{=} P[1]^{\mathbf{m}[2]} \ldots P[j]^{\mathbf{m}[j+1]} \ldots P[size(P)-1]^{\mathbf{m}[size(P)]} P[size(P)]^\omega$$

Lemma 4 below states that iterated path schemas encode all runs from flat counter systems by noting that infinite runs necessarily end by a simple loop (repeated infinitely) and the visit of loops is strictly ordered.

Lemma 4. *[8] Given an infinite run ρ in a flat counter system S, there exists an iterated path schema $\langle P, \mathbf{m} \rangle$ such that $trans(\rho) = trans(P, \mathbf{m})$.*

Encoding iterated path schemas. Thanks to Lemma 3, we show that it is possible to encode path schemas by vectors in $\mathbb{N}^K$ with $K = 1 + \beta + \gamma$. Intuitively, we encode a path schema P by two vectors $\mathbf{v}_p$ and $\mathbf{v}_t$ in $\mathbb{N}^K$ where the first element of each vector is equal to $size(P)$ and for all $i \in [2, size(P)+1]$, we have $\mathbf{v}_t[i] = 1$ if $P[i]$ is a loop and $\mathbf{v}_t[i] = 0$ otherwise. So, $\mathbf{v}_t$ encodes the *type* of each element (transition vs. loop) in the sequence defining P. Similarly, $\mathbf{v}_p[i]$ represents the number of the associated transition or loop; for instance, $\mathbf{v}_p[i] = 2$ and $\mathbf{v}_t[i] = 1$ encodes that $P[i]$ is the second loop, say l_2. Furthermore, we encode the vector $\mathbf{m}$ by a vector $\mathbf{v}_{it} \in \mathbb{N}^K$. Let us formalize this. First, we define the function $\tau : ((\{0\} \times [1, \beta]) \cup (\{1\} \times [1, \gamma])) \rightarrow \Delta \cup L$ such that $\tau(0, i) \stackrel{\text{def}}{=} \delta_i$ and $\tau(1, i) \stackrel{\text{def}}{=} l_i$. Now, we provide a set of conditions $\mathfrak{C}$ on the vectors $\mathbf{v}_t, \mathbf{v}_p, \mathbf{v}_{it} \in \mathbb{N}^K$ which have to be respected so that, we can build from them an iterated path schema.

$\mathfrak{C}.1$ $\mathbf{v}_p[1] = \mathbf{v}_t[1] = \mathbf{v}_{it}[1]$ with $\mathbf{v}_p[1] \in [1, K-1]$; for all $i \in [\mathbf{v}_{it}[1] + 2, K]$, $\mathbf{v}_p[i] = \mathbf{v}_t[i] = \mathbf{v}_{it}[i] = 0$,

$\mathfrak{C}.2$ $\mathbf{v}_t[i] \in \{0, 1\}$ for all $i \in [2, K]$,

$\mathfrak{C}.3$ if $\mathbf{v}_t[i] = 0$ then $\mathbf{v}_p[i] \in [1, \beta]$, for all $i \in [2, \mathbf{v}_p[1] + 1]$,

$\mathfrak{C}.4$ if $\mathbf{v}_t[i] = 1$ then $\mathbf{v}_p[i] \in [1, \gamma]$, for all $i \in [2, \mathbf{v}_p[1] + 1]$,

$\mathfrak{C}.5$ $\mathbf{v}_t[\mathbf{v}_p[1] + 1] = 1$,

$\mathfrak{C}.6$ there are no $i, j \in [2, \mathbf{v}_p[1]+1]$ such that $i \neq j$, $\mathbf{v}_t[i] = \mathbf{v}_t[j]$ and $\mathbf{v}_p[i] = \mathbf{v}_p[j]$,

$\mathfrak{C}.7$ $target(\tau(\mathbf{v}_t[i], \mathbf{v}_p[i])) = source(\tau(\mathbf{v}_t[i + 1], \mathbf{v}_p[i + 1]))$ for all $i \in [2, \mathbf{v}_p[1]]$,

$\mathfrak{C}.8$ for all $i \in [2, \mathbf{v}_p[1]]$, $\mathbf{v}_{it}[i] > 0$ and if $\mathbf{v}_t[i] = 0$ then $\mathbf{v}_{it}[i] = 1$.

The first four conditions ensure that the vectorial representation is coherent. The three next conditions guarantee that the encoding respects the structure of a minimal path schema, i.e. that the last element is a loop ($\mathfrak{C}.5$), that there are no two identical transitions or loops in the schema ($\mathfrak{C}.6$) and that the succession of elements effectively represents a path in the counter system ($\mathfrak{C}.7$). The last condition ensures that $\mathbf{v}_{it}$ matches the definition of the vector in an iterated path schema. It follows that given vectors $\mathbf{v}_p$, $\mathbf{v}_t$ and $\mathbf{v}_{it}$ in $\mathbb{N}^K$ that satisfy all the conditions ($\mathfrak{C}.i$), we can build a minimal path schema $P_{\mathbf{v}_t, \mathbf{v}_p}$ equal to

$$\tau(\mathbf{v}_t[2], \mathbf{v}_p[2]) \cdots \tau(\mathbf{v}_t[\mathbf{v}_p[1] + 1], \mathbf{v}_p[\mathbf{v}_p[1] + 1])$$

From the vector $\mathbf{v}_{it}$, we can define the vector $\mathbf{m}_{\mathbf{v}_{it}} \in \mathbb{N}^{\mathbf{v}_{it}[1]}$ such that for all $i \in [1, \mathbf{v}_{it}[1]]$, $\mathbf{m}_{\mathbf{v}_{it}}[i] \stackrel{\text{def}}{=} \mathbf{v}_{it}[i]$. We will see that there exists a Presburger formula $Schema(Z_t, Z_p, Z_{it})$ over the sets of variables $Z_p = \{z_p^1, \ldots, z_p^K\}$, $Z_t = \{z_t^1, \ldots, z_t^K\}$ and $Z_{it} = \{z_{it}^1, \ldots, z_{it}^K\}$ to express the conditions $(\mathfrak{C}.i)_{i \in [1,8]}$.

Lemma 5.

1. *Let P be a finite non-empty sequence of length $N \leq \beta + \gamma$ over the alphabet $\Delta \cup L$ and $\mathbf{m} \in \mathbb{N}^N$. Then, $\langle P, \mathbf{m} \rangle$ is an iterated path schema iff there are v_t, v_p and v_{it} in $\mathbb{N}^K$ respecting $\mathfrak{C}$ and such that $P = P_{\mathbf{v}_t, \mathbf{v}_p}$ and $\mathbf{m} = \mathbf{m}_{\mathbf{v}_{it}}$.*
2. *One can build a (PA) formula $Schema(Z_t, Z_p, Z_{it})$ of polynomial size in the size of the counter system S such that for all $v_t, v_p, v_{it} \in \mathbb{N}^K$, we have $v_t, v_p, v_{it} \models Schema(Z_t, Z_p, Z_{it})$ iff v_t, v_p and v_{it} satisfy $\mathfrak{C}$.*

Let us consider the following flat counter system.

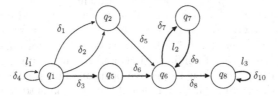

There are 10 transitions and 3 simple loops. The enumeration of edges and loops is done as shown above. Let $\langle P, \mathbf{m}\rangle$ be such that $P = \delta_3 \cdot \delta_6 \cdot l_2 \cdot \delta_8 \cdot l_3$ and $\mathbf{m} = (5, 1, 1, 146, 1)$. So, we get the resulting ω-word as $\delta_3 \cdot \delta_6 \cdot (l_2)^{146} \cdot \delta_8 \cdot (l_3)^{\omega}$. From the previous encoding, the ω-word is encoded by vectors $\mathbf{v}_p = (5, 3, 6, 2, 8, 3, 0, 0, 0, 0, 0, 0, 0, 0, 0)$, $\mathbf{v}_t = (5, 0, 0, 1, 0, 1, 0, 0, 0, 0, 0, 0, 0, 0, 0)$ and $\mathbf{v}_{it} = (5, 1, 1, 146, 1, 0, 0, 0, 0, 0, 0, 0, 0, 0, 0)$.

4.2   Encoding Runs Using Vectors

Lemma 4 states that any infinite run can be encoded by an iterated path schema. However, not every iterated path schema corresponds to a run in due form. We will see now how to check that an iterated path schema indeed represents a run starting from a given configuration c. First, we need to introduce a notion of *pseudo-run* in which only the updates are precise. Given $c \in Q \times \mathbb{Z}^n$, a *pseudo-run* ρ starting from c in S is an infinite sequence $\rho := c_0 \xrightarrow{\delta_1} \cdots \xrightarrow{\delta_{m-1}} c_m \xrightarrow{\delta_m} \cdots$ where $c_0 = c$, $c_i = \langle q_i, \mathbf{v}_i \rangle \in Q \times \mathbb{Z}^n$ for all $i \geq 0$ and for all transitions $\delta \in \Delta$ we have $\langle q, \mathbf{v} \rangle \xrightarrow{\delta} \langle q', \mathbf{v}' \rangle \overset{\text{def}}{\Leftrightarrow} q = source(\delta)$, $q' = target(\delta)$ and $\mathbf{v}' = \mathbf{v} + update(\delta)$. So, a pseudo-run $\rho = \langle q_0, \mathbf{v}_0 \rangle \xrightarrow{\delta_1} \cdots \xrightarrow{\delta_{m-1}} \langle q_m, \mathbf{v}_m \rangle \cdots$ is a run iff for all $i \in \mathbb{N}$, $\mathbf{v}_i \models guard(\delta_i)$ and $\mathbf{v}_i \in \mathbb{N}^n$. Note also that for all configurations $\langle q, \mathbf{v} \rangle$, if $\langle P, \mathbf{m}\rangle$ is an iterated path schema such that $source(P[1]) = q$ then there exists a pseudo-run starting from c such that $trans(\rho) = trans(\langle P, \mathbf{m}\rangle)$.

From these observations, we conclude that an iterated path schema $\langle P, \mathbf{m}\rangle$ augmented with $c_0 = \langle q_0, \mathbf{v}_0 \rangle$ verifying $source(P[1]) = q_0$, defines a unique pseudo-run that is denoted by $\rho(P, \mathbf{m}, c_0)$. Given a configuration $c_0 = \langle q_0, \mathbf{v}_0 \rangle$, we say that $\rho(P, \mathbf{m}, c_0)$ is *well-defined* if $source(P[1]) = q_0$. For every $i \in [0, size(P) - 1]$ let $\mathbf{p}_i \overset{\text{def}}{=} \sum_{j=1}^{j=i} \mathbf{m}[j] * length(P[j])$ with limit case $\mathbf{p}_0 = 0$. The value $\mathbf{p}_i$ is called the *position* of the ith *witness configuration* $\rho(P, \mathbf{m}, c_0)(\mathbf{p}_i)$. Intuitively, we reach the ith witness configuration after going through the first i elements of the path schema P in $\rho(P, \mathbf{m}, c_0)$. We say that $\rho(P, \mathbf{m}, c_0)$ is *positive* if for all the witness configurations $\langle q, \mathbf{v} \rangle$, we have $\mathbf{v} \in \mathbb{N}^n$. Note that since for all path schemas P, we have $size(P) \leq \beta + \gamma$, the number of witness configurations for such a pseudo-run is bounded by $\beta + \gamma$.

Now, we show how to build a (PA) formula whose set of solutions corresponds to the witness configurations of a pseudo-run associated to an iterated path schema equipped with an initial configuration. Before defining the formula, we explain some further notions. In the sequel, we use the sets of variables $X_0 = \{x_0^1, \ldots, x_0^{n+1}\}$ and $X = \{x^1, \ldots, x^{n+1}\}$ to represent configurations and $W_i =$

$\{w_i^1, \ldots, w_i^{n+1}\}$ for every $i \in [0, \beta + \gamma - 1]$ to represent pseudo-configurations and the variables $p_0, \ldots, p_{\beta+\gamma-1}$ and y to represent positions in (pseudo)-runs. Furthermore, given sets of variables X, W representing (pseudo)-configurations, a variable x and a vector $u \in \mathbb{N}^n$, we use the shortcut $X = W + x.u$ to denote the formula $\bigwedge_{i=2}^{n+1} x^i = w^i + x.u[i-1]$. Let us define the formula *Witness* that states whether a given set of configurations and natural numbers represent the witness configurations and their respective positions in a pseudo-run associated to an iterated path schema. The main idea of the formula is to check at each step whether the control states of the witness configurations match with the states of the taken transitions or loops in the path schema and then to compute the effect of the corresponding element of the iterated path schema taking into account the number of iterations.

$$Witness(W_0, \ldots, W_{\beta+\gamma-1}, p_0, \ldots, p_{\beta+\gamma-1}, Z_t, Z_p, Z_{it}, X_0) \stackrel{def}{=}$$

$$(p_0 = 0 \wedge X_0 = W_0 \wedge \bigvee_{t=0}^{1} \bigvee_{j=1}^{max(\beta,\gamma)} z_p^2 = j \wedge z_t^2 = t \wedge x_0^1 = source(\tau(t,j))) \wedge$$

$$\bigwedge_{i=1}^{\beta+\gamma-1} (i < z_t^1 \Rightarrow \bigvee_{t=0}^{1} \bigvee_{j=1}^{max(\beta,\gamma)} (z_p^{i+1} = j \wedge z_t^{i+1} = t \wedge p_i = p_{i-1} + z_{it}^{i+1} * length(\tau(t,j)) \wedge$$

$$w_i^1 = target(\tau(t,j)) \wedge W_i = W_{i-1} + z_{it}^{i+1} * update(\tau(t,i)))$$

Lemma 6 below characterizes the formula *Witness*.

Lemma 6. *Let* $w_0, \ldots, w_{\beta+\gamma-1}, c_0 \in \mathbb{N}^{n+1}$ *and* $p_0, \ldots, p_{\beta+\gamma-1} \in \mathbb{N}$ *and* v_t, v_p, v_{it} *in* $\mathbb{N}^K$ *such that* $v_t, v_p, v_{it} \models Schema(Z_t, Z_p, Z_{it})$. *We have* $w_0, \ldots,$ $w_{\beta+\gamma-1}, p_0, \ldots, p_{\beta+\gamma-1}, v_t, v_p, v_{it}, c_0 \models Witness$ *iff* $\rho(P_{v_t,v_p}, m_{v_{it}}, c_0)$ *is well-defined and positive and for all* $j \in [0, \beta + \gamma - 1]$, *if* $j < size(P_{v_t,v_p})$, *then* w_j *represents the jth witness configuration of* $\rho(P_{v_t,v_p}, m_{v_{it}}, c_0)$ *and* p_j *its position.*

Using *Witness*, one can build in logarithmic space a formula to check whether a vector c is the ith configuration $\langle q_i, v_i \rangle$ of a pseudo-run $\rho(P_{v_t,v_p}, m_{v_{it}}, c_0)$ with the property that $v_i \models guard(trans(\langle P_{v_t,v_p}, m_{v_{it}} \rangle)[i+1])$ and $v_i \in \mathbb{N}^n$ (here i is the number of transitions to reach that configuration) and then to construct a formula to check whether a pseudo-run is a run. In fact, as observed earlier, it is enough to check whether at each step the ith configuration satisfies the guard of the $(i+1)$th transition.

Lemma 7. *One can build in logarithmic-space in the size of flat counter system* S *two PA formulae* $Conf(Z_t, Z_p, Z_{it}, X_0, y, X)$ *and* $Run(Z_t, Z_p, Z_{it}, X_0)$ *such that for all* $c_0, c \in \mathbb{N}^{n+1}$, *for all* $i \in \mathbb{N}$ *and for all* $v_t, v_p, v_{it} \in \mathbb{N}^{\beta+\gamma+1}$, *we have the two following properties:*

1. $v_t, v_p, v_{it}, c_0, i, c \models Conf$ *iff* $v_t, v_p, v_{it} \models Schema$ *and* $\rho(P_{v_t,v_p}, m_{v_{it}}, c_0)$ *is well defined and* $c = \rho(P_{v_t,v_p}, m_{v_{it}}, c_0)(i)$ *and* $c[2], \cdots, c[n+1] \models guard(trans(\langle P_{v_t,v_p}, m_{v_{it}} \rangle)[i+1])$

2. $v_t, v_p, v_{it}, c_0 \models Run$ *iff* $v_t, v_p, v_{it} \models Schema$ *and* $\rho(P_{v_t,v_p}, m_{v_{it}}, c_0)$ *is well-defined and is a run.*

4.3   Encoding CTL* Formulae Using (PA)

We can encode path schemas and runs using vectors and check their validity using Presburger arithmetic formula, our next aim is to encode a given CTL* formula using a formula in (PA). The forthcoming encoding internalizes CTL* semantics and a similar idea has been already used in [10]. For each CTL* formula ϕ, we build a (PA) formula $Check_\phi(Z_t, Z_p, Z_{it}, X_0, y)$ where the variables Z_t, Z_p, Z_{it} and X_0 represent a run as in the formula Run and, y represents a position such that the formula checks whether the CTL* formula is satisfied at the current position. Formula $Check_\phi$ is defined recursively (Boolean clauses are omitted):

$$Check_p \stackrel{\text{def}}{=} \exists\, X\, (Conf(Z_t, Z_p, Z_{it}, X_0, y, X) \wedge \bigvee_{\{j \,\mid\, p \,\in\, \ell(j)\}} x^1 = j)$$

$$Check_{\psi(x_1,\ldots,x_n)} \stackrel{\text{def}}{=} \exists\, X\, (Conf(Z_t, Z_p, Z_{it}, X_0, y, X) \wedge \psi(X))$$

$$Check_{X\phi} \stackrel{\text{def}}{=} \exists\, y'\, (y' = y + 1 \wedge Check_\phi(Z_t, Z_p, Z_{it}, X_0, y'))$$

$$Check_{\phi U \phi'} \stackrel{\text{def}}{=} \exists\, y''\, (y \le y'' \wedge Check_{\phi'}(Z_t, Z_p, Z_{it}, X_0, y'')\wedge$$
$$\forall\, y'\, (y \le y' < y'' \Rightarrow Check_\phi(Z_t, Z_p, Z_{it}, X_0, y')))$$

$$Check_{E\phi} \stackrel{\text{def}}{=} \exists\, Z'_t\, \exists\, Z'_p\, \exists\, Z'_{it}\, \exists\, X\, (Conf(Z_t, Z_p, Z_{it}, X_0, y, X)\wedge$$
$$Run(Z'_t, Z'_p, Z'_{it}, X) \wedge \exists\, y'\, (y' = 0 \wedge Check_\phi(Z'_t, Z'_p, Z'_{it}, X, y')))$$

Now, we can state the main property concerning the formulae $Check_\phi$ based on Lemmas 4, 5 and 7.

Lemma 8. *Let* $c_0 \in \mathbb{N}^{n+1}$, $i \in \mathbb{N}$ *and* $v_t, v_p, v_{it} \in \mathbb{N}^K$ *be such that* v_t, v_p, v_{it}, $c_0 \models Run$. *We have* $\rho(P_{v_t, v_p}, m_{v_{it}}, c_0), i \models \phi$ *iff* $v_t, v_p, v_{it}, c_0, i \models Check_\phi(Z_t, Z_p, Z_{it}, X_0, y)$.

This allows us to conclude the main result of this section.

Theorem 9. *There is a logarithmic-space reduction from MC(*CTL*, *FlatCS)* *to the satisfiability problem for (PA).*

It is possible to extend the reduction by admitting linear past-time operators to the temporal language since we have seen that we can easily quantify over runs. However, in that case, finite prefixes in runs should not be reset.

5   Conclusion

We have been able to characterize the computational complexity for MC(CTL*, FlatCS) by showing that the problem is equivalent to the satisfiability problem for Presburger arithmetic (modulo logarithmic-space reductions). The lower bound is obtained by considering a quite strong restriction (no arithmetical constraints in formulae, the only temporal operator is EF, guards on transitions are simple linear constraints). By contrast, the restriction of the problem to LTL formulae is known to be NP-complete [8] when guards are in the linear fragment and the restriction of the problem to formulae in CTL$_{EF}$ is also equivalent to (PA). We have proposed a new way for encoding runs in flat counter systems using Presburger arithmetic formulae, but without any exponential blow up, which allows us to get a precise complexity characterization. It remains open to determine which extensions of CTL* on flat counter systems preserve decidability, if not an efficient translation into (PA).

References

1. Berman, L.: The complexity of logical theories. TCS 11, 71–78 (1980)
2. Bersani, M., Demri, S.: The complexity of reversal-bounded model-checking. In: Tinelli, C., Sofronie-Stokkermans, V. (eds.) FroCoS 2011. LNCS, vol. 6989, pp. 71–86. Springer, Heidelberg (2011)
3. Boigelot, B.: Symbolic methods for exploring infinite state spaces. PhD thesis, Université de Liège (1998)
4. Bozga, M., Iosif, R., Konečný, F.: Safety problems are NP-complete for flat integer programs with octagonal loops. In: McMillan, K.L., Rival, X. (eds.) VMCAI 2014. LNCS, vol. 8318, pp. 242–261. Springer, Heidelberg (2014)
5. Bruyère, V., Dall'Olio, E., Raskin, J.: Durations, parametric model-checking in timed automata with presburger arithmetic. In: Alt, H., Habib, M. (eds.) STACS 2003. LNCS, vol. 2607, pp. 687–698. Springer, Heidelberg (2003)
6. Comon, H., Jurski, Y.: Multiple counter automata, safety analysis and Presburger Arithmetic. In: Vardi, M.Y. (ed.) CAV 1998. LNCS, vol. 1427, pp. 268–279. Springer, Heidelberg (1998)
7. de Moura, L., Bjørner, N.S.: Z3: An efficient SMT solver. In: Ramakrishnan, C.R., Rehof, J. (eds.) TACAS 2008. LNCS, vol. 4963, pp. 337–340. Springer, Heidelberg (2008)
8. Demri, S., Dhar, A.K., Sangnier, A.: Taming past LTL and flat counter systems. In: Gramlich, B., Miller, D., Sattler, U. (eds.) IJCAR 2012. LNCS, vol. 7364, pp. 179–193. Springer, Heidelberg (2012)
9. Demri, S., Dhar, A.K., Sangnier, A.: On the complexity of verifying regular properties on flat counter systems, In: Fomin, F.V., Freivalds, R., Kwiatkowska, M., Peleg, D. (eds.) ICALP 2013, Part II. LNCS, vol. 7966, pp. 162–173. Springer, Heidelberg (2013)
10. Demri, S., Finkel, A., Goranko, V., van Drimmelen, G.: Model-checking CTL* over flat Presburger counter systems. JANCL 20(4), 313–344 (2010)
11. Dhar, A.K.: Applying Satisfiability Modulo Theories Techniques to the Verification of Infinite-State Systems. PhD thesis, Université Paris VII-Denis Diderot (2014)
12. Emerson, A., Halpern, J.: 'sometimes' and 'not never' revisited: on branching versus linear time temporal logic. JACM 33, 151–178 (1986)
13. Emerson, E.A., Lei, C.-L.: Modalities for model checking: Branching time logic strikes back. Sci. Comput. Program. 8(3), 275–306 (1987)
14. Finkel, A., Leroux, J.: How to compose presburger-accelerations: Applications to broadcast protocols. In: Agrawal, M., Seth, A.K. (eds.) FSTTCS 2002. LNCS, vol. 2556, pp. 145–156. Springer, Heidelberg (2002)
15. Göller, S., Haase, C., Ouaknine, J., Worrell, J.: Branching-time model checking of parametric one-counter automata. In: Birkedal, L. (ed.) FOSSACS 2012. LNCS, vol. 7213, pp. 406–420. Springer, Heidelberg (2012)
16. Göller, S., Lohrey, M.: Branching-time model checking of one-counter processes and timed automata. SIAM J. Comput. 42(3), 884–923 (2013)
17. Habermehl, P.: On the complexity of the linear-time mu-calculus for Petri nets. In: Azéma, P., Balbo, G. (eds.) ICATPN 1997. LNCS, vol. 1248, pp. 102–116. Springer, Heidelberg (1997)

18. Laroussinie, F., Markey, N., Schnoebelen, P.: Model checking CTL$^+$ and FCTL is hard. In: Honsell, F., Miculan, M. (eds.) FOSSACS 2001. LNCS, vol. 2030, pp. 318–331. Springer, Heidelberg (2001)

19. Leroux, J.: Presburger counter machines. Habilitation thesis, U. of Bordeaux (2012)

20. Leroux, J., Point, G.: TaPAS: The talence presburger arithmetic suite. In: Kowalewski, S., Philippou, A. (eds.) TACAS 2009. LNCS, vol. 5505, pp. 182–185. Springer, Heidelberg (2009)

21. Leroux, J., Sutre, G.: On flatness for 2-dimensional vector addition systems with states. In: Gardner, P., Yoshida, N. (eds.) CONCUR 2004. LNCS, vol. 3170, pp. 402–416. Springer, Heidelberg (2004)

22. Leroux, J., Sutre, G.: Flat counter automata almost everywhere! In: Peled, D.A., Tsay, Y.-K. (eds.) ATVA 2005. LNCS, vol. 3707, pp. 489–503. Springer, Heidelberg (2005)

23. Minsky, M.: Computation, Finite and Infinite Machines. Prentice Hall (1967)

24. Presburger, M.: Über die Vollständigkeit eines gewissen Systems der Arithmetik ganzer Zahlen, in welchem die Addition als einzige Operation hervortritt. In: Comptes Rendus du premier congrès de mathématiciens des Pays Slaves, Warszawa, pp. 92–101 (1929)

Synthesising Succinct Strategies in Safety and Reachability Games[*]

Gilles Geeraerts, Joël Goossens, and Amélie Stainer

Université libre de Bruxelles, Département d'Informatique, Brussels, Belgium

Abstract. We introduce general techniques to compute, *efficiently*, *succinct representations* of winning strategies in safety and reachability games. Our techniques adapt the *antichain* framework to the setting of games, and rely on the notion of *turn-based alternating simulation*, which is used to formalise natural relations that exist between the states of those games in many applications. In particular, our techniques apply to the realisability problem of LTL [8], to the synthesis of real-time schedulers for multiprocessor platforms [4], and to the determinisation of timed automata [3] — three applications where the size of the game one needs to solve is at least exponential in the size of the problem description, and where succinct strategies are particularly crucial in practice.

1 Introduction

Finite, turn-based, games are a very simple, yet relevant, class of games. They are played by two players ($\mathcal{S}$ and $\mathcal{R}$) on a finite graph (called the arena), whose set of vertices is partitioned into Player $\mathcal{S}$ and Player $\mathcal{R}$ vertices. A play is an infinite path in this graph, obtained by letting the players move a token on the vertices. Initially, the token is on a designated initial vertex. At each round of the game, the player who owns the vertex marked by the token decides on which successor node to move it next. A play is winning for $\mathcal{R}$ if the token eventually touches some designated 'bad' nodes (the objective for $\mathcal{R}$ is thus a reachability objective), otherwise it is winning for $\mathcal{S}$ (for whom the objective is a safety objective), hence the names of the players.

Such games are a natural model to describe the interaction of a potential controller with a given environment, where the aim of the controller (modeled by player $\mathcal{S}$) is to avoid the bad states that model system failures. They have also been used as a tool to solve other problems such as LTL realisability [8], real-time scheduler synthesis [4] or timed automata determinisation [3].

We consider, throughout the paper, a running example which is a variation of the well-known Nim game [5]. Initially, a heap of N balls is shared by the

---

[*] This research has been supported by the Belgian F.R.S./FNRS FOREST grant, number 14621993.

The research leading to these results has received funding from the European Union Seventh Framework Programme (FP7/2007-2013) under Grant Agreement n°601148 (CASSTING).

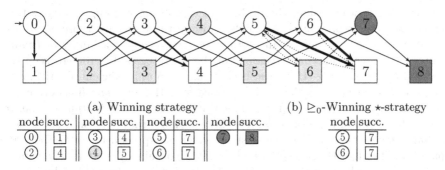

(a) Winning strategy

node	succ.	node	succ.	node	succ.	node	succ.
⓪	1	③	4	⑤	7	⑦	8
②	4	④	5	⑥	7		

(b) $\unrhd_0$-Winning $\star$-strategy

node	succ.
⑤	7
⑥	7

Fig. 1. Urn-filling Nim game with $N = 8$, and three winning strategies

players, and the urn is empty. The players play by turn and pick either 1 or 2 balls from the heap and put them into the urn. A player looses the game if he is the last to play (i.e., the heap is empty after he has played). An arena modeling this game (for $N = 8$) is given in Fig. 1 (top), where $\mathcal{S}$-states are circles, $\mathcal{R}$-states are squares, and the numbers labelling the states represent the number of balls *inside the urn*. The arena obtained from Fig. 1 *without the dotted edges* faithfully models the description of the game we have sketched above (assuming Player $\mathcal{S}$ plays first). From the point of view of player $\mathcal{S}$, the set of states that he wants to avoid (and that player $\mathcal{R}$ wants to reach) is $\mathsf{Bad} = \{⑦, ⬛8\}$, and we call *winning* all the states from which $\mathcal{S}$ can avoid Bad whatever $\mathcal{R}$ does. It is well-known [5] that a simple characterisation of the set of winning states[1] can be given. For each state v, let $\lambda(v)$ denote its label. Then, the winning states (in white in Fig 1) are all the $\mathcal{S}$-states v s.t. $\lambda(v) \bmod 3 \neq 1$ plus all the $\mathcal{R}$-states v' s.t. $\lambda(v') \bmod 3 = 1$.

It is well-known that *memory-less winning strategies* (i.e., that depend only on the current state) are sufficient for both players in those games. Memory-less strategies are often regarded as simple and straightforward to implement (remember that the winning strategy is very often the actual control policy that we want to implement in, say, an embedded controller). Yet, this belief falls short in many practical applications such as the three mentioned above because the arena is not given explicitly, and its size is *at least exponential* in the size of the original problem instance. Hence, the computation of winning strategies might be intractable in practice because it could request to traverse the whole arena. Moreover, a naive implementation of a winning strategy σ by means of a table mapping each $\mathcal{S}$-state v to its safe successor $\sigma(v)$ (like in Fig. 1 (a) for our running example), is not realistic because this table would have the size of the arena.

---

[1] In order to make our example more interesting (this will become clear in the sequel), we have added the three *dotted edges* from ⑦ to ⑥ and ⑤ respectively, and from ⑥ to ⑤ although those actions are not permitted in the original game. However, observe that those extra edges do not modify the set of winning states.

In this work, we consider the problem of computing winning strategies that can be *succinctly* represented. We call '$\star$-strategy' those succinct representations, and they can be regarded as an *abstract representation* of a family of (plain) strategies, that we call *concretisations* of the $\star$-strategies. In order to keep the description of winning $\star$-strategies succinct, and to obtain efficient algorithms to compute them, we propose heuristics inspired from the *antichain* line of research [7]. These heuristics have been developed mainly in the *verification setting*, to deal with *automata-based models*. Roughly speaking, they rely on a *simulation partial order* on the states of the system, which is exploited to *prune* the state space that the algorithms need to explore, and to obtain *efficient data structures* to store the set of states that the algorithms need to maintain. They have been applied to several problems, such as LTL model-checking [7] or multi-processor schedulability [9] with remarkable performance improvements of several orders of magnitude.

In this paper, we introduce general antichain-based techniques for solving reachability and safety games, and computing *efficiently succinct representations of winning strategies*. We propose a general and elegant theory which is built on top of the notion of *turn-based alternating simulation* (tba-simulation for short, a notion adapted from [2]), instead of *simulation*. In our running example, a tba-simulation $\trianglerighteq_0$ exists and is given by: $v \trianglerighteq_0 v'$ iff v and v' belong to the same player, $\lambda(v) \geq \lambda(v')$ and $\lambda(v) \bmod 3 = \lambda(v') \bmod 3$. Then, it is easy to see that the winning strategy of Fig. 1 (a) exhibits some kind of *monotonicity* wrt $\trianglerighteq_0$: ⑤$\trianglerighteq_0$②, and the winning strategy asks to put two balls in the urn in both cases. Hence, we can represent the winning strategy as in Fig. 1 (b). Observe that not all concretisations of this strategy are winning. For instance, playing ③ from ② is a losing move, but it is not compatible with $\trianglerighteq_0$ because ③ is not $\trianglerighteq_0$-covered by ⑦. Moreover, this succinct description of the strategy can be implemented straightforwardly: only the table in Fig. 1 (b) needs to be stored in the controller, as $\trianglerighteq_0$ can be directly computed from the description of the states.

These intuitions are formalised in Section 4, where we show that, in general, it is sufficient to store the strategy on the maximal *antichain* of the reachable winning states. In Section 5, we present *an efficient on-the-fly algorithm to compute such succinct $\star$-strategies* (adapted from the classical OTFUR algorithm to solve reachability games [6]). Our algorithm generalises the algorithm of Filiot et al. [8], with several improvements: 1. it applies to a general class of games whose arena is equipped with a tba-simulation (not only those generated from an instance of the LTL realisability problem) ; 2. it contains an additional heuristic that was not present in [8] ; 3. its proof of correctness is straightforward, and stems directly from the definition of tba-simulation. Finally, in Section 6, we show that our approach can be straightforwardly applied to the games one obtains in the three applications introduced above (LTL realisability, real-time feasibility and determinisation of timed automata) which demonstrates the wide applicability of our approach.

Note that, owing to lack of space, all proofs are to be found in the companion technical report [10]

2 Preliminaries

Turn-based finite games. A *finite turn-based game arena* is a tuple $\mathcal{A} = (V_S, V_R, E, I)$, where V_S and V_R are the finite sets of states controlled by Players S and R respectively; $E \subseteq (V_S \times V_R) \cup (V_R \times V_S)$ is the set of edges; and $I \in V_S$ is the initial state. We let $V = V_S \cup V_R$. For a finite arena $\mathcal{A} = (V_S, V_R, E, I)$ and a state $v \in V$, we let $\mathsf{Succ}(\mathcal{A}, v) = \{v' \mid (v, v') \in E\}$ and $\mathsf{Reach}(\mathcal{A}, v) = \{v' \mid (v, v') \in E^*\}$, where E^* is the reflexive and transitive closure of E. We write $\mathsf{Reach}(\mathcal{A})$ instead of $\mathsf{Reach}(\mathcal{A}, I)$, and lift the definitions of Reach and Succ to sets of states in the usual way.

The aim of Player R is to *reach* some designated set of states Bad, while the aim of S is to *avoid* it. Throughout this paper, we focus on the objective of player S, and regard our finite games as *safety games* because they correspond to the applications we target in Section 6. However, those games are symmetrical and determined, so, our results can easily be adapted to cope with *reachability games*. Formally, A *finite turn-based (safety) game* is a tuple $G = (V_S, V_R, E, I, \mathsf{Bad})$ where (V_S, V_R, E, I) is a finite turn-based game arena, and $\mathsf{Bad} \subseteq V$ is the set of bad states that S wants to avoid. The definitions of Reach and Succ carry on to games: for a game $G = (\mathcal{A}, \mathsf{Bad})$, we let $\mathsf{Reach}(G, v) = \mathsf{Reach}(\mathcal{A}, v)$, $\mathsf{Reach}(G) = \mathsf{Reach}(\mathcal{A})$ and $\mathsf{Succ}(G, v) = \mathsf{Succ}(\mathcal{A}, v)$. When the game is clear from the context, we often omit it.

Plays and strategies. During the game, players interact to produce a play, which is a finite or infinite path in the graph (V, E). Players play turn by turn, by moving a *token* on the game's states. Initially, the token is on state I. At each turn, the player who controls the state marked by the token gets to choose the next state. A *strategy* for S is a function $\sigma : V_S \to V_R$ such that for all $v \in V_S$, $(v, \sigma(v)) \in E$. We extend strategies to set of states S in the usual way: $\sigma(S) = \{\sigma(v) \mid v \in S\}$. A strategy σ for S is *winning for a state* $v \in V$ iff no bad states are reachable from v in the graph G_σ obtained from G by removing all the moves of S which are not chosen by σ, i.e. $\mathsf{Reach}(G_\sigma, v) \cap \mathsf{Bad} = \emptyset$, where $G_\sigma = (V_S, V_R, E_\sigma, I, \mathsf{Bad})$ and $E_\sigma = \{(v, v') \mid (v, v') \in E \wedge v \in V_S \implies v' = \sigma(v)\}$. We say that a strategy σ is *winning* in a game $G = (V_S, V_R, E, I, \mathsf{Bad})$ iff it is winning in G for I.

Winning states and attractors. A state $v \in V$ in G is *winning* (for Player S) iff there exists a strategy σ that is winning in G for v. We denote by Win the set of winning states (for Player S). By definition, any strategy such that $\sigma(\mathsf{Win}) \subseteq \mathsf{Win}$ is thus winning. Moreover, it is well-known that Win can be computed in polynomial time (in the size of the arena), by computing the so-called *attractor* (for Player R) of the unsafe states. In a game $G = (V_S, V_R, E, I, \mathsf{Bad})$, the sequence $(\mathsf{Attr}_i)_{i \geq 0}$ of attractors (of the Bad states) is defined as follows. $\mathsf{Attr}_0 =$

Bad and for all $i \in \mathbb{N}$, $\mathsf{Attr}_{i+1} = \mathsf{Attr}_i \cup \{v \in V_{\mathcal{R}} \mid \mathsf{Succ}\,(v) \cap \mathsf{Attr}_i \neq \emptyset\} \cup \{v \in V_{\mathcal{S}} \mid \mathsf{Succ}\,(v) \subseteq \mathsf{Attr}_i\}$. For finite games, the sequence stabilises after a finite number of steps on a set of states that we denote $\mathsf{Attr}_{\mathsf{Bad}}$. Then, v belongs to $\mathsf{Attr}_{\mathsf{Bad}}$ iff Player $\mathcal{R}$ can force the game to reach Bad from v. Thus, the set of winning states for Player $\mathcal{S}$ is $\mathsf{Win} = V \setminus \mathsf{Attr}_{\mathsf{Bad}}$. Then, the strategy σ s.t. for all $v \in V_{\mathcal{S}} \cap \mathsf{Win}$, $\sigma(v) = v'$ with $v' \in \mathsf{Win}$ is winning.

Partial orders, closed sets and antichains. Fix a finite set S. A relation $\trianglerighteq \in S \times S$ is a partial order iff $\trianglerighteq$ is reflexive, transitive and antisymmetric, i.e. for all $s \in S$: $(s, s) \in \trianglerighteq$ (reflexivity); for all $s, s', s'' \in S$, $(s, s') \in \trianglerighteq$ and $(s', s'') \in \trianglerighteq$ implies $(s, s'') \in \trianglerighteq$ (transitivity); and for all $s, s' \in S$: $(s, s') \in \trianglerighteq$ and $(s', s) \in \trianglerighteq$ implies $s = s'$ (antisymmetry). As usual, we often write $s \trianglerighteq s'$ and $s \not\trianglerighteq s'$ instead of $(s, s') \in \trianglerighteq$ and $(s, s') \notin \trianglerighteq$, respectively. The $\trianglerighteq$-*downward closure* $\downarrow^{\trianglerighteq}(S')$ of a set $S' \subseteq S$ is defined as $\downarrow^{\trianglerighteq}(S') = \{s \mid \exists s' \in S', s' \trianglerighteq s\}$. Symmetrically, the *upward closure* $\uparrow^{\trianglerighteq}(S')$ of S' is defined as: $\uparrow^{\trianglerighteq}(S') = \{s \mid \exists s' \in S' : s \trianglerighteq s'\}$. Then, a set S' is *downward closed* (resp. *upward closed*) iff $S' = \downarrow^{\trianglerighteq}(S')$ (resp. $S' = \uparrow^{\trianglerighteq}(S')$). When the partial order is clear from the context, we often write $\downarrow(S)$ and $\uparrow(S)$ instead of $\downarrow^{\trianglerighteq}(S)$ and $\uparrow^{\trianglerighteq}(S)$ respectively. Finally, a subset α of some set $S' \subseteq S$ is an *antichain* on S' with respect to $\trianglerighteq$ if for all $s, s' \in \alpha$: $s \neq s'$ implies $s \not\trianglerighteq s'$. An antichain α on S' is said to be a set of *maximal elements of S'* (or, simply a *maximal antichain of S'*) iff for all $s_1 \in S'$ there is $s_2 \in \alpha$: $s_2 \trianglerighteq s_1$. Symmetrically, an antichain α on S' is a set of *minimal elements of S'* (or a *minimal antichain of S'*) iff for all $s_1 \in S'$ there is $s_2 \in \alpha$: $s_1 \trianglerighteq s_2$. It is easy to check that if α and β are maximal and minimal antichains of S' respectively, then $\downarrow(\alpha) = \downarrow(S')$ and $\uparrow(\beta) = \uparrow(S')$. Intuitively, α (β) can be regarded as a symbolic representation of $\downarrow(S')$ ($\uparrow(S')$), which is of minimal size in the sense that it contains no pair of $\trianglerighteq$-comparable elements. Moreover, since $\trianglerighteq$ is a partial order, each subset S' of the finite set S admits a unique minimal and a unique maximal antichain, that we denote by $\lfloor S' \rfloor$ and $\lceil S' \rceil$ respectively. Observe that one can always effectively build a $\lceil S' \rceil$ and $\lfloor S' \rfloor$, simply by iteratively removing from S', all the elements that are strictly $\trianglerighteq$-dominated by (for $\lceil S' \rceil$) or that strictly dominate (for $\lfloor S' \rfloor$) another one.

Simulation relations. Fix an arena $G = (V_{\mathcal{S}}, V_{\mathcal{R}}, E, I, \mathsf{Bad})$. A relation $\trianglerighteq \subseteq V_{\mathcal{S}} \times V_{\mathcal{S}} \cup V_{\mathcal{R}} \times V_{\mathcal{R}}$ is a *simulation relation compatible*[2] *with* Bad (or simply a *simulation*) iff it is a partial order[3] and for all $(v_1, v_2) \in \trianglerighteq$: either $v_1 \in \mathsf{Bad}$ or: (i) for all $v'_2 \in \mathsf{Succ}\,(v_2)$, there is $v'_1 \in \mathsf{Succ}\,(v_1)$ s.t. $v'_1 \trianglerighteq v'_2$ and (ii) $v_2 \in \mathsf{Bad}$ implies that $v_1 \in \mathsf{Bad}$. On our example, the relation $\trianglerighteq_0 = \{(v, v') \in V_{\mathcal{S}} \times V_{\mathcal{S}} \cup V_{\mathcal{R}} \times V_{\mathcal{R}} \mid \lambda(v) \geq \lambda(v') \text{ and } \lambda(v) \bmod 3 = \lambda(v') \bmod 3\}$ is a simulation relation compatible with $\mathsf{Bad} = \{⑦, \boxed{8}\}$. Moreover, $\mathsf{Win} = \{v \in V_{\mathcal{S}} \mid \lambda(v) \bmod 3 \neq 1\} \cup \{v \in V_{\mathcal{R}} \mid \lambda(v) \bmod 3 = 1\}$ is downward closed for $\trianglerighteq_0$ and its

---

[2] See [8] for an earlier definition of a simulation relation compatible with a set of states.

[3] Observe that our results can be extended to the case where the relations are *pre-orders*, i.e. transitive and reflexive relations.

complement (the set of losing states), is upward closed. Finally, Win admits a single maximal antichain for $\unrhd_0$: MaxWin $= \{\boxed{7}, \textcircled{6}, \textcircled{5}\}$.

3   Succinct Strategies

Let us first formalise our notion of *succinct strategy* (observe that other works propose different notions of 'small strategies', see for instance [11]). As explained in the introduction, a naive way to implement a memory-less strategy σ is to store, in an appropriate data structure, the set of pairs $\{(v, \sigma(v)) \mid v \in V_{\mathcal{S}}\}$, and implement a controller that traverses the whole table to find action to perform each time the system state is updated. While the definition of strategy asks that $\sigma(v)$ be defined for all $\mathcal{S}$-states v, this information is sometimes indifferent, for instance, when v is not reachable in G_σ. Thus, we want to reduce the number of states v s.t. $\sigma(v)$ is crucial to keep the system safe.

$\star$-*strategies.* We introduce the notion of $\star$-strategy to formalise this idea: a $\star$-strategy is a function $\hat{\sigma} : V_{\mathcal{S}} \mapsto V_{\mathcal{R}} \cup \{\star\}$, where $\star$ stands for a 'don't care' information. We denote by $\mathsf{Supp}(\hat{\sigma})$ the *support* $\hat{\sigma}^{-1}(V_{\mathcal{R}})$ of $\hat{\sigma}$, i.e. the set of nodes v s.t. $\hat{\sigma}(v) \neq \star$. Such $\star$-strategies can be regarded as a representation of a family of concrete strategies. A *concretisation* of a $\star$-strategy $\hat{\sigma}$ is a strategy σ s.t. for all $v \in V_{\mathcal{S}}$, $\hat{\sigma}(v) \neq \star$ implies $\hat{\sigma}(v) = \sigma(v)$. A $\star$-strategy $\hat{\sigma}$ is *winning* if every concretisation of $\hat{\sigma}$ is winning (intuitively, $\hat{\sigma}$ is winning if $\mathcal{S}$ always wins when he plays according to $\hat{\sigma}$, whatever choices he makes when $\hat{\sigma}$ returns $\star$). The *size* of a $\star$-strategy $\hat{\sigma}(v)$ is the size of $\mathsf{Supp}(\hat{\sigma})$.

Computing succinct $\star$-strategies. Our goal is to compute *succinct* $\star$-strategies, defined as $\star$-strategies of minimal size. To characterise the hardness of this task, we consider the following decision problem, and prove that it is NP-complete:

*Problem 1 (*MinSizeStrat*).* Given a finite turn-based game G and an integer $k \in \mathbb{N}$ (in binary), decide whether there is a winning $\star$-strategy of size smaller than k in G.

Theorem 1. MinSizeStrat *is NP-complete.*

Thus, unless P=NP, there is no polynomial-time algorithm to compute a winning $\star$-strategy *of minimal size*. In most practical cases we are aware of, the situation is even worse, since the arena is not given explicitly. This is the case with the three problems we consider as applications (see Section 6), because they can be reduced to safety games whose sizes are at least *exponential* in the size of the original problem instance.

4   Structured Games and Monotonic Strategies

To mitigate the strong complexity identified in the previous section, we propose to follow the successful *antichain approach* [12,7,8]. In this line of research, the authors point out that, in practical applications (like those we identify in Section 6), system states exhibit some inherent *structure*, which is formalised by a *simulation relation* and can be exploited to improve the practical running time of the algorithms. In the present paper, we rely on the notion of *turn-based alternating simulation*, to define heuristics to (i) improve the running time of the algorithms to solve finite turn-based games and (ii) obtain succinct representations of strategies. This notion is adapted from [2].

Turn-based alternating simulations. Let $G = (V_S, V_R, E, I, \mathsf{Bad})$ be a finite safety game. A partial order $\unrhd \subseteq V_S \times V_S \cup V_R \times V_R$ is a *turn-based alternating simulation relation for G* [2] (tba-simulation for short) iff for all v_1, v_2 s.t. $v_1 \unrhd v_2$, either $v_1 \in \mathsf{Bad}$ or the three following conditions hold: (i) If $v_1 \in V_S$, then, for all $v_1' \in \mathsf{Succ}(v_1)$, there is $v_2' \in \mathsf{Succ}(v_2)$ s.t. $v_1' \unrhd v_2'$; (ii) If $v_1 \in V_R$, then, for all $v_2' \in \mathsf{Succ}(v_2)$, there is $v_1' \in \mathsf{Succ}(v_1)$ s.t. $v_1' \unrhd v_2'$; and (iii) $v_2 \in \mathsf{Bad}$ implies $v_1 \in \mathsf{Bad}$.

On the running example (Fig. 1), $\unrhd_0$ is a tba-simulation relation. Indeed, as we are going to see in Section 6, a simulation relation in a game where player S has always the opportunity to perform the same moves is necessarily alternating.

Monotonic concretisations of $\star$-strategies. Let us exploit the notion of tba-simulation to introduce a finer notion of concretisation of $\star$-strategies. Let $\hat{\sigma}$ be a $\star$-strategy. Then, a strategy σ is a $\unrhd$-*concretisation* of $\hat{\sigma}$ iff for all $v \in V_S$: (i) $v \in \mathsf{Supp}(\hat{\sigma})$ **implies** $\sigma(v) = \hat{\sigma}(v)$; and (ii) $(v \notin \mathsf{Supp}(\hat{\sigma}) \wedge v \in \downarrow^{\unrhd}(\mathsf{Supp}(\hat{\sigma})))$ **implies** $\exists \overline{v} \in \mathsf{Supp}(\hat{\sigma})$ s.t. $\overline{v} \unrhd v$ and $\sigma(\overline{v}) \unrhd \sigma(v)$. Intuitively, when $\hat{\sigma}(v) = \star$, but there is $v' \unrhd v$ s.t. $\hat{\sigma}(v') \neq \star$, then, $\sigma(v)$ must mimic the strategy $\sigma(\overline{v})$ from some state $\overline{v}$ that covers v and s.t. $\hat{\sigma}(\overline{v}) \neq \star$. Then, we say that a $\star$-strategy is $\unrhd$-*winning* if all its $\unrhd$-concretisations are winning.

Because equality is a tba-simulation, the proof of Theorem 1 can be used to show that computing a $\unrhd$-winning $\star$-strategy of size less than k is an NP-complete problem too. Nevertheless, $\unrhd$-winning $\star$-strategies can be even more compact than winning $\star$-strategy. For instance, on the running example, the smallest winning $\star$-strategy $\overline{\sigma}$ is of size 5: it is given in Fig. 1 (b) and highlighted by bold arrows in Fig. 1 (thus, $\overline{\sigma}(④) = \overline{\sigma}(⑦) = \star$). Yet, one can define a $\unrhd_0$-winning $\star$-strategy $\hat{\sigma}$ of size 2 because states ⑤ and ⑥ simulate all the winning states of S. This $\star$-strategy[4] $\hat{\sigma}$ is the one given in Fig. 1 (b) and represented by the boldest arrows in Fig. 1. Observe that, while all $\unrhd$-concretisations of $\hat{\sigma}$ are winning, not all *concretisations* of $\hat{\sigma}$ are. For instance, all concretisations σ of $\hat{\sigma}$ s.t. $\sigma(⓪) = \boxed{2}$ are not $\unrhd_0$-monotonic and losing.

Obtaining $\unrhd$-winning $\star$-strategies. The previous example clearly shows the kind of $\unrhd$-winning $\star$-strategies we want to achieve: $\star$-strategies $\hat{\sigma}$ s.t. $\mathsf{Supp}(\hat{\sigma})$ is the maximal antichain of the winning states. In Section 5, we introduce an efficient on-the-fly algorithm to compute such a $\star$-strategy. Its correctness is based on the fact that we can extract a $\unrhd$-winning $\star$-strategy from any winning (plain)

---

[4] Actually, this strategy is winning for all initial number n of balls s.t. $n \bmod 3 \neq 1$.

strategy, as shown by Proposition 1 hereunder. For all strategies σ, and all $V \subseteq V_S$, we let $\sigma|_V$ denote the $\star$-strategy $\hat{\sigma}$ s.t. $\hat{\sigma}(v) = \sigma(v)$ for all $v \in V$ and $\hat{\sigma}(v) = \star$ for all $v \notin V$. Then:

Proposition 1. *Let $G = (V_S, V_R, E, I, \mathsf{Bad})$ be a finite turn-based game and $\trianglerighteq$ be a tba-simulation relation for G. Let σ be a strategy in G, and let $\mathbf{S} \subseteq V_S$ be a set of S-states s.t.:   (i) $(\mathbf{S} \cup \sigma(\mathbf{S})) \cap \mathsf{Bad} = \emptyset$; (ii) $I \in{\downarrow}^{\trianglerighteq} (\mathbf{S})$; and (iii) $\mathsf{succ}(\sigma(\mathbf{S})) \subseteq{\downarrow}^{\trianglerighteq}(\mathbf{S})$. Then, $\sigma|_\mathbf{S}$ is a $\trianglerighteq$-winning $\star$-strategy.*

This proposition allows us to identify families of sets of states on which $\star$-strategies can be defined. One of the sets that satisfies the conditions of Proposition 1 is the maximal antichain of reachable S-states, for a given winning strategy σ:

Theorem 2. *Let $G = (V_S, V_R, E, I, \mathsf{Bad})$ be a finite turn-based game, $\trianglerighteq$ be a tba-simulation relation for G. Let σ be a winning strategy and $\mathcal{WR}_\sigma$ be a maximal $\trianglerighteq$-antichain on $\mathsf{Reach}(G_\sigma) \cap V_S$, then the $\star$-strategy $\sigma|_{\mathcal{WR}_\sigma}$ is $\trianglerighteq$-winning.*

5   Efficient Computation of Succinct Winning Strategies

The original OTFUR algorithm. The *On-The-Fly algorithm for Untimed Reachability games* (OTFUR) algorithm [6] is an efficient, on-the-fly algorithm to compute a winning strategy *for Player $\mathcal{R}$* , i.e., when considering a *reachability objective*. It is easy to adapt it to compute winning strategies for Player $\mathcal{S}$ instead. We sketch the main ideas behind this algorithm, and refer the reader to [6] for a comprehensive description. The intuition of the approach is to combine a forward exploration from the initial state with a backward propagation of the information when a losing state is found. During the forward exploration, newly discovered states are assumed winning until they are declared losing for sure. Whenever a losing state is identified (either because it is Bad, or because Bad is unavoidable from it), the information is back propagated to predecessors whose status could be affected by this information. A bookkeeping function Depend is used for that purpose: it associates, to each state v, a list $\mathsf{Depend}(v)$ of edges that need to be re-evaluated should v be declared losing. The main interest of this algorithm is that it works *on-the-fly* (thus, the arena does not need to be fully constructed before the analysis), and avoids, if possible, the entire traversal of the arena. In this section, we propose an optimized version of OTFUR for games equipped with tba-simulations. Before this, we prove that, when a finite turn-based game is equipped with a tba-simulation $\trianglerighteq$, then its set of winning states is $\trianglerighteq$-*downward closed*. This property will be important for the correctness of our algorithm.

Proposition 2. *Let G be a finite turn-based game, and let $\trianglerighteq$ be a tba-simulation for G. Then the set Win of winning states in G is downward closed for $\trianglerighteq$.*

Algorithm 1. The OTFUR optimized for games with a tba-simulation

---

Data: A finite turn-based game $G = (V_S, V_R, E, I, \mathsf{Bad})$

1   **if** $I \in \mathsf{Bad}$ **then return** *false*;

2   Passed $:= \{I\}$; Depend$(I) := \varnothing$;

3   AntiMaybe $:= \{I\}$; AntiLosing $:= \{\}$;

4   Waiting $:= \{(I, v') \mid v' \in \lfloor \mathsf{Succ}(I) \rfloor\}$;

5   **while** Waiting $\neq \varnothing \wedge I \notin\uparrow$ AntiLosing **do**

6      $e = (v, v') := pop(\mathsf{Waiting})$;

7   **if** $v \notin\uparrow$ AntiLosing **then**

8   **if** $v \in\downarrow$ AntiMaybe $\setminus$ AntiMaybe **then**

9   choose $v_m \in$ AntiMaybe s.t. $v_m \unrhd v$;

10   Depend$[v_m] :=$ Depend$[v_m] \cup \{e\}$;

11   **else**

12   **if** $v' \in\downarrow$ AntiMaybe **then**

13   **if** $v' \notin$ AntiMaybe **then**

14   choose $v_m \in$ AntiMaybe s.t. $v_m \unrhd v'$;

15   Depend$[v_m] :=$ Depend$[v_m] \cup \{e\}$;

16   **else**

17   **if** $v' \notin$ Passed **then**

18   Passed $:=$ Passed $\cup \{v'\}$;

19   **if** $v' \notin\uparrow$ AntiLosing **then**

20   **if** $(v' \in \mathsf{Bad})$ **then**

21   AntiLosing $:= \lfloor$ AntiLosing $\cup \{v'\} \rfloor$;

22   Waiting $:=$ Waiting $\cup \{e\}$; // reevaluation of e

23   **else**

24   Depend$[v'] := \{(v, v')\}$;

25   AntiMaybe $:= \lceil$ AntiMaybe $\cup \{v'\} \rceil$;

26   **if** $v \in V_S$ **then**

27   Waiting $:=$ Waiting $\cup \{(v', v'') \mid v' \in \lfloor \mathsf{Succ}\left(v'\right) \rfloor\}$;

28   **else**

29   Waiting $:=$ Waiting $\cup \{(v', v'') \mid v' \in \lceil \mathsf{Succ}\left(v'\right) \rceil\}$;

30   **else** // reevaluation of e

31   Waiting $:=$ Waiting $\cup \{e\}$;

32   **else** // reevaluation

33   Losing* $:= \quad v \in V_S \wedge \bigwedge_{v'' \in \min(\mathsf{Succ}(v))} (v'' \in\uparrow$ AntiLosing$)$;

                            $\vee \; v \in V_R \wedge \bigvee_{v'' \in \max(\mathsf{Succ}(v))} (v'' \in\uparrow$ AntiLosing$)$

34   **if** Losing* **then**

35   AntiLosing $:= \lfloor$ AntiLosing $\cup \{v\} \rfloor$;

36   AntiMaybe $:= \lceil$ Passed$\setminus \uparrow$(AntiLosing)$\rceil$;

                     // back propagation

37   Waiting $:=$ Waiting $\cup$ Depend$[v]$;

38   **else**

39   **if** $\neg$Losing$[v']$ **then** Depend$[v'] :=$ Depend$[v'] \cup \{e\}$;

40   **return** $I \notin\uparrow$ AntiLosing

Optimised OTFUR. Let us discuss Algorithm 1, our optimised version of OT-FUR for the construction of $\trianglerighteq$-winning $\star$-strategies. Its high-level principle is the same as in the original OTFUR, i.e. forward exploration and backward propagation. At all times, it maintains several sets: (i) Waiting that stores edges waiting to be explored; (ii) Passed that stores nodes that have already been explored; and (iii) AntiLosing and AntiMaybe which represent, by means of antichains (see discussion below) a set of surely losing states and a set of possibly winning states respectively[5]. The main **while** loop runs until either no more edges are waiting, or the initial state I is surely losing. An iteration of the loop first picks an edge $e = (v, v')$ from Waiting, and checks whether exploring this edge can be post-poned (line 7–15, see hereunder). Then, if v' has not been explored before (line 16), cannot be declared surely losing (line 18), and does not belong to Bad (line 19), it is explored (lines 23–28). When v' is found to be losing, e is put back in Waiting for back propagation (lines 21 or 30). The actual back-propagation is performed at lines 32–38 and triggered by an edge (v, v') s.t. $v' \in$ Passed. Let us highlight the three optimisations that rely on a tba-simulation $\trianglerighteq$:

1. By the properties of $\trianglerighteq$, we explore only the $\trianglerighteq$-minimal (respectively $\trianglerighteq$-maximal) successors of each $\mathcal{S}$ ($\mathcal{R}$) state (see lines 3, 26 and 28). We consider maximal and minimal elements only when evaluating a node in line 32.
2. By Proposition 2, the set of winning states in the game is downward-closed, hence the set of losing states is upward-closed, and we store the set of states that are losing for sure as an antichain AntiLosing of minimal losing states.
3. Symmetrically, the set of *possibly winning states* is stored as an antichain AntiMaybe of maximal states. This set allows to postpone, and potentially avoid, the exploration of some states: assume some edge (v, v') has been popped from Waiting. Before exploring it, we first check whether either v or v' belongs to $\downarrow$(AntiMaybe) (see lines 7 and 11). If yes, there is $v_m \in$ AntiMaybe s.t. $v_m \trianglerighteq v$ (resp. $v_m \trianglerighteq v'$), and the exploration of v (v') can be postponed. We store the edge (v, v') that we were about to explore in Depend[v_m], so that, if v_m is eventually declared losing (see line 36), (v, v') will be re-scheduled for exploration. Thus, the algorithm stops when all maximal $\mathcal{S}$ states have a successor that is covered by a non-losing one.

Observe that optimisations 1 and 2 rely on the upward closure of the losing states only, and were present in the antichain algorithm of [8]. Optimisation 3 is original and exploits more aggressively the notion of tba-simulation. It allows to keep at all times an antichain of potentially winning states, which is crucial to compute efficiently a winning $\star$-strategy. If, at the end of the execution, $I \notin \uparrow$(AntiLosing), we can extract from AntiMaybe a winning $\star$-strategy $\hat{\sigma}_G$ as follows. For all $v \in$ AntiMaybe $\cap V_{\mathcal{S}}$, we let $\hat{\sigma}_G(v) = v'$ such that $v' \in$ Succ$(v) \cap \downarrow$(AntiMaybe). For all $v \in V_{\mathcal{S}} \setminus$ AntiMaybe, we let $\hat{\sigma}_G(v) = \star$. Symmetrically, if $I \in \uparrow$(AntiLosing), there is no winning strategy for $\mathcal{S}$.

---

[5] We could initialise AntiLosing to Bad, but this is not always practical. In particular, when the arena is not given explicitly, we want to avoid pre-computing Bad.

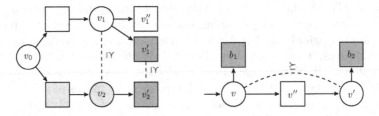

Fig. 2. A simulation and the downward closure are not sufficient to apply Algorithm 1

Theorem 3. *When called on game G, Algorithm 1 always terminates. Upon termination, either $I \in \uparrow (\mathsf{AntiLosing})$ and there is no winning strategy for $\mathcal{S}$ in G, or $\hat{\sigma}_G$ is a $\trianglerighteq$-winning $\star$-strategy.*

Why simulations are not sufficient. Let us exhibit two examples of games equipped with a simulation $\succeq$ which is not a tba-simulation, to show why tba-simulations are crucial for our optimisations. In Fig. 2 (left), $\mathsf{Bad} = \{v'_1, v'_2\}$, and the set of winning states is not $\succeq$-downward closed (gray states are losing). In the game of Fig. 2 (right), $\mathsf{Bad} = \{b_1, b_2\}$ and Algorithm 1 does not develop the successors of v' (because $v \succeq v'$, and $v \in \mathsf{AntiMaybe}$ when first reaching v'). Instead, it computes a purportedly winning $\star$-strategy $\hat{\sigma}_G$ s.t. $\hat{\sigma}_G(v) = v''$ and $\hat{\sigma}_G(v') = \star$. Clearly this $\star$-strategy is not $\succeq$-winning (actually, there is no winning strategy).

6   Applications

To apply our techniques, the game arena must be equipped with a *tba-simulation*. In many cases (see the three practical cases below), a *simulation relation* on the states of the game is already known, or can be easily defined. In general, not all simulation relations are tba-simulations, yet we can identify properties of the arena that yield this useful property. Intuitively, this occurs when Player $\mathcal{S}$ can always choose to play *the same set of actions* from all its states, and when playing the same action a in two states $v_1 \trianglerighteq v_2$ yields two states v'_1 and v'_2 with $v'_1 \trianglerighteq v'_2$ [6]. Formally, let $G = (V_{\mathcal{S}}, V_{\mathcal{R}}, E, I, \mathsf{Bad})$ be a finite turn-based game and Σ a finite alphabet. A *labeling* of G is a function $\mathsf{lab} : E \to \Sigma$. For all states $v \in V_{\mathcal{S}} \cup V_{\mathcal{R}}$, and all $a \in \Sigma$, we let $\mathsf{Succ}_a(v) = \{v' \mid (v, v') \in E \wedge \mathsf{lab}(v, v') = a\}$. Then, (G, lab) is *$\mathcal{S}$-deterministic* iff there is a set of actions $\Sigma_{\mathcal{S}} \subseteq \Sigma$ s.t. for all $v \in V_{\mathcal{S}}$: (i) $|\mathsf{Succ}_a(v)| = 1$ for all $a \in \Sigma_{\mathcal{S}}$ and (ii) $|\mathsf{Succ}_a(v)| = 0$ for all $a \notin \Sigma_{\mathcal{S}}$. Moreover, a labeling lab is *$\trianglerighteq$-monotonic* (where $\trianglerighteq$ is a simulation relation on the states of G) iff for all $v_1, v_2 \in V_{\mathcal{S}} \cup V_{\mathcal{R}}$ such that $v_1 \trianglerighteq v_2$, for all $a \in \Sigma$, for all $v'_2 \in \mathsf{Succ}_a(v_2)$: there is $v'_1 \in \mathsf{Succ}_a(v_1)$ s.t. $v'_1 \trianglerighteq v'_2$. Then:

---

[6] For example, in the urn-filling game (Fig. 1), Player $\mathcal{S}$ can always choose between taking 1 or 2 balls, from all states where at least 2 balls are left.

Theorem 4. *Let $G = (V_S, V_R, E, I, \mathsf{Bad})$ be a finite turn-based game, let $\trianglerighteq$ be a simulation relation on G and let* lab *be a $\trianglerighteq$-monotonic labeling of G. If (G, lab) is S-deterministic, then $\trianglerighteq$ is a tba-simulation relation.*

Thus, when a game G is labeled, S-deterministic, equipped with a simulation relation $\trianglerighteq$ that can be computed directly from the description of the states[7] and $\trianglerighteq$-monotonic, our approach can be applied out-of-the-box. In this case, Algorithm 1 yields, if it exists, a winning $\star$-strategy $\hat{\sigma}_G$. We describe $\hat{\sigma}_G$ by means of the set of pairs $(v, \mathsf{lab}(v, \hat{\sigma}_G(v)))$ s.t. v is in the support of $\hat{\sigma}_G$. That is, we store, for all v in the maximal antichain of winning reachable states, the *action* to be played from v instead of the *successor* $\hat{\sigma}_G(v)$). Then, a controller implementing $\hat{\sigma}_G$ works as follows: when the current state is v, the controller looks for a pair $(\overline{v}, a)$ with $\overline{v} \trianglerighteq v$, and executes a. Such a pair exists by S-determinism (and respects $\trianglerighteq$-concretisation by $\trianglerighteq$-monotonicity). The time needed to find $\overline{v}$ depends only on the size of the antichain, that we expect to be small in practice.

Three potential applications. Let us now describe very briefly three concrete problems to which our approach can be applied. They share the following characteristics, that make our technique particularly appealing: (i) they have practical applications where an efficient implementation of the winning strategy is crucial; (ii) the arena of the game is not given explicitly and is at least exponential in the size of the problem instance; and (iii) they admit a natural tba-simulation $\trianglerighteq$, that can be computed directly from the descriptions of the states. The empirical evaluation of our approach is future work, except for the first application which has already been (partially) implemented in [8] with excellent performances.

LTL realisability: roughly speaking, the realisability problem of LTL asks to compute a controller that enforces a specification given as an LTL formula. As already explained, Filiot, Jin and Raskin reduce [8] this problem to a safety game whose states are vectors of (bounded) natural numbers. They show that the partial order $\succeq$ where $v \succeq v'$ iff $v[i] \geq v'[i]$ for all coordinates i is a *simulation relation* and rely on it to define an efficient antichain algorithm (based on the OTFUR algorithm). Our technique generalises these results: Theorem 4 can be invoked to show that $\succeq$ is a *tba-simulation* and Algorithm 1 is the same as the antichain algorithm of [8], except for the third optimisation (see Section 5) which is not present in [8]. Thus, our results provide a general theory to explain the excellent performance reported in [8], and have the potential to improve it.

Multiprocessor real-time scheduler synthesis: this problem asks to compute a *correct scheduler* for a set of *sporadic tasks* running on a *platform of m identical CPUs*. A sporadic task (C, T, D) is a process that repeatedly creates *jobs*, s.t. each job creation (also called *request*) occurs at least T time units after the previous one. Each job models a computational payload. It needs at most C units of CPU time to complete, and must obtain them within a certain time frame of length D starting from the request (otherwise the job *misses* its

---

[7] This means that one can decide whether $v \trianglerighteq v'$ from the encoding of v and v' and the set of pairs $\{(v, v') \mid v \trianglerighteq v'\}$ does not need to be stored explicitly.

deadline). A scheduler is a function that assigns, at all times, jobs to available CPUs. It is *correct* iff it ensures that no job ever misses a deadline.

This problem can be reduced to a safety game [4] where the two players are the scheduler and the coalition of the tasks respectively. In this setting, a *winning* strategy for Player $\mathcal{S}$ is a *correct* scheduler. One can rely on Theorem 4 to show that the simulation relation $\succeq$ introduced in [9] (to solve a related real-time scheduling problem using antichain techniques) is a tba-simulation. An $\mathcal{S}$-deterministic and $\succeq$-monotonic labeling is obtained if we label moves of the environment by the set of tasks producing a request, and the scheduler moves by a total order on all the tasks, which is used as a priority function determining which tasks are scheduled for running.

Determinisation of timed automata: timed automata extend finite automata with a finite set of real-valued variables that are called clocks, whose value evolves with time elapsing, and that can be tested and reset when firing transitions [1]. They are a popular model for real-time systems. One of the drawbacks of timed automata is that they *cannot be made deterministic in general*. Hence, only partial algorithms exist for determinisation. So far, the most general of those techniques has been introduced in [3] and consists in turning a TA $\mathcal{A}$ into a safety game $G_{\mathcal{A},(Y,M)}$ (parametrised by a set of clocks Y and a maximal constant M). Then, a deterministic TA over-approximating $\mathcal{A}$ (with set of clocks Y and maximal constant M), can be extracted from any strategy for Player $\mathcal{S}$. If the strategy is winning, then the approximation is an *exact* determinisation. Using Theorem 4, we can define a tba-simulation $\unrhd_{\mathsf{det}}$ on the states of this game.

References

1. Alur, R., Dill, D.: A theory of timed automata. TCS 126(2), 183–235 (1994)
2. Alur, R., Henzinger, T.A., Kupferman, O., Vardi, M.Y.: Alternating refinement relations. In: Sangiorgi, D., de Simone, R. (eds.) CONCUR 1998. LNCS, vol. 1466, pp. 163–178. Springer, Heidelberg (1998)
3. Bertrand, N., Stainer, A., Jéron, T., Krichen, M.: A game approach to determinize timed automata. In: Hofmann, M. (ed.) FOSSACS 2011. LNCS, vol. 6604, pp. 245–259. Springer, Heidelberg (2011)
4. Bonifaci, V., Marchetti-Spaccamela, A.: Feasibility analysis of sporadic real-time multiprocessor task systems. In: de Berg, M., Meyer, U. (eds.) ESA 2010, Part II. LNCS, vol. 6347, pp. 230–241. Springer, Heidelberg (2010)
5. Bouton, C.: Nim, a game with a complete mathematical theory. Ann. Math. 3, 35–39 (1902)
6. Cassez, F., David, A., Fleury, E., Larsen, K.G., Lime, D.: Efficient on-the-fly algorithms for the analysis of timed games. In: Abadi, M., de Alfaro, L. (eds.) CONCUR 2005. LNCS, vol. 3653, pp. 66–80. Springer, Heidelberg (2005)
7. Doyen, L., Raskin, J.-F.: Antichain algorithms for finite automata. In: Esparza, J., Majumdar, R. (eds.) TACAS 2010. LNCS, vol. 6015, pp. 2–22. Springer, Heidelberg (2010)
8. Filiot, E., Jin, N., Raskin, J.: Antichains and compositional algorithms for LTL synthesis. FMSD 39(3), 261–296 (2011)

9. Geeraerts, G., Goossens, J., Lindström, M.: Multiprocessor schedulability of arbitrary-deadline sporadic tasks: complexity and antichain algorithm. RTS 49(2), 171–218 (2013)

10. Geeraerts, G., Goossens, J., Stainer, A.: Computing succinct strategies in safety games. CoRR abs/1404.6228, http://arxiv.org/abs/1404.6228

11. Neider, D.: Small Strategies for Safety Games. In: Bultan, T., Hsiung, P.-A. (eds.) ATVA 2011. LNCS, vol. 6996, pp. 306–320. Springer, Heidelberg (2011)

12. De Wulf, M., Doyen, L., Maquet, N., Raskin, J.-F.: Antichains: Alternative algorithms for LTL satisfiability and model-checking. In: Ramakrishnan, C.R., Rehof, J. (eds.) TACAS 2008. LNCS, vol. 4963, pp. 63–77. Springer, Heidelberg (2008)

Integer Vector Addition Systems with States

Christoph Haase[*] and Simon Halfon

Laboratoire Spécification et Vérification (LSV), CNRS
École Normale Supérieure (ENS) de Cachan, France

Abstract. This paper studies reachability, coverability and inclusion problems for Integer Vector Addition Systems with States ($\mathbb{Z}$-VASS) and extensions and restrictions thereof. A $\mathbb{Z}$-VASS comprises a finite-state controller with a finite number of counters ranging over the integers. Although it is folklore that reachability in $\mathbb{Z}$-VASS is NP-complete, it turns out that despite their naturalness, from a complexity point of view this class has received little attention in the literature. We fill this gap by providing an in-depth analysis of the computational complexity of the aforementioned decision problems. Most interestingly, it turns out that while the addition of reset operations to ordinary VASS leads to undecidability and Ackermann-hardness of reachability and coverability, respectively, they can be added to $\mathbb{Z}$-VASS while retaining NP-completeness of both coverability and reachability.

1   Introduction

Vector Addition Systems with States (VASS) are a prominent class of infinite-state systems. They comprise a finite-state controller with a finite number of counters ranging over the natural numbers. When taking a transition, an integer can be added to a counter, provided that the resulting counter value is non-negative. A configuration of a VASS is a tuple $q(\boldsymbol{v})$ consisting of a control state q and a vector $\boldsymbol{v} \in \mathbb{N}^d$, where $d > 0$ is the number of counters or, equivalently, the dimension of the VASS. The central decision problems for VASS are reachability, coverability and inclusion. Given configurations $q(\boldsymbol{v})$, $q'(\boldsymbol{v}')$ of a VASS $\mathcal{A}$, reachability is to decide whether there is a path connecting the two configurations in the transition system induced by $\mathcal{A}$. Coverability on the other hand asks whether there is a path from $q(\boldsymbol{v})$ to a configuration that is "above" $q'(\boldsymbol{v}')$, *i.e.*, a path to some $q'(\boldsymbol{w})$ such that $\boldsymbol{w} \geq \boldsymbol{v}'$, where $\geq$ is interpreted component-wise. Finally, given VASS $\mathcal{A}$ and $\mathcal{B}$, inclusion asks whether the set of counter values reachable in the transition system induced by $\mathcal{A}$ is contained in those reachable by $\mathcal{B}$. All of the aforementioned problems have extensively been studied over the course of the last forty years. One of the earliest results was obtained by Lipton, who showed that reachability and coverability are EXPSPACE-hard [20]. Later, Rackoff established a matching upper bound for coverability [23], and Mayr showed that reachability is decidable [21]. For inclusion, it is known that

---

[*] Supported by the French ANR, REACHARD (grant ANR-11-BS02-001).

J. Ouaknine, I. Potapov, and J. Worrell (Eds.): RP 2014, LNCS 8762, pp. 112–124, 2014.
© Springer International Publishing Switzerland 2014

this problem is in general undecidable [14] and Ackermann ($\mathbf{F}_\omega$)-complete [18] when restricting to VASS with a finite reachability set. Moreover, various extensions of VASS with, for instance, resets or polynomial updates on counter values have been studied in the literature. Resets allow for setting a counter to zero along a transition, and polynomial updates allow for updating a counter with an arbitrary polynomial. In general, reachability in the presence of any such extension becomes undecidable [4,6], while the complexity of coverability increases significantly to $\mathbf{F}_\omega$-completeness in the presence of resets [25].

What makes VASS hard to deal with, both in the computational and in the mathematical sense, is the restriction of the counters to non-negative integers. This restriction allows for enforcing an order in which transitions can be taken, which is at the heart of many hardness proofs. In this paper, we relax this restriction and study $\mathbb{Z}$-VASS which are VASS whose counters can take values from the integers, and extensions thereof. Thus, the effect of transitions can commute along a run of a $\mathbb{Z}$-VASS, which makes deciding reachability substantially easier, and it is in fact folklore that reachability in $\mathbb{Z}$-VASS is NP-complete. It appears, however, that many aspects of the computational complexity of standard decision problems for $\mathbb{Z}$-VASS and extensions and restrictions thereof have not received much attention in the literature.

Our Contribution. The main focus of this paper[1] is to study the computational complexity of reachability, coverability and inclusion for $\mathbb{Z}$-VASS equipped with resets ($\mathbb{Z}$-VASS$_\mathrm{R}$). Unlike in the case of VASS, we can show that reachability and coverability are naturally logarithmic-space inter-reducible. By generalizing a technique introduced by Seidl *et al.* [26] for defining Parikh images of finite-state automata in existential Presburger arithmetic, we can show that a given instance of reachability (and *a fortiori* coverability) in $\mathbb{Z}$-VASS$_\mathrm{R}$ can be reduced in logarithmic-space to an equivalent sentence in existential Presburger arithmetic, and henceforth both problems are NP-complete. Moreover, by exploiting a recent result on the complexity of Presburger arithmetic with a fixed number of quantifier alternations [12], this reduction immediately yields coNEXP-membership of the inclusion problem for $\mathbb{Z}$-VASS$_\mathrm{R}$. We also show that a matching lower bound can be established via a reduction from validity in Π_2-Presburger arithmetic. This lower bound does not require resets and thus already holds for $\mathbb{Z}$-VASS. Along the way, wherever possible we sharpen known lower bounds and propose some further open problems.

Related Work. The results obtained in this paper are closely related to decision problems for commutative grammars, *i.e.* Parikh images of, for instance, finite-state automata or context-free grammars. A generic tool that is quite powerful in this setting is to define Parikh images as the set of solutions to certain systems of linear Diophantine equations. This approach has, for instance, been taken

---

[1] A full version containing all proofs omitted due to space constraints can be obtained from http://arxiv.org/abs/1406.2590.

in [5,22,26,13,15]. As stated above, we generalize the technique of Seidl *et al.*, which has also been the starting point in [15] in order to show decidability and complexity results for pushdown systems equipped with reversal-bounded counters.

Furthermore, results related to ours have also been established by Kopczyński & To. In [19], they consider inclusion problems for regular and context-free commutative grammars, and show that for a fixed alphabet those problems are coNP- and Π_2^P-complete, respectively. As a matter of fact, the proof of the Π_2^P-upper bound is established for context-free commutative grammars in which, informally speaking, letters can be erased, which can be seen as a generalization of $\mathbb{Z}$-VASS. In general, inclusion for context-free commutative grammars is in coNEXP [16], but it is not known whether this bound is tight. Also related is the work by Reichert [24], who studies the computational complexity of reachability games on various classes of $\mathbb{Z}$-VASS. Finally, $\mathbb{Z}$-VASS are an instance of valence automata, which have recently, for instance, been studied by Buckheister & Zetzsche [3]. However, their work is more concerned with language-theoretic properties of valence automata rather than aspects of computational complexity. Language-theoretic aspects of $\mathbb{Z}$-VASS have also been studied by Greibach [11].

As discussed above, $\mathbb{Z}$-VASS achieve a lower complexity for standard decision problems in comparison to VASS by relaxing counters to range over the integers. Another approach going into a similar direction is to allow counters to range over the positive reals. It has been shown in recent work by Fraca & Haddad [7] that the decision problems we consider in this paper become substantially easier for such continuous VASS, with reachability even being decidable in P.

2   Preliminaries

In this section, we provide most of the definitions that we rely on in this paper. We first introduce some general notation and subsequently an abstract model of register machines from which we derive $\mathbb{Z}$-VASS as a special subclass. We then recall and tighten some known complexity bounds for $\mathbb{Z}$-VASS and conclude this section with a brief account on Presburger arithmetic.

General Notation. In the following, $\mathbb{Z}$ and $\mathbb{N}$ are the sets of integers and natural numbers, respectively, and $\mathbb{N}^d$ and $\mathbb{Z}^d$ are the set of dimension d vectors in $\mathbb{N}$ and $\mathbb{Z}$, respectively. We denote by $[d]$ the set of positive integers up to d, *i.e.* $[d] = \{1, \ldots, d\}$. By $\mathbb{N}^{d \times d}$ and $\mathbb{Z}^{d \times d}$ we denote the set of $d \times d$ square matrices over $\mathbb{N}$ and $\mathbb{Z}$, respectively. The identity matrix in dimension d is denoted by I_d and e_i denotes the i-th unit vector in any dimension d provided $i \in [d]$. For any d and $i, j \in [d]$, E_{ij} denotes the $d \times d$-matrix whose i-th row and j-th column intersection is equal to one and all of its other components are zero, and we use E_i to abbreviate E_{ii}. For $v \in \mathbb{Z}^d$ we write $v(i)$ for the i-th component of v for $i \in [d]$. Given two vectors $v_1, v_2 \in \mathbb{Z}^d$, we write $v_1 \geq v_2$ iff for all $i \in [d]$, $v_1(i) \geq v_2(i)$. Given a vector $v \in \mathbb{Z}^d$ and a set $S \subseteq [d]$, by $v_{|S}$ we denote the vector w derived from v with components from S reset, *i.e*, for all

$j \in [d]$, $\boldsymbol{w}(j) = \boldsymbol{v}(j)$ when $j \notin S$, and $\boldsymbol{w}(j) = 0$ otherwise. Given $i \in [d]$, $\boldsymbol{v}_{|i}$ abbreviates $\boldsymbol{v}_{|\{i\}}$. If not stated otherwise, all numbers in this paper are assumed to be encoded in binary.

Presburger Arithmetic. Recall that *Presburger arithmetic (PA)* is the first-order theory of the structure $\langle \mathbb{N}, 0, 1, +, \geq \rangle$, *i.e.*, quantified linear arithmetic over natural numbers. The size $|\Phi|$ of a PA formula is the number of symbols required to write it down, where we assume unary encoding of numbers[2]. For technical convenience, we may assume with no loss of generality that terms of PA formulas are of the form $\boldsymbol{z} \cdot \boldsymbol{x} \geq b$, where $\boldsymbol{x}$ is an n-tuple of first-order variables, $\boldsymbol{z} \in \mathbb{Z}^n$ and $b \in \mathbb{Z}$. It is well-known that the existential (Σ_1-)fragment of PA is NP-complete, see *e.g.* [2]. Moreover, validity for the Π_2-fragment of PA, *i.e.* its restriction to a $\forall^* \exists^*$-quantifier prefix, is coNEXP-complete [10,12].

Given a PA formula $\Phi(x_1, \ldots, x_d)$ in d free variables, we define

$$[\![\Phi(x_1, \ldots, x_d)]\!] = \{(n_1, \ldots, n_d) \in \mathbb{N}^d : \Phi(n_1/x_1, \ldots, n_d/x_d) \text{ is valid}\}.$$

Moreover, a set $M \subseteq \mathbb{N}^d$ is *PA-definable* if there exists a PA formula $\Phi(x_1, \ldots, x_d)$ such that $M = [\![\Phi(x_1, \ldots, x_d)]\!]$. Recall that a result due to Ginsburg & Spanier states that PA-definable sets coincide with the so-called *semi-linear sets* [9].

Integer Vector Addition Systems. The main objects studied in this paper can be derived from a general class of integer register machines which we define below.

Definition 1. *Let* $\mathfrak{A} \subseteq \mathbb{Z}^{d \times d}$, *a dimension d-integer register machine over* $\mathfrak{A}$ *($\mathbb{Z}$-RM($\mathfrak{A}$)) is a tuple* $\mathcal{A} = (Q, \Sigma, d, \Delta, \tau)$ *where*

- *Q is a finite set of control states,*
- *Σ is a finite alphabet,*
- *$d > 0$ is the dimension or the number of counters,*
- *$\Delta \subseteq Q \times \Sigma \times Q$ is a finite set of transitions,*
- *$\tau : \Sigma \to (\mathbb{Z}^d \to \mathbb{Z}^d)$ maps each $a \in \Sigma$ to an affine transformation such that $\tau(a) = \boldsymbol{v} \mapsto A\boldsymbol{v} + \boldsymbol{b}$ for some $A \in \mathfrak{A}$ and $\boldsymbol{b} \in \mathbb{Z}^d$.*

We will often consider τ as a morphism from Σ^* to the set of affine transformations such that $\tau(\epsilon) = I_d$ and for any $w \in \Sigma^*$ and $a \in \Sigma$, $\tau(wa)(\boldsymbol{v}) = \tau(a)(\tau(w)(\boldsymbol{v}))$. The set $C(\mathcal{A}) = Q \times \mathbb{Z}^d$ is called the *set of configurations of* $\mathcal{A}$. For readability, we write configurations as $q(\boldsymbol{v})$ instead of $(q, \boldsymbol{v})$. Given configurations $q(\boldsymbol{v}), q'(\boldsymbol{v}') \in C$, we write $q(\boldsymbol{v}) \xrightarrow{a}_\mathcal{A} q'(\boldsymbol{v}')$ if there is a transition $(q, a, q') \in \Delta$ such that $\boldsymbol{v}' = \tau(a)(\boldsymbol{v})$, and $q(\boldsymbol{v}) \to_\mathcal{A} q'(\boldsymbol{v}')$ if $q(\boldsymbol{v}) \xrightarrow{a}_\mathcal{A} q'(\boldsymbol{v}')$ for some $a \in \Sigma$. A *run on a word* $\gamma = a_1 \cdots a_n \in \Sigma^*$ is a finite sequence of configurations $\varrho : c_0 c_1 \cdots c_n$ such that $c_i \xrightarrow{a_{i+1}}_\mathcal{A} c_{i+1}$ for all $0 \leq i < n$, and we write

---

[2] This is with no loss of generality since binary encoding can be simulated at the cost of a logarithmic blowup of the formula size. Note that in particular all complexity lower bounds given in this paper still hold assuming unary encoding of numbers.

$c_0 \xrightarrow{\gamma}_{\mathcal{A}} c_n$ in this case. Moreover, we write $c \rightarrow_{\mathcal{A}}^* c'$ if there is a run ϱ on some word γ such that $c = c_0$ and $c' = c_n$. Given $q(\boldsymbol{v}) \in C(\mathcal{A})$, the *reachability set starting from* $q(\boldsymbol{v})$ is defined as

$$reach(\mathcal{A}, q(\boldsymbol{v})) = \{\boldsymbol{v}' \in \mathbb{Z}^d : q(\boldsymbol{v}) \rightarrow_{\mathcal{A}}^* q'(\boldsymbol{v}') \text{ for some } q' \in Q\}.$$

In this paper, we study the complexity of deciding reachability, coverability and inclusion.

$\mathbb{Z}$-RM($\mathfrak{A}$) REACHABILITY/COVERABILITY/INCLUSION

INPUT: $\mathbb{Z}$-RM($\mathfrak{A}$) $\mathcal{A}, \mathcal{B}$, configurations $q(\boldsymbol{v}), q'(\boldsymbol{v}') \in C(\mathcal{A}), p(\boldsymbol{w}) \in C(\mathcal{B})$.
QUESTION: *Reachability:* Is there a run $q(\boldsymbol{v}) \rightarrow_{\mathcal{A}}^* q'(\boldsymbol{v}')$?
          Coverability: Is there a $\boldsymbol{z} \in \mathbb{Z}^d$ s.t. $q(\boldsymbol{v}) \rightarrow_{\mathcal{A}}^* q'(\boldsymbol{z})$ and $\boldsymbol{z} \geq \boldsymbol{v}'$?
          Inclusion: Does $reach(\mathcal{A}, q(\boldsymbol{v})) \subseteq reach(\mathcal{B}, p(\boldsymbol{w}))$ hold?

If we allow an arbitrary number of control states, whenever it is convenient we may assume $\boldsymbol{v}, \boldsymbol{v}'$ and $\boldsymbol{w}$ in the definition above to be equal to $\boldsymbol{0}$. Of course, $\mathbb{Z}$-RM are very general, and all of the aforementioned decision problems are already known to be undecidable, we will further elaborate on this topic below. We therefore consider subclasses of $\mathbb{Z}$-RM($\mathfrak{A}$) in this paper which restrict the transformation mappings or the number of control states: $\mathcal{A}$ is called

- *integer vector addition system with states and resets* ($\mathbb{Z}$-*VASS_R*) if $\mathfrak{A} = \{\lambda_1 E_1 + \cdots + \lambda_d E_d : \lambda_i \in \{0,1\}, i \in [d]\}$;
- *integer vector addition system with states* ($\mathbb{Z}$-*VASS*) if $\mathfrak{A} = I_d$;
- *integer vector addition system* ($\mathbb{Z}$-*VAS*) if $\mathcal{A}$ is a $\mathbb{Z}$-VASS and $|Q| = 1$.

Classical vector addition systems with states (VASS) can be recovered from the definition of $\mathbb{Z}$-VASS by defining the set of configurations as $Q \times \mathbb{N}^d$ and adjusting the definition of $\rightarrow_{\mathcal{A}}$ appropriately. It is folklore that coverability in VASS is logarithmic-space reducible to reachability in VASS. Our first observation is that unlike in the case of VASS, reachability can be reduced to coverability in $\mathbb{Z}$-VASS, this even holds for $\mathbb{Z}$-VASS_R. Thanks to this observation, all lower and upper bounds for reachability carry over to coverability, and *vice versa*.

Lemma 2. *Reachability and coverability are logarithmic-space inter-reducible in each of the classes $\mathbb{Z}$-VASS_R, $\mathbb{Z}$-VASS and $\mathbb{Z}$-VAS. The reduction doubles the dimension.*

Proof. The standard folklore construction to reduce coverability in VASS to reachability in VASS also works for all classes of $\mathbb{Z}$-VASS_R. For brevity, we therefore only give the reduction in the converse direction.

Let $\mathcal{A}$ be from any class of $\mathbb{Z}$-VASS in dimension d and let $q(\boldsymbol{v}), q'(\boldsymbol{v}') \in C(\mathcal{A})$. We construct a $\mathbb{Z}$-VASS $\mathcal{B}$ in dimension $2d$ with the property $q(\boldsymbol{v}) \rightarrow_{\mathcal{A}}^* q'(\boldsymbol{v}')$ iff $q(\boldsymbol{v}, -\boldsymbol{v}) \rightarrow_{\mathcal{B}}^* q'(\boldsymbol{v}', -\boldsymbol{v}')$ as follows: any affine transformation $\boldsymbol{v} \mapsto A\boldsymbol{v} + \boldsymbol{b}$ is replaced by $\boldsymbol{v} \mapsto A'\boldsymbol{v} + \boldsymbol{b}'$, where

$$A' = \begin{bmatrix} A & \boldsymbol{0} \\ \boldsymbol{0} & A \end{bmatrix} \qquad b' = \begin{vmatrix} \boldsymbol{b} \\ -\boldsymbol{b} \end{vmatrix}.$$

Any run $\varrho : q_0(\boldsymbol{v}_0) \cdots q_n(\boldsymbol{v}_n)$ in $\mathcal{B}$ such that $q_0(\boldsymbol{v}_0) = q(\boldsymbol{v}, -\boldsymbol{v})$ and $q_n(\boldsymbol{v}_n) = q'(\boldsymbol{v}', -\boldsymbol{v}')$ corresponds in the first d components to a run in $\mathcal{A}$. Moreover, ϱ has the property that for any $0 \leq i \leq n$ and $q_i(\boldsymbol{v}_i)$, $\boldsymbol{v}_i(j) = -\boldsymbol{v}_i(j+d)$ for all $j \in [d]$. Therefore, $q(\boldsymbol{v}, -\boldsymbol{v}) \rightarrow_{\mathcal{B}}^* q'(\boldsymbol{w}, -\boldsymbol{w})$ for some $q'(\boldsymbol{w}, -\boldsymbol{w})$ that covers $q'(\boldsymbol{v}', -\boldsymbol{v}')$ if, and only if, $\boldsymbol{w} \geq \boldsymbol{v}'$ and $-\boldsymbol{w} \geq -\boldsymbol{v}'$, i.e., $\boldsymbol{w} = \boldsymbol{v}'$ and thus in particular whenever $\mathcal{A}$ reaches $q'(\boldsymbol{v}')$ from $q(\boldsymbol{v})$. $\qquad\Box$

Known Complexity Results for $\mathbb{Z}$-VASS. It is folklore that reachability in $\mathbb{Z}$-VASS is NP-hard. Most commonly, this is shown via a reduction from SUBSET SUM, so this hardness result in particular relies on binary encoding of numbers and the presence of control states. Here, we wish to remark the following observation.

Lemma 3. *Reachability in $\mathbb{Z}$-VAS is NP-hard even when numbers are encoded in unary.*

The proof is given in the appendix of the full version of this paper and follows straight-forwardly via a reduction from feasibility of a system of linear Diophantine equations $A\boldsymbol{x} = \boldsymbol{b}, \boldsymbol{x} \geq \boldsymbol{0}$, which is known to be NP-complete even when unary encoding of numbers is assumed [8]. Apart from that, it is folklore that reachability in $\mathbb{Z}$-VASS is in NP. To the best of the authors' knowledge, no upper bounds for reachability, coverability or inclusion for $\mathbb{Z}$-VASS$_R$ have been established so far.

Next, we recall that slightly more general transformation matrices lead to undecidability of reachability: when allowing for arbitrary diagonal matrices, i.e. affine transformations along transitions, reachability becomes undecidable already in dimension two [6]. Consequently, by a straight forward adaption of Lemma 2 we obtain the following.

Lemma 4. *Let $\mathfrak{D}_d$ be the set of all diagonal matrices in dimension d. Coverability in $\mathbb{Z}$-RM$(\mathfrak{D}_d)$ is undecidable already for $d = 4$.*

Of course, undecidability results for reachability in matrix semi-groups obtained in [1] can be applied in order to obtain undecidability results for more general classes of matrices, and those undecidability results do not even require the presence of control states.

3   Reachability in $\mathbb{Z}$-VASS$_R$ is in NP

One main idea for showing that reachability for $\mathbb{Z}$-VASS$_R$ is in NP is that since there are no constraints on the counter values along a run, a reset on a particular counter allows to forget any information about the value of this counter up to this point, i.e., a reset cuts the run. Hence, in order to determine the value of a particular counter at the end of a run, we only need to sum up the effect of the operations on this counter since the last occurrence of a reset on this counter. This in turn requires us to guess and remember the last occurrence of a reset on each counter.

Subsequently, we introduce monitored alphabets and generalized Parikh images in order to formalize our intuition behind resets. A *monitored alphabet* is an alphabet $\Sigma \uplus R$ with $R = \{r_1, \ldots, r_k\}$ being the monitored letters. Given $S \subseteq [k]$, we denote by $\Sigma_S = \Sigma \cup \{r_i : i \in S\}$ the alphabet containing only monitored letters indexed from S. Any word $\gamma \in (\Sigma \cup R)^*$ over a monitored alphabet admits a unique decomposition into *partial words*

$$\gamma = \gamma_0 r_{i_1} \gamma_1 r_{i_2} \cdots r_{i_\ell} \gamma_\ell$$

for some $\ell \leq k$ such that all i_j are pairwise distinct and for all $j \in [\ell]$, $\gamma_j \in \Sigma^*_{\{r_{i_{j+1}}, \ldots, r_{i_\ell}\}}$. Such a decomposition simply keeps track of the last occurrence of each monitored letter. For instance for $k = 4$ and $\Sigma = \{a, b\}$, the word $\gamma = aabr_1br_3abr_3ar_1$ can uniquely be decomposed as $(aabr_1br_3ab)r_3(a)r_1$.

In this paper, the *Parikh image* $\pi_\Sigma(w)$ of a word $w \in (\Sigma \uplus R)^*$ restricted to the alphabet $\Sigma = \{a_1, \ldots, a_n\}$ is the vector $\pi_\Sigma(w) \in \mathbb{N}^n$ such that $\pi(w)(i) = |w|_{a_i}$ is the number of occurrences of a_i in w. Moreover, $\mathfrak{S}_k$ denotes the permutation group on k symbols.

Definition 5. *Let $\Sigma \uplus R$ be a monitored alphabet such that $|\Sigma| = n$ and $|R| = k$. A tuple $(\boldsymbol{\alpha}, \sigma) = (\boldsymbol{\alpha}_0, \boldsymbol{\alpha}_1, \ldots, \boldsymbol{\alpha}_k, \sigma) \in (\mathbb{N}^n)^{k+1} \times \mathfrak{S}_k$ is a generalized Parikh image of $\gamma \in (\Sigma \uplus R)^*$ if there exist $0 \leq p \leq k$ and a decomposition $\gamma = \gamma_p r_{\sigma(p+1)} \gamma_{p+1} r_{\sigma(p+2)} \cdots r_{\sigma(k)} \gamma_k$ such that:*

(a) *for all $p \leq i \leq k$, $\gamma_i \in \Sigma^*_{R_i}$, where $R_i = \{r_{\sigma(i+1)}, \ldots, r_{\sigma(k)}\}$; and*
(b) *for all $0 \leq i < p$, $\boldsymbol{\alpha}_i = \mathbf{0}$ and for all $p \leq i \leq k$, $\boldsymbol{\alpha}_i = \pi_\Sigma(\gamma_i)$, the Parikh image of γ_i restricted to Σ, i.e. monitored alphabet symbols are ignored.*

The generalized Parikh image of a language $L \subseteq (\Sigma \uplus R)^*$ is the set $\Pi(L) \subseteq (\mathbb{N}^n)^{k+1} \times \mathfrak{S}_k$ of all generalized Parikh images of all words $\gamma \in L$.

This definition formalizes the intuition given by the decomposition described above with some additional padding of dummy vectors for monitored letters not occurring in γ in order to obtain canonical objects of *uniform size*. Even though generalized Parikh images are not unique, two generalized Parikh images of the same word only differ in the order of dummy monitored letters. For instance for $k = 4$, the word $\gamma = aabr_1br_3abr_3ar_1$ has two generalized Parikh images: they coincide on $\boldsymbol{\alpha}_0 = \boldsymbol{\alpha}_1 = \boldsymbol{\alpha}_2 = (0, 0)$, $\boldsymbol{\alpha}_3 = (3, 3)$, $\boldsymbol{\alpha}_4 = (1, 0)$ and $\sigma(3) = 3$, $\sigma(4) = 1$, and only differ on $\sigma(1)$ and $\sigma(2)$ that can be 2 and 4, or 4 and 2, respectively.

Generalized Parikh images can now be applied to reachability in $\mathbb{Z}$-VASS$_R$ as follows. Without loss of generality, we may assume that a $\mathbb{Z}$-VASS$_R$ in dimension d is given as $\mathcal{A} = (Q, \Sigma \uplus R, d, \Delta, \tau)$ for some alphabet $\Sigma = \{a_1, \ldots, a_n\}$ and $R = \{r_1, \ldots, r_d\}$ such that $\tau(r_i) = \boldsymbol{v} \mapsto \boldsymbol{v}_{|i}$ for any $i \in [d]$ and for any $a_i \in \Sigma$, $\tau(a_i) = \boldsymbol{v} \mapsto \boldsymbol{v} + \boldsymbol{b}_i$ for some $\boldsymbol{b}_i \in \mathbb{Z}^d$. This assumption allows for isolating transitions performing a reset and enables us to apply monitored alphabets by monitoring when a reset occurs in each dimension the last time. Consequently, the counter value realized by some $\gamma \in (\Sigma \uplus R)^*$ starting from $\mathbf{0}$ is fully determined by a generalized Parikh image of γ.

Lemma 6. *Let $\mathcal{A}$ be a $\mathbb{Z}$-VASS$_R$, $\gamma \in (\Sigma \uplus R)^*$, $(\alpha_0, \alpha_1, \ldots, \alpha_d, \sigma) \in \Pi(\gamma)$ and $B \in \mathbb{Z}^{d \times n}$ the matrix whose columns are the vectors $\boldsymbol{b}_i$. Then the following holds:*

$$\tau(\gamma)(\mathbf{0}) = \sum\nolimits_{1 \le i \le d} (B\boldsymbol{\alpha}_{i-1})_{|\{\sigma(i), \ldots, \sigma(d)\}} + B\boldsymbol{\alpha}_d.$$

It thus remains to find a suitable way to define the generalized Parikh image of the language of the non-deterministic finite state automaton (NFA) underlying a $\mathbb{Z}$-VASS$_R$. In [26], it is shown how to construct in linear time an existential Presburger formula representing the Parikh image of the language of an NFA. We generalize this construction to generalized Parikh images of NFA over a monitored alphabet, the original result being recovered in the absence of monitored alphabet symbols, *i.e.* when $k = 0$. To this end, we introduce below some definitions and two lemmas from the construction provided in [26] which we employ for our generalization. First, a *flow* in an NFA $\mathcal{B} = (Q, \Sigma, \Delta, q_0, F)$ is a triple (f, s, t) where $s, t \in Q$ are states, and $f : \Delta \to \mathbb{N}$ maps transitions $(p, a, q) \in \Delta$ to natural numbers. Let us introduce the following abbreviations:

$$\text{in}_f(q) = \sum_{(p,a,q) \in \Delta} f(p, a, q) \quad \text{and} \quad \text{out}_f(p) = \sum_{(p,a,q) \in \Delta} f(p, a, q).$$

A flow (f, s, t) is called *consistent* if for each $p \in Q$, $\text{in}_f(p) = \text{out}_f(p) + h(p)$, where $h(s) = -1$, $h(t) = 1$, and $h(p) = 0$ otherwise. A flow is *connected* if the undirected graph obtained from the graph underlying the automaton when removing edges with zero flow is connected. A consistent and connected flow simply enforces Eulerian path conditions on the directed graph underlying $\mathcal{B}$ so that any path starting in s and ending in t yields a unique such flow.

Lemma 7 ([26]). *A vector $\alpha \in \mathbb{N}^n$ is in the Parikh image of $\mathcal{L}(\mathcal{B})$ if, and only if, there is a consistent and connected flow (f, s, t) such that*

- *$s = q_0$, $t \in F$, and*
- *for each $a_i \in \Sigma$, $\alpha(i) = \sum_{(p, a_i, q) \in \Delta} f(p, a_i, q)$*

Subsequently, in order to conveniently deal with states and alphabet symbols in Presburger arithmetic, we write $Q = \{\tilde{1}, \ldots, \tilde{m}\}$, $\Sigma = \{\dot{1}, \ldots, \dot{n}\}$ and $R = \{(n + 1), \ldots, (n + k)\}$. This enables us to write within the logic terms like $p = q$ for $\tilde{p}, \tilde{q} \in Q$. Moreover, it is easy to construct a formula $\varphi_\Delta(p, a, q)$ such that $\varphi_\Delta(p, a, q)$ holds if, and only if, $(\tilde{p}, \dot{a}, \tilde{q}) \in \Delta$. In particular, φ_Δ can be constructed in linear time, independently of the encoding of the NFA and its graph structure. With this encoding, it is not difficult to see how the conditions from Lemma 7 can be checked by an existential Presburger formula.

Lemma 8 ([26]). *There exists a linear-time computable existential Presburger formula $\varphi_\mathcal{B}(\boldsymbol{f}, s, t)$ with the following properties:*

- *$\boldsymbol{f}$ represents a flow, i.e., is a tuple of variables $x_{(p,a,q)}$ for each $(p, a, q) \in \Delta$;*
- *s and t are free variables constrained to represent states of Q; and*

$-$ $(m_{\delta_1}, \ldots, m_{\delta_g}, m_s, m_t) \in [\![\varphi_{\mathcal{B}}(\boldsymbol{f}, s, t)]\!]$ if, and only if, the flow $(f_m, \tilde{m}_s, \tilde{m}_t)$ defined by $f_m(\delta_i) = m_{\delta_i}$ is connected and consistent in $\mathcal{B}$.

We can now show how to generalize the construction from [26] to monitored alphabets and generalized Parikh images. Subsequently, recall that k is the number of monitored letters.

Theorem 9. *Given an NFA $\mathcal{B} = (Q, \Sigma \uplus R, \Delta, \tilde{q}_0, F)$ over a monitored alphabet $\Sigma \uplus R$, an existential Presburger formula $\Psi_{\mathcal{B}}(\boldsymbol{\alpha}, \boldsymbol{\sigma})$ defining the generalized Parikh image of the language $\mathcal{L}(B)$ of $\mathcal{B}$ can be constructed in time $O(k^2|\mathcal{B}|)$.*

Proof. The formula we construct has free variables $\alpha_0^1, \ldots, \alpha_0^n, \alpha_1^1, \ldots, \alpha_k^n$ representing the $k+1$ vectors $\boldsymbol{\alpha_0}, \ldots, \boldsymbol{\alpha_k}$ and free variables $\boldsymbol{\sigma} = (\sigma_1, \ldots, \sigma_k)$ to represent the permutation σ. First, we construct a formula φ_{perm} expressing that $\boldsymbol{\sigma}$ is a permutation from $[k]$ to $[k]$:

$$\varphi_{\text{perm}}(\boldsymbol{\sigma}) = \bigwedge_{i \in [k]} \left(1 \le \sigma_i \le k \wedge \bigwedge_{j \in [k]} i \ne j \rightarrow \sigma_i \ne \sigma_j \right).$$

This formula has already size $O(k^2)$. Now we have to compute the flow for each of the $k+1$ parts of the runs corresponding to the $k+1$ partial words, but first we have to "guess" the starting and ending states of each of these partial runs, in order to use the formula from Lemma 8. Let $\boldsymbol{s} = (s_0, \ldots, s_k)$ and $\boldsymbol{t} = (t_0, \ldots, t_k)$, we define

$$\varphi_{\text{states}}(\boldsymbol{\sigma}, p, \boldsymbol{s}, \boldsymbol{t}) = s_0 = q_0 \wedge \bigvee_{\tilde{q} \in F} t_k = q \wedge$$

$$\bigwedge_{i \in [k]} [i \le p \rightarrow s_{i-1} = t_{i-1} \wedge t_{i-1} = s_i] \wedge [p < i \rightarrow \varphi_{\Delta}(t_{i-1}, n + \sigma_i, s_i)].$$

Here, p is used as in Definition 5. We can now express the $k+1$ flows: we need one variable per transition for each partial run.

$$\varphi_{\text{flows}}(\boldsymbol{\sigma}, p, \boldsymbol{f}, \boldsymbol{s}, \boldsymbol{t}) = \bigwedge_{0 \le i \le k} i < p \rightarrow \sum_{(p,a,q) \in \Delta} x_{(p,a,q)}^i = 0 \wedge$$

$$\wedge \bigwedge_{0 \le i \le k} p \le i \rightarrow \left(\varphi_{\mathcal{B}}(\boldsymbol{f_i}, s_i, t_i,) \wedge \bigwedge_{1 \le j < i} \bigwedge_{(p,\dot{a},q) \in \Delta} a = n + \sigma_j \rightarrow x_{(p,\dot{a},q)}^i = 0 \right),$$

where $\boldsymbol{f} = (\boldsymbol{f_0}, \ldots, \boldsymbol{f_k})$ and $\boldsymbol{f_i}$ is the tuple of free variables of the form $x_{(p,a,q)}^i$ for all $(p, a, q) \in \Delta$. This formula essentially enforces the constraints from Definition 5. The first line enforces that the "dummy flows" $\boldsymbol{f_0}, \ldots, \boldsymbol{f_{p-1}}$ have zero flow. The second line ensures that the flows $\boldsymbol{f_p}, \ldots, \boldsymbol{f_k}$ actually correspond to partial words γ_i in the decomposition described in Definition 5, and that monitored letters that, informally speaking, have expired receive zero flow.

Now putting everything together yields:

$$\Psi_{\mathcal{B}}(\boldsymbol{\alpha}, \boldsymbol{\sigma}) = \exists p, \boldsymbol{f}_0, \ldots \boldsymbol{f}_k, \boldsymbol{s}, \boldsymbol{t}. \, 0 \le p \le k \wedge \varphi_{\mathrm{perm}}(\boldsymbol{\sigma}) \wedge$$

$$\wedge \, \varphi_{\mathrm{states}}(\boldsymbol{\sigma}, p, \boldsymbol{s}, \boldsymbol{t}) \wedge \varphi_{\mathrm{flows}}(\boldsymbol{\sigma}, p, \boldsymbol{f}, \boldsymbol{s}, \boldsymbol{t}) \wedge \bigwedge_{0 \le i \le k} \bigwedge_{a \in [n]} \alpha_i^a = \sum_{(p, \dot{a}, q) \in \varDelta} x_{(p, \dot{a}, q)}^i.$$

The size of $\Psi_{\mathcal{B}}(\boldsymbol{\alpha}, \boldsymbol{\sigma})$ is dominated by the size of $\varphi_{\mathrm{flows}}(\boldsymbol{\sigma}, p, \boldsymbol{f}, \boldsymbol{s}, \boldsymbol{t})$ which is $O(k^2 |\mathcal{B}|)$. $\qquad\square$

Note that it is easy to modify $\Psi_{\mathcal{B}}$ in order to have q_0 as a free variable. By combining $\Psi_{\mathcal{B}}$ with Lemma 6, we obtain the following corollary.

Corollary 10. *Let $\mathcal{A}$ be a $\mathbb{Z}$-VASS$_R$ and $p, q \in Q$. There exists a logarithmic-space computable existential Presburger formula[3] $\Phi_{\mathcal{A}}(p, q, \boldsymbol{v}, \boldsymbol{w}, \boldsymbol{\alpha}, \boldsymbol{\sigma})$ such that $(p, q, \boldsymbol{v}, \boldsymbol{w}, \boldsymbol{\alpha}, \boldsymbol{\sigma}) \in [\![\Phi_{\mathcal{A}}]\!]$ if, and only if, there is $\gamma \in (\Sigma \uplus R)^*$ such that $\tilde{p}(\boldsymbol{v}) \xrightarrow{\gamma}_{\mathcal{A}} \tilde{q}(\boldsymbol{w})$ and $(\boldsymbol{\alpha}, \boldsymbol{\sigma}) \in \Pi(\gamma)$, where $\sigma(i) = \boldsymbol{\sigma}(i)$.*

In particular, this implies that the reachability set of $\mathbb{Z}$-VASS$_R$ is semi-linear, and that reachability in $\mathbb{Z}$-VASS$_R$ is NP-complete.

4 Inclusion for $\mathbb{Z}$-VASS

In this section, we show the following theorem.

Theorem 11. *Inclusion for $\mathbb{Z}$-VAS is NP-hard and in Π_2^P, and coNEXP-complete for $\mathbb{Z}$-VASS and $\mathbb{Z}$-VASS$_R$.*

The upper bounds follow immediately from the literature. For $\mathbb{Z}$-VAS we observe that we are asking for inclusion between linear sets. Huynh [17] shows that inclusion for semi-linear sets is Π_2^P-complete, which yields the desired upper bound. Regarding inclusion for $\mathbb{Z}$-VASS$_R$, from Corollary 10 we have that the reachability set of a $\mathbb{Z}$-VASS$_R$ is Σ_1-PA definable. Let $\mathcal{A}, \mathcal{B}$ be $\mathbb{Z}$-VASS$_R$ in dimension d, $q(\boldsymbol{v}) \in C(\mathcal{A})$, $p(\boldsymbol{w}) \in C(\mathcal{B})$, and let $\phi_{\mathcal{A}, q(\boldsymbol{v})}(\boldsymbol{x})$ and $\phi_{\mathcal{B}, p(\boldsymbol{w})}(\boldsymbol{x})$ be appropriate Σ_1-PA formulas from Corollary 10 with $\boldsymbol{x} = (x_1, \ldots, x_d)$. We have

$$reach(\mathcal{A}, q(\boldsymbol{v})) \subseteq reach(\mathcal{B}, p(\boldsymbol{w})) \Leftrightarrow \neg(\exists \boldsymbol{x}. \phi_{\mathcal{A}, q(\boldsymbol{v})}(\boldsymbol{x}) \wedge \neg(\phi_{\mathcal{B}, p(\boldsymbol{w})}(\boldsymbol{x}))) \text{ is valid.}$$

Bringing the above formula into prenex normal form yields a Π_2-PA sentence for which validity can be decided in coNEXP [12]. For that reason we focus on the lower bounds in the remainder of this section.

For $\mathbb{Z}$-VAS, an NP-lower bound follows straight-forwardly via a reduction from the feasibility problem of a system of linear Diophantine equations $A\boldsymbol{x} = \boldsymbol{b}, \boldsymbol{x} \ge \boldsymbol{0}$. Despite some serious efforts, we could not establish a stronger lower bound. Even though it is known that inclusion for semi-linear sets is Π_2^P-hard [16], this lower bound does not seem to carry over to inclusion for $\mathbb{Z}$-VAS.

---

[3] Here, we allow $\boldsymbol{v}$ and $\boldsymbol{w}$ to be interpreted over $\mathbb{Z}$, which can easily be achieved by representing an integer as the difference of two natural numbers.

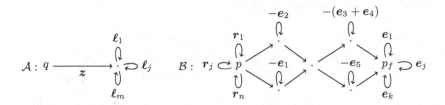

Fig. 1. Illustration of the approach to reduce validity of a Π_2-PA formula $\Phi = \forall \boldsymbol{x}.\exists \boldsymbol{y}.(t_1 \vee t_2) \wedge ((t_3 \wedge t_4) \vee v_5)$ to inclusion for $\mathbb{Z}$-VASS

Lemma 12. *Inclusion for $\mathbb{Z}$-VASS is* coNEXP-*hard even when numbers are encoded in unary.*

Proof. We reduce from validity in Π_2-PA, which is coNEXP-hard already when numbers are encoded in unary [10,12]. To this end, let $\Phi = \forall \boldsymbol{x}.\exists \boldsymbol{y}.\varphi(\boldsymbol{x}, \boldsymbol{y})$ be a formula in this fragment such that $\boldsymbol{x}$ and $\boldsymbol{y}$ are m- and n-tuples of first-order variables, respectively. As discussed in the introduction, with no loss of generality we may assume that $\varphi(\boldsymbol{x}, \boldsymbol{y})$ is a positive Boolean combination of k terms $t_1, \ldots, t_k$ of the form $t_i = \boldsymbol{a}_i \cdot \boldsymbol{x} + z_i \geq \boldsymbol{b}_i \cdot \boldsymbol{y}$ with $\boldsymbol{a}_i \in \mathbb{Z}^m, \boldsymbol{b}_i \in \mathbb{Z}^n$ and $z_i \in \mathbb{Z}$. In our reduction, we show how to construct in logarithmic space $\mathbb{Z}$-VASS $\mathcal{A}, \mathcal{B}$ with designated control states q, p such that Φ is valid iff $reach(\mathcal{A}, q(\boldsymbol{0})) \subseteq reach(\mathcal{B}, p(\boldsymbol{0}))$. Figure 1 illustrates the structure of the $\mathbb{Z}$-VASS $\mathcal{A}$ and $\mathcal{B}$. A key point behind our reduction is that the counters of $\mathcal{A}$ and $\mathcal{B}$ are used to represent evaluations of left-hand and right-hand-sides of the *terms* of $\varphi(\boldsymbol{x}, \boldsymbol{y})$.

In Figure 1, we have that $\boldsymbol{z} \in \mathbb{Z}^k$ is such that $\boldsymbol{z}(i) = z_i$. For $j \in [m]$, $\boldsymbol{\ell}_j \in \mathbb{Z}^k$ is such that $\boldsymbol{\ell}_j(i) = a_i(j)$. Likewise, for $j \in [n]$, $\boldsymbol{r}_j \in \mathbb{Z}^k$ is such that $\boldsymbol{r}_j(i) = b_i(j)$. When moving away from state q, $\mathcal{A}$ adds the absolute term of each t_i to the respective counters. It can then choose any valuation of the $\boldsymbol{x}$ and thus stores the corresponding values of the left-hand sides of each t_i in the counters. Now $\mathcal{B}$ has to match the choice of $\mathcal{A}$. To this end, it can first loop in state p in order to guess a valuation of the $\boldsymbol{y}$ and update the values of the counters accordingly, which now correspond to the right-hand sides of the t_i. Along a path from p to p_f, $\mathcal{B}$ may, if necessary, simulate the Boolean structure of φ: conjunction is simulated by sequential composition and disjunction by branching. For every conjunct of φ, $\mathcal{B}$ can non-deterministically decrement all but one term of every disjunct. Finally, once $\mathcal{B}$ reaches p_f, it may non-deterministically increase the value corresponding to the right-hand sides of every term in order to precisely match any value reached by $\mathcal{A}$. From this example, it is now clear how to construct $\mathcal{A}$ and $\mathcal{B}$ from Φ in general in logarithmic space such that Φ is valid if, and only if, $\mathcal{B}$ has a run beginning in $p(\boldsymbol{0})$ that matches the counter values reached by any run of $\mathcal{A}$ beginning in $q(\boldsymbol{0})$. Obviously, the the converse direction holds as well. □

5   Concluding Remarks

We studied reachability, coverability and inclusion problems for various classes of $\mathbb{Z}$-VASS, *i.e.*, VASS whose counter values range over $\mathbb{Z}$. Unsurprisingly, the complexity of those decision problems is lower for $\mathbb{Z}$-VASS when compared to VASS. However, the extend to which the complexity drops reveals an element of surprise: coverability and reachability for VASS in the presence of resets are $\mathbf{F}_\omega$-complete and undecidable, respectively, but both problems are only NP-complete for $\mathbb{Z}$-VASS$_R$. For the upper bound, we provided a generalization of Parikh images which we believe is a technical construction of independent interest.

Throughout this paper, the dimension of the $\mathbb{Z}$-VASS has been part of the input. A natural line of future research could be to investigate the complexity of the problems we considered in fixed dimensions.

Acknowledgments. We would like to thank the anonymous referees, Sylvain Schmitz and Philippe Schnoebelen for their helpful comments and suggestions on an earlier version of this paper.

References

1. Bell, P., Potapov, I.: On undecidability bounds for matrix decision problems. Theor. Comput. Sci. 391(1-2), 3–13 (2008)
2. Borosh, I., Treybing, L.B.: Bounds on positive integral solutions of linear Diophantine equations. Proc. AMS 55, 299–304 (1976)
3. Buckheister, P., Zetzsche, G.: Semilinearity and context-freeness of languages accepted by valence automata. In: Chatterjee, K., Sgall, J. (eds.) MFCS 2013. LNCS, vol. 8087, pp. 231–242. Springer, Heidelberg (2013)
4. Dufourd, C., Finkel, A., Schnoebelen, P.: Reset nets between decidability and undecidability. In: Larsen, K.G., Skyum, S., Winskel, G. (eds.) ICALP 1998. LNCS, vol. 1443, pp. 103–115. Springer, Heidelberg (1998)
5. Esparza, J.: Petri nets, commutative context-free grammars, and basic parallel processes. Fundam. Inform. 31(1), 13–25 (1997)
6. Finkel, A., Göller, S., Haase, C.: Reachability in register machines with polynomial updates. In: Chatterjee, K., Sgall, J. (eds.) MFCS 2013. LNCS, vol. 8087, pp. 409–420. Springer, Heidelberg (2013)
7. Fraca, E., Haddad, S.: Complexity analysis of continuous petri nets. In: Colom, J.-M., Desel, J. (eds.) PETRI NETS 2013. LNCS, vol. 7927, pp. 170–189. Springer, Heidelberg (2013)
8. Garey, M.R., Johnson, D.S.: Computers and Intractability: A Guide to the Theory of NP-Completeness. W. H. Freeman & Co., New York (1979)
9. Ginsburg, S., Spanier, E.H.: Semigroups, Presburger formulas and languages. Pac. J. Math. 16(2), 285–296 (1966)
10. Grädel, E.: Dominoes and the complexity of subclasses of logical theories. Ann. Pure Appl. Logic 43(1), 1–30 (1989)
11. Greibach, S.A.: Remarks on blind and partially blind one-way multicounter machines. Theor. Comput. Sci. 7(3), 311–324 (1978)
12. Haase, C.: Subclasses of Presburger arithmetic and the weak EXP hierarchy. In: Proc. CSL-LICS (to appear, 2014)
13. Haase, C., Kreutzer, S., Ouaknine, J., Worrell, J.: Reachability in succinct and parametric one-counter automata. In: Bravetti, M., Zavattaro, G. (eds.) CONCUR 2009. LNCS, vol. 5710, pp. 369–383. Springer, Heidelberg (2009)

14. Hack, M.: The equality problem for vector addition systems is undecidable. Theor. Comput. Sci. 2(1), 77–95 (1976)
15. Hague, M., Lin, A.W.: Model checking recursive programs with numeric data types. In: Gopalakrishnan, G., Qadeer, S. (eds.) CAV 2011. LNCS, vol. 6806, pp. 743–759. Springer, Heidelberg (2011)
16. Huynh, D.T.: The complexity of equivalence problems for commutative grammars. Inform. Control 66(1-2), 103–121 (1985)
17. Huynh, D.T.: A simple proof for the Σ_2^p upper bound of the inequivalence problem for semilinear sets. Elektron. Inform. Kybernet. 22(4), 147–156 (1986)
18. Jančar, P.: Nonprimitive recursive complexity and undecidability for Petri net equivalences. Theor. Comput. Sci. 256(1-2), 23–30 (2001)
19. Kopczyński, E., To, A.W.: Parikh images of grammars: Complexity and applications. In: Proc. LICS, pp. 80–89 (2010)
20. Lipton, R.: The reachability problem is exponential-space-hard. Technical report, Yale University, New Haven, CT (1976)
21. Mayr, E.W.: An algorithm for the general Petri net reachability problem. In: Proc. STOC, pp. 238–246. ACM, New York (1981)
22. Plandowski, W., Rytter, W.: Complexity of language recognition problems for compressed words. In: Karhumäki, J., Maurer, H.A., Păun, G., Rozenberg, G. (eds.) Jewels are Forever, pp. 262–272 (1999)
23. Rackoff, C.: The covering and boundedness problems for vector addition systems. Theor. Comput. Sci. 6(2), 223–231 (1978)
24. Reichert, J.: On the complexity of counter reachability games. In: Abdulla, P.A., Potapov, I. (eds.) RP 2013. LNCS, vol. 8169, pp. 196–208. Springer, Heidelberg (2013)
25. Schnoebelen, P.: Revisiting ackermann-hardness for lossy counter machines and reset petri nets. In: Hliněný, P., Kučera, A. (eds.) MFCS 2010. LNCS, vol. 6281, pp. 616–628. Springer, Heidelberg (2010)
26. Seidl, H., Schwentick, T., Muscholl, A., Habermehl, P.: Counting in trees for free. In: Díaz, J., Karhumäki, J., Lepistö, A., Sannella, D. (eds.) ICALP 2004. LNCS, vol. 3142, pp. 1136–1149. Springer, Heidelberg (2004)

Reachability in MDPs:
Refining Convergence of Value Iteration*

Serge Haddad[1] and Benjamin Monmege[2]

[1] LSV, ENS Cachan, CNRS & Inria, France
serge.haddad@lsv.ens-cachan.fr
[2] Université libre de Bruxelles, Belgium
benjamin.monmege@ulb.ac.be

Abstract. Markov Decision Processes (MDP) are a widely used model including both non-deterministic and probabilistic choices. Minimal and maximal probabilities to reach a target set of states, with respect to a policy resolving non-determinism, may be computed by several methods including value iteration. This algorithm, easy to implement and efficient in terms of space complexity, consists in iteratively finding the probabilities of paths of increasing length. However, it raises three issues: (1) defining a stopping criterion ensuring a bound on the approximation, (2) analyzing the rate of convergence, and (3) specifying an additional procedure to obtain the exact values once a sufficient number of iterations has been performed. The first two issues are still open and for the third one a "crude" upper bound on the number of iterations has been proposed. Based on a graph analysis and transformation of MDPs, we address these problems. First we introduce an *interval iteration algorithm*, for which the stopping criterion is straightforward. Then we exhibit convergence rate. Finally we significantly improve the bound on the number of iterations required to get the exact values.

1 Introduction

Markov Decision Processes (MDP) are a commonly used formalism for modelling systems that use both probabilistic and non-deterministic behaviors. These are generalizations of discrete-time Markov chains for which non-determinism is forbidden. MDPs have acquired an even greater gain of interest since the development of quantitative verification of systems, which in particular may take into account probabilistic aspects (see [1] for a deep study of model checking techniques, in particular for probabilistic systems). Automated verification techniques have been extensively studied to handle such probabilistic models, leading to various tools like the PRISM probabilistic model checker [9].

Value Iteration for Reachability Problems. In the tutorial paper [5], the authors cover some of the algorithms for the model-checking of MDPs and Markov

---

* The research leading to these results has received funding from the European Union Seventh Framework Programme (FP7/2007-2013) under Grant Agreement n601148 (CASSTING).

J. Ouaknine, I. Potapov, and J. Worrell (Eds.): RP 2014, LNCS 8762, pp. 125–137, 2014.
© Springer International Publishing Switzerland 2014

chains. The first simple, yet intriguing, problem lies in the computation of minimum and maximum probabilities to reach a target set of states of an MDP. Exact polynomial time methods, like linear programming, exist to compute those probabilities, but they seem unable to scale on large systems. Nonetheless, they are based on the fact that these probabilities are indeed fixpoints of some operators. Usually, numerical approximate methods are rather used in practice, the most used one being *value iteration*. The algorithm consists in asymptotically reaching the previous fixpoints by iterating the operators. However, it raises three issues. Since the algorithm must terminates after a finite number of iterations one has to define a stopping criterion ensuring a bound on the difference between the computed and the exact values. From a theoretical point of view, establishing the rate of convergence with respect to the parameters of the MDP (number of states, smallest positive transition probability, etc.) helps to estimate the complexity of value iteration. Sometimes for further application the exact values and/or the optimal policy are required. This is generally done by performing an additional rounding procedure once a sufficient number of iterations has been performed. The first two issues are still open and for the third one a "crude" upper bound on the number of iterations has been proposed [3, Sec 3.5].

Our Contributions. Generally the numerical computations of optimal reachability probabilities are preceded by a qualitative analysis that computes the sets of states for which this probability is 0 or 1 and performs an appropriate transformation of the MDP. We adopt here an alternative approach based on the maximal end component (MEC) decomposition of an MDP (that can be computed in polynomial time [4]). We show that for an MDP featuring a particular MEC decomposition, some safety probability is null with an additional convergence rate with respect to the length of the run. Then we design a min- (respectively, max-) reduction that ensures this feature while preserving the minimal (respectively, maximal) reachability probabilities. In both cases, we establish that the reachability probabilities are unique fixed points of some operator.

So we iterate these operators starting from the maximal and the minimal possible vectors. These iterations naturally yield an *interval iteration algorithm* for which the stopping criterion is straightforward since, at any step, the two current vectors constitute a framing of the reachability probabilities. Similar computations of parallel under- and over-approximations have been used in [7], in order to detect steady-state on-the-fly during the transient analysis of continuous-time Markov chains. In [8], under- and over-approximations of reachability probabilities in MDPs are obtained by substituting to the MDP a stochastic game. Combining it with a CEGAR-based procedure leads to an iterative procedure with approximations converging to the exact values. However the speed of convergence is only studied from an experimental point of view. Afterwards, we provide probabilistic interpretations for the adjacent sequences of the interval iteration algorithm. Combining such an interpretation with the safety convergence rate of the reduced MDP allows us to exhibit a convergence rate for interval iteration algorithm. At last, exploiting this convergence rate, we significantly improve the bound on the number of iterations required to get the exact values by a rounding procedure.

Related Work. Interestingly, our approach has been realized in parallel of Brázdil et al [2] that solves a different problem with similar ideas. There, authors use some machine learning algorithm, namely real-time dynamic programming, in order to avoid to apply the full operator at each step of the value iteration, but rather to partially apply it based on some statistical test. Using the same idea of lower and upper approximations, they prove that their algorithm *almost surely* converges towards the optimal probability, in case of MDPs without non-trivial end components. In the presence of non-trivial end components, rather than computing in advance a simplified equivalent MDP as we do, they rather compute the simplification on-the-fly. It allows them to also obtain results in the case where the MDP is not explicitly given. However, no analysis of the speed of convergence of their algorithm is provided, nor are given explicit stopping criteria enabling an exact computation of values.

Outline. Section 2 introduces MDPs and the reachability/safety problems. It also includes MEC decomposition, dedicated MDP transformations and characterization of minimal and maximal reachability probabilities as unique fixed points of operators. Section 3 presents our main contributions: the interval iteration algorithm, the analysis of the convergence rate and a better bound for the number of iterations required for obtaining the exact values by rounding. Due to space constraints, a complete version, with full proofs, can be found in [6].

2   Reachability Problems for Markov Decision Processes

2.1   Problem Specification

We mainly follow the notations of [5]. We denote by $Dist(S)$ the set of *distributions* over a finite set S, i.e., every mapping $p\colon S \to [0,1]$ from S to the set $[0,1]$ such that $\sum_{s \in S} p(s) = 1$. The support of a distribution p, denoted by $\mathrm{Supp}(p)$, is the subset of S defined by $\mathrm{Supp}(p) = \{s \in S \mid p(s) > 0\}$.

A *Markov Decision Process* (MDP) is a tuple $\mathcal{M} = (S, \alpha_{\mathcal{M}}, \delta_{\mathcal{M}})$ where S is a finite set of states; $\alpha_{\mathcal{M}} = \bigcup_{s \in S} A(s)$ where every $A(s)$ is a non empty finite set of actions with $A(s) \cap A(s') = \emptyset$ for all $s \neq s'$; and $\delta_{\mathcal{M}}\colon S \times \alpha_{\mathcal{M}} \to Dist(S)$ is a partial probabilistic transition function defined for (s,a) if and only if $a \in A(s)$.

The dynamic of the system is defined as follows. Given a current state s, an action $a \in A(s)$ is chosen non deterministically. The next state is then randomly selected, using the corresponding distribution $\delta_{\mathcal{M}}(s, a)$, i.e., the probability that a transition to s' occurs equals $\delta_{\mathcal{M}}(s, a)(s')$. In a more suggestive way, one denotes $\delta_{\mathcal{M}}(s, a)(s')$ by $\delta_{\mathcal{M}}(s'|s, a)$ and $\sum_{s' \in S'} \delta_{\mathcal{M}}(s'|s, a)$ by $\delta_{\mathcal{M}}(S'|s, a)$.

More formally, an *infinite path* through an MDP is a sequence $\pi = s_0 \xrightarrow{a_0} s_1 \xrightarrow{a_1} \cdots$ where $s_i \in S$, $a_i \in A(s_i)$ and $\delta_{\mathcal{M}}(s_{i+1}|s_i, a_i) > 0$ for all $i \in \mathbb{N}$: in the following, state s_i is denoted by $\pi(i)$. For every $i \in \mathbb{N}$, $\pi_{\uparrow i}$ denotes the suffix of π starting in s_i, i.e., $\pi_{\uparrow i} = s_i \xrightarrow{a_i} s_{i+1} \cdots$. A *finite path* $\rho = s_0 \xrightarrow{a_0} s_1 \xrightarrow{a_1} \cdots \xrightarrow{a_{n-1}} s_n$ is a prefix of an infinite path ending in a state s_n, denoted by $\mathrm{last}(\rho)$. We denote by $\mathsf{Path}_{\mathcal{M},s}$ (respectively, $\mathsf{FPath}_{\mathcal{M},s}$) the set of infinite paths (respectively, finite paths) starting in state s, whereas $\mathsf{Path}_{\mathcal{M}}$ (respectively, $\mathsf{FPath}_{\mathcal{M}}$) denotes the set of all infinite paths (respectively, finite paths).

To associate a probability space with an MDP, we need to eliminate the non-determinism of the behaviour. This is done by introducing policies (also called schedulers or strategies). A *policy* of an MDP $\mathcal{M} = (S, \alpha_{\mathcal{M}}, \delta_{\mathcal{M}})$ is a function $\sigma \colon \mathsf{FPath}_{\mathcal{M}} \to Dist(\alpha_{\mathcal{M}})$ such that $\sigma(\rho)(a) > 0$ only if $a \in A(\mathrm{last}(\rho))$. One denotes $\sigma(\rho)(a)$ by $\sigma(a|\rho)$. We denote by $Pol_{\mathcal{M}}$ the set of all policies of $\mathcal{M}$. A policy σ is *deterministic* when $\sigma(\rho)$ is a Dirac distribution for every $\rho \in \mathsf{FPath}_{\mathcal{M}}$ (in that case, $\sigma(\rho)$ denotes the action $a \in A(\mathrm{last}(\rho))$ associated to probability one); it is *stationary* (also called memoryless) if $\sigma(\rho)$ only depends on $\mathrm{last}(\rho)$.

A policy σ and an initial state $s \in S$ yields a discrete-time Markov chain $\mathcal{M}_s^\sigma$ (see [5, Definition 10]), whose states are the finite paths of $\mathsf{FPath}_{\mathcal{M},s}$. The probability measure $Pr_{\mathcal{M}^\sigma,s}$ over paths of the Markov chain starting in s (with basic cylinders being generated by finite paths) defines a probability measure $Pr_{\mathcal{M},s}^\sigma$ over $\mathsf{Path}_{\mathcal{M},s}$, capturing the behavior of $\mathcal{M}$ from state s under policy σ. Let $\rho_n = s_0 \xrightarrow{a_0} s_1 \xrightarrow{a_1} \cdots \xrightarrow{a_{n-1}} s_n$ and $\rho_{n+1} = s_0 \xrightarrow{a_0} s_1 \xrightarrow{a_1} \cdots s_n \xrightarrow{a_n} s_{n+1}$, the probability measure is inductively defined by

$$Pr_{\mathcal{M},s_0}^\sigma(\rho_{n+1}) = Pr_{\mathcal{M},s_0}^\sigma(\rho_n) \sum_{a \in A(s_n)} \sigma(a|\rho_n)\, \delta_{\mathcal{M}}(s_{n+1}|s_n, a)\,.$$

One specifies properties on infinite paths as follows. Given a subset $S' \subseteq S$ of states and $\pi = s_0 \xrightarrow{a_0} s_1 \xrightarrow{a_1} \cdots \in \mathsf{Path}_{\mathcal{M}}$, $\pi \models S'$ iff $s_0 \in S'$. The atomic proposition $\{s\}$ is more concisely denoted by s. One also uses Boolean operators $\neg$, $\wedge$ and $\vee$ for building formulas. We finally use temporal operators F (for *Finally*) and G (for *Globally*). For a property φ, we let $\pi \models \mathsf{F}\,\varphi$ if there exists $i \in \mathbb{N}$ such that the suffix $\pi_{\uparrow i}$ of π verifies $\pi_{\uparrow i} \models \varphi$. The dual operator G is defined by $\mathsf{G}\,\varphi \equiv \neg\,\mathsf{F}\,\neg\varphi$. One also considers restricted scopes of these operators: $\pi \models \mathsf{F}^{\leq n}\,\varphi$ if there exists $0 \leq i \leq n$ such that $\pi_{\uparrow i} \models \varphi$, and $\mathsf{G}^{\leq n}\,\varphi \equiv \neg\,\mathsf{F}^{\leq n}\,\neg\varphi$. Given a property φ on infinite paths one denotes $Pr_{\mathcal{M},s}^\sigma(\{\pi \in \mathsf{Path}_{\mathcal{M},s} \mid \pi \models \varphi\})$ more concisely by $Pr_{\mathcal{M},s}^\sigma(\varphi)$.

Given a subset of target states T, *reachability* properties are specified by $\mathsf{F}\,T$ and *safety* properties by $\mathsf{G}\,\neg T$. Our main goal is to compute the infimum and supremum reachability and safety probabilities, with respect to the policies, i.e., for $\varphi \in \{\mathsf{F}\,T, \mathsf{G}\,\neg T\}$: $Pr_{\mathcal{M},s}^{\min}(\varphi) = \inf_{\sigma \in Pol_{\mathcal{M}}} Pr_{\mathcal{M},s}^\sigma(\varphi)$ and $Pr_{\mathcal{M},s}^{\max}(\varphi) = \sup_{\sigma \in Pol_{\mathcal{M}}} Pr_{\mathcal{M},s}^\sigma(\varphi)$. Since $Pr_{\mathcal{M},s}^\sigma(\mathsf{G}\,\neg T) = 1 - Pr_{\mathcal{M},s}^\sigma(\mathsf{F}\,T)$, one immediately gets: $Pr_{\mathcal{M},s}^{\max}(\mathsf{G}\,\neg T) = 1 - Pr_{\mathcal{M},s}^{\min}(\mathsf{F}\,T)$, and $Pr_{\mathcal{M},s}^{\min}(\mathsf{G}\,\neg T) = 1 - Pr_{\mathcal{M},s}^{\max}(\mathsf{F}\,T)$.

Thus we focus on reachability problems and without loss of generality, all the states of T may be merged in a single state called s_+ with $A(s_+) = \{loop_+\}$ such that $\delta_{\mathcal{M}}(s_+|s_+, loop_+) = 1$. In the sequel, the vector $(Pr_{\mathcal{M},s}^\sigma(\varphi))_{s \in S}$ (respectively, $(Pr_{\mathcal{M},s}^{\min}(\varphi))_{s \in S}$ and $(Pr_{\mathcal{M},s}^{\max}(\varphi))_{s \in S}$) of probabilities will be denoted by $Pr_{\mathcal{M}}^\sigma(\varphi)$ (respectively, $Pr_{\mathcal{M}}^{\min}(\varphi)$ and $Pr_{\mathcal{M}}^{\max}(\varphi)$).

2.2 MEC Decomposition and Transient Behaviour

In our approach, we first reduce an MDP by a qualitative analysis based on *end components*. We adopt here a slightly different definition of the usual one by allowing trivial end components (see later on). Preliminarily, the *graph* of an MDP $\mathcal{M}$ is defined as follows: the set of its vertices is S and there is an edge from s to s' if there is some $a \in A(s)$ with $\delta_{\mathcal{M}}(s'|s, a) > 0$.

Definition 1 (end component). *Let* $\mathcal{M} = (S, \alpha_{\mathcal{M}}, \delta_{\mathcal{M}})$. *Then* (S', α') *with* $\emptyset \neq S' \subseteq S$ *and* $\alpha' \subseteq \bigcup_{s \in S'} A(s)$ *is an* end component *if (i) for all* $s \in S'$ *and* $a \in A(s) \cap \alpha'$, $\mathrm{Supp}(\delta_{\mathcal{M}}(s, a)) \subseteq S'$; *(ii) the graph of* (S', α') *is strongly connected.*

Given two end components, one says that (S', α') is smaller than (S'', α''), denoted by $(S', \alpha') \preceq (S'', \alpha'')$, if $S' \subseteq S''$ and $\alpha' \subseteq \alpha''$. Given some state s, there is a minimal end component containing s namely $(\{s\}, \emptyset)$. Such end components are called *trivial* end components. The union of two end components that share a state is also an end component. Hence, *maximal* end components (MEC) do not share states and cover all states of S. Furthermore, we consider *bottom* MEC (BMEC): a MEC (S', α') is a BMEC if $\alpha' = \bigcup_{s \in S'} A(s)$. For instance $(\{s_+\}, \{loop_+\})$ is a BMEC. Every MDP contains at least one BMEC.

Fig. 1-(a) shows the decomposition in MEC of an MDP. There are two BMECs $(\{s_+\}, \{loop_+\})$ and $(\{b, b'\}, \{d, e\})$, one trivial MEC $(\{t\}, \emptyset)$ and another MEC $(\{s, s'\}, \{a, c\})$.

The set of MECs of an MDP can be computed in polynomial time (see for instance [4]). It defines a partition of $S = \biguplus_{i=k}^{K} S_k \uplus \biguplus_{\ell=1}^{L} \{t_\ell\} \uplus \biguplus_{m=0}^{M} B_m$ where $\{t_\ell\}$ is the set of states of a trivial MEC, B_m is the set of states a BMEC and S_k's are the set of states of the other MECs. By convention, $B_0 = \{s_+\}$. The next proposition is the key ingredient of our approach.

Proposition 2. *Let* $\mathcal{M}$ *be an MDP such that its MEC decomposition only contains trivial MECs and BMECs, i.e.,* $S = \biguplus_{\ell=1}^{L} \{t_\ell\} \uplus \biguplus_{m=0}^{M} B_m$. *Then:*

1. *There is a partition* $S = \biguplus_{0 \leqslant i \leqslant I} G_i$ *such that* $G_0 = \biguplus_{m=0}^{M} B_m$ *and for all* $1 \leqslant i \leqslant I$, $s \in G_i$ *and* $a \in A(s)$, *there is* $s' \in \bigcup_{j < i} G_j$ *such that* $\delta_{\mathcal{M}}(s'|s, a) > 0$.
2. *Let* η *be the smallest positive probability occurring in the distributions of* $\mathcal{M}$. *Then for all* $n \in \mathbb{N}$, *and for all* $s \in S$, $Pr_{\mathcal{M}, s}^{\max}(\mathsf{G}^{\leqslant nI} \neg G_0) \leqslant (1 - \eta^I)^n$.
3. *For all* $s \in S$, $Pr_{\mathcal{M}, s}^{\max}(\mathsf{G} \neg G_0) = 0$.

Proof. (Sketch) 1. One builds the partition of S by induction. We first let $G_0 = \biguplus_{m=0}^{M} B_m$. Then, assuming that $G_0, \ldots, G_i$ have been defined, we let $G_{i+1} = \{s \in S \setminus \bigcup_{j \leqslant i} G_j \mid \forall a \in A(s) \ \exists s' \in \bigcup_{j < i} G_j \ \delta_{\mathcal{M}}(s'|s, a) > 0\}$. The construction stops when some G_i is empty. If G_I is the last non-empty set, it can easily be checked that $S = \bigcup_{i \leqslant I} G_i$.

2. One observes that the path property $\mathsf{G}^{\leqslant n} \neg G_0$ only depends on the prefix of length n. So there is only a finite number of policies up to n and we denote σ_n the policy that achieves $Pr_{\mathcal{M}, s}^{\max}(\mathsf{G}^{\leqslant n} \neg G_0)$. Observe also that after a path of length $k < n$ leading to state $s \notin G_0$, policy σ_n may behave as policy σ_{n-k} starting in s. The property may then be shown by using the fact that for all

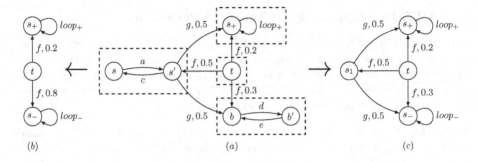

Fig. 1. (a) An MDP and its MEC decomposition, (b) its min-reduction, and (c) its max-reduction

state s and policy σ, there is a path of length at most I in $\mathcal{M}^\sigma$ from s to ρ with last(ρ) $\in G_0$, showing that $Pr^\sigma_{\mathcal{M},s}(G^{\leq I} \neg G_0) \leq (1 - \eta^I)$.

3. The last assertion is a straightforward consequence of the previous one.   □

This proposition shows the interest of eliminating MECs that are neither trivial ones nor BMECs. In the following, we consider the partition $S = \biguplus_{i=k}^K S_k \uplus \biguplus_{\ell=1}^L \{t_\ell\} \uplus \biguplus_{m=0}^M B_m$ where $\{t_\ell\}$'s are trivial MECs, B_m's are BMECs and S_k's are all the other MECs. A quotienting of an MDP has been introduced in [4, Algorithm 3.3] in order to decrease the complexity of the computation for reachability properties. We now introduce two variants of reductions for MDPs depending on the kind of probabilities we want to compute.

2.3   Characterization of Minimal Reachability Probabilities

The reduction in the case of minimal reachability probabilities consists in merging all non-trivial MECs different from ($\{s_+\}$, $\{loop_+\}$) into a fresh state s_-: all these states merged into s_- will have a zero minimal reachability probability.

Definition 3 (min-reduction). *Let $\mathcal{M}$ be an MDP with the partition of $S = \biguplus_{i=k}^K S_k \uplus \biguplus_{\ell=1}^L \{t_\ell\} \uplus \biguplus_{m=0}^M B_m$. We define $\mathcal{M}^\bullet = (S^\bullet, \alpha_{\mathcal{M}^\bullet}, \delta_{\mathcal{M}^\bullet})$ by:*
- *$S^\bullet = \{s_-, s_+, t_1, \ldots, t_L\}$, and for all $s \in S$, $s^\bullet$ is defined by: (1) $s^\bullet = t_l$ if $s = t_\ell$, (2) $s^\bullet = s_+$ if $s = s_+$, and (3) $s^\bullet = s_-$ otherwise.*
- *$A^\bullet(s_-) = \{loop_-\}$, $A^\bullet(s_+) = \{loop_+\}$ and for all $1 \leq \ell \leq L$, $A^\bullet(t_\ell) = A(t_\ell)$.*
- *For all $1 \leq \ell, \ell' \leq L$, $a \in A^\bullet(t_\ell)$,*

$$\delta_{\mathcal{M}^\bullet}(s_- | t_\ell, a) = \delta_{\mathcal{M}}(\textstyle\biguplus_{i=k}^K S_k \uplus \biguplus_{m=1}^M B_m | t_\ell, a),$$
$$\delta_{\mathcal{M}^\bullet}(s_+ | t_\ell, a) = \delta_{\mathcal{M}}(s_+ | t_\ell, a), \qquad \delta_{\mathcal{M}^\bullet}(t_{\ell'} | t_\ell, a) = \delta_{\mathcal{M}}(t_{\ell'} | t_\ell, a),$$
$$\delta_{\mathcal{M}^\bullet}(s_+ | s_+, loop_+) = \delta_{\mathcal{M}}(s_- | s_-, loop_-) = 1.$$

An MDP $\mathcal{M}$ is called *min-reduced* if $\mathcal{M} = \mathcal{N}^\bullet$ for some MDP $\mathcal{N}$. The min-reduction of an MDP is illustrated in Fig. 1-(b). The single trivial MEC ($\{t\}, \emptyset$) is preserved while MECs ($\{b, b'\}, \{d, e\}$) and ($\{s, s'\}, \{a, c\}$) are merged in s_-.

Proposition 4. *Let $\mathcal{M}$ be an MDP and $\mathcal{M}^\bullet$ be its min-reduced MDP. Then for all $s \in S$, $Pr^{\min}_{\mathcal{M},s}(\mathsf{F}\, s_+) = Pr^{\min}_{\mathcal{M}^\bullet,s^\bullet}(\mathsf{F}\, s_+)$.*

We now establish another property of the min-reduced MDP that allows us to use Proposition 2.

Lemma 5. *Let $\mathcal{M}^\bullet$ be the min-reduced MDP of an MDP $\mathcal{M}$. Then every state $s \in S^\bullet \setminus \{s_-, s_+\}$ is a trivial MEC.*

In order to characterize $Pr^\sigma_{\mathcal{M}}(\mathsf{F}\, s_+)$ with a fixpoint equation, we define the set of S-vectors as $\mathcal{V} = \{x = (x_s)_{s \in S} \mid \forall s \in S \setminus \{s_-, s_+\}\ 0 \leqslant x_s \leqslant 1 \wedge x_{s_+} = 1 \wedge x_{s_-} = 0\}$. We also introduce the operator $f_{\min}: \mathcal{V} \to \mathcal{V}$ by letting for all $x \in \mathcal{V}$: $f_{\min}(x)_s = \min_{a \in A(s)} \sum_{s' \in S} \delta_{\mathcal{M}}(s'|s,a)x_{s'}$ for every $s \in S \setminus \{s_-, s_+\}$, $f_{\min}(x)_{s_-} = 0$ and $f_{\min}(x)_{s_+} = 1$.

We claim that there is a single fixed point of $f_{\min}$. In order to establish that claim, given a stationary deterministic strategy σ, we introduce the operator $f_\sigma: \mathcal{V} \to \mathcal{V}$ defined for all $x \in \mathcal{V}$ by: $f_\sigma(x)_s = \sum_{s' \in S} \delta_{\mathcal{M}}(s'|s,\sigma(s))x_{s'}$ for every $s \in S \setminus \{s_-, s_+\}$, $f_\sigma(x)_{s_-} = 0$ and $f_\sigma(x)_{s_+} = 1$.

Proposition 6. *Let $\mathcal{M}$ be a min-reduced MDP. $Pr^\sigma_{\mathcal{M}}(\mathsf{F}\, s_+)$ is the unique fixed point of f_σ. $Pr^{\min}_{\mathcal{M}}(\mathsf{F}\, s_+)$ is the unique fixed point of $f_{\min}$ and it is obtained by a stationary deterministic policy.*

2.4 Characterization of Maximal Reachability Probabilities

The reduction for maximal reachability probabilities is more complex. Indeed, we cannot merge any non-trivial MEC different from $(\{s_+\}, \{loop_+\})$ into the state s_- anymore, since some of these states may have a non-zero maximal reachability probability. Hence, we consider a fresh state s_k for each MEC S_k and simply merge all BMECs B_m's different from $(\{s_+\}, \{loop_+\})$ into state s_-.

Definition 7 (max-reduction). *Let $\mathcal{M}$ be a MDP with the partition of $S = \biguplus_{i=k}^K S_k \uplus \biguplus_{\ell=1}^L \{t_\ell\} \uplus \biguplus_{m=0}^M B_m$. Then the max-reduced $\mathcal{M}^\bullet = (S^\bullet, \alpha_{\mathcal{M}^\bullet}, \delta_{\mathcal{M}^\bullet})$ is defined by:*

- *$S^\bullet = \{s_-, s_+, t_1, \ldots, t_L, s_1, \ldots, s_K\}$. For all $s \in S$, one defines $s^\bullet$ by: (1) $s^\bullet = t_l$ if $s = t_l$, (2) $s^\bullet = s_+$ if $s = s_+$, (3) $s^\bullet = s_k$ if $s \in S_K$, and (4) $s^\bullet = s_-$ otherwise.*
- *$A^\bullet(s_-) = \{loop_-\}$, $A^\bullet(s_+) = \{loop_+\}$ for all $1 \leqslant \ell \leqslant L$, $A^\bullet(t_\ell) = A(t_\ell)$, and for all $1 \leqslant k \leqslant K$, $A^\bullet(s_k) = \{a \mid \exists s \in S_k\ a \in A(s) \wedge \mathrm{Supp}(\delta_{\mathcal{M}}(s,a)) \not\subseteq S_k\}$.*
- *For all $1 \leqslant \ell, \ell' \leqslant L$, $a \in A^\bullet(t_\ell)$, $1 \leqslant k, k' \leqslant K$, $b \in A^\bullet(s_k) \cap A_s$ with $s \in S_k$,*

$$\delta_{\mathcal{M}^\bullet}(s_-|t_\ell,a) = \delta_{\mathcal{M}}(\biguplus_{m=1}^M B_m|t_\ell,a), \quad \delta_{\mathcal{M}^\bullet}(s_+|t_\ell,a) = \delta_{\mathcal{M}}(s_+|t_\ell,a),$$
$$\delta_{\mathcal{M}^\bullet}(t_{\ell'}|t_\ell,a) = \delta_{\mathcal{M}}(t_{\ell'}|t_\ell,a), \quad \delta_{\mathcal{M}^\bullet}(s_k|t_\ell,a) = \delta_{\mathcal{M}}(S_k|t_\ell,a),$$
$$\delta_{\mathcal{M}^\bullet}(s_-|s_k,b) = \delta_{\mathcal{M}}(\biguplus_{m=1}^M B_m|s,b), \quad \delta_{\mathcal{M}^\bullet}(s_+|s_k,b) = \delta_{\mathcal{M}}(s_+|s,b),$$
$$\delta_{\mathcal{M}^\bullet}(t_\ell|s_k,b) = \delta_{\mathcal{M}}(t_\ell|s,b), \quad \delta_{\mathcal{M}^\bullet}(s_{k'}|s_k,b) = \delta_{\mathcal{M}}(S_{k'}|s,b),$$
$$\delta_{\mathcal{M}^\bullet}(s_+|s_+,loop_+) = \delta_{\mathcal{M}}(s_-|s_-,loop_-) = 1.$$

Observe that $\mathcal{M}^\bullet$ is indeed an MDP since $A^\bullet(s_k)$ cannot be empty (otherwise S_k would be BMEC). Fig. 1-(c) illustrates the max-reduction of an MDP. The single trivial MEC $(\{t\}, \emptyset)$ is preserved while MEC $(\{b, b'\}, \{d, e\})$ is merged in s_-. The MEC $(\{s, s'\}, \{a, c\})$ is now merged into s_1 with only action g preserved.

The following propositions are similar to Proposition 4 and Lemma 5 for the min-reductions.

Proposition 8 ([4, Thm. 3.8]). *Let $\mathcal{M}$ be an MDP and $\mathcal{M}^\bullet$ be its max-reduced MDP. Then for all $s \in S$, $Pr_{\mathcal{M},s}^{\max}(\mathsf{F}\, s_+) = Pr_{\mathcal{M}^\bullet, s^\bullet}^{\max}(\mathsf{F}\, s_+)$.*

Lemma 9. *Let $\mathcal{M}^\bullet$ be the max-reduced MDP of an MDP $\mathcal{M}$. Then every state $s \in S^\bullet \setminus \{s_-, s_+\}$ is a trivial MEC.*

As for minimal reachability probabilities, we introduce operator $f_{\max}\colon \mathcal{V} \to \mathcal{V}$ by letting for all $x \in \mathcal{V}$: $f_{\max}(x)_s = \max_{a \in A(s)} \sum_{s' \in S} \delta_{\mathcal{M}}(s, a)(s') x_{s'}$ for all $s \in S \setminus \{s_-, s_+\}$, $f_{\max}(x)_{s_-} = 0$ and $f_{\max}(x)_{s_+} = 1$.

We observe that Lemma 9 combined with Proposition 2 ensures that in a max-reduced MDP $\mathcal{M}$, for any policy σ, $S \setminus \{s_-, s_+\}$ is a set of transient states of $\mathcal{M}^\sigma$. This helps to prove that Proposition 6 also holds for max-reduced MDPs:

Proposition 10. *Let $\mathcal{M}$ be a max-reduced MDP. $Pr_{\mathcal{M}}^\sigma(\mathsf{F}\, s_+)$ is the unique fixed point of f_σ. $Pr_{\mathcal{M}}^{\max}(\mathsf{F}\, s_+)$ is the unique fixed point of $f_{\max}$ and it is obtained by a stationary deterministic policy.*

Discussion. Usually, algorithms that compute maximal and minimal reachability probabilities first determine the set of states for which those probabilities are 0 or 1, and merge them in states s_- and s_+ respectively (see for instance [5, Algorithms 1–4]). For the case of minimal reachability probabilities, the MDP obtained after this transformation—which is a quotient of our $\mathcal{M}^\bullet$—fulfills the hypotheses of Proposition 2 and our further development is still valid.

Unfortunately, it does not hold in the maximal case: for the MDP on the left of Fig. 1-(a), the obtained MDP, that we call $\mathcal{M}'$, simply merges $\{b, b'\}$ into s_-, without merging $\{s, s'\}$ (since the maximal probability to reach s_+ from s or s' is equal to 0.5, when choosing action b in s'). Moreover, Proposition 10 does not hold either in $\mathcal{M}'$ for maximal probabilities[1]. In fact, the vector of maximal probabilities in $\mathcal{M}'$ is only the smallest fixed point of $f_{\max}$. Indeed, the reader can check that the vector which is equal to 0 for s_-, 0.7 for t, and 1 for all the other states is also a fixed point of $f_{\max}$, whereas the maximal reachability probability to reach s_+ from s or s' is equal to 0.5. Notice that in the max-reduction $\mathcal{M}^\bullet$ of this MDP, the MEC $(\{s, s'\}, \{a, c\})$ is merged into a single state, hence removing this non-unicity problem, as shown in Proposition 10.

While this issue does not preclude the standard computation of the probabilities, the approach we have followed enables us to solve the convergence issues of the previous methods. This is the subject of the next section.

---

[1] This is already observed in [5], but a wrong statement is made in [1, Thm. 10.100].

3 Value Iteration for Reachability Objectives

This section presents the value iteration algorithm used, for example in the PRISM model-checker [9], to compute optimal reachability probabilities of an MDP. After stating convergence issues of this method, we give a new algorithm, called *interval iteration algorithm*, and the strong guarantees that it gives.

3.1 Convergence Issues

The idea of the value iteration algorithm is to compute the fixed points of $f_{\min}$ and $f_{\max}$ (more precisely, the smallest fixed points of $f_{\min}$ and $f_{\max}$) by iterating them on a given initial vector, until a certain convergence criterion is met. More precisely, as recalled in [5], we let $x^{(0)}$ defined by $x_{s_+}^{(0)} = 1$ and $x_s^{(0)} = 0$ for $s \neq s_+$ (observe that $x^{(0)}$ is the minimal vector of $\mathcal{V}$ for the pointwise order), and we then build one of the two sequences $\underline{x} = (\underline{x}^{(n)})_{n \in \mathbb{N}}$ or $\overline{x} = (\overline{x}^{(n)})_{n \in \mathbb{N}}$ defined by

- $\underline{x}^{(0)} = x^{(0)}$ and for all $n \in \mathbb{N}$, $\underline{x}^{(n+1)} = f_{\min}(\underline{x}^{(n)})$;
- $\overline{x}^{(0)} = x^{(0)}$ and for all $n \in \mathbb{N}$, $\overline{x}^{(n+1)} = f_{\max}(\overline{x}^{(n)})$.

Since $f_{\min}$ and $f_{\max}$ are monotonous operators and due to the choice of the initial vector, $\underline{x}$ and $\overline{x}$ are non-decreasing bounded sequences, hence convergent. Let $\underline{x}^{(\infty)}$ and $\overline{x}^{(\infty)}$ be their respective limits. By continuity of $f_{\min}$ and $f_{\max}$, $\underline{x}^{(\infty)}$ (respectively, $\overline{x}^{(\infty)}$) is a fixed point of $f_{\min}$ (respectively, $f_{\max}$). Due to Propositions 6 and 10, $\underline{x}^{(\infty)}$ (respectively, $\overline{x}^{(\infty)}$) is the vector $Pr_{\mathcal{M}}^{\min}(\mathsf{F}\, s^+)$ (respectively, $Pr_{\mathcal{M}}^{\max}(\mathsf{F}\, s^+)$) of minimal (respectively, maximal) reachability probabilities.

In practice, several stopping criteria can be chosen. In the model-checker PRISM [9], two criteria are implemented. For a vector $x \in \mathcal{V}$, we let $\|x\| = \max_{s \in S} |x_s|$. For $x \in \{\underline{x}, \overline{x}\}$ and a given threshold $\varepsilon > 0$, the *absolute criterion* consists in stopping once $\|x^{(n+1)} - x^{(n)}\| \leqslant \varepsilon$, whereas the *relative criterion* considers $\max_{s \in S}(x_s^{(n+1)} - x_s^{(n)})/x_s^{(n)} \leqslant \varepsilon$. However, as noticed in [5], no guarantees are obtained when using such value iteration algorithms, whatever the stopping criterion. As an example, consider the MDP (indeed the Markov chain) of Fig. 2. It is easy to check that (minimal and maximal) reachability probability of $s^+ = 0$ in state n is $1/2$. However, if ε is chosen as $1/2^n$ (or any value above), the sequence of vectors computed by the value iteration algorithm will be $x^{(0)} = (1, 0, 0, \ldots, 0, 0, \ldots, 0)$, $x^{(1)} = (1, 1/2, 0, \ldots, 0, 0, \ldots, 0)$, $x^{(2)} = (1, 1/2, 1/4, \ldots, 0, 0, \ldots, 0)$, $\ldots$, $x^{(n)} = (1, 1/2, 1/4, \ldots, 1/2^n, 0, \ldots, 0)$, at which point the absolute stopping criterion is met. Hence, the algorithm outputs $x_n^{(n)} = 1/2^n$ as the reachability probability of $s_+ = \{0\}$ in state n.

Example 11. The use of PRISM confirms this phenomenon. On this MDP, choosing $n = 10$ and threshold $\varepsilon = 10^{-3} < 1/2^{10}$, the absolute stopping criterion leads to the probability $9.77 \times 10^{-4} \approx 1/2^{10}$, whereas the relative stopping criterion leads to the probability 0.198. It has to be noticed that the tool indicates that the value iteration has converged, and does not warn the user that a possible problem may have arisen.

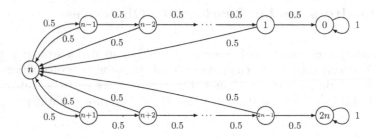

Fig. 2. A Markov chain with problems of convergence in value iteration

---

Algorithm 1. Interval iteration algorithm for minimum reachability

---

Input: Min-reduced MDP $\mathcal{M} = (S, \alpha_\mathcal{M}, \delta_\mathcal{M})$, convergence threshold ε

1 $x_{s_+} := 1;\ x_{s_-} := 0;\ y_{s_+} := 1;\ y_{s_-} := 0$

2 **foreach** $s \in S \setminus \{s_+, s_-\}$ **do** $x_s := 0;\ y_s := 1$

3 **repeat**

4 $\quad$ **foreach** $s \in S \setminus \{s_+, s_-\}$ **do**

5 $\quad\quad$ $x'_s := \min_{a \in A(s)} \sum_{s' \in S} \delta_\mathcal{M}(s, a)(s')\, x_{s'}$

6 $\quad\quad$ $y'_s := \min_{a \in A(s)} \sum_{s' \in S} \delta_\mathcal{M}(s, a)(s')\, y_{s'}$

7 $\quad$ $\delta := \max_{s \in S}(y'_s - x'_s)$

8 $\quad$ **foreach** $s \in S \setminus \{s_+, s_-\}$ **do** $x'_s := x_s;\ y'_s := y_s$

9 **until** $\delta \leqslant \varepsilon$

10 **return** $(x_s)_{s \in S}, (y_s)_{s \in S}$

We consider a modification of the algorithm in order to obtain a convergence guarantee when stopping the value iteration algorithm. We provide (1) stopping criteria for approximation and exact computations and, (2) rate of convergence.

3.2   Stopping Criterion for ε-Approximation

Here, we introduce two other sequences. For that, let vector $y^{(0)}$ be the maximal vector of $\mathcal{V}$, defined by $y_{s_-}^{(0)} = 0$ and $y_s^{(0)} = 1$ for $s \neq s_-$. We then define inductively the two sequences $\underline{y}$ and $\overline{y}$ of vectors by

 - $\underline{y}^{(0)} = y^{(0)}$ and for all $n \in \mathbb{N}$, $\underline{y}^{(n+1)} = f_{\min}(\underline{y}^{(n)})$;
 - $\overline{y}^{(0)} = y^{(0)}$ and for all $n \in \mathbb{N}$, $\overline{y}^{(n+1)} = f_{\max}(\overline{y}^{(n)})$.

Because of the new choice for the initial vector, notice that $\underline{y}$ and $\overline{y}$ are non-increasing sequences. Hence, with the same reasoning as above, we know that these sequences converge, and that their limit, denoted by $\underline{y}^{(\infty)}$ and $\overline{y}^{(\infty)}$ respectively, are the minimal (respectively, maximal) reachability probabilities. In particular, notice that $\underline{x}$ and $\underline{y}$, as well as $\overline{x}$ and $\overline{y}$, are adjacent sequences, and that $\underline{x}^{(\infty)} = \underline{y}^{(\infty)} = Pr_\mathcal{M}^{\min}(\mathsf{F}\, s^+)$ and $\overline{x}^{(\infty)} = \overline{y}^{(\infty)} = Pr_\mathcal{M}^{\max}(\mathsf{F}\, s^+)$.

Let us first consider a min-reduced MDP $\mathcal{M}$. Then, our new value iteration algorithm computes both in the same time sequences $\underline{x}$ and $\underline{y}$ and stops as soon as $\|\underline{y}^{(n)} - \underline{x}^{(n)}\| \leqslant \varepsilon$. In case this criterion is satisfied, which will happen after

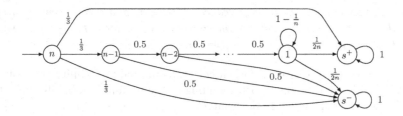

Fig. 3. A Markov chain with less iterations for the initial state

a finite (yet possibly large and not bounded *a priori*) number of iterations, we can guarantee that we obtained over- and underapproximations of $Pr_{\mathcal{M}}^{\min}(\mathsf{F}\,s^+)$ with precision at least ε on every component. Because of the simultaneous computation of lower and upper bounds, we call this algorithm *interval iteration algorithm*, and specify it in Algorithm 1. A similar algorithm can be designed for maximum reachability probabilities, by considering max-reduced MDPs and replacing min operations of lines 5 and 6 by max operations.

Theorem 12. *For every min-reduced (respectively, max-reduced) MDP $\mathcal{M}$, and threshold ε, if the interval iteration algorithm returns the vectors x and y on those inputs, then for all $s \in S$, $Pr_{\mathcal{M},s}^{\min}(\mathsf{F}\,s_+)$ (respectively, $Pr_{\mathcal{M},s}^{\max}(\mathsf{F}\,s_+)$) is in the interval $[x_s, y_s]$ of length at most ε.*

Example 13. For the same example as the one in Example 11, our algorithm converges after 10548 steps, and outputs, for the initial state $s = n$, $x_n = 0.4995$ and $y_n = 0.5005$, given a good confidence to the user.

Notice that it is possible to speed up the convergence if we are only interested in the optimal reachability probability of a given state s_0. Indeed, we can simply replace the stopping criterion $\|y^{(n)} - x^{(n)}\| \leqslant \varepsilon$ by $y_{s_0}^{(n)} - x_{s_0}^{(n)} \leqslant \varepsilon$.

Example 14. Let us look at the MDP (in fact a Markov chain) of Fig. 3 with initial state $s_0 = n$. Assume that we select threshold $\varepsilon = 2^{-(n-1)}$. For state s_0, the algorithm stops after $n-1$ iterations with interval $\left[\frac{1}{3}, \frac{1}{3}(1 + 2^{-(n-2)})\right]$ for the reachability probability. However, for the reaching probability of state 1, the interval after k iterations is $\left[\frac{1}{2n}\sum_{0\leqslant i<k}(1 - \frac{1}{n})^i, \frac{1}{2n}\sum_{0\leqslant i<k}(1 - \frac{1}{n})^i + (1 - \frac{1}{n})^k\right]$. So it will stop when $(1-\frac{1}{n})^k \leqslant 2^{-(n-1)}$, i.e., $k \geqslant -\frac{(n-1)}{\log_2(1-\frac{1}{n})}$ implying $k = \Theta(n^2)$.

3.3   Rate of Convergence

We now establish guarantees on the rate of convergence of the interval iteration algorithm. Notice that the results also apply to the usual value iteration algorithm, even though the proof relies on the introduction of adjacent sequences. In the sequel, we assume that there is at least one transition probability $0 < \delta < 1$ (otherwise the problems are trivial).

Theorem 15. *For a min- or max-reduced MDP $\mathcal{M}$, and a convergence threshold ε, the interval iteration algorithm converges in at most $I\lceil \frac{\log \varepsilon}{\log(1-\eta')}\rceil$ steps, where I and η are introduced in Proposition 2.*

Proof. Let σ be the policy corresponding to the minimal probability of satisfying $\mathsf{G}^{\leqslant n} \neg s_-$ and σ' be the policy corresponding to the minimal probability of satisfying $\mathsf{F}^{\leqslant n} s_+$. In particular, notice that $Pr_{\mathcal{M},s}^{\sigma}(\mathsf{G}^{\leqslant nI} \neg s_-) \leqslant Pr_{\mathcal{M},s}^{\sigma'}(\mathsf{G}^{\leqslant nI} \neg s_-)$.

Since $\mathsf{G}^{\leqslant n} \neg s_- \equiv \mathsf{G}^{\leqslant n} \neg (s_- \vee s_+) \vee \mathsf{F}^{\leqslant n} s_+$, with the disjunction being exclusive, we have for all $s \in S$,

$$Pr_{\mathcal{M},s}^{\min}(\mathsf{G}^{\leqslant nI} \neg s_-) - Pr_{\mathcal{M},s}^{\min}(\mathsf{F}^{\leqslant nI} s_+)) = Pr_{\mathcal{M},s}^{\sigma}(\mathsf{G}^{\leqslant nI} \neg s_-) - Pr_{\mathcal{M},s}^{\sigma'}(\mathsf{F}^{\leqslant nI} s_+)$$
$$\leqslant Pr_{\mathcal{M},s}^{\sigma'}(\mathsf{G}^{\leqslant nI} \neg s_-) - Pr_{\mathcal{M},s}^{\sigma'}(\mathsf{F}^{\leqslant nI} s_+) = Pr_{\mathcal{M},s}^{\sigma'}(\mathsf{G}^{\leqslant nI} \neg (s_- \vee s_+) \leqslant (1-\eta^I)^n$$

due to Proposition 2. It is easy to show by induction that $\underline{x}^{(n)} = Pr_{\mathcal{M}}^{\min}(\mathsf{F}^{\leqslant n} s_+)$ and $\underline{y}^{(n)} = Pr_{\mathcal{M}}^{\min}(\mathsf{G}^{\leqslant n} \neg s_-)$. Then, we have $\|\underline{y}^{(nI)} - \underline{x}^{(nI)}\| \leqslant (1-\eta^I)^n$. In conclusion, the stopping criterion is met when $(1-\eta^I)^n \leqslant \varepsilon$, i.e., after at most $I\lceil \frac{I \log \varepsilon}{\log(1-\eta^I)}\rceil$ steps. A similar proof can be made for maximal probabilities. $\square$

It may also be noticed, from similar arguments, that for all n, $\|\underline{y}^{((n+1)I)} - \underline{x}^{((n+1)I)}\| \leqslant (1-\eta^I)\|\underline{y}^{(nI)} - \underline{x}^{(nI)}\|$ (and similarly for the maximum case), implying that the value iteration algorithm has a linear rate of convergence.

Remark 16. One may use this convergence rate to delay the computation of one of the two adjacent sequences of Algorithm 1. Indeed assume that only $x^{(n)}$ is computed until step n. To use the stopping criterion provided by the adjacent sequences, one sets the upper sequence with $y_s^{(n)} = \min(x_s^{(n)} + (1-\eta^I)^{\lfloor \frac{n}{I} \rfloor}, 1)$ for all $s \notin \{s_-, s_+\}$, $y_{s_+}^{(n)} = 1$, and $y_{s_-}^{(n)} = 0$ and then applies the algorithm. In the favorable cases, this could divide by almost 2 the computation time.

3.4 Stopping Criterion for Exact Computation

In [3], a convergence guarantee was given for MDPs with rational transition probabilities. For such an MDP $\mathcal{M}$, let d be the largest denominator of transition probabilities (expressed as irreducible fractions), N the number $|S|$ of states, and M the number of transitions with non-zero probabilities. A bound $\gamma = d^{4M}$ was announced so that, after γ^2 iterations, the obtained probabilities lie in intervals that could only contain one possible probability value for the system, permitting to claim for the convergence of the algorithm. So after γ^2 iterations, the actual probability might me computed by considering the rational of the form α/γ closest to the current estimate. However, no proof of this result is given in [3].

Using our simultaneous computation of under- and over-approximations of the probabilities, we provide an alternative stopping criterion for exact computation that moreover exhibits an optimal policy. Its proof is based on the fact that optimal probabilities are rational for which we can control the size of the denominator, and strongly relies on the existence of stationary optimal policies.

Theorem 17. *Let $\mathcal{M}$ be a reduced MDP with rational transition probabilities. Optimal reachability probabilities and optimal policies can be computed by the interval iteration algorithm in at most $\mathcal{O}((1/\eta)^N N^3 \log d)$.*

The theorem also holds for the value iteration algorithm. Observe that our stopping criterion is significantly better than the bound d^{8M} claimed in [3] since $N \leqslant M$ and $1/\eta \leqslant d$. Furthermore M may be in $\Omega(N^2)$ even with a single action per state and $1/\eta$ may be significantly smaller than d as for instance in the extreme case $\eta = \frac{1}{2} - \frac{1}{10^n}$ and $d = 10^n$ for some large n.

4   Conclusion

We have provided a framework allowing to guarantee good properties when value iteration algorithm is used to compute optimal reachability probabilities of Markov decision processes. Our study pointed out some difficulties related to non-trivial end components in MDPs, that was not clearly described previously. Moreover, we gave results over the convergence speed, as well as criteria for obtaining exact convergence. As future works, it seems particularly interesting to test this algorithm on real instances, as it is done in [2], where authors moreover apply machine learning techniques.

Acknowledgments. We thank the reviewer that pointed out the similarities between our approach and [2] (to be presented at the next ATVA, in Nov. 2014).

References

1. Baier, C., Katoen, J.-P.: Principles of Model Checking. MIT Press (2008)
2. Brázdil, T., Chatterjee, K., Chmelík, M., Forejt, V., Křetínský, J., Kwiatkowska, M., Parker, D., Ujma, M.: Verification of Markov decision processes using learning algorithms. Research Report arXiv:1402.2967 (2014)
3. Chatterjee, K., Henzinger, T.A.: Value iteration. In: Grumberg, O., Veith, H. (eds.) 25 Years of Model Checking. LNCS, vol. 5000, pp. 107–138. Springer, Heidelberg (2008)
4. de Alfaro, L.: Formal Verification of Probabilistic Systems. PhD thesis, Stanford University (1997)
5. Forejt, V., Kwiatkowska, M., Norman, G., Parker, D.: Automated verification techniques for probabilistic systems. In: Bernardo, M., Issarny, V. (eds.) SFM 2011. LNCS, vol. 6659, pp. 53–113. Springer, Heidelberg (2011)
6. Haddad, S., Monmege, B.: Reachability in MDPs: Refining convergence of value iteration. Technical Report LSV-14-07, LSV, ENS Cachan (2014), http://www.lsv.ens-cachan.fr/Publis/RAPPORTS_LSV/PDF/rr-lsv-2014-07.pdf
7. Katoen, J.-P., Zapreev, I.S.: Safe on-the-fly steady-state detection for time-bounded reachability. In: QEST 2006, pp. 301–310 (2006)
8. Kattenbelt, M., Kwiatkowska, M.Z., Norman, G., Parker, D.: A game-based abstraction-refinement framework for Markov decision processes. Formal Methods in System Design 36(3), 246–280 (2010)
9. Kwiatkowska, M., Norman, G., Parker, D.: PRISM 4.0: Verification of probabilistic real-time systems. In: Gopalakrishnan, G., Qadeer, S. (eds.) CAV 2011. LNCS, vol. 6806, pp. 585–591. Springer, Heidelberg (2011)

On the Expressiveness of Metric Temporal Logic over Bounded Timed Words*

Hsi-Ming Ho

Department of Computer Science, University of Oxford
Wolfson Building, Parks Road, Oxford, OX1 3QD, UK

Abstract. It is known that Metric Temporal Logic (MTL) is strictly less expressive than the Monadic First-Order Logic of Order and Metric (FO[$<, +1$]) in the pointwise semantics over bounded time domains (i.e., timed words of bounded duration) [15]. In this paper, we present an extension of MTL which has the same expressive power as FO[$<, +1$] in both the pointwise and continuous semantics over bounded time domains.

1 Introduction

One of the most prominent specification formalisms used in verification is *Linear Temporal Logic* (LTL), which is typically interpreted over the non-negative integers or reals. A celebrated result of Kamp [9] states that, in either case, LTL has precisely the same expressive power as the *Monadic First-Order Logic of Order* (FO[$<$]). These logics, however, are inadequate to express specifications for systems whose correct behaviour depends on quantitative timing requirements. Over the last three decades, much work has therefore gone into lifting classical verification formalisms and results to the real-time setting. *Metric Temporal Logic* (MTL), which extends LTL by constraining the temporal operators by time intervals, was introduced by Koymans [10] in 1990 and has emerged as a central real-time specification formalism.

MTL enjoys two main semantics, depending intuitively on whether atomic formulas are interpreted as *state predicates* or as (instantaneous) *events*. In the former, the system is assumed to be under observation at every instant in time, leading to a 'continuous' semantics based on *flows* or *signals*, whereas in the latter, observations of the system are taken to be (finite or infinite) sequences of timestamped snapshots, leading to a 'pointwise' semantics based on *timed words*. Timed words are the leading interpretation, for example, for systems modelled as timed automata [1]. In both cases, the time domain is usually taken to be the non-negative real numbers. Both semantics have been extensively studied; see, e.g., [12] for a historical account.

Alongside these developments, researchers proposed the *Monadic First-Order Logic of Order and Metric* (FO[$<, +1$]) as a natural quantitative extension of

---

* More extensive technical details as well as all proofs can be found in the full version of this paper [5].

J. Ouaknine, I. Potapov, and J. Worrell (Eds.): RP 2014, LNCS 8762, pp. 138–150, 2014.
© Springer International Publishing Switzerland 2014

FO[<]. Unfortunately, Hirshfeld and Rabinovich [4] showed that no 'finitary' extension of MTL—and *a fortiori* MTL itself—could have the same expressive power as FO[<, +1] over the reals.[1] Still, in the continuous semantics, MTL can be made expressively complete for FO[<, +1] by extending the logic with an infinite family of *'counting modalities'* [7] or considering only *bounded* time domains [11, 13]. Nonetheless, and rather surprisingly, MTL with counting modalities remains strictly less expressive than FO[<, +1] over bounded time domains in the pointwise semantics, i.e., over timed words of bounded duration, as we will see in Section 3.

The main result of this paper is to show that MTL, equipped with both the forwards and backwards temporal modalities 'generalised Until' ($\mathfrak{U}$) and 'generalised Since' ($\mathfrak{S}$), has precisely the same expressive power as FO[<, +1] over bounded time domains in the pointwise semantics (and also, trivially, in the continuous semantics). This extended version of Metric Temporal Logic, written MTL[$\mathfrak{U}, \mathfrak{S}$], therefore yields a definitive real-time analogue of Kamp's theorem over bounded domains.

It is worth noting that MTL[$\mathfrak{U}, \mathfrak{S}$] satisfiability and model checking (against timed automata) are decidable over bounded time domains, thanks to the decidability of FO[<, +1] over such domains as established in [11, 13]. Unfortunately, FO[<, +1] has non-elementary complexity, whereas the time-bounded satisfiability and model-checking problems for MTL are EXPSPACE-complete [11, 13]. However, it can easily be seen by inspecting the relevant constructions that the complexity bounds for MTL carry over to our new logic MTL[$\mathfrak{U}, \mathfrak{S}$].

2   Preliminaries

2.1   Timed Words

A *time sequence* $\tau = \tau_1 \tau_2 \ldots \tau_n$ is a non-empty finite sequence over non-negative reals (called *timestamps*) that satisfies the requirements below (we denote the length of τ by $|\tau|$):

- *Initialisation*[2]: $\tau_1 = 0$
- *Strict monotonicity*: For all $i, 1 \le i < |\tau|$, we have $\tau_i < \tau_{i+1}$.

A **timed word** over finite alphabet Σ is a pair $\rho = (\sigma, \tau)$, where $\sigma = \sigma_1 \sigma_2 \ldots \sigma_n$ is a non-empty finite word over Σ and τ is a time sequence of the same length. We refer to each (σ_i, τ_i) as an *event*. In this sense, a timed word

---

[1] Hirshfeld and Rabinovich's result was only stated and proved for the continuous semantics, but we believe that their approach would also carry through for the pointwise semantics. In any case, using different techniques Prabhakar and D'Souza [15] and Pandya and Shah [14] independently showed that MTL is strictly weaker than FO[<, +1] in the pointwise semantics.

[2] This requirement is natural in the present context as all the logics we consider in this paper are *translation invariant*: two timed words are indistinguishable by formulas (of these logics) if they only differ by a fixed delay.

can be regarded as a sequence of events. We denote by $|\rho|$ the number of events in ρ. A *position* in ρ is a number i such that $1 \leq i \leq |\rho|$. The *duration* of ρ is defined as $\tau_{|\rho|}$. A $\mathbb{T}$-timed word is a timed word all of whose timestamps are in $\mathbb{T}$, where $\mathbb{T}$ is either $[0, N)$, for some $N \in \mathbb{N}$, or $\mathbb{R}_{\geq 0}$.

Note that we are focussing on finite timed words. Our results carry over to the case of (Zeno) infinite timed words as well, with some modifications.

2.2   Metric Logics

We first define a metric predicate logic FO[$<, +1$] and its pointwise interpretation. This logic will serve as a 'yardstick' of expressiveness. In the sequel, we write $\Sigma_{\mathbf{P}} = 2^{\mathbf{P}}$ for a set of monadic predicates $\mathbf{P}$.

Definition 1. *Given a set of monadic predicates $\mathbf{P}$, the set of FO[$<, +1$] formulas is generated by the grammar*

$$\vartheta ::= P(x) \mid x < x' \mid d(x, x') \sim c \mid \mathbf{true} \mid \vartheta_1 \wedge \vartheta_2 \mid \neg\vartheta \mid \exists x\, \vartheta\,,$$

where $P \in \mathbf{P}$, x, x' are variables, $\sim \in \{=, \neq, <, >, \leq, \geq\}$ and $c \in \mathbb{N}$.[3]

With each $\mathbb{T}$-timed word $\rho = (\sigma, \tau)$ over $\Sigma_{\mathbf{P}}$ we associate a structure M_ρ. Its universe U_ρ is the finite subset $\{\tau_i \mid 1 \leq i \leq |\rho|\}$ of $\mathbb{T}$. The order relation $<$ and monadic predicates in $\mathbf{P}$ are interpreted in the expected way. For example, $P(\tau_i)$ holds in M_ρ iff $P \in \sigma_i$. The binary *distance* predicate $d(x, x') \sim c$ holds iff $|x - x'| \sim c$. The satisfaction relation is defined inductively as usual. We write $M_\rho, t_1, \ldots, t_n \models \vartheta(x_1, \ldots, x_n)$ (or $\rho, t_1, \ldots, t_n \models \vartheta(x_1, \ldots, x_n)$) if $t_1, \ldots, t_n \in U_\rho$ and $\vartheta(t_1, \ldots, t_n)$ holds in M_ρ. We say that FO[$<, +1$] formulas $\vartheta_1(x)$ and $\vartheta_2(x)$ are *equivalent* over $\mathbb{T}$-timed words if for all $\mathbb{T}$-timed words ρ and $t \in U_\rho$,

$$\rho, t \models \vartheta_1(x) \iff \rho, t \models \vartheta_2(x)\,.$$

Formulas of metric temporal logics are built from monadic predicates using Boolean connectives and **modalities**. A k-ary modality is defined by an FO[$<, +1$] formula $\varphi(x, X_1, \ldots, X_k)$ with a single free first-order variable x and k free monadic predicates $X_1, \ldots, X_k$. For example, the MTL modality $\mathsf{U}_{(0,5)}$ is defined by

$$\mathsf{U}_{(0,5)}(x, X_1, X_2) = \exists x' \left(x < x' \wedge d(x, x') < 5 \wedge X_2(x') \right.$$
$$\left. \wedge \forall x'' \left(x < x'' \wedge x'' < x' \implies X_1(x'') \right) \right).$$

The MTL formula $\varphi_1 \, \mathsf{U}_{(0,5)} \, \varphi_2$ (using infix notation) is obtained by substituting MTL formulas φ_1, φ_2 for X_1, X_2, respectively.

---

[3] Note that whilst we still refer to the logic as FO[$<, +1$], we adopt here an equivalent definition using a binary distance predicate $d(x, x')$ (as in [16]) in place of the usual $+1$ function symbol.

Definition 2. *Given a set of monadic predicates* **P**, *the set of* MTL *formulas is generated by the grammar*

$$\varphi ::= P \mid \textbf{true} \mid \varphi_1 \wedge \varphi_2 \mid \neg\varphi \mid \varphi_1 \, \mathsf{U}_I \, \varphi_2 \mid \varphi_1 \, \mathsf{S}_I \, \varphi_2,$$

where $P \in \textbf{P}$ and $I \subseteq (0, \infty)$ is an interval with endpoints in $\mathbb{N} \cup \{\infty\}$.

The (future-only) fragment $\mathsf{MTL}_{\mathsf{fut}}$ is obtained by banning subformulas of the form $\varphi_1 \, \mathsf{S}_I \, \varphi_2$. If I is not present as a subscript to a given modality then it is assumed to be $(0, \infty)$. We sometimes use pseudo-arithmetic expressions to denote intervals, e.g., '≥ 1' denotes $[1, \infty)$ and '$= 1$' denotes the singleton $\{1\}$. We also employ the usual syntactic sugar, e.g., $\textbf{false} \equiv \neg\textbf{true}$, $\mathsf{F}_I\varphi \equiv \textbf{true} \, \mathsf{U}_I \varphi$, $\overleftarrow{\mathsf{F}}_I\varphi \equiv \textbf{true} \, \mathsf{S}_I \, \varphi$, $\mathsf{G}_I\varphi \equiv \neg\mathsf{F}_I\neg\varphi$ and $\mathsf{X}_I\varphi \equiv \textbf{false} \, \mathsf{U}_I \, \varphi$, etc. For the sake of completeness, we give a traditional inductive definition of the satisfaction relation of MTL below.

Definition 3. *The satisfaction relation $(\rho, i) \models \varphi$ for an MTL formula φ, a timed word $\rho = (\sigma, \tau)$ and a position i in ρ is defined as follows:*

- $(\rho, i) \models P$ iff $P(\tau_i)$ holds in M_ρ
- $(\rho, i) \models \textbf{true}$
- $(\rho, i) \models \varphi_1 \wedge \varphi_2$ iff $(\rho, i) \models \varphi_1$ and $(\rho, i) \models \varphi_2$
- $(\rho, i) \models \neg\varphi$ iff $(\rho, i) \not\models \varphi$
- $(\rho, i) \models \varphi_1 \mathsf{U}_I\varphi_2$ iff there exists $j, i < j \leq |\rho|$ such that $(\rho, j) \models \varphi_2$, $\tau_j - \tau_i \in I$, and $(\rho, k) \models \varphi_1$ for all k with $i < k < j$
- $(\rho, i) \models \varphi_1 \mathsf{S}_I\varphi_2$ iff there exists $j, 1 \leq j < i$ such that $(\rho, j) \models \varphi_2$, $\tau_i - \tau_j \in I$ and $(\rho, k) \models \varphi_1$ for all k with $j < k < i$.

Note that we adopt strict versions of temporal modalities, e.g., φ_2 holds at i does not imply that $\varphi_1 \, \mathsf{U} \, \varphi_2$ holds at i. We write $\rho \models \varphi$ if $(\rho, 1) \models \varphi$.

2.3 Relative Expressiveness

Let L, L' be two metric logics. We say that L' is ***expressively complete for*** L over $\mathbb{T}$-timed words if for any formula $\vartheta(x) \in L$, there is an equivalent formula $\varphi(x) \in L'$ over $\mathbb{T}$-timed words.

3 Expressiveness

In this section, we present a sequence of successively more expressive extensions of $\mathsf{MTL}_{\mathsf{fut}}$ over bounded timed words. Along the way we highlight the key features that give rise to the differences in expressiveness. The necessity of a 'new' extension (such as the one in the next section) is justified by the fact that no known extension can lead to expressive completeness.

3.1 Definability of Time 0

Recall that $\mathsf{MTL_{fut}}$ and $\mathsf{FO}[<,+1]$ have the same expressiveness over continuous domains of the form $[0, N)$ [11,13], a result that fails over $[0, N)$-timed words. To account for this difference between the two semantics, observe that a distinctive feature of the continuous interpretation of $\mathsf{MTL_{fut}}$ is exploited in [11,13]: in any $[0, N)$-flow, the formula $\mathsf{F}_{=(N-1)}\mathbf{true}$ holds in $[0, 1)$ and nowhere else. One can make use of conjunctions of similar formulas to determine which unit interval the current instant is in. Unfortunately, this trick does not work for $\mathsf{MTL_{fut}}$ in the pointwise semantics. However, it can be achieved in MTL by using past modalities. Let

$$\varphi_{i,i+1} = \overleftarrow{\mathsf{F}}_{[i,i+1)}(\neg\overleftarrow{\mathsf{F}}\,\mathbf{true})$$

and $\Phi_{unit} = \{\varphi_{i,i+1} \mid i \in \mathbb{N}\}$. It is clear that $\varphi_{i,i+1}$ holds only in $[i, i+1)$ and nowhere else. Denote by $\mathsf{MTL_{fut}}[\Phi_{unit}]$ the extension of $\mathsf{MTL_{fut}}$ obtained by allowing these formulas as subformulas. This very restrictive use of past modalities strictly increases the expressiveness of $\mathsf{MTL_{fut}}$. Indeed, our main result depends crucially on the use of these formulas.

Proposition 1. $\mathsf{MTL_{fut}}[\Phi_{unit}]$ *is strictly more expressive than* $\mathsf{MTL_{fut}}$ *over* $[0, N)$-*timed words.*

3.2 Past Modalities

The following proposition says that the conservative extension in the last subsection is not sufficient for obtaining expressive completeness: non-trivial nesting of future modalities and past modalities provides more expressiveness.

Proposition 2. MTL *is strictly more expressive than* $\mathsf{MTL_{fut}}[\Phi_{unit}]$ *over* $[0, N)$-*timed words.*

3.3 Counting Modalities

The modality $C_n(x, X)$ asserts that X holds at least at n points in the open interval $(x, x+1)$. The modalities C_n for $n \geq 2$ are called *counting modalities*. It is well-known that these modalities are inexpressible in MTL over $\mathbb{R}_{\geq 0}$-flows [3]. For this reason, they (or variants thereof) are often used to separate the expressiveness of various metric logics (cf., e.g., [2,14,15]). For example, the $\mathsf{FO}[<,+1]$ formula

$$\vartheta_{pqr}(x) = \exists y \left(x < y \wedge P(y) \wedge \exists y' \left(y < y' \wedge d(y,y') > 1 \wedge d(y,y') < 2 \wedge Q(y') \right.\right.$$

$$\left.\left. \wedge \exists y'' \left(y' < y'' \wedge d(y,y'') > 1 \wedge d(y,y'') < 2 \wedge R(y'') \right) \right) \right)$$

has no equivalent in MTL over $\mathbb{R}_{\geq 0}$-timed words [14]. Indeed, it was shown recently that in the continuous semantics, MTL with counting modalities and their past versions (which we denote by $\mathsf{MTL}[\{C_n, \overleftarrow{C}_n\}_{n=2}^{\infty}]$) is expressively complete for FO[$<, +1$] [7]. However, counting modalities add no expressiveness to MTL in the time-bounded setting. To see this, observe that the following formula is equivalent to ϑ_{pqr} over $[0, N)$-timed words (we make use of formulas in Φ_{unit} defined in Section 3.1)

$$F\left(\bigvee_{i \in [0, N-1]} \left(P \wedge \varphi_{i,i+1} \wedge \left(F_{>1}\left(Q \wedge F(R \wedge \varphi_{i+1,i+2})\right) \right.\right.\right.$$

$$\vee F_{<2}\left(R \wedge \varphi_{i+2,i+3} \wedge \overleftarrow{F}(Q \wedge \varphi_{i+2,i+3})\right)$$

$$\left.\left.\left. \vee \left(F_{>1}(Q \wedge \varphi_{i+1,i+2}) \wedge F_{<2}(R \wedge \varphi_{i+2,i+3})\right)\right)\right)\right).$$

The same idea can be generalised to handle counting modalities and their past counterparts.

Proposition 3. MTL *is expressively complete for* MTL[$\{C_n, \overleftarrow{C}_n\}_{n=2}^{\infty}$] *over* $[0, N)$-*timed words.*

3.4 Non-Local Properties: One Reference Point

Proposition 3 shows that part of the expressiveness hierarchy over $\mathbb{R}_{\geq 0}$-timed words collapses in the time-bounded setting. Nonetheless, MTL is still not expressive enough to capture all of FO[$<, +1$]. Recall that another feature of the continuous interpretation of MTL$_{fut}$ used in the proof in [11, 13] is that $F_{=k}\varphi$ holds at t *iff* φ holds at $t + k$. Suppose that we want to specify the following property over $\mathbf{P} = \{P, Q\}$ at the current time t_1 for some integer constant $a > 0$:

- There is an event at time $t_2 > t_1 + a$ where Q holds
- P holds at all events in $(t_1 + a, t_2)$.

In the continuous semantics, by introducing a special monadic predicate P_ϵ that holds at all 'no-event' points in the flow, the property can easily be expressed as

$$\varphi_{cont1} = F_{=a}\left((P \vee P_\epsilon) \cup Q\right).$$

See Figure 1 for an illustration. Filled boxes denote events at which $\neg P \wedge Q$ holds whereas hollow boxes denote events at which $P \wedge \neg Q$ holds. The formula φ_{cont1} holds at t_1 in the continuous semantics.

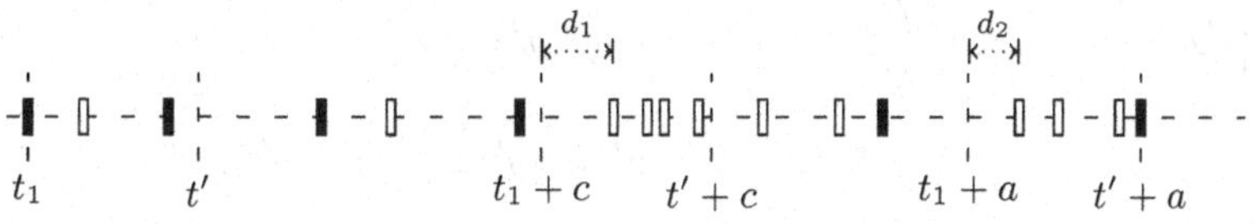

Fig. 1. φ_{cont1} holds at t_1 in the continuous semantics

In essence, when the current time is t_1, the continuous interpretation of MTL allows one to speak of properties 'around' $t_1 + a$ regardless of whether there is an event at $t_1 + a$. The same is not readily possible with the pointwise interpretation of MTL if there is no event at $t_1 + a$. To handle this issue within the pointwise semantic framework, we introduce a relatively simple family of modalities $\mathcal{B}_I^{\rightarrow}$ ('Beginning') and their past versions $\mathcal{B}_I^{\leftarrow}$. They can be used to specify the *first* events in given intervals. For example, the following modality asserts that X holds at the first event in (a, b):

$$\mathcal{B}_{(a,b)}^{\rightarrow}(x, X) = \exists x' \left(x < x' \wedge d(x, x') > a \wedge d(x, x') < b \wedge X(x') \right.$$
$$\left. \wedge \nexists x'' \left(x < x'' \wedge x'' < x' \wedge d(x, x'') > a \right) \right).$$

Now the property above can be defined as $\mathcal{B}_{(a,\infty)}^{\rightarrow}(Q \vee (P \cup Q))$. We refer to the extension of MTL with $\mathcal{B}_I^{\rightarrow}, \mathcal{B}_I^{\leftarrow}$ as MTL[$\mathcal{B}^{\leftrightarrows}$].

The following proposition states that this extension is indeed non-trivial.

Proposition 4. MTL[$\mathcal{B}^{\leftrightarrows}$] *is strictly more expressive than* MTL *over* $[0, N)$-*timed words.*

3.5   Non-local Properties: Two Reference Points

Adding modalities $\mathcal{B}_I^{\rightarrow}, \mathcal{B}_I^{\leftarrow}$ to MTL allows one to specify properties with respect to a distant time point even when there is no event at that point. However, the following proposition shows that this is still not enough for expressive completeness.

Proposition 5. FO[$<, +1$] *is strictly more expressive than* MTL[$\mathcal{B}^{\leftrightarrows}$] *over* $[0, N)$-*timed words.*

Proof. This is similar to a proof in [15, Section 7]. Given $m \in \mathbb{N}$, we construct two models as follows. Let

$$\mathcal{G}_m = (\emptyset, 0)(\emptyset, \frac{0.5}{2m+3})(\emptyset, \frac{1.5}{2m+3}) \dots (\emptyset, 1 - \frac{0.5}{2m+3})$$
$$(\emptyset, 1 + \frac{0.5}{2m+2})(\emptyset, 1 + \frac{1.5}{2m+2}) \dots \dots (\emptyset, 2 - \frac{0.5}{2m+2}).$$

$\mathcal{H}_m$ is constructed as $\mathcal{G}_m$ except that the event at time $\frac{m+1.5}{2m+3}$ is missing.

Figure 2 illustrates the models for the case $m = 2$ where hollow boxes represent events at which no monadic predicate holds. It can be proved that no MTL[$\mathcal{B}^{\leftrightarrows}$] formula of modal depth $\leq m$ distinguishes $\mathcal{G}_m$ and $\mathcal{H}_m$ while the FO[$<, +1$] formula

$$\exists x \left(\nexists y \, (y < x) \wedge \exists x' \left(d(x, x') > 1 \wedge d(x, x') < 2 \right. \right.$$
$$\wedge \exists x'' \left(x' < x'' \wedge \nexists y' \, (x' < y' \wedge y' < x'') \right.$$
$$\left. \left. \left. \wedge \nexists y'' \left(d(x', y'') < 1 \wedge d(x'', y'') > 1 \right) \right) \right) \right)$$

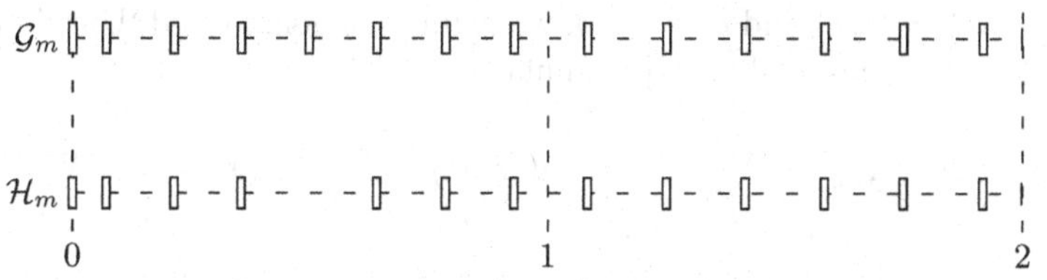

Fig. 2. Models $\mathcal{G}_m$ and $\mathcal{H}_m$ for $m = 2$

distinguishes $\mathcal{G}_m$ and $\mathcal{H}_m$ for any $m \in \mathbb{N}$.   □

One way to understand this phenomenon is to consider the arity of MTL operators. Let the current time be t_1. Suppose that we want to specify the following property ($a > c > 0$):

- There is an event at $t_2 > t_1 + a$ where Q holds
- P holds at all events in $(t_1 + c, t_1 + c + (t_2 - t_1 - a))$.

In the continuous semantics one can simply write

$$\varphi_{cont2} = \big(\mathsf{F}_{=c}(P \vee P_\epsilon)\big) \, \mathsf{U} \, (\mathsf{F}_{=a}Q).$$

Observe how this formula (effectively) talks about properties around two points: $t_1 + c$ and $t_1 + a$. In the same vein, the following formula distinguishes $\mathcal{G}_m$ and $\mathcal{H}_m$ in the continuous semantics:

$$\varphi_{cont3} = \mathsf{F}_{(1,2)}\big(\neg P_\epsilon \wedge (\overleftarrow{\mathsf{F}}_{=1}P_\epsilon) \, \mathsf{U} \, (\neg P_\epsilon)\big).$$

In the next section, we propose new modalities that add this ability to MTL in the pointwise semantics. We show later that this ability is exactly the missing piece of expressiveness.

4 New Modalities

4.1 Generalised 'Until' and 'Since'

We introduce a family of modalities which can be understood as generalisations of the usual 'Until' and 'Since' modalities. Let $I \subseteq (0, \infty)$ be an interval with endpoints in $\mathbb{N} \cup \{\infty\}$ and $c \in \mathbb{N}$. The formula $\varphi_1 \, \mathfrak{U}_I^c \, \varphi_2$ (using infix notation), when imposed at t_1, asserts that

- There is an event at t_2 where φ_2 holds and $t_2 - t_1 \in I$
- φ_1 holds at all events in $\Big(c, c + \big(t_2 - (t_1 + \inf(I))\big)\Big)$.

Formally, for $I = (a, b)$ and $a \geq c \geq 0$, we define the generalised 'Until' modality $\mathfrak{U}^c_{(a,b)}$ by the following $\mathsf{FO}[<, +1]$ formula:

$$\mathfrak{U}^c_{(a,b)}(x, X_1, X_2) = \exists x' \left(x < x' \wedge d(x, x') > a \wedge d(x, x') < b \wedge X_2(x') \right.$$
$$\wedge \forall x'' \left(x < x'' \wedge d(x, x'') > c \wedge x'' < x' \right.$$
$$\left. \left. \wedge d(x', x'') > (a - c) \implies X_1(x'') \right) \right).$$

Symmetrically, we define the generalised 'Since' modality $\mathfrak{S}^c_{(a,b)}$ for $I = (a, b)$ and $a \geq c \geq 0$:

$$\mathfrak{S}^c_{(a,b)}(x, X_1, X_2) = \exists x' \left(x' < x \wedge d(x, x') > a \wedge d(x, x') < b \wedge X_2(x') \right.$$
$$\wedge \forall x'' \left(x'' < x \wedge d(x, x'') > c \wedge x' < x'' \right.$$
$$\left. \left. \wedge d(x', x'') > (a - c) \implies X_1(x'') \right) \right).$$

The modalities for I being a half-open interval or a closed interval can be defined similarly. We will refer to the logic obtained by adding these modalities to MTL as $\mathsf{MTL}[\mathfrak{U}, \mathfrak{S}]$. Note that the usual 'Until' and 'Since' modalities can be written in terms of generalised modalities. For instance,

$$\varphi_1 \, \mathsf{U}_{(a,b)} \, \varphi_2 = \varphi_1 \, \mathfrak{U}^a_{(a,b)} \, \varphi_2 \wedge \neg \left(\mathbf{true} \, \mathfrak{U}^0_{(0,a]} \, (\neg \varphi_1) \right).$$

4.2 More Liberal Bounds

In the definition of modalities $\mathfrak{U}^c_I$ and $\mathfrak{S}^c_I$ in the last subsection, we stressed that $I \subseteq (0, \infty)$ and $\inf(I) \geq c \geq 0$. This is because more liberal usage of bounds are indeed merely syntactic sugar. For instance, one may define

$$\mathfrak{U}^{10}_{(2,5)}(x, X_1, X_2) = \exists x' \left(x < x' \wedge d(x, x') > 2 \wedge d(x, x') < 5 \wedge X_2(x') \right.$$
$$\wedge \forall x'' \left(x < x'' \wedge d(x, x'') > 10 \right.$$
$$\left. \left. \wedge d(x', x'') < 8 \implies X_1(x'') \right) \right),$$

but this is indeed equivalent to

$$\mathsf{F}_{(2,5)} \varphi_2 \wedge \neg \left((\neg \varphi_2) \, \mathfrak{U}^2_{(10,13)} \, (\neg \varphi_1 \wedge \neg (\overleftarrow{\mathsf{F}}_{=8} \neg \varphi_2)) \right)$$

over $[0, N)$-timed words. In fact, we can even use $c \in \mathbb{Z}$ and $I \subseteq (-\infty, \infty)$ for free. For example, over $[0, N)$-timed words, $\varphi_1 \, \mathfrak{U}^{-7}_{(5,10)} \, \varphi_2$ is equivalent to

$$\mathsf{F}_{(5,10)} \left(\varphi_2 \wedge (\varphi_1 \mathfrak{S}^{12}_{(5,10)} \mathbf{true}) \right) \wedge \left((\mathbf{false} \, \mathfrak{U}^0_{(5,10)} \varphi_2) \vee \left(\varphi' \mathsf{U} ((\mathbf{false} \, \mathfrak{U}^0_{(5,10)} \varphi_2) \wedge \varphi') \right) \right)$$

where $\varphi' = \varphi_1 \, \mathfrak{S}^7_{(0,5)} \, (\mathbf{true} \wedge \neg (\overleftarrow{\mathsf{F}}_{=7} \neg \varphi_1))$. Other cases can be handled with similar ideas.

We can now give an MTL$[\mathfrak{U}, \mathfrak{S}]$ formula that distinguishes, in the pointwise semantics, the models $\mathcal{G}_m$ and $\mathcal{H}_m$ in Section 3.5:

$$F_{(1,2)}\left(\textbf{true} \wedge \left(\textbf{false } \mathfrak{U}^{-1}_{(0,\infty)} \textbf{ true}\right)\right).$$

Compare this with the formula φ_{cont3} defined in Section 3.5, which distinguishes $\mathcal{G}_m$ and $\mathcal{H}_m$ in the continuous semantics.

5   The Translation

We give a translation from an arbitrary FO$[<, +1]$ formula with one free variable into an equivalent MTL$[\mathfrak{U}, \mathfrak{S}]$ formula (over $[0, N)$-timed words). Our proof strategy is similar to that in [11]: we eliminate the metric by introducing extra predicates, convert to LTL, and then replace the new predicates by their equivalent MTL$[\mathfrak{U}, \mathfrak{S}]$ formulas.

5.1   Eliminating the Metric

We introduce fresh monadic predicates $\overline{\textbf{P}} = \{P_i \mid P \in \textbf{P}, 0 \le i \le N - 1\}$ as in [11] and, additionally, $\overline{\textbf{Q}} = \{Q_i \mid 0 \le i \le N - 1\}$. Intuitively, $P_i(x)$ holds (for $x \in [0, 1)$) iff $P \in \textbf{P}$ holds at time $i + x$ in the corresponding $[0, N)$-timed word, and $Q_i(x)$ holds iff there is an event at time $i + x$ in the corresponding $[0, N)$-timed word, regardless of whether any $P \in \textbf{P}$ holds there. Let $\varphi_{event} = \forall x \left(\bigvee_{i \in [0, N-1]} Q_i(x)\right) \wedge \forall x \left(\bigwedge_{i \in [0, N-1]} (P_i(x) \implies Q_i(x))\right)$ and $\varphi_{init} = \exists x \left(\nexists x' (x' < x) \wedge Q_0(x)\right)$. There is an obvious 'stacking' bijection (indicated by overlining) between $[0, N)$-timed words over $\Sigma_{\textbf{P}}$ and $[0, 1)$-timed words over $\Sigma_{\overline{\textbf{P}} \cup \overline{\textbf{Q}}}$ satisfying $\varphi_{event} \wedge \varphi_{init}$.

Let $\vartheta(x)$ be an FO$[<, +1]$ formula with one free variable and in which each quantifier uses a fresh new variable. Without loss of generality, we assume that $\vartheta(x)$ contains only existential quantifiers (this can be achieved by syntactic rewriting). Replace the formula by

$$\left(Q_0(x) \wedge \vartheta[x/x]\right) \vee \left(Q_1(x) \wedge \vartheta[x + 1/x]\right) \vee \ldots \vee \left(Q_{N-1}(x) \wedge \vartheta[x + (N-1)/x]\right)$$

where $\vartheta[e/x]$ denotes the formula obtained by substituting all free occurrences of x in ϑ by (an expression) e. Then, similarly, recursively replace every subformula $\exists x' \, \theta$ by

$$\exists x' \left(\left(Q_0(x') \wedge \theta[x'/x']\right) \vee \ldots \vee \left(Q_{N-1}(x') \wedge \theta[x' + (N-1)/x']\right)\right).$$

Note that we do not actually have the $+1$ function in our structures; it only serves as annotation here and will be removed later, e.g., $x' + k$ means that $Q_k(x')$ holds. We then carry out the following syntactic substitutions:

- For each inequality of the form $x_1 + k_1 < x_2 + k_2$, replace it with
  - $x_1 < x_2$ if $k_1 = k_2$

- **true** if $k_1 < k_2$
- $\neg$**true** if $k_1 > k_2$
- For each distance formula, e.g., $d(x_1 + k_1, x_2 + k_2) \leq 2$, replace it with
  - **true** if $|k_1 - k_2| \leq 1$
  - $(\neg(x_1 < x_2) \wedge \neg(x_2 < x_1)) \vee (x_2 < x_1)$ if $k_2 - k_1 = 2$
  - $(\neg(x_1 < x_2) \wedge \neg(x_2 < x_1)) \vee (x_1 < x_2)$ if $k_1 - k_2 = 2$
  - $\neg$**true** if $|k_1 - k_2| > 2$
- Replace terms of the form $P(x_1 + k)$ with $P_k(x_1)$.

This gives a non-metric first-order formula $\overline{\vartheta}(x)$ over $\overline{\mathbf{P}} \cup \overline{\mathbf{Q}}$. Denote by $frac(t)$ the fractional part of a non-negative real t. It is not hard to see that for each $[0, N)$-timed word $\rho = (\sigma, \tau)$ over $\Sigma_{\mathbf{P}}$ and its stacked counterpart $\overline{\rho}$, the following holds:

- $\rho, t \models \vartheta(x)$ implies $\overline{\rho}, \overline{t} \models \overline{\vartheta}(x)$ where $\overline{t} = frac(t)$
- $\overline{\rho}, \overline{t} \models \overline{\vartheta}(x)$ implies there exists $t \in U_\rho$ with $frac(t) = \overline{t}$ s.t. $\rho, t \models \vartheta(x)$.

Moreover, if $\rho, t \models \vartheta(x)$, then the integral part of t indicates which clause in $\overline{\vartheta}(x)$ is satisfied when x is substituted with $\overline{t} = frac(t)$, and vice versa.

By Kamp's theorem [9], $\overline{\vartheta}(x)$ is equivalent to an LTL[U, S] formula $\overline{\varphi}$ of the following form:

$$(Q_0 \wedge \overline{\varphi}_0) \vee (Q_1 \wedge \overline{\varphi}_1) \vee \ldots \vee (Q_{N-1} \wedge \overline{\varphi}_{N-1}).$$

5.2 From Non-Metric to Metric

We now construct an MTL[$\mathfrak{U}$, $\mathfrak{S}$] formula that is equivalent to $\vartheta(x)$ over $[0, N)$-timed words. Note that we make heavy use of the formulas in Φ_{unit} defined in Section 3.1.

Proposition 6. *Let $\overline{\psi}$ be a subformula of $\overline{\varphi}_i$ for some $i \in [0, N-1]$. There is an MTL[$\mathfrak{U}$, $\mathfrak{S}$] formula ψ such that for any $[0, N)$-timed word ρ, $t \in \rho$ and $frac(t) = \overline{t} \in \overline{\rho}$, we have*

$$\overline{\rho}, \overline{t} \models \overline{\psi} \iff \rho, t \models \psi.$$

Proof. The MTL[$\mathfrak{U}$, $\mathfrak{S}$] formula ψ is constructed inductively as follows:

- *Base step.* Consider the following cases:
  - $\overline{\psi} = P_j$: Let

  $$\psi = (\varphi_{0,1} \wedge \mathsf{F}_{=j}P) \vee \ldots \vee (\varphi_{j,j+1} \wedge P) \vee \ldots \vee (\varphi_{N-1,N} \wedge \overset{\leftarrow}{\mathsf{F}}_{=((N-1)-j)}P).$$

  - $\overline{\psi} = Q_j$: Similarly we let

  $$\psi = (\varphi_{0,1} \wedge \mathsf{F}_{=j}\mathbf{true}) \vee \ldots \vee (\varphi_{j,j+1} \wedge \mathbf{true}) \vee \ldots \vee (\varphi_{N-1,N} \wedge \overset{\leftarrow}{\mathsf{F}}_{=((N-1)-j)}\mathbf{true}).$$

– *Induction step.* The case for boolean operations is trivial and hence omitted.

• $\overline{\psi} = \overline{\psi}_1 \, \mathsf{U} \, \overline{\psi}_2$: By IH we have ψ_1 and ψ_2. Let

$$\psi^{j,k,l} = \psi_1 \, \mathfrak{U}^k_{(j,j+1)} \, (\psi_2 \wedge \varphi_{l,l+1}) \,.$$

The desired formula is

$$\psi = \bigvee_{i \in [0,N-1]} \left(\varphi_{i,i+1} \wedge \bigvee_{\substack{j \in [-i,\ldots,(N-1)-i] \\ l=i+j}} \left(\bigwedge_{k \in [-i,\ldots,(N-1)-i]} \psi^{j,k,l} \right) \right) \,.$$

• $\overline{\psi} = \overline{\psi}_1 \, \mathsf{S} \, \overline{\psi}_2$: This is symmetric to the case for $\overline{\psi}_1 \, \mathsf{U} \, \overline{\psi}_2$.

The claim holds by a straightforward induction on the structure of $\overline{\psi}$ and ψ.
□

Construct corresponding formulas φ_i for each $\overline{\varphi}_i$ using the proposition above. Substitute them into $\overline{\varphi}$ and replace all Q_i by $\varphi_{i,i+1}$ to obtain our final formula φ. We claim that it is equivalent to $\vartheta(x)$ over $[0,N)$-timed words.

Proposition 7. *For any $[0,N)$-timed words ρ and $t \in U_\rho$, we have*

$$\rho, t \models \varphi(x) \iff \rho, t \models \vartheta(x) \,.$$

Proof. Follows directly from Section 5.1 and Proposition 6.
□

We are now ready to state our main result.

Theorem 1. MTL$[\mathfrak{U}, \mathfrak{S}]$ *is expressively complete for* FO$[<,+1]$ *over* $[0,N)$-*timed words.*

6 Conclusion

Our main result is that over bounded timed words, MTL extended with our new modalities 'generalised until' and 'generalised since' is expressively complete for FO$[<,+1]$. Along the way we obtain a strict hierarchy of metric temporal logics, based on their expressiveness over bounded timed words:

$$\mathsf{MTL_{fut}} \subsetneq \mathsf{MTL_{fut}}[\varPhi_{unit}] \subsetneq \mathsf{MTL} \subsetneq \mathsf{MTL}[\mathcal{B}^{\leftrightarrows}] \subsetneq \mathsf{MTL}[\mathfrak{U}, \mathfrak{S}] = \mathsf{FO}[<,+1].$$

We are currently working on adapting the result to the case of $\mathbb{R}_{\geq 0}$-timed words. This might require a separation theorem (in the style of [8]) that works in the pointwise semantics [6].

References

1. Alur, R., Dill, D.: A theory of timed automata. Theoretical Computer Science 126(2), 183–235 (1994)
2. Bouyer, P., Chevalier, F., Markey, N.: On the expressiveness of TPTL and MTL. In: Sarukkai, S., Sen, S. (eds.) FSTTCS 2005. LNCS, vol. 3821, pp. 432–443. Springer, Heidelberg (2005)
3. Hirshfeld, Y., Rabinovich, A.: Expressiveness of metric modalities for continuous time. In: Grigoriev, D., Harrison, J., Hirsch, E.A. (eds.) CSR 2006. LNCS, vol. 3967, pp. 211–220. Springer, Heidelberg (2006)
4. Hirshfeld, Y., Rabinovich, A.: Expressiveness of metric modalities for continuous time. Logical Methods in Computer Science 3(1) (2007)
5. Ho, H.M., Ouaknine, J., Worrell, J.: On the expressiveness of metric temporal logic over bounded timed words (2014), http://www.cs.ox.ac.uk/people/hsi-ming.ho/exp-full.pdf, full version
6. Ho, H.M., Ouaknine, J., Worrell, J.: Online monitoring of metric temporal logic. In: Bonakdarpour, B., Smolka, S.A. (eds.) RV 2014. LNCS, vol. 8734, pp. 178–192. Springer, Heidelberg (2014), http://www.cs.ox.ac.uk/people/hsi-ming.ho/monitoring-rv.pdf
7. Hunter, P.: When is metric temporal logic expressively complete? In: Proceedings of CSL 2013. LIPIcs, vol. 23, pp. 380–394. Schloss Dagstuhl - Leibniz-Zentrum fuer Informatik (2013)
8. Hunter, P., Ouaknine, J., Worrell, J.: Expressive completeness of metric temporal logic. In: Proceedings of LICS 2013, pp. 349–357. IEEE Computer Society Press (2013)
9. Kamp, J.: Tense logic and the theory of linear order. Ph.D. thesis, University of California, Los Angeles (1968)
10. Koymans, R.: Specifying real-time properties with metric temporal logic. Real-Time Systems 2(4), 255–299 (1990)
11. Ouaknine, J., Rabinovich, A., Worrell, J.: Time-bounded verification. In: Bravetti, M., Zavattaro, G. (eds.) CONCUR 2009. LNCS, vol. 5710, pp. 496–510. Springer, Heidelberg (2009)
12. Ouaknine, J., Worrell, J.: Some recent results in metric temporal logic. In: Cassez, F., Jard, C. (eds.) FORMATS 2008. LNCS, vol. 5215, pp. 1–13. Springer, Heidelberg (2008)
13. Ouaknine, J., Worrell, J.: Towards a theory of time-bounded verification. In: Abramsky, S., Gavoille, C., Kirchner, C., Meyer auf der Heide, F., Spirakis, P.G. (eds.) ICALP 2010. LNCS, vol. 6199, pp. 22–37. Springer, Heidelberg (2010)
14. Pandya, P.K., Shah, S.S.: On expressive powers of timed logics: Comparing boundedness, non-punctuality, and deterministic freezing. In: Katoen, J.-P., König, B. (eds.) CONCUR 2011. LNCS, vol. 6901, pp. 60–75. Springer, Heidelberg (2011)
15. Prabhakar, P., D'Souza, D.: On the expressiveness of MTL with past operators. In: Asarin, E., Bouyer, P. (eds.) FORMATS 2006. LNCS, vol. 4202, pp. 322–336. Springer, Heidelberg (2006)
16. Wilke, T.: Specifying timed state sequences in powerful decidable logics and timed automata. In: Langmaack, H., de Roever, W.-P., Vytopil, J. (eds.) FTRTFT 1994 and ProCoS 1994. LNCS, vol. 863, pp. 694–715. Springer, Heidelberg (1994)

Trace Inclusion for One-Counter Nets Revisited

Piotr Hofman[1] and Patrick Totzke[2]

[1] University of Bayreuth, Germany
[2] LaBRI, Univ. Bordeaux & CNRS, France

Abstract. One-counter nets (OCN) consist of a nondeterministic finite control and a single integer counter that cannot be fully tested for zero. They form a natural subclass of both One-Counter Automata, which allow zero-tests and Petri Nets/VASS, which allow multiple such weak counters. The trace inclusion problem has recently been shown to be undecidable for OCN. In this paper, we contrast the complexity of two natural restrictions which imply decidability.

We show that trace inclusion between a OCN and a *deterministic* OCN is NL-complete, even with arbitrary binary-encoded initial counter-values as part of the input. Secondly, we show that the the trace *universality* problem of nondeterministic OCN, which is equivalent to checking trace inclusion between a finite and a OCN-process, is Ackermann-complete.

1 Introduction

A fundamental question in formal verification is if the behaviour of one process can be reproduced by – or equals that of – another given process. These inclusion and equivalence problems, respectively have been studied for various notions of behavioural preorders and equivalences and for many computational models. Trace inclusion/equivalence asks if the set of *traces*, all emittable sequences of actions, of one process is contained in/equal to that of another. Other than for instance Simulation preorder, trace inclusion lacks a strong locality of failures, which makes this problem intractable or even undecidable already for very limited models of computation.

We consider one-counter nets, which consist of a finite control and a single integer counter that cannot be fully tested for zero, in the sense that an empty counter can only restrict possible moves. They are subsumed by One-counter automata (OCA) and thus Pushdown Systems, which allow explicit zero-tests by reading a bottom marker on the stack. At the same time, OCN are a subclass of Petri Nets or Vector Addition Systems with states (VASS): they are exactly the one-dimensional VASS and thus equivalent to Petri Nets with at most one unbounded place.

Related work. Valiant and Paterson [17] show the decidability of the trace equivalence problem for *deterministic* one-counter automata (DOCA). This problem has recently been shown to be NL-complete by Böhm, Göller, and Jančar

J. Ouaknine, I. Potapov, and J. Worrell (Eds.): RP 2014, LNCS 8762, pp. 151–162, 2014.
© Springer International Publishing Switzerland 2014

[2], assuming fixed initial counter-values. The equivalence of deterministic push-down automata is known to be decidable [13] and primitive recursive [14, 9], but the exact complexity is still open.

Valiant [16] proves the undecidability of both trace inclusion for DOCA and universality for nondeterministic OCA. Jančar, Esparza, and Moller [11] consider trace inclusion between Petri Nets and finite systems and prove decidability in both directions. Jančar [10] showed that trace inclusion becomes undecidable if one compares processes of Petri Nets with at least two unbounded places. In [7], the authors show that trace inclusion is undecidable already for (nondetermin-istic) one-counter nets. Simulation preorder however, is known to be decidable and PSPACE-complete for this model [1, 12, 6], which implies a PSPACE upper bound for trace inclusion on DOCN as trace inclusion and simulation coincide for deterministic systems.

Higuchi, Wakatsuki, and Tomita [5] compare the classes of *languages* defined by DOCN with various acceptance modes and consider the respective inclusion problems. They derive procedures that exhaustively search for a bounded witness that work in time and space polynomial in the size of the automata if the initial counter-values are fixed. We show that for monotone relations like trace inclusion or the inclusion of languages defined by acceptance with final states, it suffices to search for witnesses in a particular compact representation.

Our contribution. We fix the complexity of two well-known decidable decision problems regarding the traces of one-counter processes. We show that trace inclusion between *deterministic* OCNs is NL-complete. Our upper bound holds even if only the supposedly larger process is deterministic and if (binary encoded) initial counter-values are part of the input. We use short certificates for the existence of (possibly long) distinguishing traces. The sizes of certificates are polynomial in the number of states of the finite control and they can be verified in space logarithmic in the binary representation of the initial counter-values.

Our second result is that trace universality of *nondeterministic* OCN is Ackermann-complete. This problem is (logspace) inter-reducible with checking trace inclusion between a finite process and a process of a OCN.

2 Background

We write $\mathbb{N}$ for the set of non-negative integers. For any set A, let A^* denote the set of finite strings over A and $\varepsilon \in A^*$ the empty string.

Definition 1 (One-Counter Nets). *A* one-counter net *(OCN) is given as triple $\mathcal{N} = (Q, Act, \delta)$ where Q is a finite set of control states, Act is a finite set of action labels and $\delta \subseteq Q \times Act \times \{-1, 0, 1\} \times Q$ is a set of transitions, each written as $p \xrightarrow{a,d} p'$. A process of $\mathcal{N}$ consists of a state $p \in Q$ and a counter-value $m \in \mathbb{N}$. We will simply write pm for such a pair. Processes can evolve according to the transition rules of the net: For any $a \in Act$, $p, q \in Q$ and $m, n \in \mathbb{N}$ there is a step $pm \xrightarrow{a} qn$ iff there exists $(p \xrightarrow{a,d} q) \in \delta$ such that*

$$n = m + d \geq 0. \tag{1}$$

The net $\mathcal{N}$ is deterministic *(a DOCN) if for every $p \in Q$ and $a \in Act$, there is at most one transition $(p, a, d, q) \in \delta$. It is* complete *if for every $p \in Q$ and $a \in Act$ at least one transition $(p, a, d, q) \in \delta$ exists.*

Definition 2 (Traces). *Let pm be a process of the OCN $\mathcal{N}$. The* traces *of pm are the elements of the set*

$$T_{\mathcal{N}}(pm) = \{a_1 a_2 \ldots a_k \in Act^* \mid \exists qn \; pm \xrightarrow{a_0} \circ \xrightarrow{a_1} \circ \cdots \circ \xrightarrow{a_k} qn\}.$$

We will omit the index $\mathcal{N}$ if it is clear from the context. Trace inclusion *is the decision problem that asks if $T_A(pm) \subseteq T_B(p'm')$ holds for given processes pm and $p'm'$ of nets A and B, respectively.* Trace universality *asks if $Act^* \subseteq T(pm)$ holds for a given process pm.*

An important property of one-counter nets is that the step relation and therefore also trace inclusion is monotone with respect to the counter:

Lemma 1 (Monotonicity). *If $pm \xrightarrow{a} p'm'$ then $p(m+1) \xrightarrow{a} p'(m'+1)$. This in particular means that $T(pm) \subseteq T(p(m+1))$ holds for any OCN-process pm.*

Remark 1. In this paper we consider what are called *realtime* automata, in which no silent (ε-labelled) transitions are present. For deterministic OCN, this is no restriction: the usual syntactic requirement for DPDA, that no state with outgoing ε-transition may have outgoing transitions labelled by $a \neq \varepsilon$, together with the monotonicity of steps in OCN, implies that all states on ε-cycles are essentially deadlocks. One can thus eliminate ε-labelled transitions in logspace.

We will w.l.o.g. assume input nets in a certain form, justified by the next lemma. A pair A, B of OCNs is in *normal form* if A is deterministic and B is complete. The proof is a simple construction and can be found in [8].

Lemma 2 (Normal Form). *Given OCNs A and B with state sets N and M, one can in logarithmic space construct nets A', B' in normal form, with states N and $M' \supseteq M$, respectively, such that for all $(p, n, q, m) \in N \times \mathbb{N} \times M \times \mathbb{N}$*

$$T_A(pm) \subseteq T_B(qn) \iff T_{A'}(pm) \subseteq T_{B'}(qn). \tag{2}$$

Moreover, the constructed net B' is deterministic if the original net B is.

Due to the undecidability of trace inclusion for OCN [7], a direct consequence of Lemma 2 is that $T_A(pm) \subseteq T_B(qn)$ is already undecidable if we allow the net B to be nondeterministic. Unless otherwise stated, we will from now on assume a DOCN $A = (Q_A, Act, \delta_A)$ and a complete DOCN $B = (Q_B, Act, \delta_B)$.

3   Trace Inclusion for Deterministic One-Counter Nets

We characterize witnesses for non-inclusion $T_A(pm) \not\subseteq T_B(qn)$, starting with some notation to express paths and their effects.

Definition 3 (OCN Paths). *Let* $\mathcal{N} = (Q, Act, \delta)$ *be a OCN and* $t = (p, a, d, p')$ $\in \delta$. *We write* $source(t) = p$, $target(t) = p'$ *and* $\Delta(t) = d$ *for its source and target states and effect, respectively. A* path *in* $\mathcal{N}$ *is a sequence* $\pi = t_0 t_1 \ldots t_k \in \delta^*$ *of transitions where* $target(t_i) = source(t_{i+1})$ *for every* $i < k$. *Let* $^i\pi$ *denote its prefix of length* i. *The* effect $\Delta(\pi)$ *and* guard $\Gamma(\pi)$ *of* π *are*

$$\Delta(\pi) = \sum_{i=0}^{k} \Delta(t_i) \qquad and \qquad \Gamma(\pi) = -\min\{\Delta(^i\pi) \mid 0 \leq i \leq k\}.$$

The path π *is* enabled *in process* pm *(write* $pm \xrightarrow{\pi}$*) if* $\Gamma(\pi) \leq m$. *We write* $pm \xrightarrow{\pi} p'm'$ *if* π *takes* pm *to* $p'm'$, *i.e., if* $pm \xrightarrow{\pi}$, $target(\pi) = p'$ *and* $m' = m + \Delta(\pi)$.

The guard $\Gamma(\pi)$ is the minimal counter-value that is sufficient to traverse the path π while maintaining a non-negative counter-value along the way. This value is always non-negative. Notice that the absolute values of the effect and guard of a path are bounded by its length. We consider the synchronous product of the control graphs of two given deterministic one-counter nets.

Definition 4 (Products). *The* product *of nets* $\mathcal{A}$ *and* $\mathcal{B}$ *is the finite graph with nodes* $V = Q_{\mathcal{A}} \times Q_{\mathcal{B}}$ *and* $(Act \times \{-1, 0, 1\} \times \{-1, 0, 1\})$*-labelled edges* E, *where*

$$(p, q) \xrightarrow{a, d_A, d_B} (p', q') \in E \text{ iff } p \xrightarrow{a, d_A} p' \in \delta_{\mathcal{A}} \text{ and } q \xrightarrow{a, d_B} q' \in \delta_{\mathcal{B}}.$$

A path *in the product is a sequence* $\pi = T_0 T_1 \cdots T_k \in E^*$ *and defines paths* $\pi_{\mathcal{A}}$ *and* $\pi_{\mathcal{B}}$ *in nets* $\mathcal{A}$ *and* $\mathcal{B}$, *respectively. It is* enabled *in* (pm, qn) *if* $\pi_{\mathcal{A}}$ *and* $\pi_{\mathcal{B}}$ *are enabled in* pm *and* qn, *respectively. In this case we write* $(pm, qn) \xrightarrow{\pi} (p'm', q'n')$ *to mean that* $pm \xrightarrow{\pi_{\mathcal{A}}} p'm'$ *and* $qn \xrightarrow{\pi_{\mathcal{B}}} q'n'$. *We lift the definitions of source and target nodes to paths in the product:* $source(\pi) = (source(\pi_{\mathcal{A}}), source(\pi_{\mathcal{B}})) \in V$, $target(\pi) = (target(\pi_{\mathcal{A}}), target(\pi_{\mathcal{B}})) \in V$. *Moreover, write* $\Delta_A(\pi)$, $\Delta_B(\pi)$, $\Gamma_A(\pi)$ *and* $\Gamma_B(\pi)$ *for the effects and guards of* π *in nets* $\mathcal{A}$ *and* $\mathcal{B}$, *respectively.*

Since both $\mathcal{A}$ and $\mathcal{B}$ are deterministic and $\mathcal{B}$ is complete, Due to our normal form assumption, a trace $w \in T_A(pm)$ uniquely determines a path from state (p, q) in their product. We therefore identify witnesses for non-inclusion with the paths they induce in the product.

Definition 5 (Witnesses). *Assume* $T_A(pm) \not\subseteq T_B(qn)$ *for processes* pm *and* qn *of* $\mathcal{A}$ *and* $\mathcal{B}$. *A* witness *for* (pm, qn) *is a path* π *in the product of* $\mathcal{A}$ *and* $\mathcal{B}$ *such that* $(pm, qn) \xrightarrow{\pi} (p'm', q'n')$ *and for some* $a \in Act$, $p'm' \xrightarrow{a}$ *but* $q'n' \xrightarrow{a}\!\!\!\!/\ $.

Every witness π for (pm, qn) completely exhausts the counter in the process of $\mathcal{B}$: $(pm, qn) \xrightarrow{\pi} (p'm', q'0)$. This is because a process of a complete net can only *not* make an a-step in case the counter is empty.

Example 1. Consider two nets given by self-loops $p \xrightarrow{a, 0} p$ and $q \xrightarrow{a, -1} q$, respectively. Their product is the cycle $L = (p, q) \xrightarrow{a, 0, -1} (p, q)$ with effects $\Delta_A(L) = 0$

and $\Delta_B(L) = -1$. The only witness for (pm, qn) for initial counter-values $m, n \in \mathbb{N}$ is L^n, which has length polynomial in the sizes of the nets *and* the initial counter-values, but not in the sizes of the nets alone.

The previous example shows that if binary-encoded initial counter-values are part of the input, we can only bound the length of shortest witnesses exponentially. However, we will see that it suffices to consider witnesses of a certain regular form only. This leads to small certificates for non-inclusion, which can be stepwise guessed and verified in space logarithmic in the size of the nets. A crucial ingredient for our characterization is the monotonicity of witnesses, a direct consequence of the monotonicity of the steps in OCNs (Lemma 1):

Lemma 3. *If π is a witness for (pm, qn) then for all $m' \geq m$ and $n' \leq n$ some prefix of π is a witness for (pm', qn').*

The intuition behind the further characterization of witnesses is that in order to show non-inclusion, one looks for a path that is enabled in the process of $\mathcal{A}$ and moreover exhausts the counter in the process of $\mathcal{B}$. Since any sufficiently long path will revisit control states in the product, we can compare such paths with respect to their effect on the counters and see that some are "better" than others. For instance, a cycle that only increments the counter in $\mathcal{B}$ and decrements the one in $\mathcal{A}$ is surely suboptimal considering our goal to find a (shortest) witness. The characterization Theorem 1 essentially states that if a witness exists, then also one that, apart from short paths, combines only the most productive cycles.

Definition 6 (Loops). *A non-empty path π in the product is called a* cycle *if $source(\pi) = target(\pi)$. Such a cycle is a* loop *if none of its proper subpaths is a cycle. The* slope *of loop π is the ratio $S(\pi) = \Delta_{\mathcal{A}}(\pi)/\Delta_{\mathcal{B}}(\pi)$, where for $n > 0$ and $k \in \mathbb{Z}$ we let $n/0 = \infty > k$, $0/0 = 0$ and $-n/0 = -\infty < k$. Based on the effect of a loop we distinguish four types of loops: $(<, <), (>, \geq), (\leq, \geq)$, and $(\geq, <)$. The type of π is $Type(\pi) = (\blacktriangleleft, \blacktriangleright)$ iff $\Delta_{\mathcal{A}}(\pi) \blacktriangleleft 0$ and $\Delta_{\mathcal{B}}(\pi) \blacktriangleright 0$.*

Note that no loop is longer than $|V|$ because it visits exactly one node twice.

Example 2. Consider two DOCN such that their product is the graph depicted below, where we identify transitions with their action labels for simplicity and let $v_0 = (p, p') \in V$. The paths $t_0 t_1 t_2$, $t_3 t_4$ and t_6 are loops with slopes $3/1$, $2/1$ and $1/1$ and types $(>, \geq), (>, \geq)$ and $(<, <)$, respectively. The path $(t_0 t_1 t_2)(t_3 t_4)^9 t_5 (t_6)^{20}$ is a witness for $(p0, p'10)$ of length 42. By replacing 8 occurrences of the loop $(t_3 t_4)$ with $(t_0 t_1 t_2)^8$ we derive the longer witness $(t_0 t_1 t_2)^9 (t_3 t_4) t_5 (t_6)^{20}$, which has essentially the same structure but is more efficient in

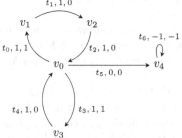

the sense that for the same effect on $\mathcal{B}$ it achieves a higher counter-effect on $\mathcal{A}$.

Theorem 1. *Fix a DOCN $\mathcal{A}$, a complete DOCN $\mathcal{B}$, and let $K \in \mathbb{N}$ be the number of nodes in their product. There is a bound $c \in \mathbb{N}$ that depends polynomially on K, such that the following holds for any two processes pm and qn of $\mathcal{A}$ and $\mathcal{B}$. If $T(pm) \not\subseteq T(qn)$, then there is a witness for (pm, qn) that is either no longer than c or has one of the following forms:*

1. *$\pi_0 L_0^{l_0} \pi_1$, where L_0 is a loop of type $(\geq, <)$ and π_0, π_1 are no longer than c,*
2. *$\pi_0 L_0^{l_0} \pi_1 L_1^{l_1} \pi_2$, where L_0 and L_1 are loops of type $(>, \geq)$ and $(<, <)$ with $S(L_0) > S(L_1)$ and π_0, π_1, π_2 are no longer than c,*
3. *$\pi_0 L_0^{l_0} \pi_1$, where L_0 is a loop of type $(<, <)$ and π_0, π_1 are no longer than c,*

where in all cases, the number of iterations $l_0, l_1 \in \mathbb{N}$ are polynomial in K and the initial counter-values m and n of the given processes.

Proof (sketch). The overall idea of the proof is to explicitly rewrite witnesses into one of the canonical forms of Theorem 1. More specifically, we introduce a system of path-rewriting rules which simplify witnesses by removing, reducing or changing some loops as in Example 2. We show that the rules preserve witnesses and any sequence of successive rule applications must eventually terminate with a normalized path, to which none of the rules is applicable. Such a witness can be decomposed as

$$\pi = \pi_0 L_0^{l_0} \pi_1 L_1^{l_1} \dots \pi_k L_k^{l_k} \pi_{k+1} \tag{3}$$

where the L_i are (pairwise different) loops and the π_i are short, i.e. polynomially bounded in K. Moreover the rules are designed in such a way that almost all l_i are polynomially bounded. By almost all we mean except one in the first and third form of the witness or two in the witness of the second form. This means that unravelling of those loops with polynomially bounded l_i and glueing them with surrounding π_i to get paths π_0, π_1, π_2 does not blow up of the length of π_0, π_1, π_2 above polynomial bound c. $\square$

Notice that the bound c in the claim of Theorem 1 depends only on the number of states. We now derive a decision procedure for trace inclusion that works in logarithmic space. The NL lower bound already holds for the trace inclusion problem of DFA, which can be shown by a streightforward reduction from s-t-connectivity.

Theorem 2. *Let pm and qn be processes of OCN $\mathcal{A}$ and DOCN $\mathcal{B}$, respectively, where m, n are given in binary. There is a nondeterministic algorithm that decides $T(pm) \subseteq T(qn)$ in logarithmic space.*

Proof. Let $\mathcal{A} = (Q_{\mathcal{A}}, Act, \delta_{\mathcal{A}})$ and $\mathcal{B} = (Q_{\mathcal{B}}, Act, \delta_{\mathcal{B}})$, and let $K \in \mathbb{N}$ be the number of states in their product. By Lemma 2, we can assume w.l.o.g. that $\mathcal{A}$ is deterministic and $\mathcal{B}$ is complete and deterministic and so Theorem 1 applies.

If the initial counter-values are $m = n = 0$, Theorem 1 implies a polynomial bound on the length of shortest witnesses. In that case, one can simply stepwise guess and verify a witness, explicitly storing the intermediate processes with binary encoded counter-values in logarithmic space. Such a procedure is impossible with arbitrary initial counter-values as part of the input, because one does not even have the space to memorize them.

For the general case, we argue that one can nondeterministically guess a template (consisting of short paths) and verify in logspace that there is indeed some witness that fits this template. Theorem 1 allows us to either guess a short ($\leq c \in poly(K)$) witness or one of forms 1,2 or 3, together with matching short paths π_i, L_i. The effect and guard of these paths are bounded by their lengths and hence by c. This means $\mathcal{O}(\log K)$ space suffices to stepwise compute the binary representation of these values and verify that the conditions the form imposes on the types and slopes of the loops are met. It remains to check if exponents $l_0, l_1 \in \mathbb{N}$ exist, that complete the description of a witness π. To see why these checks can be implemented in logarithmic space, first recall that one can verify inequalities of the form

$$m \cdot A + B \geq n \cdot C + D \tag{4}$$

in $\mathcal{O}(log(A + B + C + D))$ space, if $m, n \in \mathbb{N}$ are given in binary (see [8] for details).

For templates of the first two forms, it suffices to check if $m \geq \Gamma_{\mathcal{A}}(\pi_0 L_0)$, because the type of L_0 implies that $\Gamma_{\mathcal{A}}(\pi_0 L_0^l) \leq \Gamma_{\mathcal{A}}(\pi_0 L_0)$ for all $1 < l \in \mathbb{N}$. This means that the process pm of $\mathcal{A}$ can go to, and repeat the loop L_0 arbitrarily often. In case its effect in $\mathcal{B}$ is negative (in templates of form 1), this immediately implies the existence of a suitable l_0. For templates of form 2) the existence of $l_0, l_1 \in \mathbb{N}$ completing the description of a witness is guaranteed because the slope of the first loop is bigger than that of the second.

For templates of the third kind recall that, because $\mathcal{B}$ is complete, a path $\pi = \pi_0 L_0^{l_0} \pi_1$ is a witness iff there is some edge T in the product such that $\Delta_{\mathcal{B}}(T) = -1$ and both $m \geq \Gamma_{\mathcal{A}}(\pi T)$ and $n + \Delta_{\mathcal{B}}(\pi T) = -1$. Equivalently, we can write this as

$$m + \Delta_{\mathcal{A}}(\pi_0 L_0^{l_0}) = m + \Delta_{\mathcal{A}}(\pi_0) + \Delta_{\mathcal{A}}(L_0) \cdot l_0 \geq \Gamma_{\mathcal{A}}(\pi_1 T) \text{ and} \tag{5}$$
$$n + 1 = -\Delta_{\mathcal{B}}(\pi T) = -\Delta_{\mathcal{B}}(\pi_0) - \Delta_{\mathcal{B}}(L_0) \cdot l_0 - \Delta_{\mathcal{B}}(\pi_1 T). \tag{6}$$

Eliminating l_0, we see that this is true iff

$$m + \Delta_{\mathcal{A}}(\pi_0) + \Delta_{\mathcal{A}}(L_0) \cdot \frac{\Delta_{\mathcal{B}}(\pi_0) + \Delta_{\mathcal{B}}(\pi_1) + n}{-\Delta_{\mathcal{B}}(L_0)} \geq \Gamma_{\mathcal{A}}(\pi_1). \tag{7}$$

Simplifying further we can bring this into the form $m \cdot A - n \cdot B \geq C$ where A, B, C are polynomial in c. The condition can be checked in $\mathcal{O}(\log K)$ space. □

4   Universality of Nondeterministic One-Counter Nets

To contrast the result of the previous section we now turn to the problem of checking trace inclusion between a finite process and a nondeterministic OCN.

This problem is known to be decidable, even for general Petri nets [11] and it can be easily seen to be (logspace) inter-reducible with the trace universality problem, because OCNs are closed under products with finite systems.

For OCN, trace universality can be decided using a simple well-quasi-order based saturation method that determinizes the net on the fly. We will see that this procedure is optimal: The problem is Ackermannian, i.e. it is non-primitive recursive and lies exactly at level ω of the Fast Growing Hierarchy [4].

Let $\mathbb{N}_\perp$ be the set of non-negative integers plus a special least element $\perp$ and let max be the total function that returns the maximal element of any nonempty finite subset and $\perp$ otherwise. Consider a set $S \subseteq Q \times \mathbb{N}$ of processes of a OCN $\mathcal{N} = (Q, Act, \delta)$. We lift the definition of traces to sets of processes in the natural way: the *traces* of S are $T(S) = \bigcup_{qn \in S} T(qn)$. By the monotonicity of trace inclusion (Lemma 1), the traces of a finite set of processes are determined only by the traces of its maximal elements.

Definition 7. *Let $Q = \{q_1, q_2, \ldots, q_k\}$ be the states-set of some OCN. For a finite set $S \subseteq Q \times \mathbb{N}$ define the* macrostate *as the vector $M_S \in \mathbb{N}_\perp^k$ where for each $0 < i \le k$, $M_S(i) = M_S(q_i) = \max\{n \mid q_i n \in S\}$. In particular, the macrostate for a singleton set $S = \{q_i n\}$ is the vector with value n at the i-th coordinate and $\perp$ on all others. The* norm *of a macrostate $M \in \mathbb{N}_\perp^k$ is $|M|_\infty = \max\{M(i) \mid 0 < i \le k\}$. We define a step relation $\overset{a}{\Longrightarrow}$ for all $a \in Act$ on the set of macrostates as follows:*

$$(n_1, n_2, \ldots, n_k) \overset{a}{\Longrightarrow} (m_1, m_2, \ldots, m_k) \tag{8}$$

iff $m_i = \max\{n \mid \exists n_j \ne \perp. q_j n_j \overset{a}{\longrightarrow} q_i n\}$ for all $0 < i \le k$. The traces *of macrostate M are $T(M) = \bigcup_{0 < i \le k} T(q_i M(i))$, where $T(q\perp) = \emptyset$. For two macrostates M, N we say M is* covered *by N and write $M \sqsubseteq N$, if it is pointwise smaller, i.e., $M(i) \le N(i)$ for all $0 < i \le k$. For convenience, we will write $\{q_1 = n_1, q_2 = n_2, \ldots, q_l = n_l\}$ for the macrostate with value $M(i) = n_i$ whenever $q_i = n_i$ is listed and $\perp$ otherwise.*

Steps on macrostates correspond to the classical powerset construction and each macrostate represents the finite set of possible processes the OCN can be in, where all non-maximal ones (w.r.t. their counter-value) are pruned out.

The next lemma directly follows from these definitions and monotonicity (Lemma 1).

Lemma 4.

1. *The covering-order $\sqsubseteq$ is a well-quasi-order on $\mathbb{N}_\perp^k$, the set of all macrostates. Moreover, $M \sqsubseteq N$ implies $T(M) \subseteq T(N)$.*
2. *If $M \overset{a}{\Longrightarrow} N$ then $|N|_\infty \le |M|_\infty + 1$.*
3. *For any finite set $S \subseteq Q \times \mathbb{N}$ it holds that $T(S) = T(M_S)$.*

Dealing with macrostates allows us to treat universality as a reachability problem: By point 3 of Lemma 4 we see that a process qn is *not* trace universal,

$Act^* \neq T(qn)$, if and only if $M_{\{qn\}} \Longrightarrow^* (\bot, \bot, \ldots, \bot)$. We take the perspective of a pathfinder, whose goal it is to reach $(\bot)^k$.

We can decide universality by stepwise guessing a shortest terminating path from the initial macrostate, and thus a witness for non-universality. Whenever we see a macrostate that covers one of its predecessors, we can safely discard this candidate, because omitting the intermediate path would result in a shorter witness by Lemma 4.1.

We show non-primitive recursiveness by reduction from the control state reachability problem for incrementing counter machines [3, 4].

Definition 8 (Counter machines). *A (Minsky)-counter machine (CM) is an automaton with a finite set of states Q, finitely many counters $C_1, C_2, \ldots, C_k$, and transitions are of the form $Q \times Act \times Q$ where Act is $\{\text{inc}, \text{dec}, \text{ifz}\} \times \{1, 2, \ldots, k\}$. A configuration of such a CM consists of a state and a valuation of the counters. Performing a transition $(p, (op, i), q)$ changes a configuration precisely: the state changes from p to q and we make operation op on the counter c_i, where inc, dec and ifz mean increment, decrement and zero-test, respectively. Such a step is forbidden if the requested operation is dec and the value of c_i is 0, or if $c_i > 0$ and the operation is ifz.*

An incrementing counter machine (ICM) is a CM in which counters can spontaneously increment without performing any transitions. Such increments we call incrementing errors. Control state reachability is the decision problem that asks if there is a run of a given CM from an initial configuration to some given state $q_f \in Q$.

Our reduction is based on the following simple observation. Consider a OCN $\mathcal{N} = (Q, Act, \delta)$ that contains a *universal* state u: it has self-loops $u \xrightarrow{a,0} u \in \delta$ for every action $a \in Act$. A Pathfinder who wants to prove non-universality must avoid macrostates with $M(u) \neq \bot$, because no continuation of a path leading to such a macrostate can be a witness. We can use this idea to construct macrostates that prevent Pathfinder from making certain actions.

Definition 9 (Obstacles). *Let $S \subseteq Act$ be a set of actions in a OCN that contains a universal state u. A state $q \in Q$ is called an S-obstacle if $q \xrightarrow{a,0} u \in \delta$ for all actions $a \in S$. We say q ignores S, if $q \xrightarrow{a,0} q \in \delta$ for all $a \in S$.*

Note that if a macrostate contains an S-obstacle, then Pathfinder must avoid all actions of S. In order to remove an obstacle, Pathfinder must play an action that is not the label of any of its incoming transitions.

Theorem 3. *Trace universality for OCN is not primitive recursive.*

Proof. By reduction (using logspace) from the control state reachability problem for ICM, which has non-primitive recursive complexity [3]. We construct a OCN-process $Init(0)$ that is not universal iff a given ICM reaches a final state from its initial configuration. The idea is to enforce a faithful simulation of the ICM by pathfinder, who wants to show non-universality of the OCN by stepwise rewriting the initial macrostate $\{Init = 0\}$ to the all-bottom-macrostate $\bot^l$.

We construct a OCN $\mathcal{N}$ which has a unique action for every transition of the ICM, as well as actions τ_i that indicate incrementing errors for every counter c_i, and actions $\sharp$ and $\$$ to mark the beginning and end of a run, respectively. This way we make sure there is a strict correspondence between words and ICM-runs. The states of $\mathcal{N}$ are

- a new initial state *Init* and a universal state u,
- a state q_i for every state q_i of the ICM,
- a state C_i for every counter c_i of the ICM,
- a state z, which ignores every action but the end marker $\$$. State z will be used to access the constant 0.

A configuration $q(c_1, c_2, \ldots, c_k)$ of the ICM is represented by a macrostate $\{q = 0, z = 0, C_1 = c_1, C_2 = c_2, \ldots, C_k = c_k\}$. We will define the transitions of $\mathcal{N}$ such that the only way for Pathfinder to reach $\perp^l$ is by rewriting the initial macrostate $\{Init = 0\}$ to the one representing the initial ICM configuration and then to stepwise announce the transitions of an accepting run of the ICM. Using the idea of obstacles, we define the rules of the net $\mathcal{N}$ so that the only way Pathfinder can avoid the universal state u and reach the macrostate $\perp^l$ is by first transforming the initial macrostate $\{Init = 0\}$ to the one that represents the initial ICM configuration and then announcing transitions (as well as actions demanding increment errors) of a valid and accepting run of the ICM.

Initialization. To set up $M_0 = \{q_0 = 0, z = 0, C_0 = 0, C_1 = 0, \ldots, C_k = 0\}$, representing the initial ICM configuration, we add $\sharp$-labelled transitions with effect 0 from *Init* to q_0, z and C_i for all $0 \leq i \leq k$. Moreover, we make *Init* an obstacle for every action but $\sharp$. This way, Pathfinder has to play $\sharp$ as the first move (and set up M_0) in order to avoid a universal macrostate.

Finite control. For any transition $t = q \xrightarrow{(a,i)} q'$ of the ICM, we add a transition $q \xrightarrow{t,0} q'$ to $\mathcal{N}$ that, in a macrostate-step, will replace the value 0 in dimension q by $\perp$ and introduce value 0 in dimension q'. Moreover, we make every state q an obstacle for all actions announcing ICM-transitions not originating in q. This prevents Pathfinder from announcing transitions from q unless the current macrostate has $M(q) = 0$ and $M(q_i) = \perp$ for all $q_i \neq q$.

Simulation of the Counters. Every transition operates on one of the counters c_i for $0 \leq i \leq k$. Below we list the corresponding transitions in the OCN $\mathcal{N}$ for this counter. Every state of $\mathcal{N}$ not explicitly mentioned ignores the action in question. In the macrostate, the values of these states are therefore unchanged.

Increments For ICM-transitions t that increase the ith counter, $\mathcal{N}$ contains a t-labelled transition from state C_i to C_i with effect $+1$. Additionally, to deal with spontaneous increment errors, there is a τ_i-labelled increasing self-loop in state C_i. All other states ignore the τ_i.

Decrements For ICM-transitions t that decrease the ith counter, $\mathcal{N}$ contains a t-labelled transition from state C_i to C_i with effect -1.
This means that the next macrostate M could lose the value for this counter and have $M(C_i) = \bot$ if previously, the value was 0. In that case, the decrementing step from value 0 to value 0 is valid in the ICM because it can first (silently) increment and then do the (visible) decrement step. In order to avoid losing the state C_i in the macrostate, the OCN contains a transition $z \xrightarrow{t,0} C_i$ from the constant-zero state z to state C_i. Recall that z is present in the macrostate because z ignores every action except end marker \$. Consequently, no correctly set up macrostate will set $M(C_i) = \bot$.

Zero-tests For ICM-transitions t that test the ith counter for 0, we add a t-labelled transition $C_i \xrightarrow{t,-1} u$ from state C_i to the universal state. This prevents Pathfinder from using these actions if the current macrostate has $M(C_i) > 0$ because it would make the next macrostate universal. If however $M(C_i) = 0$, such a step is safe because the punishing transition is not enabled in the OCN-process $C_i 0$.

Lastly, we only add transitions to $\mathcal{N}$ so that the final state q_f is the only original ICM-state which is not an obstacle for \$. This prevents Pathfinder from playing the end-marker \$ unless the simulation has reached the final state. □

In order to estimate an upper bound, we recall a recent result of Figueira, Figueira, Schmitz, and Schnoebelen [4], that allows us to provide the exact complexity of the OCN trace universality problem in terms of its level in the Fast-Growing Hierarchy. The main idea is to estimate the maximal length of a path in the well quasi order based algorithm using bounds on the difference of sizes of consecutive configurations. A full proof can be found in [8].

Theorem 4. *Trace universality of OCN is Ackermannian (Complete for $\mathfrak{F}_\omega$).*

5   Conclusion

We have shown NL-completeness of the trace inclusion problem for deterministic one-counter nets, where initial counter-values are part of the input. Our proof is based on a characterization of the shape of possible witnesses in terms of a small number of polynomially-sized templates. Realizability of such templates can be verified in space logarithmic only in the size of the underlying state space. To prove the characterization theorem we use witness rewriting rules, the correctness of which crucially depends on the monotonicity of trace inclusion w.r.t. counter-values. In fact, we only make use of this property in the net on the left but similarly one can define rules that exploit only the monotonicity in the process on the right. With some additional effort one can extend this argument also for trace inclusion between DOCN and DOCA or vice versa (see [15]).

The second part of the paper explores the complexity of the universality problem for nondeterministic OCN, and trace inclusion between finite systems and OCN that easily reduces to OCN universality. Here we show that the simplest known algorithm which uses a well-quasi-order based saturation technique has already optimal complexity: The problem is Ackermannian, i.e., not primitive recursive.

Acknowledgement. We thank Mary Cryan, Diego Figueira and Sylvain Schmitz for helpful discussions and the anonymous reviewers of an earlier draft for their constructive feedback. Piotr Hofman acknowledges a partial support by the Polish NCN grant 2013/09/B/ST6/01575.

References

[1] Abdulla, P.A., Cerans, K.: Simulation Is Decidable for One-Counter Nets. In: Sangiorgi, D., de Simone, R. (eds.) CONCUR 1998. LNCS, vol. 1466, pp. 253–268. Springer, Heidelberg (1998)

[2] Böhm, S., Göller, S., Jančar, P.: Equivalence of Deterministic One-Counter Automata is NL-complete. In: STOC, pp. 131–140 (2013)

[3] Demri, S., Lazić, R.: LTL with the freeze quantifier and register automata. ACM Trans. Comput. Logic 10(3), 16:1–16:30 (2009)

[4] Figueira, D., Figueira, S., Schmitz, S., Schnoebelen, P.: Ackermannian and Primitive-Recursive Bounds with Dickson's Lemma. In: LICS, pp. 269–278 (2011)

[5] Higuchi, K., Wakatsuki, M., Tomita, E.: Some Properties of Deterministic Restricted One-Counter Automata. In: IEICE E79-D.8, pp. 914–924 (July 1996)

[6] Hofman, P., Lasota, S., Mayr, R., Totzke, P.: Simulation Over Onecounter Nets is PSPACE-Complete. In: FSTTCS, pp. 515–526 (2013)

[7] Hofman, P., Mayr, R., Totzke, P.: Decidability of Weak Simulation on One-Counter Nets. In: LICS, pp. 203–212 (2013)

[8] Hofman, P., Totzke, P.: Trace Inclusion for One-Counter Nets Revisited. In: CoRR abs/1404.5157 (2014) (full version of this paper)

[9] Jančar, P.: Equivalences of Pushdown Systems Are Hard. In: Muscholl, A. (ed.) FOSSACS 2014 (ETAPS). LNCS, vol. 8412, pp. 1–28. Springer, Heidelberg (2014)

[10] Jančar, P.: Undecidability of Bisimilarity for Petri Nets and Some Related Problems. TCS 148(2), 281–301 (1995)

[11] Jančar, P., Esparza, J., Moller, F.: Petri Nets and Regular Processes. J. Comput. Syst. Sci. 59(3), 476–503 (1999)

[12] Jančar, P., Kučera, A., Moller, F.: Simulation and Bisimulation over One-Counter Processes. In: STACS, pp. 334–345 (2000)

[13] Sénizergues, G.: L(A) = L(B)? ENTCS 9, 43 (1997)

[14] Stirling, C.: Deciding DPDA Equivalence Is Primitive Recursive. In: ICALP, pp. 821–832 (2002)

[15] Totzke, P.: Inclusion Problems for One-Counter Systems. PhD thesis. LFCS, University of Edinburgh (2014)

[16] Valiant, L.: Decision Procedures for Families of Deterministic Pushdown Automata. PhD thesis. University of Warwick (1973)

[17] Valiant, L., Paterson, M.S.: Deterministic One-Counter Automata. JCSS 10(3), 340–350 (1975)

Mean-Payoff Games with Partial-Observation[*]
(Extended Abstract)

Paul Hunter, Guillermo A. Pérez, and Jean-François Raskin

Département d'Informatique, Université Libre de Bruxelles (U.L.B.), Belgium
{paul.hunter,guillermo.perez,jraskin}@ulb.ac.be

Abstract. Mean-payoff games are important quantitative models for open reactive systems. They have been widely studied as games of perfect information. In this paper we investigate the algorithmic properties of several subclasses of mean-payoff games where the players have asymmetric information about the state of the game. These games are in general undecidable and not determined according to the classical definition. We show that such games are determined under a more general notion of winning strategy. We also consider mean-payoff games where the winner can be determined by the winner of a finite cycle-forming game. This yields several decidable classes of mean-payoff games of asymmetric information that require only finite-memory strategies, including a generalization of perfect information games where positional strategies are sufficient. We give an exponential time algorithm for determining the winner of the latter.

1 Introduction

Mean-payoff games (MPGs) are two-player, infinite duration, turn-based games played on finite edge-weighted graphs. The two players alternately move a token around the graph; and one of the players (Eve) tries to maximize the (limit) average weight of the edges traversed, whilst the other player (Adam) attempts to minimize the average weight. Such games are particularly useful in the field of verification of models of reactive systems, and the perfect information versions of these games have been extensively studied [4,7,8,10]. One of the major open questions in the field of verification is whether the following decision problem, known to be in the intersection of the classes NP and coNP [10][1], can be solved in polynomial time: Given a threshold ν, does Eve have a strategy to ensure a mean-payoff value of at least ν?

In game theory the concepts of imperfect, partial and limited information indicate situations where players have asymmetric knowledge about the state of the game. In the context of verification games this partial knowledge is reflected in one or both players being unable to determine the precise location of the token amongst several equivalent vertices, and such games have also been extensively

---

[*] This work was supported by the ERC inVEST (279499) project.
[1] From results in [17] and [12] it follows that the problem is also in UP ∩ coUP.

J. Ouaknine, I. Potapov, and J. Worrell (Eds.): RP 2014, LNCS 8762, pp. 163–175, 2014.
© Springer International Publishing Switzerland 2014

studied [2, 3, 9, 13, 16]. Adding partial-observation to verification games results in an enormous increase in complexity, both algorithmically and in terms of strategy synthesis. For example, it was shown in [9] that for MPGs with partial-observation, when the mean payoff value is defined using lim sup, the analogue of the above decision problem is undecidable; and whilst memoryless strategies suffice for MPGs with perfect information, infinite memory may be required. The first result of this paper is to show that this is also the case when the mean payoff value is defined using the stronger lim inf operator, closing two open questions posed in [9]. As a consequence, we generalize a result from [6] which uses the undecidability result from [9] to show several classical problems for mean-payoff automata are also undecidable.

To simplify our definitions and algorithmic results we initially consider a restriction on the set of observations which we term *limited-observation*. In games of limited-observation the current observation contains only those vertices consistent with the observable history, that is the observations are the *belief set of Eve* (see, e.g. [5]). This is not too restrictive as any MPG with partial-observation can be realized as a game of limited-observation via a subset construction. In Section 9 we consider the extension of our definitions to MPGs with partial-observation via this construction.

Our focus for the paper will be on games at the observation level, in particular we are interested in *observation-based strategies* for both players. Whilst observation-based strategies for Eve are usual in the literature, observation-based strategies for Adam have not, to the best of our knowledge, been considered. Such strategies are more advantageous for Adam as they encompass several simultaneous concrete strategies. Further, in games of limited-observation there is guaranteed to be at least one concrete strategy consistent with an observation-based strategy. Our second result is to show that although MPGs with partial-observation are not determined under the usual definition of strategy, they are determined when Adam can use an observation-based strategy.

In games of perfect information one aspect of MPGs that leads to simple (but not quite efficient) decision procedures is their equivalence to finite cycle-forming games. Such games are played as their infinite counterparts, however when the token revisits a vertex the game is stopped. The winner is determined by a finite analogue of the mean-payoff condition on the cycle now formed. Ehrenfeucht and Mycielski [10] and Björklund et al. [4][2] used this equivalence to show that positional strategies are sufficient to win MPGs with perfect information. Critically, a winning strategy in the finite game translates directly to a winning strategy in the MPG, so such games are especially useful for strategy synthesis.

We extend this idea to games of partial-observation by introducing a finite, perfect information, cycle-forming game played at the observation level. That is, the game finishes when an observation is revisited (though not necessarily the first time). In this reachability game winning strategies can be translated to finite-memory winning strategies in the MPG. This leads to a large, natural subclass of MPGs with partial-observation, *forcibly terminating* games, where

---

[2] A recent result of Aminof and Rubin [1] corrects some errors in [4].

Table 1. Summary of results for the classes of games studied.

	Forcibly Terminating	Forcibly FAC		FAC	
		limited-obs.	partial-obs.	limited-obs.	partial-obs.
Memory	Finite	Exponential	2-Exponential	Positional	Exponential
Class membership	Undecidable	PSPACE-complete	NEXP-hard, in EXPSPACE	coNP-complete	coNEXP-complete
Winner determination	R-complete	PSPACE-complete	EXP-complete	NP ∩ coNP	EXP-complete

determining the winner is decidable and finite memory observation-based strategies suffice.

Unfortunately, recognizing if an MPG is a member of this class is undecidable, and although determining the winner is decidable, we show that this problem is complete (under polynomial-time reductions) for the class of all decidable problems. Motivated by these negative algorithmic results, we investigate two natural refinements of this class for which winner determination and class membership are decidable. The first, *forcibly first abstract cycle* games (forcibly FAC games, for short), is the natural class of games obtained when our cycle-forming game is restricted to simple cycles. Unlike the perfect information case, we show that winning strategies in this finite simple cycle-forming game may still require memory, though this memory is at most exponential in the size of the game. The second refinement, *first abstract cycle* (FAC) games, is a further structural refinement that guarantees a winner in the simple cycle-forming game. We show that in this class of games positional observation-based strategies suffice.

Table 1 summarizes the results of this paper. For space reasons the full details of all proofs can be found in the technical report [11].

2 Preliminaries

Mean-payoff games. A *mean-payoff game (MPG) with partial-observation* is a tuple $G = \langle Q, q_I, \Sigma, \Delta, w, Obs \rangle$, where Q is a finite set of states, $q_I \in Q$ is the initial state, Σ is a finite set of actions, $\Delta \subseteq Q \times \Sigma \times Q$ is the transition relation, $w : \Delta \to \mathbb{Z}$ is the weight function, and $Obs \in \texttt{Partition}(Q)$ is a set of observations. We assume Δ is total. We say that G is a *mean-payoff game with limited-observation* if additionally, (1) $\{q_I\} \in Obs$, and (2) for each $(o, \sigma) \in Obs \times \Sigma$ the set $\{q' \mid \exists q \in o$ and $(q, \sigma, q') \in \Delta\}$ is a union of elements of Obs. If every element of Obs is a singleton, then we say G is a *mean-payoff game with perfect information*. For simplicity, we denote by $\texttt{post}_\sigma(s) = \{q' \in Q \mid \exists q \in s : (q, \sigma, q') \in \Delta\}$ the set of σ-successors of a set of states $s \subseteq Q$.

In this work, unless explicitly stated otherwise, we depict states from an MPG with partial-observation as circles and transitions as arrows labelled by an action-weight pair: σ, w. Observations are represented by dashed boxes.

Abstract and concrete paths. A *concrete path* in an MPG with partial-observation is a sequence $q_0\sigma_0q_1\sigma_1\ldots$ where for all $i \geq 0$ we have $q_i \in Q$, $\sigma_i \in \Sigma$ and $(q_i, \sigma_i, q_{i+1}) \in \Delta$. An *abstract path* is a sequence $o_0\sigma_0o_1\sigma_1\ldots$ where $o_i \in Obs$, $\sigma_i \in \Sigma$ and for all i there exists $q_i \in o_i$ and $q_{i+1} \in o_{i+1}$ with $(q_i, \sigma_i, q_{i+1}) \in \Delta$. Given an abstract path ψ, let $\gamma(\psi)$ be the (possibly empty) set of concrete paths that agree with the observation and action sequence. Note that in games of limited-observation this set is never empty. Also, given abstract (respectively concrete) path ρ, let $\rho[..n]$ represent the prefix of ρ up to the $(n+1)$-th observation (state), which we express as $\rho[n]$; similarly, we denote by $\rho[l..]$ the suffix of ρ starting from the l-th observation (state) and by $\rho[l..n]$ the finite subsequence starting and ending in the aforementioned locations. An *abstract (respectively concrete) cycle* is an abstract (concrete) path $\chi = o_0\sigma_0\ldots o_n$ where $o_0 = o_n$. We say χ is *simple* if $o_j \neq o_i$ for $0 \leq i < j < n$. Given $k \in \mathbb{N}$ define χ^k to be the abstract (concrete) cycle obtained by traversing χ k times. A *cyclic permutation* of χ is an abstract (concrete) cycle $o'_0\sigma'_0\ldots o'_n$ such that $o'_j = o_{j+k \pmod{n}}$ and $\sigma'_j = \sigma_{j+k \pmod{n}}$ for some k. If $\chi' = o'_0\sigma'_0\ldots o'_m$ is a cycle with $o'_0 = o_i$ for some i, the *interleaving* of χ and χ' is the cycle $o_0\sigma_0\ldots o_i o'_0\ldots o'_m\sigma_i\ldots o_n$.

Given a concrete path $\pi = q_0\sigma_0q_1\sigma_1\ldots$, the *payoff* up to the $(n+1)$-th element is given by

$$w(\pi[..n]) = \sum_{i=0}^{n-1} w(q_i, \sigma_i, q_{i+1}).$$

If π is infinite, we define two *mean-payoff* values $\underline{MP}$ and $\overline{MP}$ as:

$$\underline{MP}(\pi) = \liminf_{n\to\infty} \frac{1}{n}w(\pi[..n]) \qquad \overline{MP}(\pi) = \limsup_{n\to\infty} \frac{1}{n}w(\pi[..n])$$

Plays and strategies. A *play* in an MPG with partial-observation G is an infinite abstract path starting at $o_I \in Obs$ where $q_I \in o_I$. Denote by $\mathtt{Plays}(G)$ the set of all plays and by $\mathtt{Prefs}(G)$ the set of all finite prefixes of such plays ending in an observation. Let $\gamma(\mathtt{Plays}(G))$ be the set of concrete paths of all plays in the game, and $\gamma(\mathtt{Prefs}(G))$ be the set of all finite prefixes of all concrete paths.

An *observation-based strategy for Eve* is a function from finite prefixes of plays to actions, i.e. $\lambda_\exists : \mathtt{Prefs}(G) \to \Sigma$. A play $\psi = o_0\sigma_0o_1\sigma_1\ldots$ is *consistent* with $\lambda_\exists$ if $\sigma_i = \lambda_\exists(\psi[..i])$ for all i. An *observation-based strategy for Adam* is a function $\lambda_\forall : \mathtt{Prefs}(G) \times \Sigma \to Obs$ such that for any prefix $\pi = o_0\sigma_0\ldots o_n \in \mathtt{Prefs}(G)$ and action σ, $\lambda_\forall(\pi, \sigma) \cap \mathtt{post}_\sigma(\pi[n]) \neq \emptyset$. A play $\psi = o_0\sigma_0o_1\sigma_1\ldots$ is consistent with $\lambda_\forall$ if $\lambda_\forall(\psi[..i], \sigma_i) = o_{i+1}$ for all i. A *concrete strategy for Adam* is a function $\mu_\forall : \gamma(\mathtt{Prefs}(G)) \times \Sigma \to Q$ such that for any concrete prefix $\pi = q_0\sigma_0\ldots q_n \in \gamma(\mathtt{Prefs}(G))$ and action σ, $\mu_\forall(\pi, \sigma) \in \mathtt{post}_\sigma(\{\pi[n]\})$. A play $\psi = o_0\sigma_0o_1\sigma_1\ldots$ is consistent with $\mu_\forall$ if there exists a concrete path $\pi \in \gamma(\psi)$ such that $\mu_\forall(\pi[..i], \sigma_i) = \pi[i+1]$ for all i.

We say an observation-based strategy for Eve $\lambda_\exists$ has *memory* m if there is a set M with $|M| = m$, an element $m_0 \in M$, and functions $\alpha_u : M \times Obs \to M$ and $\alpha_o : M \times Obs \to \Sigma$ such that for any play prefix $\rho = o_0\sigma_0\ldots o_n$ we have $\lambda_\exists(\rho) = \alpha_o(m_n, o_n)$, where m_n is defined inductively by $m_{i+1} = \alpha_u(m_i, o_i)$ for

$i \geq 0$. An observation-based strategy for Adam $\lambda_\forall$ has *memory m* if there is a set M with $|M| = m$, an element $m_0 \in M$, and functions $\alpha_u : M \times Obs \times \Sigma \to M$ and $\alpha_o : M \times Obs \times \Sigma \to Obs$ such that for any play prefix ending in an action $\rho = o_0\sigma_0 \ldots o_n\sigma_n$, we have $\lambda_\forall(\rho) = \alpha_o(m_n, o_n, \sigma_n)$, where m_n is defined inductively by $m_{i+1} = \alpha_u(m_i, o_i, \sigma_i)$. An observation-based strategy (for either player) with memory 1 is *positional*.

Note that for any concrete strategy μ of Adam there is a unique observation-based strategy λ_μ such that all plays consistent with μ are consistent with λ_μ. Conversely there may be several, but possibly no, concrete strategies that correspond to a single observation-based strategy. In games of limited-observation there is guaranteed to be at least one concrete strategy for every observation-based strategy.

Given a threshold $\nu \in \mathbb{R}$, we say a play ψ is *winning for Eve* if $\underline{MP}(\pi) \geq \nu$ for all concrete paths $\pi \in \gamma(\psi)$, otherwise it is *winning for Adam*. Given ν, one can construct an equivalent game in which Eve wins if and only if $\underline{MP}(\pi) \geq 0$ if and only if she wins the original game, so without loss of generality we will assume $\nu = 0$. A strategy λ is *winning* for a player if all plays consistent with λ are winning for that player. We say that a player *wins* G if (s)he has a winning strategy.

It was shown in [9] that in MPGs with partial-observation where finite memory strategies suffice Eve wins the $\underline{MP}$ version of the game if and only if she wins the $\overline{MP}$ version. As the majority of games considered in this paper only require finite memory, we can take either definition. For simplicity and consistency with Section 3 we will use $\underline{MP}$.

Reachability games. A *reachability game* $G = \langle Q, q_I, \Sigma, \Delta, \mathcal{T}_\exists, \mathcal{T}_\forall \rangle$ is a tuple where Q is a (not necessarily finite) set of states; Σ is a finite set of actions; $\Delta \subseteq Q \times \Sigma \times Q$ is a finitary transition function; $q_I \in Q$ is the initial state; and $\mathcal{T}_\exists, \mathcal{T}_\forall \subseteq Q$ are the terminating states. Notions of plays and strategies in the reachability game follow from the definitions for MPGs, however we extend plays to include finite paths that end in $\mathcal{T}_\exists$ or in $\mathcal{T}_\forall$. In the first case we declare Eve as the winner whereas the latter corresponds to Adam winning the game. In general, the game might not terminate. In this case we say neither player wins.

3   Undecidability of Liminf Games

Mean-payoff games with partial-observation were extensively studied in [9]. In that paper the authors show that, with the mean payoff condition defined using $\underline{MP}$ and $>$, determining whether Eve has a winning strategy is undecidable and when defined using $\overline{MP}$ and $\geq$, strategies with infinite memory may be necessary. The analogous, and more general, questions using $\underline{MP}$ and $\geq$ were left open. In this section we answer these questions, showing that both results still hold.

Proposition 1. *There exist MPGs with partial-observation for which Eve requires infinite memory observation-based strategies to ensure $\underline{MP} \geq 0$.*

Consider the game in Figure 2 and consider the strategy of Eve that plays (regardless of location) $aba^2ba^3ba^4b\ldots$ As b is played infinitely often in this strategy, the only concrete paths consistent with this strategy are $\pi = q_0q_1^\omega$ and $\pi = q_0q_1^kq_2^lq_3^\omega$ for non-negative integers k, l. In both cases $\underline{MP} \geq 0$, so the strategy is winning.

Against a finite memory strategy of Eve, Adam plays to ensure the game remains in $\{q_1, q_2\}$. As Eve's strategy has finite memory, her choice of actions must be ultimately periodic. Now there are two cases, if she plays a finite number of b's then Adam has a concrete winning strategy which consists in guessing when she will play the last b and moving to q_2. If, on the other hand, she plays b infinitely often then Adam can choose to stay in q_1 and again win the game.

Theorem 1. *Let G be an MPG with partial-observation. Determining whether Eve has an observation-based strategy to ensure $\underline{MP} \geq 0$ is undecidable.*

In [6], the authors present a reduction from blind MPGs to mean-payoff automata. This reduction, together with the undecidability result from [9], imply several classical automata-theoretical problems for mean-payoff automata are also undecidable. In [6], the authors study the non-strict $\geq$ relation between quantitative languages. It follows from the undecidability result presented above, that even when one considers the strict order, $>$, these problems remain undecidable.

Corollary 1. *The strict quantitative universality, and strict quantitative language inclusion problems are undecidable for non-deterministic and alternating mean-payoff automata.*

4   Observable Determinacy

One of the key features of MPGs with perfect information is that they are determined, that is, it is always the case that one player has a winning strategy. This is not true in games of partial or limited-observation as can be seen in Figure 1. Any concrete strategy of Adam reveals to Eve the successor of q_0 and

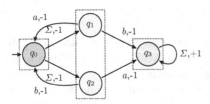

Fig. 1. A non-determined MPG with limited-observation ($\Sigma = \{a, b\}$).

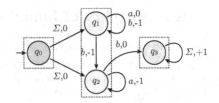

Fig. 2. An MPG with limited-observation which Eve requires infinite memory to win.

she can use this information to play to q_3. Conversely Adam can defeat any strategy of Eve by playing to whichever of q_1 or q_2 means the play returns to q_0 on Eve's next choice (recall Eve cannot distinguish q_1 and q_2 and must therefore choose an action to apply to the observation $\{q_1, q_2\}$). This strategy of Adam can be encoded as an observation-based strategy: "from $\{q_1, q_2\}$ with action a or b, play to $\{q_0\}$". It transpires that, under an assumption about large cardinals[3], any such counter-play by Adam is always encodable as an observable strategy.

Theorem 2 (Observable determinacy). *Assuming the existence of a measurable cardinal, one player always has a winning observation-based strategy in an MPG with limited-observation.*

The existence of a measurable cardinal implies Σ_1^1-Determinacy [14] – a weak form of the "Axiom of Determinacy". The observable determinacy of MPGs with limited-observation then follows from the following result:

Lemma 1. *The set of plays that are winning for Eve in an MPG with limited-observation is co-Suslin.*

5   Strategy Transfer

In this section we will construct a reachability game from an MPG with limited-observation in which winning strategies for either player are sufficient (but not necessary) for winning strategies in the original MPG.

Let us fix a mean-payoff game with limited-observation $G = \langle Q, q_I, \Sigma, \Delta, Obs, w \rangle$. We will define a reachability game on the weighted unfolding of G.

Let $\mathcal{F}$ be the set of functions $f : Q \to \mathbb{Z} \cup \{+\infty, \bot\}$. Our intention is to use functions in $\mathcal{F}$ to keep track of the minimum weight of all concrete paths ending in the given vertex. A function value of $\bot$ indicates that the given vertex is not in the current observation, and intuitively a function value of $+\infty$ is used to indicate to Eve that the token is not located at such a vertex. The added complication permits our winning condition to include games where Adam wins by ignoring paths going through the given vertex. The *support* of f is $\mathrm{supp}(f) = \{q \in Q \mid f(q) \neq \bot\}$. We say that $f' \in \mathcal{F}$ is a σ-successor of $f \in \mathcal{F}$ if:

- $\mathrm{supp}(f') \in Obs \wedge \mathrm{supp}(f') \subseteq \mathrm{post}_\sigma(\mathrm{supp}(f))$; and
- for all $q \in \mathrm{supp}(f')$, $f'(q)$ is either $\min\{f(q') + w(q', \sigma, q) \mid q' \in \mathrm{supp}(f) \wedge (q', \sigma, q) \in \Delta\}$ or $+\infty$.

We define a family of partial orders, $\preceq_k$ ($k \in \mathbb{N}$), on $\mathcal{F}$ by setting $f \preceq_k f'$ if $\mathrm{supp}(f) = \mathrm{supp}(f')$ and $f(q) + k \leq f'(q)$ for all $q \in \mathrm{supp}(f)$ (where $+\infty + k = +\infty$).

Denote by $\mathfrak{F}_G$ the set of all sequences $f_0 \sigma_0 f_1 \ldots \sigma_{n-1} f_n \in (\mathcal{F} \cdot \Sigma)^* \mathcal{F}$ such that for all $0 \leq i < n$, f_{i+1} is a σ_i-successor of f_i. Observe that for each function-action sequence $\rho = f_0 \sigma_0 \ldots f_n \in \mathfrak{F}_G$ there is a unique abstract path $\mathrm{supp}(\rho) =$

---

[3] This assumption is independent of the theory of ZFC.

$o_0\sigma_0\ldots o_n$ such that $o_i = \mathbf{supp}(f_i)$ for all i. Conversely for each abstract path $\psi = o_0\sigma_0\ldots o_n$ there may be many corresponding function-action sequences in $\mathbf{supp}^{-1}(\psi)$.

The *reachability game associated with* G, i.e. $\Gamma_G = \langle \Pi_G, \Sigma, f_I, \delta, \mathcal{T}_\exists, \mathcal{T}_\forall \rangle$, is formally defined as follows: $f_I \in \mathcal{F}$ is the function for which $f(q) \mapsto 0$ if $q = q_I$ and $f(q) \mapsto \perp$ otherwise. Π_G is the subset of $\mathfrak{F}_G$ where for all $f_0\sigma_0 f_1 \ldots \sigma_{n-1} f_n \in \Pi_G$ we have $f_0 = f_I$ and for all $0 \le i < j < n$ we have $f_i \not\preceq_0 f_j$ and $f_j \not\preceq_1 f_i$; δ is the natural transition function, that is, if x and $x \cdot \sigma \cdot f$ are elements of Π_G then $(x, \sigma, x \cdot \sigma \cdot f) \in \delta$; $\mathcal{T}_\exists$ is the set of all $f_0\sigma_0 f_1 \ldots \sigma_{n-1} f_n \in \Pi_G$ such that for some $0 \le i < n$ we have $f_i \preceq_0 f_n$; and $\mathcal{T}_\forall$ is the set of all $f_0\sigma_0 f_1 \ldots \sigma_{n-1} f_n \in \Pi_G$ such that for some $0 \le i < n$ we have $f_n \preceq_1 f_i$ and $f_i(q) \ne +\infty$ for some $q \in \mathbf{supp}(f_i)$.

Note that the directed graph defined by Π_G and δ is a tree, but not necessarily finite. To gain an intuition about Γ_G, let us say an abstract cycle ρ is *good* if there exists $f_0\sigma_0\ldots f_n \in \mathbf{supp}^{-1}(\rho)$ such that $f_i(q) \ne +\infty$ for all q and all i and $f_0 \preceq_0 f_n$. Let us say ρ is *bad* if there exists $f_0\sigma_0\ldots f_n \in \mathbf{supp}^{-1}(\rho)$ such that $f_0(q) \ne +\infty$ for some $q \in \mathbf{supp}(f_0)$ and $f_n \preceq_1 f_0$. Then it is not difficult to see that Γ_G is essentially an abstract cycle-forming game played on G which is winning for Eve if a good abstract cycle is formed and winning for Adam if a bad abstract cycle is formed.

Theorem 3. *Let G be an MPG with limited-observation and let Γ_G be the associated reachability game. If Adam (Eve) has a winning strategy in Γ_G then (s)he has a finite-memory observation-based winning strategy in G.*

The idea behind the strategy for the mean-payoff game is straightforward. If Eve wins the reachability game then she can transform her strategy into one that plays indefinitely by returning, whenever the play reaches $\mathcal{T}_\exists$, to the natural previous position – namely the position that witnesses the membership of $\mathcal{T}_\exists$. By continually playing her winning strategy in this way Eve perpetually completes good abstract cycles and this ensures that all concrete paths consistent with the play have non-negative mean-payoff value. Likewise if Adam has a winning strategy in the reachability game, he can continually play his strategy by returning to the natural position whenever the play reaches $\mathcal{T}_\forall$. By doing this he perpetually completes bad abstract cycles and this ensures that there is a concrete path consistent with the play that has strictly negative mean-payoff value. The finiteness of the size of the memory required for this strategy follows from the following result.

Lemma 2. *If λ is a winning strategy for Adam or Eve in Γ_G, then there exists $N \in \mathbb{N}$ such that for all plays π consistent with λ, $|\pi| \le N$.*

Although the following results are not used until Section 7, they give an intuition toward the correctness of the strategies described above.

Lemma 3. *Let ρ be an abstract cycle.*

  (i) If ρ is good (bad) then an interleaving of ρ with another good (bad) cycle is also good (bad).

(ii) If ρ is good then for all k and all concrete cycles $\pi \in \gamma(\rho^k)$, $w(\pi) \geq 0$.
(iii) If ρ is bad then $\exists k \geq 0, \pi \in \gamma(\rho^k)$ such that $w(\pi) < 0$.

Corollary 2. *No cyclic permutation of a good abstract cycle is bad.*

6   Forcibly Terminating Games

The reachability game defined in the previous section gives a sufficient condition for determining the winner in an MPG with limited-observation. However, as there may be plays where no player wins, such games are not necessarily determined. The first subclass of MPGs with limited-observation we investigate is the class of games where the associated reachability game is determined.

Definition 1. *An MPG with limited-observation is* forcibly terminating *if in the corresponding reachability game Γ_G either Adam has a winning strategy to reach locations in $\mathcal{T}_\forall$ or Eve has a winning strategy to reach locations in $\mathcal{T}_\exists$.*

It follows immediately from Theorem 3 that finite memory strategies suffice for both players in forcibly terminating games. Note that an upper bound on the memory required is the number of vertices in the reachability game restricted to a winning strategy, and this is exponential in N, the bound obtained in Lemma 2.

Theorem 4 (Finite-memory determinacy). *One player always has a winning observation-based strategy with finite memory in a forcibly terminating MPG.*

We now consider the complexity of two natural decision problems associated with forcibly terminating games: the problem of recognizing if an MPG is forcibly terminating and the problem of determining the winner of a forcibly terminating game. Both results follow directly from the fact that we can accurately simulate a Turing Machine with an MPG with limited-observation.

Theorem 5. *Let M be a Deterministic Turing Machine. Then there exists an MPG with limited-observation G, constructible in polynomial time, such that Eve wins Γ_G if and only if M halts in the accept state and Adam wins Γ_G if and only if M halts in the reject state.*

Corollary 3 (Class membership). *Let G be an MPG with limited-observation. Determining if G is forcibly terminating is undecidable.*

Corollary 4 (Winner determination). *Let G be a forcibly terminating MPG. Determining if Eve wins G is* R-complete.

Proof. R-hardness follows from Theorem 5. For decidability, Lemma 2 implies that an alternating Turing Machine simulating a play on Γ_G will terminate.

7   Forcibly First Abstract Cycle Games

In this section and the next we consider restrictions of forcibly terminating games in order to find subclasses with more efficient algorithmic bounds. The negative algorithmic results from the previous section largely arise from the fact that the abstract cycles required to determine the winner are not necessarily simple cycles. Our first restriction of forcibly terminating games is the restriction of the abstract cycle-forming game to simple cycles.

More precisely, let G be an MPG with limited-observation and Γ_G be the associated reachability game. Define $\Pi'_G \subseteq \Pi_G$ as the set of all sequences $x = f_0 \sigma_0 f_1 \sigma_1 \dots f_n \in \Pi_G$ such that $\mathrm{supp}(f_i) \neq \mathrm{supp}(f_j)$ for all $0 \leq i < j < n$ and denote by Γ'_G the reachability game $\langle \Pi'_G, \Sigma, f_I, \delta', \mathcal{T}'_\exists, \mathcal{T}'_\forall \rangle$ where δ' is δ restricted to Π'_G, $\mathcal{T}'_\exists = \mathcal{T}_\exists \cap \Pi'_G$ and $\mathcal{T}'_\forall = \mathcal{T}_\forall \cap \Pi'_G$.

Definition 2. *An MPG with limited-observation is* forcibly first abstract cycle *(or forcibly FAC) if in the associated reachability game Γ'_G either Adam has a winning strategy to reach locations in $\mathcal{T}'_\forall$ or Eve has a winning strategy to reach locations in $\mathcal{T}'_\exists$.*

One immediate consequence of the restriction to simple abstract cycles is that the bound in Lemma 2 is at most $|Obs|$. In particular an alternating Turing Machine can, in linear time, simulate a play of the reachability game and decide which player, if any, has a winning strategy. Hence the problems of deciding if a given MPG with partial-observation is forcibly FAC and deciding the winner of a forcibly FAC game are both solvable in PSPACE. The next results show that there is a matching lower bound for both these problems.

Theorem 6 (Class membership). *Let G be an MPG with limited-observation. Determining if G is forcibly FAC is* PSPACE-*complete.*

PSPACE-hardness follows from a reduction from the satisfiability of quantified boolean formulas. The construction is similar to the construction used to prove PSPACE-hardness for Generalized Geography in [15]. That is, the game proceeds through diamond gadgets – the choice of each player on which side to go through corresponds to the selection of the value for the quantified variable. The (abstract) play then passes through a gadget for the formula in the obvious way (Adam choosing for $\wedge$ and Eve choosing for $\vee$), returning to a diamond gadget when a variable is reached. If the variable has been seen before the cycle is closed and the game ends, otherwise the play proceeds to the bottom of the diamond gadget which has been seen before, thus ending the game one step later. We set up the concrete paths within the observations in such a way that if the cycle closes at the variable then it is good (and thus Eve wins) and if it closes at the bottom of the gadget then it is not good. Corollary 2 implies that the cycle closed is never bad, so either Eve wins and the game is forcibly FAC, or neither player wins and it is not forcibly FAC.

We can slightly modify the above construction in such a way that if the game does not finish when the play returns to a variable then Adam can close a bad cycle. This results in a forcibly FAC game that Eve wins if and only if the formula is satisfied. Hence,

Theorem 7 (Winner determination). *Let G be a forcibly FAC MPG. Determining if Eve wins G is* PSPACE-*complete.*

It also follows from the $|Obs|$ upper bound on plays in Γ'_G that there is an exponential upper bound on the memory required for a winning strategy for either player. Furthermore, we can show this bound is tight – the games constructed in the proof of Theorem 7 can be used to show that there are forcibly FAC games that require exponential memory for winning strategies.

Theorem 8 (Exponential memory determinacy). *One player always has a winning observation-based strategy with exponential memory in a forcibly FAC MPG. Further, for any $n \in \mathbb{N}$ there exists a forcibly FAC MPG, of size polynomial in n, such that any winning strategy has memory at least 2^n.*

8   First Abstract Cycle Games

We now consider a structural restriction that guarantees Γ'_G is determined.

Definition 3. *An MPG with limited-observation is a* first abstract cycle game *(FAC) if in the associated reachability game Γ'_G all leaves are in $\mathcal{T}'_\forall \cup \mathcal{T}'_\exists$.*

Intuitively, in an FAC game all simple abstract cycles (that can be formed) are either good or bad. It follows then from Corollary 2 that any cyclic permutation of a good cycle is also good and any cyclic permutation of a bad cycle is also bad. Together with Lemma 3, this implies the abstract cycle-forming games associated with FAC games can be seen to satisfy the following three assumptions: (1) A play stops as soon as an abstract cycle is formed, (2) The winning condition and its complement are preserved under cyclic permutations, and (3) The winning condition and its complement are preserved under interleavings. These assumptions correspond to the assumptions required in [1] for positional strategies to be sufficient for both players[4]. That is,

Theorem 9 (Positional determinacy). *One player always has a positional winning observation-based strategy in an FAC MPG.*

As we can check in polynomial time if a positional strategy is winning in an FAC MPG, we immediately have:

Corollary 5 (Winner determination). *Let G be an FAC MPG. Determining if Eve wins G is in* NP $\cap$ coNP.

A path in Γ'_G to a leaf not in $\mathcal{T}'_\forall \cup \mathcal{T}'_\exists$ provides a short certificate to show that an MPG with limited-observation is not FAC. Thus deciding if an MPG is FAC is in coNP. A matching lower bound can be obtained using a reduction from the complement of the HAMILTONIAN CYCLE problem.

---

[4] These conditions supercede those of [4] which were shown in [1] to be insufficient for positional strategies.

Theorem 10 (Class membership). *Let G be an MPG with limited-observation. Determining if G is FAC is* coNP-*complete.*

9   MPGs with Partial-Observation

The translation from partial-observation to limited-observation games allows us to extend the notions of FAC and forcibly FAC games to the larger class of MPGs with partial-observation. In this section we will investigate the resulting algorithmic effect of this translation on the decision problems we have been considering.

We say an MPG with partial-observation is *(forcibly) first belief cycle*, or FBC, if the corresponding MPG with limited-observation is (forcibly) FAC.

9.1   FBC and Forcibly FBC MPGs

Our first observation is that FBC MPGs generalize the class of *visible weight games* studied in [9]. An MPG with partial-observation is considered a visible weights game if its weight function satisfies the condition that all σ-transitions between any pair of observations have the same weight. We base some of our results for FBC and forcibly FBC games on lower bounds established for problems on visible weights games.

Lemma 4. *Let G be a visible weights MPG with partial-observation. Then G is FBC.*

We now turn to the decision problems we have been investigating throughout the paper. Given the exponential blow-up in the construction of the game of limited-observation, it is not surprising that there is a corresponding exponential increase in the complexity of the class membership problem.

Theorem 11 (Class membership). *Let G be an MPG with partial-observation. Determining if G is FBC is* coNEXP-*complete and determining if G is forcibly FBC is in* EXPSPACE *and* NEXP-*hard.*

Somewhat surprisingly, for the winner determination problem we have an EXP-time algorithm to match the EXP-hardness lower bound from visible weights games. This is in contrast to the class membership problem in which an exponential increase in complexity occurs when moving from limited to partial-observation.

Theorem 12 (Winner determination). *Let G be a forcibly FBC MPG. Determining if Eve wins G is* EXP-*complete.*

Corollary 6. *Let G be an FBC MPG. Determining if Eve wins G is* EXP-*complete.*

References

1. Aminof, B., Rubin, S.: First cycle games. In: Mogavero, F., Murano, A., Vardi, M.Y. (eds.) SR. EPTCS, vol. 146, pp. 91–96 (2014)
2. Berwanger, D., Chatterjee, K., Doyen, L., Henzinger, T.A., Raje, S.: Strategy construction for parity games with imperfect information. In: van Breugel, F., Chechik, M. (eds.) CONCUR 2008. LNCS, vol. 5201, pp. 325–339. Springer, Heidelberg (2008)
3. Berwanger, D., Doyen, L.: On the power of imperfect information. In: FSTTCS, pp. 73–82 (2008)
4. Björklund, H., Sandberg, S., Vorobyov, S.: Memoryless determinacy of parity and mean payoff games: a simple proof. TCS 310(1), 365–378 (2004)
5. Chatterjee, K., Doyen, L.: Partial-observation stochastic games: How to win when belief fails. In: LICS, pp. 175–184. IEEE (2012)
6. Chatterjee, K., Doyen, L., Edelsbrunner, H., Henzinger, T.A., Rannou, P.: Mean-payoff automaton expressions. In: Gastin, P., Laroussinie, F. (eds.) CONCUR 2010. LNCS, vol. 6269, pp. 269–283. Springer, Heidelberg (2010)
7. Chatterjee, K., Doyen, L., Henzinger, T.A.: Quantitative languages. In: Kaminski, M., Martini, S. (eds.) CSL 2008. LNCS, vol. 5213, pp. 385–400. Springer, Heidelberg (2008)
8. Chatterjee, K., Doyen, L., Henzinger, T.A., Raskin, J.-F.: Generalized mean-payoff and energy games. In: FSTTCS, pp. 505–516 (2010)
9. Degorre, A., Doyen, L., Gentilini, R., Raskin, J.-F., Toruńczyk, S.: Energy and mean-payoff games with imperfect information. In: Dawar, A., Veith, H. (eds.) CSL 2010. LNCS, vol. 6247, pp. 260–274. Springer, Heidelberg (2010)
10. Ehrenfeucht, A., Mycielski, J.: Positional strategies for mean payoff games. International Journal of Game Theory 8, 109–113 (1979)
11. Hunter, P., Pérez, G.A., Raskin, J.-F.: Mean-payoff games with partial-observation (extended abstract). CoRR (2014)
12. Jurdziński, M.: Deciding the winner in parity games is in UP ∩ coUP. IPL 68(3), 119–124 (1998)
13. Kupferman, O., Vardi, M.Y.: Synthesis with incomplete informatio. Advances in Temporal Logic 16, 109–127 (2000)
14. Martin, D.A., Steel, J.R.: Projective determinacy. Proceedings of the National Academy of Sciences of the United States of America 85(18), 6582 (1988)
15. Papadimitriou, C.H.: Computational complexity. John Wiley and Sons Ltd. (2003)
16. Reif, J.H.: The complexity of two-player games of incomplete information. Journal of Computer and System Sciences 29(2), 274–301 (1984)
17. Zwick, U., Paterson, M.: The complexity of mean payoff games on graphs. TCS 158(1), 343–359 (1996)

Parameter Synthesis for Probabilistic Timed Automata Using Stochastic Game Abstractions

Aleksandra Jovanović and Marta Kwiatkowska

Department of Computer Science, University of Oxford, Oxford, OX1 3QD, UK

Abstract. We propose a method to synthesise optimal values of timing parameters for probabilistic timed automata, in the sense that the probability of reaching some set of states is either maximised or minimised. Our first algorithm, based on forward exploration of the symbolic states, can only guarantee parameter values that correspond to upper (resp. lower) bounds on maximum (resp. minimum) reachability probability. To ensure precise reachability probabilities, we adapt the game-based abstraction refinement method. In the parametric setting, our method is able to determine all the possible maximum (or minimum) reachability probabilities that arise for different values of timing parameters, and yields optimal valuations represented as a set of symbolic constraints between parameters.

1 Introduction

Stochastic aspect is very important for modelling numerous classes of systems, such as communication and security protocols, due to component failures, unreliable channels or randomisation. The correctness of such systems can be guaranteed only with some probability. Many of them also operate under timing constraints. In such cases, the probability of a property being true depends on those timing aspects in the system: for example, increasing a certain delay might increase the maximum or minimum probability of reaching an error state.

Automatic synthesis of timing constraints to ensure the satisfaction of a given property has received a lot of attention lately. Its aim is to overcome the disadvantage of model checking, which requires complete knowledge of the system. This is often difficult to obtain, especially in the early design stages, when the whole environment is not yet known. The use of parameters instead of concrete values gives more freedom to the designers. A parametric timed model can specify that a transition is enabled for a time units, where a is a parameter. The goal is then to automatically synthesize the values of model's parameters such that the specification is guaranteed. Parameterisation, however, makes verification more difficult, as most problems become undecidable.

In this paper, we are dealing with the synthesis of timing parameters for probabilistic real-time systems modelled as probabilistic timed automata (PTA) [18]. PTA have been introduced as an extension of timed automata (TA) [1] for modelling and analysing systems which exhibit real-time, nondeterministic and probabilistic behaviour. They are finite-state automata extended with clocks,

J. Ouaknine, I. Potapov, and J. Worrell (Eds.): RP 2014, LNCS 8762, pp. 176–189, 2014.
© Springer International Publishing Switzerland 2014

real-valued variables which increase at the same, constant rate. A fundamental property of PTA is the maximum/minimum probability of reaching a certain set of states in the model (i.e. the reachability probabilities). These probabilities allow one to express a broad range of properties, from quality of service to reliability, for example, deadline properties: "the maximum probability of an airbag failing to deploy within 0.02 seconds". PTA have been successfully used to analyse protocols such as FireWire, Bluetooth, IEEE 802.11, etc. These are embedded in a networked environment and their properties are almost always expressed parametrically, as concrete values make sense only when the network environment is known. It is thus desirable to provide a tool to automatically derive the constraints on parameters for probabilistic systems, so that their correctness is ensured with optimal probability.

Contributions. We propose an algorithm for parameter synthesis for PTA based on the symbolic state-space exploration. As the forward approach gives only upper (resp. lower) bounds on max. (resp. min.) reachability probability, we adapt the game-based abstraction refinement method. This method has been introduced in [13] for Markov decision processes, and extended in [15] for PTA, for the computation of exact max/min reachability probabilities. As we consider parametric models, these probabilities are not unique and depend on particular parameter valuations. Our algorithm allows us to choose the valuations for which these probabilities are either maximised or minimised, and to synthesise them as a finite set of symbolic constraints on parameters. To the best of our knowledge, this is the first paper dealing with optimal timing parameter synthesis for probabilistic timed automata. A full version of this paper is available as [10].

Related Work. An orthogonal line of work on parameter synthesis for untimed probabilistic models is that of [7], where the authors consider Markov chains and transition probabilities as parameters. Regarding timed systems, parametric timed automata have been introduced in [2] as a means to specify parametric timing constraints. The *reachability-emptiness* problem, which asks whether there exists a parameter valuation such that the automaton has an accepting run, is undecidable. Subsequent research has thus concentrated on finding subclasses for which certain problems would be decidable by restricting the use of parameters [9] or by restricting the parameter domain [11]. In [6], the authors consider fully deterministic networks of timed automata with priorities and parametric guards, and extended MTL with counting formulas. They develop an algorithm based on constraint solving and Monte Carlo sampling to synthesise timing delays. There is little work, however, on timing parameter synthesis for probabilistic real-time systems. In [8], a technique is proposed to approximate parametric rate values for continuous-time Markov chains for bounded reachability probabilities. In [3], the authors apply their *Inverse* method for parameter synthesis for TA to PTA. The method starts from reference parameter values of a TA, and derives the constraints on parameters such that the obtained models are time-abstract equivalent. Time-abstract equivalence preserves untimed properties, and thus the parameter values derived on the non-probabilistic version of the model preserve reachability probabilities. Termination is not guaranteed and the derived constraints are not weakest in general. In [4], the authors consider a fully deterministic parametric model, where the remaining time in a node is unique and given as a parameter, and provide a method to compute the expected time to reach some node as a function of model's parameters.

2   Preliminaries

A discrete probability distribution over a set S is a function $\mu : S \mapsto [0,1]$, such that $\sum_{s \in S} \mu(s) = 1$ and the set $\{s \mid s \in S \wedge \mu(s) > 0\}$ is finite. By $\mathrm{Dist}(S)$ we denote the set of such distributions. μ_p is a point distribution if $\mu_p(s) = 1$ for some $s \in S$. We now define *Markov decision processes*, a formalism for modelling systems which exhibit both nondeterministic and probabilistic behaviour.

Definition 1 (Markov decision processes). *An MDP is a tuple* $\mathcal{M} = (S, s_0,$ $\Sigma, \mathsf{Steps}_{\mathcal{M}})$, *where S is a set of states, s_0 is a set of initial states, Σ is a set of actions and* $\mathsf{Steps}_{\mathcal{M}} : S \times \Sigma \mapsto \mathrm{Dist}(S)$ *is a probabilistic transition function.*

A transition in $\mathcal{M}$ from state s is first made by nondeterministically selecting an action $\delta \in \Sigma$ and then the successor state s' is chosen randomly according to the probability distribution $\mathsf{Steps}_{\mathcal{M}}(s, \delta)$. A *path* is a sequence of such transitions and represents a particular resolution of both nondeterminism and probability. A state s is *reachable* in $\mathcal{M}$ if there exists a path from the initial state of $\mathcal{M}$ to s. A strategy $\mathcal{A}$ is a function from finite paths to distributions which resolves nondeterminism in an MDP. For a fixed strategy $\mathcal{A}$, the behaviour of an MDP is purely probabilistic, and we can define the probability $p_s^{\mathcal{A}}(F)$ of reaching a target set $F \subseteq S$ from s under $\mathcal{A}$. By quantifying over all strategies in $\mathcal{M}$, we can define the minimum and maximum probability of reaching F:
$$p_{\mathcal{M}}^{min}(F) = \inf_{s \in s_0} \inf_{\mathcal{A}} p_s^{\mathcal{A}}(F) \text{ and } p_{\mathcal{M}}^{max}(F) = \sup_{s \in s_0} \sup_{\mathcal{A}} p_s^{\mathcal{A}}(F)$$
These values can be computed efficiently together with the corresponding strategies using, e.g., *value iteration*, which approximates the probability value.

Stochastic 2-player games [5] are turn-based games involving two players and probability. They generalise MDPs by allowing two types of nondeterministic choice, each controlled by a separate player.

Definition 2 (Stochastic games). *A stochastic game is a tuple* $\mathcal{G} = (S, (S_1,$ $S_2),$ $s_0, \Sigma, \mathsf{Steps}_{\mathcal{G}})$, *where S is a set of states partitioned into sets S_1 and S_2, s_0 is a set of initial states, Σ is a set of actions and* $\mathsf{Steps}_{\mathcal{G}} : S_1 \times \Sigma \times S_2 \mapsto 2^{\mathrm{Dist}(S)}$ *is a probabilistic transition function.*

S_1 and S_2 represent the sets of states controlled by player 1 and player 2, respectively. The behaviour of a game is as follows: first player 1, in state $s \in S_1$, selects an available action $\delta \in \Sigma$, which takes the game into a state $s' \in S_2$. Player 2 then selects a probability distribution μ from the set $\mathsf{Steps}_{\mathcal{G}}(s, \delta, s')$. Finally, the successor state s'' is chosen according to μ. A resolution of nondeterminism in $\mathcal{G}$ is a pair of strategies σ_1, σ_2 for player 1 and player 2, respectively, under which we can define the probability $p_s^{\sigma_1, \sigma_2}(F)$ of reaching a subset $F \subseteq S$ from state s.

Clocks and parameters. Let $\mathbb{R}$, $\mathbb{R}_{\geqslant 0}$ and $\mathbb{Z}$ be the sets of reals, non-negative reals and integers, respectively. Let X be a finite set. A linear expression on X is an expression of the form $\lambda := k \mid k \cdot x \mid \lambda + \lambda$, where $k \in \mathbb{Z}$ and $x \in X$.

Now let $X = \{x_1, ..., x_n\}$ be a finite set of clock variables. A clock valuation $u : X \mapsto \mathbb{R}_{\geqslant 0}$ is a function assigning a non-negative real number to each $x \in X$. Let $\mathbf{0}$ be a valuation that assigns 0 to all clocks in X. For any $R \subseteq X$ and any valuation u on X, we write $u[R]$ for the valuation on X such that $u[R](x) = 0$ if $x \in R$ and $u[R](x) = u(x)$ otherwise. For $t \geqslant 0$, $u + t$ denotes the valuation which assigns $(u + t)(x) = u(x) + t$ to all $x \in X$. Let $P = \{p_1, ..., p_m\}$ be a finite set of parameters. A (linear parametric) constraint on $X \cup P$ is an expression of the form $\gamma := x_i \sim c \mid x_i - x_j \sim c \mid \gamma \wedge \gamma$ where $1 \leqslant i \neq j \leqslant n$, $x_i, x_j \in X$, $\sim \in \{<, \leqslant\}$ and c is a linear expression on P. By $\mathcal{C}(X, P)$ we denote the set of such parametric constraints and by $\mathcal{C}'(X, P)$ we denote the set of (non-diagonal) constraints of the form: $\gamma' := x_i \sim c \mid \gamma' \wedge \gamma'$. For any valuation v on P and any linear constraint γ on $X \cup P$, $v(\gamma)$ is the linear constraint on X obtained by replacing each parameter $p \in P$ by the (concrete) value $v(p)$. Given some arbitrary order on $X \cup P$, a valuation can be viewed as a real-valued vector of size $|X \cup P|$. The set of valuations satisfying some linear constraints is then a convex polyhedron of $\mathbb{R}^{|X \cup P|}$. A zone is a polyhedron defined only by conjunctions of the constraints of the form $x - y \sim c$ or $x \sim c$ with $x, y \in X$, $c \in \mathbb{Z}$ and $\sim \in \{<, \leqslant\}$. If v is a valuation on both clocks and parameters $X \cup P$ (as v is used throughout the paper, unless specified otherwise) then by $v_{|P}$ (resp. $v_{|X}$) we denote the projection of v onto P (resp. X). We now give a formal definition of *Parametric Probabilistic Timed Automata* (PPTA), which are PTA extended with timing parameters.

Definition 3 (PPTA). *A PPTA is a tuple* $\mathcal{P} = (L, l_0, X, P, \Sigma, \mathsf{prob}, \mathsf{Inv})$ *where: L is a finite set of locations; $l_0 \in L$ is the initial location; X is a finite set of clocks; P is a finite set of parameters; Σ is a finite set of actions; prob : $L \times \Sigma \times \mathcal{C}(X, P) \mapsto \mathsf{Dist}(2^X \times L)$ is a probabilistic transition function; and $\mathsf{Inv} : L \mapsto \mathcal{C}'(X, P)$ is a function that assigns an invariant to each location.*

For any rational valuation v on P, the structure $v(\mathcal{P})$ obtained from $\mathcal{P}$ by replacing every constraint γ by $v(\gamma)$ is a PTA. The behaviour of a PPTA $\mathcal{P}$ is described by the behaviour of all PTA $v(\mathcal{P})$ obtained by considering all possible parameter valuations. A (concrete) state of $v(\mathcal{P})$ is a pair $(l, u) \in L \times \mathbb{R}_{\geqslant 0}^X$ such that the clock valuation u satisfies the invariant (notation $u \models v(\mathsf{Inv}(l))$). A transition in the semantics of $v(\mathcal{P})$ is a timed-action pair (t, δ). In each state certain amount of time $t \in \mathbb{R}_{\geqslant 0}$ can elapse, as long as $u + t \models v(\mathsf{Inv}(l))$. Time elapse is followed by the choice of an action $\delta \in \Sigma$, for which the set of clocks R to reset and successor locations l' are selected randomly according to the probability distribution $\mathsf{prob}(l, \delta, \gamma)$. The action δ can only be taken once its constraint $v(\gamma)$ (called guard) is satisfied by the current clock valuation. Each element $(R, l') \in 2^X \times L$, such that $\mathsf{prob}(l, \delta, \gamma)(R, l') > 0$, is called an edge and the set of all such edges, denoted $\mathsf{edges}(l, \delta, \gamma)$, is assumed to be an ordered list $\langle e_1, ..., e_n \rangle$. We now formally define the semantics of a PPTA under a parameter valuation v.

Definition 4 (Semantics of a PPTA). *Let* $\mathcal{P} = (L, l_0, X, P, \Sigma, \mathsf{prob}, \mathsf{Inv})$ *be a PPTA and* v *be a* $\mathbb{R}$*-valuation on* P *(*$v : P \mapsto \mathbb{R}$*). The semantics of* $v(\mathcal{P})$ *is given by the infinite-state MDP* $\mathcal{M}_{v(\mathcal{P})} = (Q, q_0, \mathbb{R}_{\geqslant 0} \times \Sigma, \mathsf{Steps}_{\mathcal{M}_{v(\mathcal{P})}})$ *where:*

- $Q = \{(l, u) \in L \times X \mapsto \mathbb{R}_{\geqslant 0} \mid u \models v(\mathsf{Inv}(l))\}$, $q_0 = (l_0, \mathbf{0})$
- $\mathsf{Steps}_{\mathcal{M}_{v(\mathcal{P})}}((l, u), (t, \delta)) = \mu$ *iff* $\exists (R, l') \in \mathsf{edges}(l, \delta, \gamma)$ *such that* $u + t \models v(\gamma) \wedge u + t' \models \mathsf{Inv}(l)$ *for all* $0 \leqslant t' \leqslant t$, *and for any* $(l', u') \in Q$:
$$\mu(l', u') = \sum\{|\, \mathsf{prob}(l, \delta, \gamma)(R, l') \mid R \in 2^X \wedge u' = (u + t)[R] \,|\}$$

Note that the definition of μ involves summation over the cases in which multiple clock resets result in the same target state (l', u'), expressed as a multiset, since some of the probabilities might be the same.

We study the *optimal timing parameter synthesis* problem for PPTA, i.e., automatically finding values of parameters such that the probability (either maximum or minimum) of reaching a certain set of locations is *optimised*. For example, in the case of property "the maximum probability of an airbag failing to deploy", we would want to choose the timing parameters that minimise this probability value. On the other hand, we would want to maximise "the maximum probability that the protocol successfully terminates".

3   Synthesis with Forward Reachability

A naive approach to parameter synthesis for PTA is to restrict parameter values to bounded intervals of integers (or rationals that can be scaled to integers) and perform verification for each such (non-parametric) model using a probabilistic model checker, e.g. PRISM [16]. However, this approach is shown to be inefficient for (non-probabilistic) TA compared to symbolic techniques, especially when the sets of possible parameter values are large [11]. This is why we aim to formulate a symbolic algorithm for deriving constraints on parameters that ensure the optimisation of some reachability probability in the model. For the symbolic exploration of the state-space, we use the notion of *parametric symbolic state* and forward symbolic operations on valuation sets given below, defined in [11].

Definition 5 (Parametric symbolic state). *A (parametric) symbolic state of a PPTA* $\mathcal{P}$, *with set of clocks* X *and set of parameters* P, *is a pair* $S = (l, \zeta)$ *where* l *is a location of* $\mathcal{P}$ *and* ζ *is a set of valuations* v *on* $X \cup P$.

- *future* (time successors): $\zeta^{\nearrow} = \{v' \mid v \in \zeta \wedge v'(x) = v(x) + d, d \geqslant 0 \text{ if } x \in X; v'(x) = v(x) \text{ if } x \in P\}$
- *reset of clocks* in $R \subseteq X$: $\zeta[R] = \{v[R] \mid v \in \zeta\}$
- *successor by edge* $e = (R, l')$ in the distribution $\mathsf{prob}(l, \delta, \gamma)$: $\mathsf{Succ}((l, \zeta), e) = (l', (\zeta \cap \gamma)[R]^{\nearrow} \cap \mathsf{Inv}(l'))$
- *initial symbolic state:* $Init(\mathcal{P}) = (l_0, \{v \in \mathbb{R}^{X \cup P} \mid v_{|X} \in \{\mathbf{0}_X\}^{\nearrow} \wedge v(\mathsf{Inv}(l_0))\})$.

The sets of valuations of all reachable symbolic states of a PPTA are convex polyhedra [9], since the set of valuations of the initial symbolic state is a convex polyhedron and all the operations preserve convexity.

Forward Reachability Exploration. The forward exploration, which builds an MDP-based abstraction of a given PTA [18], is an extension of the well-known zone-based forward reachability algorithm, ubiquitous for model-checking TA. This algorithm performs the exploration of the state-space by successively computing symbolic states using Succ, starting from the initial state. For probabilistic models, on-the-fly techniques are not used, as the goal is to compute the probability of reaching a state, instead of just checking the existence of a path.

In Fig. 1 we present our extension of the forward reachability algorithm from [18] to *parametric* probabilistic timed automata. It takes a PPTA $\mathcal{P}$ and some subset of its locations F as input, and returns the *reachability graph* $(Sym, Trans)$. Sym is the set of all reachable parametric symbolic states S of the model and $Trans$ is the set of symbolic transitions. $Waiting$ is the set of those symbolic states which have not yet been explored. As long as there are symbolic states unexplored $(Waiting \neq \varnothing)$, successor states are computed for each possible edge using Succ operator. Each symbolic transition $T \in Trans$ is of the form $T = ((l, \zeta), \delta, \langle(l_1, \zeta_1), ..., (l_n, \zeta_n)\rangle)$, where $n = |\mathsf{edges}(l, \delta, \gamma)|$. A symbolic transition T induces probability distribution μ_T over symbolic states Sym. For any $(l', \zeta') \in Sym$: $\mu_T(l', \zeta') = \sum\{|\ \mathsf{prob}(l, \delta, \gamma)e_i \mid e_i \in \mathsf{edges}(l, \delta, \gamma) \wedge \zeta_i = \zeta'\ |\}$.

Using these distributions, the algorithm BUILDMDP($Sym, Trans$) constructs an MDP similarly to that of [18] for PTA, which can then be analysed to compute the reachability probabilities. For PTA, and therefore for PPTA, this approach only gives upper (resp. lower) bounds on maximum (resp. minimum) reachability probability in the model. This is because the reachability graph is too coarse to preserve precise time the actions can be taken, and thus constructs an over-approximation of the possible strategies.

Let us highlight the differences between our algorithm and its non-parametric counterpart from [18]. In the non-parametric case, all the symbolic states (l, ζ) containing some location $l \in F$ are collected into a set $Reached$. Then, in the constructed MDP, the max. (or min.) probability of ending up in $Reached$ is calculated. In our setting, we are interested in finding the *optimal* parameter valuations (that maximise or minimise some reachability probability). We thus need to keep separate those symbolic states containing different parameter valuations and calculate the max/min reachability probability for each one. We divide the set $Reached$ into subsets $Reached_i$, each of which contains the symbolic states (l_i, ζ_i) with equivalent parameter values (obtained by projection onto parameters $\zeta_{i|P}$). Another difference arises when building symbolic transitions $Trans$. This follows from the property of TA (and therefore PTA) proven in [9], which states that weakening (resp. strengthening) the guards in any TA $\mathcal{T}$, e.g decreasing lower and increasing upper (resp. increasing lower and decreasing upper) bounds on clocks, yields an automaton whose reachable states include (resp. are subset of) those of $\mathcal{T}$. We therefore add, for any two symbolic states $(l_i, \zeta_i), (l_j, \zeta_j) \in Sym$ which satisfy $\zeta_{i|X} \subseteq \zeta_{j|X} \wedge \zeta_{i|P} \subseteq \zeta_{j|P} \wedge l_i = l_j$, a transition (point distribution) from (l_j, ζ_j) to (l_i, ζ_i), in order to obtain the correct probabilities in the MDP. By $\{Reached_i\}_{|P}$ in Fig. 1, we denote the parameter values contained in $Reached_i$.

```
// PARREACH(P, F)
Sym := ∅;  Trans := ∅;  Reached := ∅;  Waiting := {Init(P)};  n := 0;  Reached₀ := ∅
while Waiting ≠ ∅
    choose and remove (l, ζ) from Waiting
    Sym := Sym ∪ {(l, ζ)}
    for δ ∈ Σ such that edges(l, δ, γ) ≠ ∅
        for each eᵢ ∈ edges(l, δ, γ) = ⟨e₁, ..., eₙ⟩
            (lᵢ', ζᵢ') := Succ((l, ζ), eᵢ)
            if (lᵢ', ζᵢ') ∉ Sym ∧ ζᵢ' ≠ ∅ ∧ lᵢ' ∉ F then Waiting := Waiting ∪ {(lᵢ', ζᵢ')}
            else if (lᵢ', ζᵢ') ∉ Sym ∧ ζᵢ' ≠ ∅ then Reached := Reached ∪ {(lᵢ', ζᵢ')}
        Trans := Trans ∪ {((l, ζ), δ, ⟨(l₁, ζ₁), ..., (lₙ, ζₙ)⟩)}
//Additional transitions from a state to its subsets
for each (l, ζ) ∈ Sym
    if ∃(l', ζ') ∈ Sym such that l = l' ∧ ζ|X ⊆ ζ'|X ∧ ζ|P ⊆ ζ'|P then
        Trans := Trans ∪ {((l', ζ'), ∅, ⟨(l, ζ)⟩)}
//Divide Reached into subsets Reachedᵢ according to different parameter valuations
for each (l, ζ) ∈ Reached
    if (ζ|P = {Reachedᵢ}|P for some Reachedᵢ where i ∈ [0..n]) then
        Reachedᵢ := Reachedᵢ ∪ {(l, ζ)}
    else Reachedₙ := Reachedₙ ∪ {(l, ζ)}; n + +;
return (Sym, Trans)
// BUILDPARMDP(Sym, Trans)
sym₀ = {(l, ζ) ∈ Sym | l = l₀}
for (l, ζ) ∈ Sym and T ∈ Trans(l, ζ)
    Steps_M((l, ζ), T) := μ_T
return M = (Sym, sym₀, Trans, Steps_M)
```

Fig. 1. Parametric forward reachability and construction of the corresponding MDP

Example 1. Let us consider a PPTA shown in Fig. 2. We are interested in the values of the parameter b which maximise the probability of the medium successfully *send*-ing the data (reaching location l_2). The MDP constructed from the reachability graph is shown in Fig. 3. There are three symbolic states holding l_2 with different parameter valuations, $Reached_1 = \{(l_2, x = y \wedge b \leqslant 1)\}$, $Reached_2 = \{(l_2, x = y \wedge b \leqslant 3)\}$ and $Reached_3 = \{(l_2, x = y \wedge b \leqslant 5)\}$. Using PRISM, we calculated maximal probabilities of reaching those states in the MDP: $p^{max}(\Diamond Reached_1) = 0.65$, $p^{max}(\Diamond Reached_2) = 0.8775$, and $p^{max}(\Diamond Reached_3) = 0.957125$, where $\Diamond \phi$ means that ϕ must hold eventually. If we want to *maximise* the probability of reaching l_2, it is clear that we should choose $b \leqslant 1$.

The forward reachability algorithm provides only upper (resp. lower) bound on the max. (resp. min.) reachability probability. In Example 1, this method actually gives the correct values, but consider now the automaton of Fig. 4, inspired by [18]. The probability of reaching l_3 obtained using forward approach (the resulting MDP is shown in Fig. 5) is 1, regardless of the value of a. By careful inspection, we observe that the max. probability is 1 only if $a = 0$ (when the transition from l_0 is taken at $x = y = 0$), and otherwise it is at most 0.5.

Theorem 1. *For a PPTA P and a subset of its locations F, if $(Sym, Trans) =$ PARREACH(P, F) and $M =$ BUILDMDP$(Sym, Trans)$, then:*

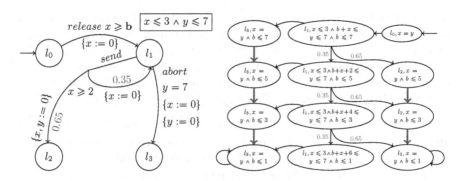

Fig. 2. PPTA   **Fig. 3.** MDP for PPTA of Fig. 2

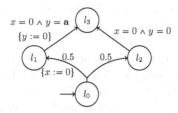
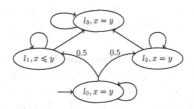

Fig. 4. PPTA   **Fig. 5.** MDP for PPTA of Fig. 4

- $p_{\mathcal{M}}^{min}(Reached) \leqslant p_{\mathcal{P}}^{min}(F)$ and $p_{\mathcal{M}}^{max}(Reached) \geqslant p_{\mathcal{P}}^{max}(F)$;
- if $\mathcal{M}$ gives the precise reachability probabilities in $\mathcal{P}$ and if some $(l_k, \zeta_k) \in$ *Reached* has the optimum (max. or min.) reachability probability, among all $(l_j, \zeta_j) \in$ *Reached*, then $\{\zeta_{k|P} \backslash (\bigcup_{\forall j \neq k, l_j \in F} \zeta_{j|P})\}$ is the solution to the optimal parameter synthesis problem.

The *reachability-emptiness* problem for parametric timed automata is undecidable [2], and the algorithm for forward reachability exploration for this model might not terminate [11,9]. Since our algorithm for PPTA can be viewed as its extension, termination cannot be guaranteed either.

To resolve the limitation of the forward approach, namely, that it can only compute bounds on the reachability probabilities, in the next section we adapt the *game-based abstraction refinement* method from [15] to synthesise the optimal timing parameter values for PPTA. We choose this approach as it can compute precise min. and max. probabilities and is shown to perform better then the alternative model checking technique for PTA, digital clocks [17].

4   Synthesis with Game-Based Abstraction Refinement

In [14], stochastic two-player games are used as abstractions for MDPs. In such a game, the two players represent nondeterminism introduced by the abstraction

(player 1) and nondeterminism from the original model (player 2). By quantifying over all possible strategies for players 1 and 2, we can obtain both the lower bound (lb) and upper bound (ub) on either the max. or min. reachability probability in the original MDP. If a game $\mathcal{G}$ is constructed from an MDP $\mathcal{M}$ using the approach from [14], where F is a subset of states of $\mathcal{M}$, we have:
$$p_{\mathcal{G}}^{lb,min}(F) \leqslant p_{\mathcal{M}}^{min}(F) \leqslant p_{\mathcal{G}}^{ub,min}(F) \text{ and } p_{\mathcal{G}}^{lb,max}(F) \leqslant p_{\mathcal{M}}^{max}(F) \leqslant p_{\mathcal{G}}^{ub,max}(F).$$
In case of maximum probability we have: $p_{\mathcal{G}}^{lb,max}(F) \stackrel{def}{=} \sup_{s\in s_0}\inf_{\sigma_1}\sup_{\sigma_2}p_s^{\sigma_1,\sigma_2}(F)$
and $p_{\mathcal{G}}^{ub,max}(F) \stackrel{def}{=} \sup_{s\in s_0}\sup_{\sigma_1}\sup_{\sigma_2}p_s^{\sigma_1,\sigma_2}(F)$. Using similar techniques to value iteration for MDPs [5], these probabilities can be efficiently approximated, together with the corresponding strategy pairs which achieve them.

In [15], the concept of gamed-based abstractions is used for PTA in order to compute the maximum and minimum reachability probabilities. The method starts from the MDP obtained via forward reachability algorithm, and subsequently builds and refines the stochastic game abstraction. In this section, we generalise this method by taking into account timing parameters.

Game-Based Abstraction for PPTA. The game-based abstraction is constructed by analysing transitions outgoing from each location in a PPTA. The transitions are divided into subsets according to the common part of the symbolic state in which they are enabled. This analysis is based on the *validity* operator [15]. In the non-parametric case, this operator takes the symbolic transition $T = ((l, \zeta), \delta, \langle(l_1, \zeta_1), ..., (l_n, \zeta_n)\rangle)$ and returns false if the part of ζ from which it is possible to let time pass and then perform action δ, such that taking the ith edge (R_i, l_i) gives some state $(l_i, v) \in (l_i, \zeta_i)$, is empty. Such analysis requires several backward operators, defined for the parametric domain in [12]:
- *past* (time predecessors): $\zeta^{\swarrow} = \{v' \mid v \in \zeta \wedge v'(x) \geqslant 0, v'(x) + d = v(x), d \geqslant 0 \text{ if } x \in X; v'(x) = v(x) \text{ if } x \in P\}$
- *inverse reset of clocks* in set $R \subseteq X$: $\zeta[R]^{-1} = \{v' \mid \exists v \in \zeta \text{ s.t. } v'(x) = 0 \text{ if } x \in R \wedge v'(x) = v(x) \text{ otherwise}\}$

We extend the validity operator to parametric domain and replace Boolean operations with the corresponding set-theoretic operations, in order to obtain the valuations on $X \cup P$ from which it is possible to perform such a transition: $valid(T) = \zeta \cap ((\gamma \cap (\cap_{i=1}^n(\zeta_i[R]^{-1})))^{\swarrow})$. The transition T is therefore *valid* if the set of valuations (polyhedron) $valid(T)$ is non-empty. The projection of these valuations onto parameters gives the corresponding values of parameters. In order to construct a stochastic game, the notion of validity is extended to sets of symbolic transitions with the same source. Again, we replace Boolean with set-theoretic operators: $valid(\mathbb{T}) = (\cap_{T\in\mathbb{T}} valid(T)) \cap (\cap_{T\in Trans(l,\zeta)\setminus\mathbb{T}} \neg valid(T))$. $valid(\mathbb{T})$ defines the set of valuations $v \models \zeta$ on $X \cup P$, such that from (l, v) it is possible to perform any symbolic transition $T \in \mathbb{T}$, but it is not possible to perform any other transition of $Trans(l, \zeta)$. In a symbolic state (l, ζ) of a stochastic game abstraction of a PPTA, player 1 first picks a subset $\mathbb{T}$ of symbolic transitions (in other words, part of the symbolic state in which these transitions are valid), and player 2 then picks a transition $T \in \mathbb{T}$. Fig. 6 shows the algorithm for the construction of a stochastic game from a given reachability graph, which yields (by quantifying over all possible strategies for player 1 and player 2) upper and lower bounds on the max/min reachability probabilities in a PPTA.

//BUILDGAME(Sym, $Trans$)
$sym_0 = \{(l, \zeta) \in S \mid l = l_0\}$
for $(l, \zeta) \in S$
    for $\mathbb{T} \subseteq Trans(l, \zeta)$ s.t. $\mathbb{T} \neq \varnothing$ and $valid(\mathbb{T}) \neq \varnothing$
        $\mathsf{Steps}_{\mathcal{G}}((l, \zeta), \mathbb{T}) := \{\mu_T \mid T \in \mathbb{T}\}$
return $\mathcal{G} = (Sym, sym_0, 2^{Trans}, \mathsf{Steps}_{\mathcal{G}})$

Fig. 6. Algorithm for stochastic game abstraction

// REFINE(Sym, $Trans$, (l, ζ), $\mathbb{T}_{lb}$, $\mathbb{T}_{ub}$)
$\zeta_{lb} := valid(\mathbb{T}_{lb})$; $\zeta_{ub} := valid(\mathbb{T}_{ub})$
$Sym^{new} := \{(l, \zeta_{lb}), (l, \zeta_{ub}), (l, \zeta \wedge \neg(\zeta_{lb} \vee \zeta_{ub}))\} \setminus \{\varnothing\}$
$Sym^{ref} := (Sym \setminus \{(l, \zeta)\}) \uplus S^{new}$; $Trans^{ref} := \varnothing$
for each $T = (S_0, \delta, \langle S_1, ..., S_n \rangle) \in Trans$
    if $(l, \zeta) \notin \{S_0, S_1, ..., S_n\}$ **then**
        $Trans^{ref} := Trans^{ref} \cup \{T\}$
    else $\mathbb{T}^{new} := \{(S_0', \delta, \langle S_1', ..., S_n' \rangle) \mid S_i' \in Sym^{new}$ if $S_i = (l, \zeta) \wedge S_i' = S_i$ otherwise$\}$
        for $T^{new} \in \mathbb{T}^{new}$ such that $valid(T^{new}) \neq \varnothing$
            $Trans^{ref} := Trans^{ref} \cup \{T^{new}\}$
return $(Sym^{ref}, Trans^{ref})$

Fig. 7. Algorithm for parametric abstraction refinement

Theorem 2. *If* $(Sym, Trans) = $ PARREACH$(\mathcal{P}, F)$, $\mathcal{G} = $ BUILDGAME$(Sym, Trans)$ *and* $* \in \{min, max\}$ *then:* $p_{\mathcal{G}}^{lb,*}(Reached) \leq p_{\mathcal{P}}^{*}(F) \leq p_{\mathcal{G}}^{ub,*}(Reached)$.

Example 2. A game constructed from the forward reachability graph of a PPTA in Fig. 2 is shown in Fig. 8. We represent player 1 states by ellipses containing symbolic states (l, ζ), and player 2 states by a black dot. In two of its states (containing l_1 and l_2), player 1 can choose between the part of the state where both transitions are valid and the part where only one transition is valid (a self-loop). The analysis of this game, however, gives values 0 and 1 for lower and upper bound, respectively, on the maximum probability of reaching l_3. We address this issue below by applying a method to refine the abstraction.

Parametric Abstraction Refinement. Stochastic game abstractions might be too imprecise for reachability probabilities, as shown in Example 2. The abstraction refinement method proceeds by iteratively computing refined abstractions until suitable precision is obtained. The game-based abstraction refinement for MDPs from [13] uses the difference between lower and upper bounds on max/min reachability probability computed thus far as the quantitative measure of precision. This method has been subsequently used in [15] for the abstraction refinement for PTA. We now explain our extension for the parametric

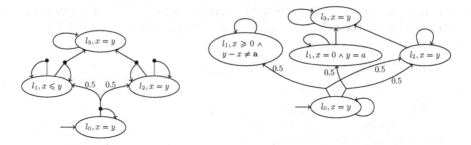

Fig. 8. Game-based abstraction   **Fig. 9.** Refinement of a symbolic state

case, which leads to parameter values corresponding to precise probabilities in the model.

After the construction and analysis of a stochastic game, the refinement algorithm, presented in Fig. 7, takes the reachability graph $(Sym, Trans)$, splits one symbolic state per iteration and modifies symbolic transitions accordingly. The split of a symbolic state (l, ζ) is done with respect to player 1 strategy choices, $\mathbb{T}_{ub}$ and $\mathbb{T}_{lb}$, in (l, ζ), which achieve lower and upper bounds (such choices must exist in a state where these bounds differ, [14]). The symbolic state (l, ζ) is therefore split into $(l, valid(\mathbb{T}_{lb})), (l, valid(\mathbb{T}_{ub}))$, and $(l, \zeta \wedge \neg(valid(\mathbb{T}_{lb}) \vee valid(\mathbb{T}_{ub})))$. By construction, both $valid(\mathbb{T}_{lb})$ and $valid(\mathbb{T}_{ub})$ are non-empty and $valid(\mathbb{T}_{lb}) \neq valid(\mathbb{T}_{ub})$, and thus the split produces strict refinement. The MDP of Fig. 5, after a refinement of one symbolic state, is shown in Fig. 9.

The complete game-based abstraction refinement scheme, shown in Fig. 10, provides a means to compute the precise values for max/min reachability probability, each corresponding to a particular parameter valuation. We can then choose those valuations that optimise (either maximise or minimise) these probabilities. Algorithm SYNTH uses function ANALYZEGAME of [5] to compute bounds on max/min probability of reaching some set of locations in a stochastic game and the corresponding strategies. The choice $\mathbb{T}_i$ of player 1, in some (l, ζ), is a set of symbolic transitions T, and also represents the part of ζ in which these transitions are valid. To find the optimal parameter valuations, we first need to take the projection onto the parameters for each $valid(\mathbb{T}_i)$ in the optimal strategy of player 1 (the strategy for reaching some $Reached_k$ which gives the optimal probability), and take their intersection. Then, for some $(l_k, \zeta_k) \in Reached_k$ (all of them have the equivalent $\zeta_{k|P}$), we obtain the solution as $\{\bigcap_i valid(\mathbb{T}_i)_{|P} \cap (\zeta_{k|P} \backslash (\bigcup_{\forall j \neq k, l_j \in F} \zeta_{j|P}))\}$.

Theorem 3. *For a PPTA $\mathcal{P}$, a subset of its location F and $* \in \{min, max\}$, let $(Sym, Trans) = $ PARREACH$(\mathcal{P}, F)$. If $(Sym^{ref}, Trans^{ref})$ is the result returned by applying* REFINE *to $(Sym, Trans)$, $\mathcal{G}$ by* BUILDGAME$(Sym, Trans)$ *and $\mathcal{G}^{ref}$ by* BUILDGAME$(Sym^{ref}, Trans^{ref})$ *then:*

- *$(Sym^{ref}, Trans^{ref})$ is a reachability graph for $(\mathcal{P}, F)$;*
- *$p_{\mathcal{G}}^{lb,*}(Reached) \leqslant p_{\mathcal{G}^{ref}}^{lb,*}(Reached)$ and $p_{\mathcal{G}}^{ub,*}(Reached) \geqslant p_{\mathcal{G}^{ref}}^{ub,*}(Reached)$;*

- If $p^* = p_{\mathcal{G}_{ref}}^{lb,*}(l_k, \zeta_k) = p_{\mathcal{G}_{ref}}^{ub,*}(l_k, \zeta_k)$, for some $(l_k, \zeta_k) \in$ Reached, is the optimum $*$ reachability probability, among all $(l_j, \zeta_j) \in$ Reached, then the solution to the optimal parameter synthesis can be extracted from the strategy σ_1 of Player 1 (which achieves p^*) and ζ_k.

```
// SYNTH(P, F, *, ε, ⋆)
(Sym, Trans) = PARREACH(P, F); G = BUILDGAME(Sym, Trans); p* := 0; σ_{p*} := ∅
for each Reached_i ∈ Reached
    (p_G^{lb,*}, p_G^{ub,*}, σ_1^{lb}, σ_1^{ub}) := ANALYSEGAME(G, Reached_i, *)
    while p_G^{ub,*} - p_G^{lb,*} > ε
        choose (l, ζ) ∈ Sym
            (Sym^{ref}, Trans^{ref}) = REFINE(Sym, Trans, (l, ζ), σ_1^{lb}(l, ζ), σ_1^{ub}(l, ζ))
            G = BUILDGAME(Sym^{ref}, Trans^{ref})
            (p_G^{lb,*}, p_G^{ub,*}, σ_1^{lb}, σ_1^{ub}) := ANALYSEGAME(G, Reached_i, *)
    if p* ~ p_G^{lb,*} then  // put < (resp. >) instead of ~ when ⋆ is maximisation
        p* := p_G^{lb,*}; σ_{p*} := σ_1^{lb}                              (resp. minimisation)
return [p*, σ_{p*}]
```

Fig. 10. Parameter synthesis using game-based abstraction refinement loop

The algorithm is designed to terminate when the difference between the upper and lower bound falls below some threshold ϵ for reasons of computational efficiency. We show that this is, however, not necessary. If the initial forward reachability exploration terminates (PARREACH), then our algorithm, similarly to its non-parametric counterpart from [15], is guaranteed to terminate in a finite number of steps with a precise answer.

Theorem 4 (Termination). Let $* \in \{min, max\}$. If forward reachability algorithm (PARREACH) terminates, then the algorithm for parameter synthesis SYNTH terminates after a finite number of steps and returns $p^* = p^{lb,*} = p^{ub,*}$.

Example 3. We return to the PPTA in Fig. 4. The final stochastic game, after two refinement iterations, contains six symbolic states. The validity of each new symbolic transition T_i, obtained in the refinement process, gives the following parameter valuations:

- $T_1 = ((l_0, x = y), \varnothing, \langle (l_1, x = 0 \land y = a), (l_2, x = y = 0) \rangle) \neq \varnothing$ if $a = 0$
- $T_2 = ((l_0, x = y), \varnothing, \langle (l_1, x = 0 \land y = a), (l_2, x = y > 0) \rangle) \neq \varnothing$ if $a \neq 0$
- $T_3 = ((l_0, x = y), \varnothing, \langle (l_1, x \geqslant 0 \land y \neq a), (l_2, x = y = 0) \rangle) \neq \varnothing$ if $a \neq 0$
- $T_4 = ((l_0, x = y), \varnothing, \langle (l_1, x \geqslant 0 \land y \neq a), (l_2, x = y > 0) \rangle) \neq \varnothing$ for $a \in \mathbb{R}_{\geqslant 0}$.

The set of transitions $\mathbb{T}_1 = \{T_2, T_3, T_4\}$ is valid if $a \neq 0$, in which case the max. probability of reaching l_3 is 0.5, and $\mathbb{T}_2 = \{T_1, T_4\}$, is valid if $a = 0$, in which case the max. probability of reaching l_3 is 1. If we wish to maximise this probability, the algorithm obtains the constraint $a = 0$.

5   Conclusion

We presented a technique for PPTA which derives symbolic constraints on parameters of the model, such that the max/min probability of reaching some set of locations is optimised. We focused on probabilistic reachability, but can easily consider more expressive target sets that refer to locations and clocks by syntactically modifying the model as in [18]. Computing expected time properties using game abstractions is still open for PTA. Termination of our algorithm depends on whether the forward reachability exploration terminates. Unlike for TA/PTA, where the extrapolation operator on zones can be used, in the parametric case we need to impose certain restrictions to ensure termination. One possibility is to restrict the parameter domain to bounded integers as in [11]. We are currently implementing the algorithm in PRISM.

Acknowledgments. This research is supported by ERC AdG VERIWARE.

References

1. Alur, R., Dill, D.L.: A theory of timed automata. TCS 126, 183–235 (1994)
2. Alur, R., Henzinger, T.A., Vardi, M.Y.: Parametric real-time reasoning. In: STOC 1993, pp. 592–601. ACM Press (1993)
3. André, É., Fribourg, L., Sproston, J.: An extension of the inverse method to probabilistic timed automata. FMSD 42, 119–145 (2013)
4. Chamseddine, N., Duflot, M., Fribourg, L., Picaronny, C., Sproston, J.: Computing expected absorption times for parametric determinate probabilistic timed automata. In: QEST 2008, pp. 254–263. IEEE CS Press (2008)
5. Condon, A.: The complexity of stochastic games. Information and Computation 96, 203–224 (1992)
6. Diciolla, M., Kim, C.H.P., Kwiatkowska, M., Mereacre, A.: Synthesising optimal timing delays for timed i/o automata. In: EMSOFT 2014, ACM (2014)
7. Hahn, E.M., Hermanns, H., Zhang, L.: Probabilistic reachability for parametric markov models. In: SPIN, pp. 88–106 (2009)
8. Han, T., Katoen, J.-P., Mereacre, A.: Approximate parameter synthesis for probabilistic time-bounded reachability. In: RTSS, pp. 173–182. IEEE Computer Society (2008)
9. Hune, T., Romijn, J., Stoelinga, M., Vaandrager, F.W.: Linear parametric model checking of timed automata. Journal of Logic and Algebraic Programming 53-53, 183–220 (2002)
10. Jovanović, A., Kwiatkowska, M.: Parameter synthesis for probabilistic timed automata using stochastic game abstractions. Technical Report CS-RR-14-06, Oxford University (June 2014)
11. Jovanović, A., Lime, D., Roux, O.H.: Integer parameter synthesis for timed automata. In: Piterman, N., Smolka, S.A. (eds.) TACAS 2013 (ETAPS 2013). LNCS, vol. 7795, pp. 401–415. Springer, Heidelberg (2013)
12. Jovanović, A., Lime, D., Roux, O.H.: Synthesis of bounded integer parameters for parametric timed reachability games. In: Van Hung, D., Ogawa, M. (eds.) ATVA 2013. LNCS, vol. 8172, pp. 87–101. Springer, Heidelberg (2013)
13. Kattenbelt, M., Kwiatkowska, M., Norman, G., Parker, D.: A game-based abstraction-refinement framework for Markov decision processes. FMSD 36(3), 246–280 (2010)
14. Kwiatkowska, M., Norman, G., Parker, D.: Game-based abstraction for Markov decision processes. In: QEST 2006, pp. 157–166. IEEE CS Press (2006)

15. Kwiatkowska, M., Norman, G., Parker, D.: Stochastic games for verification of probabilistic timed automata. In: Ouaknine, J., Vaandrager, F.W. (eds.) FOR-MATS 2009. LNCS, vol. 5813, pp. 212–227. Springer, Heidelberg (2009)
16. Kwiatkowska, M., Norman, G., Parker, D.: PRISM 4.0: Verification of probabilistic real-time systems. In: Gopalakrishnan, G., Qadeer, S. (eds.) CAV 2011. LNCS, vol. 6806, pp. 585–591. Springer, Heidelberg (2011)
17. Kwiatkowska, M., Norman, G., Parker, D., Sproston, J.: Performance analysis of probabilistic timed automata using digital clocks. FMSD 29, 33–78 (2006)
18. Kwiatkowska, M., Norman, G., Segala, R., Sproston, J.: Automatic verification of real-time systems with discrete probability distributions. TCS 282, 101–150 (2002)

On Functions Weakly Computable by Petri Nets and Vector Addition Systems[*]

J. Leroux[1] and Ph. Schnoebelen[2]

[1] LaBRI, Univ. Bordeaux & CNRS, France
[2] LSV, ENS Cachan & CNRS, France

Abstract. We show that any unbounded function weakly computable by a Petri net or a VASS cannot be sublinear. This answers a long-standing folklore conjecture about weakly computing the inverses of some fast-growing functions. The proof relies on a pumping lemma for sets of runs in Petri nets or VASSes.

1 Introduction

Petri nets (PN), Vector Addition Systems (VAS) and Vector Addition Systems with States (VASS) are essentially equivalent computational models based on simple operations on positive integer counters: decrements and increments. Such systems can be used to compute number-theoretical functions, exactly like with Minsky machines or Turing machines. However, they cannot compute all recursive functions since they are less expressive than Minsky machines. In particular they lack zero-tests, or, more precisely, they cannot initiate a given action on the condition that a counter's value is zero, only on the condition that it is not zero.

The standard definition for a function computed by a Petri net or a VASS is due to Rabin and is called "functions weakly computable by a Petri net", or just "WCPN functions" (all definitions will be found in the following sections). This notion has been used since the early days of Petri nets and has proved very useful in hardness or impossibility proofs: The undecidability of equivalence problems for nets and VASSes, and the Ackermann-hardness of the same problems for bounded systems, have been proved using the fact that multivariate polynomials with positive integer coefficients —aka positive Diophantine polynomials— and, respectively, the fast-growing functions $(F_i)_{i \in \mathbb{N}}$ in the Grzegorczyk hierarchy, are all WCPN [13,25,17].

The above results rely on showing how some useful functions are WCPN. But not much is known about exactly which functions are WCPN or not. It is known that all WCPN functions are monotonic. They are all primitive-recursive. The class of WCPN functions is closed under composition. A folklore conjecture states that the inverses of the fast-growing functions are not WCPN. It is stated as fact in [30, p.252] but no reference is given. In this paper, we settle the issue by proving that if $f : \mathbb{N} \to \mathbb{N}$ is WCPN and unbounded then it is in $\Omega(x)$, i.e., $f(x)$ eventually dominates $c \cdot x$ for some constant $c > 0$. Thus any function that is sublinear, like $x \mapsto \lfloor \sqrt{x} \rfloor$, or $x \mapsto \lfloor \log x \rfloor$, are not WCPN. In particular, this applies to the inverse F_i^{-1} of any fast-growing function with $i \geq 2$. The proof technique is interesting in its own right: it relies on a pumping lemma on sets of runs in VASSes or Petri nets.

[*] Work supported by the ReacHard project, ANR grant 11-BS02-001-01.

J. Ouaknine, I. Potapov, and J. Worrell (Eds.): RP 2014, LNCS 8762, pp. 190–202, 2014.
© Springer International Publishing Switzerland 2014

Beyond Petri nets and VASSes. Petri nets and VASSes are a classic example of well-structured systems [1,10]. In recent years, weakly computing numerical functions has proved to be a fundamental tool for understanding the expressive power and the complexity of some families of well-structured systems that are more powerful than Petri nets and VASSes [31,14,11]. For such systems, the hardness proofs rely on weakly computing fast-growing functions $(F_\alpha)_{\alpha \in Ord}$ that extend Grzegorczyk's hierarchy. These hardness proofs also crucially rely on weakly computing the inverses of the F_α's.

There are several extensions of Petri nets for which reachability (or coverability or termination) remains decidable: pushdown VASSes [23], nets with nested zero-tests [27], recursive VASSes [4] and Branching VASSes [6], VASSes with pointers to counters [5], etc. In many cases, it is not known how these extensions compare in expressive power and in complexity. We believe that weakly computable functions can be a useful tool when addressing theses questions.

Outline of the paper. Section 2 recalls the standard definitions for VASSes and fixes some notations. Section 3 recalls the definitions for WCPN functions and the classic results about them. Our main result is proved in Section 4.

2 Vector Addition Systems with States

Following Hopcroft and Pansiot [15], we adopt Vector Addition Systems with States (VASS) as our mathematical setting (rather than Petri nets or plain VASes) because they offers a good compromise between ease of description for specific systems, and convenient mathematical notation for reasoning about them. Nevertheless, all these models are essentially equivalent for our purposes.

Vectors of integers. $\mathbb{Z}$ and $\mathbb{N}$ denote the sets of integers and, resp., non-negative integers. For $d \in \mathbb{N}$, a d-dimensional *vector* is a tuple $a = \langle a_1, \ldots, a_d \rangle$ in $\mathbb{Z}^d$. We use 0 to denote $\langle 0, \ldots, 0 \rangle$ when the dimension is understood. Vectors can be concatenated: for $a \in \mathbb{Z}^d$ and $b \in \mathbb{Z}^{d'}$ we may write $\langle a, b \rangle$ for the vector $\langle a_1, \ldots, a_d, b_1, \ldots, b_{d'} \rangle \in \mathbb{N}^{d+d'}$.

Vectors in $\mathbb{Z}^d$ are ordered with $a = \langle a_1, \ldots, a_d \rangle \sqsubseteq b = \langle b_1, \ldots, b_d \rangle \overset{\text{def}}{\Leftrightarrow} a_1 \leq b_1 \wedge \cdots \wedge a_d \leq b_d$, and can be added with $(a + b) \overset{\text{def}}{=} \langle a_1 + b_1, \ldots, a_d + b_d \rangle$. Note that $(\mathbb{Z}^d, +, 0)$ is a commutative monoid, having $(\mathbb{N}^d, +, 0)$ as submonoid. Clearly, $a \in \mathbb{N}^d$ iff $0 \sqsubseteq a$. By Dickson's Lemma, $(\mathbb{N}^d, \sqsubseteq)$ is a well-ordering (more details in Section 4). In the following, we reserve $x, y, u, \ldots$ for vectors in $\mathbb{N}^d$ and write $\|x\|, \ldots,$ for their norms, defined by $\|\langle x_1, \ldots, x_d \rangle\| \overset{\text{def}}{=} x_1 + \cdots + x_d$.

VASSes and their operational semantics. A VASS is a triple $\mathcal{A} = \langle d, Q, T \rangle$ where $d \in \mathbb{N}$ is a *dimension* (i.e., a number of counters), Q is a non-empty finite set of *(control) locations*, and $T \subseteq Q \times \mathbb{Z}^d \times Q$ is a finite set of *(transition) rules*. We usually write $q, q', \ldots$ for locations, and $t, \ldots$ for rules.

Fix some VASS $\mathcal{A} = \langle d, Q, T \rangle$. The operational semantics of $\mathcal{A}$ is given in the form of a transition system $(Conf, \rightarrow)$. Formally, $Conf \overset{\text{def}}{=} Q \times \mathbb{N}^d$ is the set of *configurations*, with typical elements $c, c', \ldots$ The labeled transition relation $\rightarrow \subseteq Conf \times \mathbb{Z}^d \times Conf$ is a set of triples (c, a, c') called *steps*. As is standard, we write $c \overset{a}{\rightarrow} c'$ rather than

$(c, a, c') \in \to$. Steps are defined by $(q, x) \xrightarrow{a} (q', y) \overset{\text{def}}{\Leftrightarrow} (q, a, q') \in T \wedge y = x + a$. The vector a in a rule (q, a, q') is called a *translation*.

Graphical description. It is convenient to present VASSes in graphic form. See an example in Fig. 1. Here the locations and rules are depicted as a directed graph, as is standard with such automata-theoretical notions. Indeed, we see a d-dim VASS as being an automaton acting on d registers, or *counters*, capable of storing a natural number. These counters are named in our graphical depictions (see x and z in Fig. 1) so that we may use programming languages notations for the translation a in a rule (q, a, q'). For example, in Fig. 1, the loop labeled with "x--; x--; z++" is a rule (q_2, a, q_2) with $a = \langle -2, 1 \rangle$, the other rule being $(q_1, 0, q_2)$.

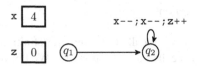

Fig. 1. A VASS depicted as an automaton acting on counters

Runs and reachability. For $k \in \mathbb{N}$, a length-k *run* from c to c' is a sequence ρ of the form $c_0 a_1 c_1 \cdots a_k c_k$ that alternates between configurations and vectors and such that $c_0 = c$, $c_k = c'$, and $c_{i-1} \xrightarrow{a_i} c_i$ for all $i = 1, \ldots, k$. For a run ρ as above, we let $\text{src}(\rho)$ and $\text{tgt}(\rho)$ denote c_0 and, respectively, c_k. We write $c \xrightarrow{*} c'$ when there is a run ρ from c to c', in which case we say that c' is *reachable* from c.

Continuing our previous example, the reachability relation for the VASS from Fig. 1 can be captured[1] with the following:

$$(q_i, x, z) \xrightarrow{*} (q_j, x', z') \quad \text{iff} \quad \begin{cases} 0 \le x - x' = 2(z' - z) & \text{if } j = 2, \text{ or} \\ x = x' \wedge z = z' & \text{if } i = j = 1. \end{cases} \quad (1)$$

Lifting steps and runs. It is well known and easy to see that steps can be lifted up by vectors $z \in \mathbb{N}^d$. For a configuration $c = (q, x)$, we write $c + z$ for the configuration $(q, x + z)$. The following properties will be useful in later sections:

Lemma 2.1 (Lifting steps and runs). *For all $c, c' \in \text{Conf}, a \in \mathbb{Z}^d$, and $u, v \in \mathbb{N}^d$:*

$$c \xrightarrow{a} c' \text{ implies } c + u \xrightarrow{a} c' + u, \quad (2)$$

$$c \xrightarrow{*} c' \text{ implies } c + u \xrightarrow{*} c' + u, \quad (3)$$

$$c + u \xrightarrow{*} c + v \text{ implies } \forall x \in \mathbb{N} : c + x \cdot u \xrightarrow{*} c + x \cdot v. \quad (4)$$

Proof of (4). With $c + u \xrightarrow{*} c + v$ and Eq. (3) one obtains $c + u + i \cdot u + j \cdot v \xrightarrow{*} c + i \cdot u + v + j \cdot v$ for any $i, j \in \mathbb{N}$. Chaining such runs yields

$$c + x \cdot u \xrightarrow{*} c + (x - 1) \cdot u + v \xrightarrow{*} c + (x - 2) \cdot u + 2 \cdot v \xrightarrow{*} \cdots \xrightarrow{*} c + x \cdot v. \quad \square$$

---

[1] The "$\Rightarrow$" direction is proved by induction on the length of the run, where every additional step respects the invariant stated by Eq. 1. The "$\Leftarrow$" direction is obvious when $j = 1$, and proved by concatenating steps of the form $(q_2, x, z) \to (q_2, x - 2, z + 1)$ when $j = 2$.

3   Weakly Computable Functions

In this section we recall the classic notion of weak PN computers and weakly computable functions. We recall the main known results, most of them from the 70's or early 80's, when the applications were limited to a few hardness or impossibility proofs. This material is classic but has been partly forgotten.

As we argued in the introduction, the notion of weakly computable functions has recently gained new relevance with the development of well-structured systems that go beyond Petri nets and VASSes in expressive power, while sharing some of their characteristics. In particular, we expect that it will help understanding the expressive power of extensions like VASSes with nested zero-tests [27] or with a pushdown stack [23].

3.1   Weak PN Computers and Weakly Computable Functions

The expected way for a finite-state register machine $\mathcal{A}$ to compute a numerical function $f : \mathbb{N} \to \mathbb{N}$ is to start in some initial location with some input value n stored in a designated input counter and from that configuration eventually reach a final or accepting location with $f(n)$ in a designated output counter. In order for $\mathcal{A}$ to be correct, it should be impossible that it reaches its accepting location with a value differing from $f(n)$ in the output counter. In that case, we say that $\mathcal{A}$ *strongly computes* f. This notion of correctness is fine with Minsky machines but it is too strong for VASSes and does not lead to an interesting family of computable functions. In fact, Petri nets and VASSes are essentially nondeterministic devices, and the above notion of strongly computing some function does not accommodate nondeterminism nicely.

With this in mind, Rabin defined a notion of "weakly computing f" that combines the following two principles:

Completeness: For any $n \in \mathbb{N}$, there is a computation with input n and output $f(n)$;
Safety: Any computation from input n to some output r satisfies $r \leq f(n)$.

This leads to our first definition:

Definition 3.1 (Weak PN computers). *Let* $f : \mathbb{N}^n \to \mathbb{N}^m$ *be a total function. A weak PN computer for* f *is a d-dimensional VASS* $\mathcal{A}$*, with* $d \geq n + m$ *and two designated locations* q_{init} *and* q_{final}*, that satisfies the following two properties. Here we write* ℓ *for* $d - n - m$*, and we decompose vectors* $\boldsymbol{w} \in \mathbb{N}^d$ *as concatenations* $\boldsymbol{w} = \boldsymbol{x}, \boldsymbol{y}, \boldsymbol{z}$ *where* $\boldsymbol{x} \in \mathbb{N}^n$*,* $\boldsymbol{y} \in \mathbb{N}^\ell$ *and* $\boldsymbol{z} \in \mathbb{N}^m$*.*

$$\forall \boldsymbol{x} : \exists \boldsymbol{x}', \boldsymbol{y}' : (q_{init}, \boldsymbol{x}, 0, 0) \xrightarrow{*} (q_{final}, \boldsymbol{x}', \boldsymbol{y}', f(\boldsymbol{x})) , \tag{CO}$$

$$\forall \boldsymbol{x}, \boldsymbol{x}', \boldsymbol{y}', \boldsymbol{z}' : (q_{init}, \boldsymbol{x}, 0, 0) \xrightarrow{*} (q_{final}, \boldsymbol{x}', \boldsymbol{y}', \boldsymbol{z}') \text{ implies } \boldsymbol{z}' \sqsubseteq f(\boldsymbol{x}) . \tag{SA}$$

We say that f *is* weakly computable*, or WCPN, if there is a weak PN computer for it.*

For convenience, Definition 3.1 assumes that the (n-dimensional) input is given in the first n counters of $\mathcal{A}$, and that the m-dimensional result is found in its last m counters. Note that $\mathcal{A}$ may use its ℓ extra counters for auxiliary calculations.

Example 3.2 (A weak computer for halving). The VASS from Fig. 1 is a weak computer for $f : x \mapsto \lfloor \frac{x}{2} \rfloor$. We just have to designate q_1 and q_2 as the required q_{init} and, resp., q_{final}. To show that (CO) and (SA) hold, one sets $z = 0$ in Eq. (1). This gives

$$(q_1, x, 0) \xrightarrow{*} (q_2, x', z') \text{ iff } z' = \frac{x - x'}{2},$$

entailing both (CO) —pick $x' = (x \mod 2)$— and (SA) —since $z', x' \in \mathbb{N}$—. ☐

Only monotonic functions can be weakly computed in the above sense. This is an immediate consequence of the monotonicity of steps in VASSes (see Lemma 2.1).

Proposition 3.3 (Monotonicity of WCPN functions). *If $f : \mathbb{N}^n \to \mathbb{N}^m$ is WCPN then $x \sqsubseteq x'$ implies $f(x) \sqsubseteq f(x')$.*

Proof. Assume that $x \sqsubseteq x'$ and pick any weak PN computer for f. By (CO), there is a run $(q_{\text{init}}, x, 0, 0) \xrightarrow{*} (q_{\text{final}}, v, y, f(x))$. By Eq. (3), there is also a run $(q_{\text{init}}, x', 0, 0) \xrightarrow{*} (q_{\text{final}}, v + x' - x, y, f(x))$. Thus $f(x) \sqsubseteq f(x')$ by (SA). ☐

3.2 More Weakly Computable Functions

Example 3.4 (A weak computer for multiplication, from [26]). Fig. 2 describes $\mathcal{A}_\times$, a weak computer for $f : x_1, x_2 \mapsto x_1 \times x_2$. To show that (SA) holds, we associate with

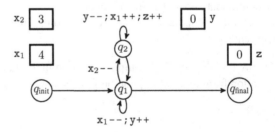

Fig. 2. $\mathcal{A}_\times$, a VASS weakly computing $x_1, x_2 \mapsto x_1 \times x_2$

any configuration c of $\mathcal{A}_\times$ a value $M(c) \in \mathbb{N}$ given by

$$M(q, x_1, x_2, y, z) \stackrel{\text{def}}{=} \begin{cases} z + (x_1 + y) \cdot x_2 + y & \text{if } q = q_2, \\ z + (x_1 + y) \cdot x_2 & \text{otherwise.} \end{cases} \tag{5}$$

By considering all rules of $\mathcal{A}_\times$ in turn, one checks that $c \to c'$ implies $M(c) \geq M(c')$. Thus given an arbitrary run from $c_0 = (q_{\text{init}}, x_1, x_2, 0, 0)$ to $c_k = (q_{\text{final}}, x_1', x_2', y', z')$ it holds that $M(c_0) \geq M(c_k)$, i.e., $x_1 \cdot x_2 \geq z' + x_1' \cdot x_2' + y' \cdot x_2'$. This entails $z' \leq x_1 \cdot x_2$ as required by (SA).

We let the reader check that (CO) holds. [Hint: steps $c \to c'$ that only use the rule from q_1 to q_2 when $x_1 = 0$, and from q_2 to q_1 when $y = 0$, satisfy $M(c) = M(c')$.] ☐

Weakly computing functions has mainly been used in hardness or impossibility proofs. For example, weakly computing multiplication can be used to show that reachability sets are not always semilinear: it is easy to adapt the construction underlying $\mathcal{A}_\times$ and design a VASS that, starting from a fixed c_0, generates the set of triples $\{\langle y_1, y_2, y \rangle \in \mathbb{N}^3 \mid 0 \leq y \leq y_1 \cdot y_2\}$ in some designated counters. The reachability set of this VASS cannot be semilinear.

Proposition 3.5. *The class of WCPN functions is closed by composition.*

Proof (Idea). The obvious way of gluing a weak PN computer for g after a weak PN computer for f produces a weak PN computer for $g \circ f$. To prove that the resulting VASS satisfies (SA), one observes that any run can be reordered by firing all rules in the f part before the rules in the g part.   □

Since the class of WCPN functions contains addition, multiplication, projections, and tuplings, one deduces that all positive Diophantine polynomials (multivariate polynomials with coefficients in $\mathbb{N}$) are weakly computable. This was used by Rabin in his reduction of Hilbert's 10th Problem to the inclusion problem for VASS reachability sets [3,13]. Hack strengthened this reduction to show that already the equality problem was undecidable [13]. (Later, Jančar showed that all behavioural equivalences are undecidable for VASSes —already for dimension $d = 5$—, using a simpler reduction with some notion of weak computer that is not numerical [18].)

3.3 Iterable Weak PN Computers

There are other easy and useful examples of WCPN functions that are not positive Diophantine polynomials, like min and max, or even *half* seen previously. In order to show the weak computability of more functions, in particular functions that are not polynomially or exponentially bounded, Mayr [24] introduced the following notion:

Definition 3.6 (Iterable Weak PN Computers). *Let* $f : \mathbb{N} \to \mathbb{N}$ *be a weakly computable unary function. A weak PN computer $\mathcal{A}$ for f is* iterable *if it satisfies*

$$\forall w, w' : (q_{init}, w) \xrightarrow{*} (q_{final}, w') \text{ implies } \|w'\| \leq f(\|w\|) . \tag{IT}$$

A unary function is iterably weakly computable, *or IWCPN, if there exists an iterable weak PN computer for it.*

In Definition 3.6, $\|w\|$ counts all the tokens (using Petri net terminology) in the starting configuration. The property stated by Eq. (IT) is useful in constructions that include $\mathcal{A}$ and where one cannot guarantee that all computations by $\mathcal{A}$ will start from clean configurations with zeroes in y and z.

Example 3.7 (Halving). The weak PN computer for halving (Fig. 1) is *not iterable* since, by Eq. (1), it has runs like $(q_{init}, 0, 1) \xrightarrow{*} (q_{final}, 0, 1)$ and $(q_{init}, 1, 0) \xrightarrow{*} (q_{final}, 1, 0)$ that have $\|w\| = \|w'\| = 1$, hence $\|w'\| \not\leq f(\|w\|) = \lfloor \frac{1}{2} \rfloor = 0$.   □

In fact, it is impossible to design an iterable weak PN computer for halving, as a consequence of the following proposition.

Proposition 3.8 (Strict Monotonicity of IWCPN functions). *If* $f : \mathbb{N} \to \mathbb{N}$ *is IWCPN then* $f(x) < f(x+1)$ *for all* $x \in \mathbb{N}$.

Proof. Assume a given iterable weak PN computer for f and let $x \in \mathbb{N}$. From (CO), we derive $(q_{\text{init}}, x, \mathbf{0}, 0) \xrightarrow{*} (q_{\text{final}}, x', \mathbf{y}', f(x))$. By lifting, we get $(q_{\text{init}}, x+1, \mathbf{0}, 0) \xrightarrow{*} (q_{\text{final}}, x'+1, \mathbf{y}', f(x))$. Now (IT) gives $x'+1 + \|\mathbf{y}'\| + f(x) \le f(x+1)$, which entails $f(x) < f(x+1)$. □

Example 3.9 (Doubling is IWCPN). One may design an iterable weak computer for

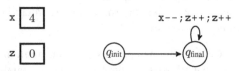

Fig. 3. $\mathcal{A}_{dbl}$, a VASS weakly computing $x \mapsto 2 \cdot x$

$x \mapsto 2 \cdot x$ (doubling) by a slight modification of Fig. 1. The resulting VASS, called $\mathcal{A}_{dbl}$, is depicted in Fig. 3. It satisfies

$$(q_{\text{init}}, x, z) \xrightarrow{*} (q_{\text{final}}, x', z') \quad \text{iff} \quad 0 \le 2(x - x') = z' - z.$$

These runs have thus $\|\mathbf{w}'\| = x' + z' = 2x - x' + z$. On the other hand $f(\|\mathbf{w}\|) = f(x + z) = 2x + 2z$. Hence $\|\mathbf{w}'\| \le f(\|\mathbf{w}'\|)$ as required by (IT). □

As expected, the functions weakly computed by iterable weak PN computers are iterable. Given a unary f and some $n \in \mathbb{N}$, we write $f^n(x)$ for the n-fold application $f(f(f(\cdots(x)\cdots)))$ of f. In particular $f^0(x) = x$. One can then show the following:

Proposition 3.10 ([24,26]). *If* f *is IWCPN, then* $iter(f) : x, y \mapsto f^x(y)$ *is IWCPN.*

Indeed, the whole point of (IT) is to entail the correctness of the obvious construction for iterating a weak PN computer.

With Proposition 3.10, and since doubling is IWCPN, we deduce that $iter(dbl)$: $x, y \mapsto dbl^x(y) = 2^x y$ is IWCPN. From that we deduce that $tower : x \mapsto 2^{2^{\cdots^{2}}} \Big\} x$ times is IWCPN. Continuing, all the fast-growing functions $(F_i)_{i \in \mathbb{N}}$ in the Grzegorczyk hierarchy are IWCPN. This was used by Mayr to show that the inclusion problem for finite reachability sets is not primitive recursive [24,25]. The problem is in fact $\mathbf{F}_\omega$-complete in the recent classification of Schmitz [28]. Using the same IWCPN functions, Jančar showed that all behavioural equivalences are Ackermann-hard between bounded VASSes [17].

While the fast-growing hierarchy extends beyond the $(F_i)_{i \in \mathbb{N}}$, the functions at the higher levels —starting with F_ω which is one possible form for Ackermann's function— are not WCPN. The following Proposition is folklore, but we could not find it explicitly stated in the literature:

Proposition 3.11. *Any weakly computable function f is primitive recursive.*

Proof. For a VASS $\mathcal{A}$ and a starting configuration $c_0 \in Conf$, let $S_{\mathcal{A}}(c_0) \in \mathbb{N}$ be the maximum norm of a configuration occurring in the Karp-Miller tree $T_{KM}(c_0)$ rooted in c_0. (We assume familiarity with Karp-Miller trees, otherwise see [19, Section 4A]. Note that these trees really contain "extended configurations" in $Q \times (\mathbb{N} \cup \{\omega\})^d$ but one only uses the finite values for their norm, as in, e.g., $\|(q, 7, \omega, 2)\| = 7 + 2 = 9$.)

For $k \in \mathbb{N}$, let now $S_{\mathcal{A}}(k) \overset{\text{def}}{=} \max \{S_{\mathcal{A}}(c) \mid \|c\| \le k\}$, i.e., $S_{\mathcal{A}}(k)$ is the size of the largest configuration in a Karp-Miller tree for $\mathcal{A}$ starting in some initial configuration of size at most k. It is shown in [9, Section 7C] that $S_{\mathcal{A}} : \mathbb{N} \to \mathbb{N}$ is primitive recursive (using a different norm for vectors, but this is of no consequence here). If now $\mathcal{A}$ is a weak PN computer for some $f : \mathbb{N}^n \to \mathbb{N}^m$, then by (CO) and for any $x \in \mathbb{N}^n$, the tree $T_{KM}((q_{\text{init}}, x, 0, 0))$ contains an extended configuration $c_x = (q_{\text{final}}, x', y', z')$ that covers $(q_{\text{final}}, 0, 0, f(x))$ since every reachable configuration is covered in T_{KM}. Furthermore, by (SA), no configuration reachable in q_{final} can have values above $f(x)$ in the last m counters. Hence the z' part of c_x has no ω's and $z' = f(x)$.

Finally, one can compute $f(x)$ by building a Karp-Miller tree of size that is primitive recursive in $\|x\|$ and by reading $f(x)$ on one of its leaves. $\square$

3.4   Alternative Definitions

The literature contains other proposals for a notion of weakly computable functions, all of them based on Rabin's seminal idea. One may define the function weakly computed by $\mathcal{A}$ as the maximum number of times a given transition [13], or all transitions [12], can be fired between $(q_{\text{init}}, x, 0)$ and q_{final}. While this does not give a larger class of weakly computable functions, other proposals are richer as we now show.

Weakly Computing Eagerly. An interesting notion is that of "eagerly" weakly computable functions. For this, we modify the Correctness and Safety requirement in Definition 3.1, replacing them with

$$\forall x : (q_{\text{init}}, x, 0, 0) \overset{*}{\to} (q_{\text{final}}, 0, 0, f(x)), \tag{CO'}$$

$$\forall x, z' : (q_{\text{init}}, x, 0, 0) \overset{*}{\to} (q_{\text{final}}, 0, 0, z') \text{ implies } z' \sqsubseteq f(x), \tag{SA'}$$

and we then say that f is EWCPN.

The idea here is that $\mathcal{A}$ must have consumed inputs and auxiliary counters *at the end of the computation*. This is meaningful in some reductions —e.g., reducing reachability in VASSes to some problem on some weakly computable function—. To the best of our knowledge, it has never been considered in the literature on VASSes and Petri nets. The fact is that it does not behave as nicely as the classical definition (see below). However, it is a natural option with some extensions like VASSes extended with resets as in [2,8], or with nested zero-tests as in [27].

Fact 3.12. *The class of EWCPN functions strictly extends the WCPN functions.*

Proof. Obviously, any WCPN function can be computed eagerly: a weak PN computer for f is made eager by adding decrementing rules that can empty the input and auxiliary counters. To see that the extension is strict, note that EWCPN functions are not always monotonic. For example, *parity* : $x \mapsto x \mod 2$ is easily seen to be EWCPN. $\square$

Since EWCPN functions are not necessarily monotonic, it is not clear whether the composition of two EWCPN functions is EWCPN itself. We introduced this notion because our main result (Theorem 4.7) holds for the larger class of EWCPN functions.

Families of Weak PN Computers. Very often, reductions showing hardness do not need a *fixed* weak PN computer for some f. They can accommodate a family $(\mathcal{A}_i)_{i \in \mathbb{N}}$ such that each $\mathcal{A}_i$ weakly computes $f(i)$, or $f(x)$ for all $x = 0, \ldots, i$. The family needs to be simple in computational terms —typically *"polynomial-time uniform"*— so that it can be used in reductions. Since the $\mathcal{A}_i$'s that weakly compute the fast-growing F_i's are uniformly generated, they provide a family weakly computing the function F_ω (equivalently, Ackermann's function) defined by $F_\omega(x) = F_x(x)$.

For slow-growing functions, one often needs a family that is polynomial-time uniform *in the size of $f(x)$*. A recent example is Lazić's polynomial-time uniform family of pushdown VASSes (VASSes extended with a stack) that weakly computes the inverse of $tower : x \mapsto 2^{2^{\cdot^{\cdot^{\cdot^2}}}} \Big\} x$ times [21].

4   Well-Quasi-ordering Runs in VASSes

Recall that a *quasi-order* (qo) on a set S is a binary relation $\preceq$ on S that is reflexive and transitive. A *partial order* is an antisymmetric quasi-order. A *well-quasi-order* (wqo) on S is a quasi-order $\preceq$ such that every infinite sequence $s_0, s_1, s_2, \ldots$ in S contains an increasing pair $s_i \preceq s_j$ for some $i < j$. See [20] or [29] for more on wqos.

Example 4.1. It is well-known that $(\mathbb{N}, \leq)$ is a wqo, while $(\mathbb{Z}, \leq)$ or $(\mathbb{Q}_{\geq 0}, \leq)$ are not. As another example, the pigeonhole principle shows that the partial order $(S, =)$ is a wqo if, and only if, S is finite.   □

In practice, many wqos are defined by applying well-known constructions on standard, already known, wqos.

Definition 4.2 (Products of wqos and Dickson's Lemma). *Let* $(S_1, \preceq_1), \ldots, (S_n, \preceq_n)$ *be qos. Their product is the qo* $(S_\times, \preceq_\times)$ *with* $S_\times \stackrel{def}{=} S_1 \times \cdots \times S_n$ *and* $\preceq_\times$ *given by*

$$(s_1, \ldots, s_n) \preceq_\times (s'_1, \ldots, s'_n) \stackrel{def}{\Leftrightarrow} s_1 \preceq_1 s'_1 \wedge \ldots \wedge s_n \preceq_n s'_n .$$

It is well-known that $(S_\times, \preceq_\times)$ *is a wqo if all* $(S_i, \preceq_i)$ *are.*

This last result is standardly called Dickson's Lemma, after Dickson's proof of his "Lemma A" in [7], showing in essence that any subset of $\mathbb{N}^d$ has finitely many minimal elements. For our purpose, Dickson's Lemma shows that $(\mathbb{N}^d, \sqsubseteq)$ is a wqo.

Definition 4.3 (Sequence extensions of wqos and Higman's Lemma). *The sequence extension* $(S^*, \preceq_*)$ *of a qo* $(S, \preceq)$ *has for its support the set* S^* *of all finite sequences* $s_1 \cdots s_k$ *over* S, *and these sequences are ordered by*

$$s_1 \cdots s_k \preceq_* s'_1 \cdots s'_\ell \stackrel{def}{\Leftrightarrow} \begin{cases} \text{there are indexes } 1 \leq n_1 < \cdots < n_k \leq \ell \\ \text{such that } s_1 \preceq s'_{n_1} \wedge \cdots \wedge s_k \preceq s'_{n_k}. \end{cases}$$

It is well-known that $(S^*, \preceq_*)$ *is a wqo if* $(S, \preceq)$ *is.*

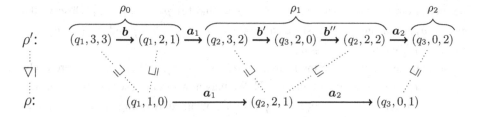

Fig. 4. Example for Def. 4.4: A factorization of $\rho' = \rho_0 a_1 \rho_1 a_2 \rho_2$ witnessing $\rho \trianglelefteq \rho'$

This last result is called Higman's Lemma.

In the rest of this section, we assume a fixed VASS $\mathcal{A} = (d, Q, T)$. We now define three orderings, respectively between the configurations of $\mathcal{A}$, between its steps, and between its runs, in the following way:

$$(q_1, \boldsymbol{x}_1) \sqsubseteq (q_2, \boldsymbol{x}_2) \overset{\text{def}}{\Leftrightarrow} q_1 = q_2 \wedge \boldsymbol{x}_1 \sqsubseteq \boldsymbol{x}_2 , \tag{6}$$

$$(c_1 \overset{a_1}{\rightarrow} c_1') \preccurlyeq (c_2 \overset{a_2}{\rightarrow} c_2') \overset{\text{def}}{\Leftrightarrow} c_1 \sqsubseteq c_2 \wedge a_1 = a_2 \wedge c_1' \sqsubseteq c_2' . \tag{7}$$

Since Q and T are finite, $(Q, =)$ and $(T, =)$ are wqos, hence $(Conf, \sqsubseteq)$ and $(Conf \times T \times Conf, \preccurlyeq)$ are wqos by Dickson's Lemma.

Definition 4.4 (Ordering runs, see Fig. 4). *For two runs ρ, ρ' of $\mathcal{A}$, we write $\rho \trianglelefteq \rho'$ if $\rho = c_0 a_1 c_1 \ldots a_k c_k$ and ρ' can be factored as some $\rho' = \rho_0 a_1 \rho_1 \ldots a_k \rho_k$ where, for all $j = 0, \ldots, k$, the ρ_j factor is a run such that $c_j \sqsubseteq \mathrm{src}(\rho_j)$ and $c_j \sqsubseteq \mathrm{tgt}(\rho_j)$.*

Lemma 4.5. *The relation $\trianglelefteq$ is a wqo over the runs of $\mathcal{A}$.*

Proof. This is essentially [22, Lemma 4.1] or [16, Theorem 6.5]. A more direct proof is by observing that

$$\rho \trianglelefteq \rho' \text{ iff } \begin{cases} \mathrm{src}(\rho) \sqsubseteq \mathrm{src}(\rho') \wedge \mathrm{tgt}(\rho) \sqsubseteq \mathrm{tgt}(\rho') \wedge \\ (c_0 \overset{a_1}{\rightarrow} c_1)(c_1 \overset{a_2}{\rightarrow} c_2) \cdots (c_{k-1} \overset{a_k}{\rightarrow} c_k) \preccurlyeq_* (c_0' \overset{a_1'}{\rightarrow} c_1') \cdots (c_{\ell-1}' \overset{a_\ell'}{\rightarrow} c_\ell') , \end{cases}$$

where $\preccurlyeq_*$ is the sequence extension of the ordering of steps defined with Eq. (7). Since $\preccurlyeq$ (over steps) and $\sqsubseteq$ (over configurations) are wqos, $\trianglelefteq$ is a wqo over the runs of $\mathcal{A}$. $\square$

The ordering on runs comes with the following Pumping Lemma:

Lemma 4.6 (Pumping Lemma). *Let $\rho \trianglelefteq \rho'$ and let $\boldsymbol{u}, \boldsymbol{v} \in \mathbb{N}^d$ such that $\mathrm{src}(\rho') = \mathrm{src}(\rho) + \boldsymbol{u}$ and $\mathrm{tgt}(\rho') = \mathrm{tgt}(\rho) + \boldsymbol{v}$. Then*

$$\forall x \in \mathbb{N} : \left(\mathrm{src}(\rho) + x \cdot \boldsymbol{u}\right) \overset{*}{\rightarrow} \left(\mathrm{tgt}(\rho) + x \cdot \boldsymbol{v}\right) .$$

Proof. Assume that ρ is some $c_0 \overset{a_1}{\rightarrow} c_1 \cdots \overset{a_k}{\rightarrow} c_k$ and that $\rho \trianglelefteq \rho'$ is witnessed by factoring ρ' under the form $\rho_0 a_1 \rho_1 \ldots a_k \rho_k$. For $j = 0, \ldots, k$, write $\boldsymbol{u}_j$ and $\boldsymbol{v}_j$ for the vectors in $\mathbb{N}^d$ such that $\mathrm{src}(\rho_j) = c_j + u_j$ and $\mathrm{tgt}(\rho_j) = c_j + v_j$. Observe that $u_j = v_{j-1}$ for any $j > 0$ since there are steps $c_{j-1} \xrightarrow{a_j} c_j$ and $c_{j-1} + v_{j-1} = \mathrm{tgt}(\rho_{j-1}) \xrightarrow{a_j} \mathrm{src}(\rho_j) = c_j + u_j$.

Since there is a run ρ_j of the form $c_j + u_j \xrightarrow{*} c_j + v_j$, by Lemma 2.1 there is also $c_j + x \cdot u_j \xrightarrow{*} c_j + x \cdot v_j$ for any $x \in \mathbb{N}$. We may now insert these runs between steps $c_{j-1} + x \cdot v_{j-1} \xrightarrow{a_j} c_j + x \cdot v_{j-1} = c_j + x \cdot u_j$, obtained by lifting up $c_{j-1} \xrightarrow{a_j} c_j$, see Eq. (2). This gives $c_0 + x \cdot u \xrightarrow{*} c_k + x \cdot v$ as required.   □

(Alternatively, it is shown in [16, Lemma 6.7] that if $\rho \trianglelefteq \rho' \trianglelefteq \rho_x$ for some run ρ_x, then there exists a run ρ_{x+1} such that $\rho_x \trianglelefteq \rho_{x+1}$, $\mathrm{src}(\rho_{x+1}) = \mathrm{src}(\rho_x) + u$, and $\mathrm{tgt}(\rho_{x+1}) = \mathrm{tgt}(\rho_x) + v$. Using induction over $x \in \mathbb{N}$, and starting with $\rho_0 = \rho$ and $\rho_1 = \rho'$, one can provide for any x a run ρ_x witnessing $\mathrm{src}(\rho) + x \cdot u \xrightarrow{*} \mathrm{tgt}(\rho) + x \cdot v$.)

Theorem 4.7. *Let $f : \mathbb{N} \to \mathbb{N}$ be an unbounded unary EWCPN function. Then there exist $r, s \in \mathbb{N}$ with $s > 0$ and such that $f(r + s \cdot x)$ is in $\Omega(x)$.*

Proof. Fix an eager weak PN computer $\mathcal{A}$ for f. For every $r \in \mathbb{N}$, $\mathcal{A}$ has a run ρ_r of the form $(q_{\mathrm{init}}, r, 0, 0) \xrightarrow{*} (q_{\mathrm{final}}, 0, 0, f(r))$. Since f is unbounded, there exists an infinite subset $R \subseteq \mathbb{N}$ such that $(f(r))_{r \in R}$ is strictly increasing. Since the runs are well-ordered by $\trianglelefteq$ (Lemma 4.5) there exists two indexes $r < r'$ in R such that $\rho_r \trianglelefteq \rho_{r'}$. By introducing $s = r' - r$, Lemma 4.6 shows that for every $x \in \mathbb{N}$, we have

$$(q_{\mathrm{init}}, r + s \cdot x, 0, 0) \xrightarrow{*} (q_{\mathrm{final}}, 0, 0, f(r) + x \cdot [f(r') - f(r)]) .$$

With (SA'), we deduce that $f(r + s \cdot x) \geq f(r) + x \cdot [f(r') - f(r)]$ for every $x \in \mathbb{N}$. The lemma follows from $f(r') - f(r) > 0$.   □

Corollary 4.8. *Let $f : \mathbb{N} \to \mathbb{N}$ be an unbounded unary WCPN function. Then $f(x)$ is in $\Omega(x)$.*

Proof. Direct from Theorem 4.7 since, by Proposition 3.3, f is non-decreasing.   □

Thus any sublinear function like $x \mapsto \lceil \sqrt{x} \rceil$ or $x \mapsto \lceil \log x \rceil$ is *not weakly computable* even in the eager sense. (We note that any monotonic bounded function is WCPN, e.g., as a max of finitely many threshold functions of the form "x $\mapsto$ if u $\sqsubseteq$ x then v$_{\mathrm{hi}}$ else v$_{\mathrm{lo}}$" with v$_{\mathrm{lo}} \sqsubseteq$ v$_{\mathrm{hi}}$.)

Corollary 4.8 can be extended beyond unary functions as follows. A function $f : \mathbb{N}^n \to \mathbb{N}$ is said to be unbounded on a component i, with $1 \leq i \leq n$, if, for some natural numbers $r_1, \dots, r_{i-1}, r_{i+1}, \dots, r_n \in \mathbb{N}$, the following unary function is unbounded:

$$x \mapsto f(r_1, \dots, r_{i-1}, x, r_{i+1}, \dots, r_n).$$

For example, $(x_1, x_2) \mapsto x_1$ is a WCPN function that is unbounded on the first component. From Corollary 4.8, and the monotonicity property given by Proposition 3.3, it follows that every WCPN function $f : \mathbb{N}^n \to \mathbb{N}$ has $f(x_1, \dots, x_n)$ in $\Omega(\max_{i \in I} x_i)$, where I is the set of unbounded components for f.

5 Concluding Remarks

We proved that Petri nets and VASSes cannot weakly compute numerical functions that are sublinear. This was a folklore conjecture that, to the best of our knowledge, had not yet been settled.

Traditionally, weakly computable functions have been used to prove hardness results. Recent hardness proofs for well-structured systems crucially rely on the ability to weakly compute both fast-growing *and slow-growing* functions. For Petri nets and VASSes, a weak computer for some slow-growing function could perhaps have been used (depending on its structure) to improve the currently best lower bound for the reachability problem. It was thus important to check whether such weak commputer exist.

Our negative result raises the question of whether more functions can be weakly computed in extensions of VASSes like the pushdown VASSes of [23] or the nets with nested zero-tests of [27].

References

1. Abdulla, P.A., Čerāns, K., Jonsson, B., Tsay, Y.-K.: Algorithmic analysis of programs with well quasi-ordered domains. Information & Computation 160(1-2), 109–127 (2000)
2. Araki, T., Kasami, T.: Some decision problems related to the reachability problem for Petri nets. Theoretical Computer Science 3(1), 85–104 (1976)
3. Baker Jr., H.G.: Rabin's proof of the undecidability of the reachability set inclusion problem of vector addition systems. Memo 79, Computation Structures Group, Project MAC, M.I.T. (July 1973)
4. Bouajjani, A., Emmi, M.: Analysis of recursively parallel programs. In: POPL 2012, pp. 203–214. ACM (2012)
5. Demri, S., Figueira, D., Praveen, M.: Reasoning about data repetitions with counter systems. In: LICS 2013, pp. 33–42. IEEE (2013)
6. Demri, S., Jurdziński, M., Lachish, O., Lazić, R.: The covering and boundedness problems for branching vector addition systems. Journal of Computer and System Sciences 79(1), 23–38 (2013)
7. Dickson, L.E.: Finiteness of the odd perfect and primitive abundant numbers with n distinct prime factors. Amer. Journal Math. 35, 413–422 (1913)
8. Dufourd, C., Finkel, A., Schnoebelen, Ph.: Reset nets between decidability and undecidability. In: Larsen, K.G., Skyum, S., Winskel, G. (eds.) ICALP 1998. LNCS, vol. 1443, pp. 103–115. Springer, Heidelberg (1998)
9. Figueira, D., Figueira, S., Schmitz, S., Schnoebelen, Ph.: Ackermannian and primitive-recursive bounds with Dickson's Lemma. In: LICS 2011, pp. 269–278. IEEE (2011)
10. Finkel, A., Schnoebelen, Ph.: Well-structured transition systems everywhere! Theoretical Computer Science 256(1–2), 63–92 (2001)
11. Haase, C., Schmitz, S., Schnoebelen, Ph.: The power of priority channel systems. In: D'Argenio, P.R., Melgratti, H. (eds.) CONCUR 2013 – Concurrency Theory. LNCS, vol. 8052, pp. 319–333. Springer, Heidelberg (2013)
12. Hack, M.: Decidability Questions for Petri Nets. PhD thesis, Massachusetts Institute of Technology, Available as report MIT/LCS/TR-161 (June 1976)
13. Hack, M.: The equality problem for vector addition systems is undecidable. Theoretical Computer Science 2(1), 77–95 (1976)

14. Haddad, S., Schmitz, S., Schnoebelen, Ph.: The ordinal-recursive complexity of timed-arc Petri nets, data nets, and other enriched nets. In: LICS 2012, pp. 355–364. IEEE (2012)
15. Hopcroft, J., Pansiot, J.-J.: On the reachability problem for 5-dimensional vector addition systems. Theoretical Computer Science 8(2), 135–159 (1979)
16. Jančar, P.: Decidability of a temporal logic problem for Petri nets. Theoretical Computer Science 74(1), 71–93 (1990)
17. Jančar, P.: Nonprimitive recursive complexity and undecidability for Petri net equivalences. Theoretical Computer Science 256(1-2), 23–30 (2001)
18. Jančar, P.: Undecidability of bisimilarity for Petri nets and some related problems. Theoretical Computer Science 148(2), 281–301 (1995)
19. Karp, R.M., Miller, R.E.: Parallel program schemata. Journal of Computer and System Sciences 3(2), 147–195 (1969)
20. Kruskal, J.B.: The theory of well-quasi-ordering: A frequently discovered concept. Journal of Combinatorial Theory, Series A 13(3), 297–305 (1972)
21. Lazić, R.: The reachability problem for vector addition systems with a stack is not elementary. CoRR, abs/1310.1767 (2013)
22. Leroux, J.: Vector addition systems reachability problem (a simpler solution). In: The Alan Turing Centenary Conference (Turing-100). EasyChair Proceedings in Computing, vol. 10, pp. 214–228. EasyChair (2012)
23. Leroux, J., Praveen, M., Sutre, G.: Hyper-Ackermannian bounds for pushdown vector addition systems. In: CSL-LICS 2014. ACM (2014)
24. Mayr, E.W.: The complexity of the finite containment problem for Petri nets. Master's thesis, Massachusetts Institute of Technology, Available as report MIT/LCS/TR-181 (June 1977)
25. Mayr, E.W., Meyer, A.R.: The complexity of the finite containment problem for Petri nets. Journal of the ACM 28(3), 561–576 (1981)
26. Müller, H.: Weak Petri net computers for Ackermann functions. Elektronische Informationsverarbeitung und Kybernetik 21(4-5), 236–246 (1985)
27. Reinhardt, K.: Reachability in Petri nets with inhibitor arcs. Electr. Notes Theor. Comput. Sci. 223, 239–264 (2008)
28. Schmitz, S.: Complexity hierarchies beyond elementary. Research Report 1312.5686 [cs.CC], Computing Research Repository (December 2013)
29. Schmitz, S., Schnoebelen, Ph.: Algorithmic aspects of WQO theory. Lecture notes (2012)
30. Schnoebelen, Ph.: Verifying lossy channel systems has nonprimitive recursive complexity. Information Processing Letters 83(5), 251–261 (2002)
31. Schnoebelen, Ph.: Revisiting Ackermann-hardness for lossy counter machines and reset Petri nets. In: Hliněný, P., Kučera, A. (eds.) MFCS 2010. LNCS, vol. 6281, pp. 616–628. Springer, Heidelberg (2010)

Generalized Craig Interpolation for Stochastic Satisfiability Modulo Theory Problems*

Ahmed Mahdi and Martin Fränzle

Carl von Ossietzky Universität,
Ammerländer Heerstraße 114-118, 26111 Oldenburg, Germany
{mahdi,fraenzle}@informatik.uni-oldenburg.de

Abstract. Craig interpolation is widely used in solving reachability and model-checking problems by SAT or SMT techniques, as it permits the computation of invariants as well as discovery of meaningful predicates in CEGAR loops based on predicate abstraction. Extending such algorithms from the qualitative to the quantitative setting of probabilistic models seems desirable. In 2012, Teige et al. [1] succeeded to define an adequate notion of generalized, stochastic interpolants and to expose an algorithm for efficiently computing them for stochastic Boolean satisfiability problems, i.e., SSAT. In this work we present a notion of *Generalized Craig Interpolant* for the stochastic SAT modulo theories framework, i.e., SSMT, and introduce a mechanism to compute such stochastic interpolants for non-polynomial SSMT problems based on a *sound* and, w.r.t. the arithmetic reasoner, *relatively complete* resolution calculus. The algorithm computes interpolants in SAT, SMT, SSAT, and SSMT problems. As this extends the scope of SSMT-based model-checking of probabilistic hybrid automata from the bounded to the unbounded case, we demonstrate our interpolation principle on an unbounded probabilistic reachability problem in a probabilistic hybrid automaton.

1 Introduction

Stochastic satisfiability modulo theories (SSMT) was proposed in 2008 [2] in order to extend SMT-based bounded model-checking to probabilistic hybrid systems. SSMT extends the satisfiability modulo theories (SMT) problem by randomized quantification or, equivalently, generalizes the stochastic boolean satisfiability problem (SSAT) [3] to background theories. An SSMT formula consists of a quantifier prefix and an SMT formula. The quantifier prefix is an alternating sequence of existentially quantified variables and variables bound by randomized quantifiers. All the quantified variables have discrete (finite) domains. Due to the presence of probabilistic assignments due to randomized quantification, the semantics of an SSMT formula Φ is no longer qualitative in the sense that Φ is satisfiable or unsatisfiable, as for propositional or predicate logic,

---

* Research supported by the German Research Council (DFG) as part of the Transregional Collaborative Research Center SFB/TR 14 AVACS (http://www.avacs.org).

J. Ouaknine, I. Potapov, and J. Worrell (Eds.): RP 2014, LNCS 8762, pp. 203–215, 2014.
© Springer International Publishing Switzerland 2014

but rather *quantitative* [2,4]. For an SSMT formula Φ, we ask for the maximum probability of satisfaction or, if formulated as a decision problem, whether this probability of satisfaction exceeds a threshold. Intuitively, a solution of Φ is a strategy in form of a tree suggesting optimal assignments to the existential variables depending on the probabilistically determined values of preceding randomized variables, in order to maximize the probability of satisfying the SMT formula. SSMT as proposed by Fränzle et al. [2] can encode bounded probabilistic reachability problems of probabilistic hybrid automaton (PHA) over discrete time. That means many practical problems exhibiting uncertainty can be described as SSMT problems or sometimes even its propositional subset SSAT, in particular probabilistic planning problems [5,6], belief networks [7], trust management [8], or depth-bounded PHA reachability [2,9] and stability problems [4]. Probabilistic bounded model-checking (PBMC) problems, for example, ask whether the probability of *reaching bad states* from the PHA's initial states stays below a given threshold, irrespective of how non-determinism in the PHA is resolved. Solving a PBMC problem can be achieved by taking its equivalent SSMT encoding and solving it with an SSMT solver, like Teige's SiSAT tool [4].

Non-polynomial SSMT problems, i.e., SSMT formulae involving transcendental arithmetic, are generally undecidable due to the undecidable underlying arithmetic theory. There are some decidable classes of SSMT however; e.g., SSMT formulae without free variables due to the finite domains of bound variables, or SSMT formulae over decidable background theories, like linear order [10]. Undecidability implies that the Craig interpolation problem also cannot be solved exactly in general. In this paper, we propose a Craig interpolation procedure for SSMT that is sound and complete when the theory is linear order, and we extend it to non-polynomial SSMT by using interval constraint propagation (ICP) [11], then obviously sacrificing completeness, yet maintaining soundness.

Essentially, we first use ICP for reducing the general, non-polynomial SSMT problem to an SSMT problem of linear order over the reals. As an unsatisfied SSMT problem may well have satisfying assignments —just not sufficiently many to exceed the target probability threshold—, we then have to compute a *generalized interpolant*, which is a Craig interpolant for $A \wedge (B \wedge \neg S_{A,B})$, where $S_{A,B}$ represents the satisfying assignments of the formula $A \wedge B$. We do so by extending Púdlak's rules [12] to compute that generalized Craig interpolant. Instrumental to that adaptation of Púdlak's rules is the observation that the theory of linear order, with simple bounds as its atoms, admits a resolution rule akin to the propositional counterpart.

Related Work: Teige in [1] proposed generalized Craig interpolation for stochastic boolean satisfiability (SSAT) problems. Our work extends this to SSMT involving non-polynomial arithmetic constraints. Kupferschmid in [13] was the first to suggest Craig interpolation for non-polynomial and thus undecidable SMT problems by means of ICP and resolution in SMT of linear order. Our approach employs the same mechanism for dealing with arithmetic constraints, but extends the approach to SSMT problems, thus necessitating computation of generalized rather than traditional Craig interpolants. Numerous authors proposed different mechanisms to compute Craig interpolants for SAT and decidable SMT problems, e.g., [14,15,16,17,18,19,20]. A recent approach for computing small CNF interpolants [21] could be integrated with our work, then replacing Púdlak's rules.

This paper is structured as follows. In Section 2 we define the syntax and semantics of stochastic satisfiability modulo theories. Section 3 presents the SSMT-resolution calculus. In Section 4 we define generalized Craig interpolants for SSMT and expose a computation procedure. Section 5 demonstrates use of SSMT interpolation in probabilistic model-checking, with full details given in [22]. Finally, Section 6 presents the conclusion.

2 Stochastic Satisfiability Modulo Theory (SSMT)

In this section, we introduce the syntax and semantics of stochastic satisfiability modulo theories (SSMT) formulae, as originally proposed in [2].

Definition 1 (Syntax of SSMT). *A stochastic satisfiability modulo theories (SSMT) formula Φ is of the form $\mathcal{Q} : \varphi$ where*

1. *φ is an arbitrary SMT formula with respect to the theory of non-polynomial arithmetic over the reals and integers, called the* matrix *of the formula, and*
2. *$\mathcal{Q} = Q_1 x_1 \in \mathcal{D}_{x_1} \odot .... \odot Q_n x_n \in \mathcal{D}_{x_n}$ is a quantifier prefix binding some variables $x_i \in Var(\varphi)$ over finite domains $\mathcal{D}_{x_i}$ by a sequence of existential and randomized quantifiers Q_i; i.e., $\exists$ and $\mathbb{Y}$ respectively.*

Free, i.e., unbound by quantifiers, variables are permitted in SSMT formulae. For simplicity, we assume that the matrix φ of an SSMT formula $\mathcal{Q} : \varphi$ is in CNF form, as one can convert any formula to a CNF of linear size by introducing auxiliary variables [23].

Definition 2 (Semantics of SSMT). *The semantics of an SSMT formula Φ is given by its maximum probability of satisfaction $Pr(\Phi)$ defined as follows:*

$$Pr(\varepsilon : \varphi) = \begin{cases} 0 \text{ if } \varphi \text{ is unsatisfiable,} \\ 1 \text{ if } \varphi \text{ is satisfiable,} \end{cases}$$

$$Pr(\exists x \in \mathcal{D}_x \odot \mathcal{Q} : \varphi) = max_{v \in \mathcal{D}_x} Pr(\mathcal{Q} : \varphi[v/x]),$$

$$Pr(\mathbb{Y}^{d_x} x \in \mathcal{D}_x \odot \mathcal{Q} : \varphi) = \sum_{v \in \mathcal{D}_x} d_x(v) \cdot Pr(\mathcal{Q} : \varphi[v/x]).$$

The semantics of an SSMT formula is a $1\frac{1}{2}$ player game shown in Fig. 1. In naïve SSMT solving, the quantifier tree would be fully unravelled and all resulting instances of the matrix passed to an SMT solver. Pruning rules also shown in Fig. 1 yet permit to skip investigating a major portion of the instances in general.

3 Resolution for SSMT

The existing SSMT solving algorithms of Teige [4] are tightly integrated with the CDCL(ICP)[1] proof search of the iSAT tool [24] and do, in principle, traverse the

---

[1] CDCL = conflict-driven clause learning, ICP = interval constraint propagation.

$\varPhi = \exists x \in \{2,3,4\}, \mathbf{H}_{[1 \mapsto 0.2, 2 \mapsto 0.4, 3 \mapsto 0.4]} y \in \{1,2,3\} : (x+y > 3 \vee 2 \cdot y - x > 3) \wedge (x < 4)$

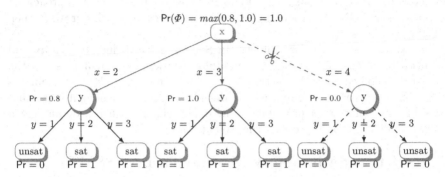

Fig. 1. $1\frac{1}{2}$ player game semantics of an SSMT formula. In recursive solvers, traversal of the dashed part of the quantifier tree will be skipped due to pruning [4].

quantifier tree of the formula as in Fig. 1 to recursively compute the maximum satisfaction probability bottom-up. Note that this does by no means imply that they are bound to traverse the whole, exponentially sized quantifier tree, as Teige proposed various mechanisms to drastically prune that tree and thus accelerate the actual computation. In the contrast to the CDCL(ICP) approach, the SSMT resolution calculus, as proposed by the authors of this paper in [10] based on Teige's SSAT resolution [25], solves SSMT problems by a resolution mechanism. SSMT-resolution works by deriving attributed clauses c^p, where c is a clause and p a probability. When such a clause c^p is derived during resolution, it expresses that the maximum probability of violation of c is p. If the probabilistic variant $\emptyset^p$ of a conflict clause happens to be derived at the end of resolution, then the maximum probability that the formula holds is p. The related SSAT-resolution calculus proposed by Teige [25,1] is *sound* and *complete*. The same applies for SSMT resolution if the theory is confined to linear order over the reals, yet if (e.g., non-polynomial) arithmetic is involved, the resolution calculus of SSMT is *sound* but only *relatively complete* with interval constraint propagation (ICP) [26] being its "oracle" for resolving arithmetic [10].

All derived clauses c^p are forced to have a tight bound p in the sense that under each assignment which falsifies c, the satisfaction probability of the remaining subproblem is exactly p.[2] Before illustrating the resolution rules, we define the symbolic falsifying assignment *falsify$_c$* that captures variable assignments falsifying a clause c. A simple bound $x \sim a \in \mathbb{SB}$ means that a variable x is restricted by comparison operator, i.e., $\sim \in \{>, \geq, <, \leq\}$, relative to value a, where the latter value is a real number. Also, we assign to each variable a domain which is a bounded interval. Let c be a non-tautological disjunction of simple bounds. We define the falsification function *falsify$_c$* that falsifies c as following:

---

[2] In [10] we relaxed the condition to a probability of less than or equal to p. The stronger form used here makes interpolation simpler.

Definition 3 (Falsification function). *Let $\mathbb{C}$ be a set of all non-tautological clauses with a typical element c such that c consists of a disjunction of simple bounds, i.e., $sb_1 \vee ... \vee sb_n$. The falsification function $falsify_c : \mathbb{C} \to \mathbb{C}$ is defined as follows:*

- $falisfy_c(c) := \bigvee_{i=1}^{n} f\!f_s(sb_i)$,
- $f\!f_s : \mathbb{SB} \to \mathbb{SB}$ *s.t.* $f\!f_s(x \sim a) := x \sim' a$ *where $\sim'$ is the converse relation to $\sim$, e.g., $\leq'$ is $>$.*

where $x \in X$, $a \in \mathbb{R}$, $\sim, \sim' \in \{\leq, <, \geq, >\}$ and x has a well-defined domain.

In order to extend the SSAT resolution rules to SSMT formulae, we assume w.l.o.g. that any clause c where resolution is applied consists of disjunctions of simple bounds only, as ICP yields a reduction to simple bounds by propagating arithemtic constraints into simple bounds [4,10]. We will introduce four resolution rules that define the resolution calculus for SSMT problems. Rule RR.1 derives a clause c^0 from an original clause $c \in \varphi$ such that c is not a tautological clause. One can consider RR.1 correspond to the quantifier-free base case where φ is *false* under any assignment that falsifies c (cf. [10] for details).

$$\frac{(c \in \varphi)}{c^0} \tag{RR.1}$$

Rule RR.2 reflects the quantifier-free base case in which φ is true under any assignment that is conform to the partial assignment τ, since $\models \varphi[\tau(x_1)/x_1]...[\tau(x_i)/x_i]$. The constructed c^1 represents the negation of the satisfiable partial assignment τ of φ.

$$\frac{\left(\begin{array}{c} c \subseteq \{x \sim a \mid x \in Var(c)\}, \not\models c, \mathcal{Q}(c) = \mathcal{Q}_1 x_1...\mathcal{Q}_i x_i, \\ \text{for each } \tau : Var(\varphi) \downarrow_i \to \mathbb{SB} \text{ with } \forall x \in Var(\varphi) : \tau(x) \text{ in } f\!f_s(x \sim a) : \\ \models \varphi[\tau(x_1)/x_1]...[\tau(x_i)/x_i] \end{array} \right)}{c^1} \tag{RR.2}$$

Rule RR.3 computes the actual probability of a resolvent depending on the type of the quantifier governing the pivot variable, where a bound on the pivot variable is used as the resolution literal. Definition 2 enforces that the domain of any quantified variable is discrete, which implies that we can evaluate the probability by simply summing up or selecting the maximum of the probabilities of satisfying assignments for $\forall$- or $\exists$-quantified variable x, resp.

$$\frac{\left(\begin{array}{c} (x \sim a \vee c_1)^{p_1}, (x \sim' b \vee c_2)^{p_2}, (x \in \mathcal{D}_x \wedge x \sim a \wedge x \sim' b \vdash \textsf{False}) \\ \mathcal{Q}_x \in \mathcal{Q}, \not\models (c_1 \vee c_2) \\ p = \begin{cases} max(p_1, p_2) & \text{if } \mathcal{Q}_x = \exists x \in \mathcal{D}_x \\ p_1 \cdot Pr(x \sim' b) + p_2 \cdot Pr(x \sim a) & \text{if } \mathcal{Q}_x = \forall^{Pr} x \in \mathcal{D}_x \end{cases} \end{array} \right)}{(c_1 \vee c_2)^p} \tag{RR.3}$$

Rule RR.3e is a counterpart of RR.3 for free variables in SSMT formulae. All free variables are implicitly existentially quantified at innermost level, yet —in contrast to explicit quantification— to continuous domains in general.

$$
\frac{
\left(
\begin{array}{c}
(x \sim a \vee c_1)^{p_1}, (x \sim' b \vee c_2)^{p_2}, \mathcal{Q}_x \notin \mathcal{Q}, x \text{ has domain } \mathcal{D}_x \\
(x \in \mathcal{D}_x \wedge x \sim a \wedge x \sim' b) \vdash \texttt{False}, \not\models (c_1 \vee c_2) \\
p = max(p_1, p_2)
\end{array}
\right)
}{
(c_1 \vee c_2)^p
}
\tag{RR.3e}
$$

Note that the SSMT-resolution calculus is *sound* and *relatively complete* w.r.t. to its underlying arithmetic reasoner ICP. On SSMT problems over the theory of linear order, SSMT resolution is *complete* (cf. [10,22] for more details). An example of SSMT resolution is shown together with interpolation in Sect. 4.

4   Interpolation for SSMT

Craig interpolation is a logical concept suggested by Craig in 1957 [27] that has been widely used in model theory and automatic verification. In its classical, non-probabilistic form, a Craig interpolant provides a reason for mutual inconsistency between two formulae. Formally, it is defined as follows:

Definition 4 (Craig Interpolation). *Given two propositional logic formulae A and B in a logics $\mathcal{L}$ such that $\models_\mathcal{L} A \to \neg B$, a Craig interpolant for (A, B) is a quantifier-free $\mathcal{L}$-formula $\mathcal{I}$ such that $\models_\mathcal{L} A \to \mathcal{I}$, $\models_\mathcal{L} \mathcal{I} \to \neg B$, and the (necessarily free) variables of $\mathcal{I}$ form a subset of the shared (and thus free) variables between A and B, i.e., $Var(\mathcal{I}) \subseteq Var(A) \cap Var(B)$.*

Depending on the logics $\mathcal{L}$, such Craig interpolants, which provide a reason why A is not satisfiable together with B, can be computed by various mechanisms. If $\mathcal{L}$ admits quantifier-elimination, then this can in principle be used; various more efficient schemes have been devised for propositional logic and for SAT-modulo-theory by exploiting the connection between resolution and variable elimination [12,28]. Following the latter line, Teige et al. [1] succeeded to generalize the Púdlak rules [12] from the propositional SAT case to stochastic SAT, where a more general definition of interpolant is needed, based on S-resolution [25] for SSAT. In the sequel of this paper, we will do the same for SSMT, thereby exploiting SSMT resolution [10].

4.1   Generalized Craig Interpolants

Traditional interpolation requires that $A \wedge B$ is unsatisfiable for the formulae A and B to interpolate. The precondition $A \wedge B \models \texttt{False}$, which would translated to $Pr(A \wedge B) = 0$ in a stochastic setting, however is too restrictive for use in probabilistic model-checking, as a residual chance of failure — which amounts to satisfying a path condition $A \wedge B$ in that context — is well acceptable in many engineering problems [4,1]. As an example consider the quantitative safety target "The probability that a plane will crash is at most 10^{-9} per year". For a violation of this quantitative safety goal, we cannot find a classical interpolant in general.

Teige proposed a general concept which can be used to form an adequate lattice of interpolants for stochastic problems.

Definition 5 (Generalized Craig Interpolant [1]). *Let A and B be some SMT formulae where $V_A := Var(A) \setminus Var(B) = \{a_1, ..., a_\alpha\}$, $V_B := Var(B) \setminus Var(A) = \{b_1, ..., b_\beta\}$, $V_{A,B} := Var(A) \cap Var(B)$, $A^\exists = \exists a_1, ..., a_\alpha : A$, and $\overline{B}^\forall = \neg \exists b_1, ..., b_\beta : B$. An SMT formula $\mathcal{I}$ is called a generalized Craig interpolant for (A, B) if and only if the following properties are satisfied: $Var(\mathcal{I}) \subseteq V_{A,B}$, $\models_{\mathcal{L}} (A^\exists \wedge \overline{B}^\forall) \to \mathcal{I}$, and $\models_{\mathcal{L}} \mathcal{I} \to (A^\exists \vee \overline{B}^\forall)$*

For SMT calculi admitting quantifier elimination, like the linear fragments of integer [29] and rational [30] as well as the polynomial fragment of real arithmetic [31,32], the four quantifier-free SMT formulae equivalent to $A^\exists \wedge \overline{B}^\forall$, to $A^\exists$, to $\overline{B}^\forall$, and to $A^\exists \vee \overline{B}^\forall$ can serve as generalized Craig interpolants for (A, B). These fragments of arithmetic are, however, very confined. A —necessarily incomplete— interpolation procedure can, however, be obtained for the non-polynomial case based on ICP, which reduces arithmetic reasoning to bound reasoning, i.e., to the decidable case of the theory of linear order over the reals and integers.

An interpolation procedure for SMT involving transcendental functions based on the latter principle has been pioneered by Kupferschmid et al. [13] without, however, addressing the stochastic case of generalized Craig interpolants (GCI). GCI for the propositional case of SSAT, on the other hand, have been explored by Teige et al. [1]. We will here reconcile these lines in order to compute GCI for SSMT.

4.2   Computation of Generalized Craig Interpolants

In this subsection, we present a formal way of computing the Craig interpolants for SSMT formulae by defining certain rules based on the SSMT resolution calculus. In order to compute systemically the Craig interpolants, one can use Púdlak's technique [12] (symmetric) or McMillan's technique [14] (asymmetric) which are both built on top of the resolution calculus for propositional logic.

We use SSMT resolution for computing generalized Craig interpolants. For this purpose, the rules of SSMT resolution are extended to deal with pairs $(c^p, \mathcal{I})$ of annotated clauses c^p and an SMT formulae $\mathcal{I}$, where $\mathcal{I}$ represents a partial generalized interpolant [1,13]. Whenever a pair $(\emptyset^p, \mathcal{I})$ denoting the empty clause is derived, a generalized Craig interpolant for the given SSMT formula has been computed. We compute the interpolant according to the three rules GR.1, GR.2, and GR.3 given below. The first Rule GR.1 represents a base case assigning initial interpolants to each clause of A and B.

$$\frac{c \vdash_{RR.1} c^0, \quad \mathcal{I} = \begin{cases} \text{False}, c \in A \\ \text{True}, c \in B \end{cases}}{(c^0, \mathcal{I})} \tag{GR.1}$$

Rule GR.2 does not exist in non-stochastic interpolation, as it refers to rule RR.2 of SSMT resolution, where the partial assignment satisfies $A \wedge B$, which

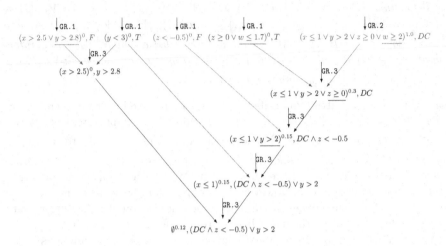

Fig. 2. Generalized Craig interpolant for Example 1. The green part is A and the blue one is B. The red part represents $\neg S_{A,B}$ with a don't-care interpolant.

is impossible in the traditional setting. If we take the negation of the satisfying assignments of $A \wedge B$; i.e., $\neg S_{A,B}$, then $A \wedge \neg S_{A,B}$, and $\neg S_{A,B} \wedge B$ are unsatisfiable. Therefore, we can choose the interpolant freely over the shared variable between A and B, i.e., $V_{A,B}$.

$$\frac{\vdash_{RR.2} c^1 \qquad \mathcal{I} \text{ is any formula over } V_{A,B}}{(c^1, \mathcal{I})} \qquad (GR.2)$$

The third rule extends Púdlak's rule for resolution in the direction of SMT simple bounds. Whenever we have two disjoint simple bounds in different clauses, we can apply SSMT resolution, i.e., one of rules RR.3 or RR.3e.

$$\frac{\begin{array}{c} ((x \sim a \vee c_1)^{p_1}, \mathcal{I}_1), ((x \sim' b \vee c_2)^{p_2}, \mathcal{I}_2), \\ (x \sim a \vee c_1)^{p_1}, (x \sim' b \vee c_2)^{p_2} \vdash_{RR.3(e)} (c_1 \vee c_2)^p, \\ \mathcal{I} = \begin{cases} \mathcal{I}_1 \vee \mathcal{I}_2 & \text{if } x \in V_A \\ \mathcal{I}_1 \wedge \mathcal{I}_2 & \text{if } x \in V_B \\ (x \sim a \vee \mathcal{I}_1) \wedge (x \sim' b \vee \mathcal{I}_2) & \text{if } x \in V_{A,B} \end{cases} \end{array}}{((c_1 \vee c_2)^p, \mathcal{I})} \qquad (GR.3)$$

Lemma 1. *Let* $\Phi = \mathcal{Q} : (A \wedge B)$ *with* $\mathcal{Q} = \mathcal{Q}_1 x_1 ... \mathcal{Q}_n x_n$ *be some SSMT formula, and the pair* $(c^p, \mathcal{I})$ *be derivable from* Φ *by interpolating SSMT-resolution, where* $\mathcal{Q}(c) = \mathcal{Q}_1 x_1 ... \mathcal{Q}_i x_i$. *Then, for each* $\tau : Var(\varphi) \downarrow_i := \{x_1, ..., x_i\}$ *for* $i \leq n$ *with* $\forall x \in Var(c) : \tau(x) = f\!f_s(x \sim a)$, *where* $x \sim a \in c$, *it holds that:*

1. $Var(\mathcal{I}) \subseteq V_{A,B}$,

2. $Pr(\mathcal{Q}_{i+1}x_{i+1}...\mathcal{Q}_n x_n : (A \wedge \neg S_{A,B} \wedge \neg \mathcal{I})[\tau(x_1)/x_1]...[\tau(x_i)/x_i]) = 0$, and
3. $Pr(\mathcal{Q}_{i+1}x_{i+1}...\mathcal{Q}_n x_n : (\mathcal{I} \wedge B \wedge \neg S_{A,B})[\tau(x_1)/x_1]...[\tau(x_i)/x_i]) = 0$.

The proof of this Lemma is stated in [22]. By using the previous lemma with the relatively complete SSMT resolution calculus, we get the following corollary:

Corollary 1 (Generating generalized SSMT interpolants). *If interpolating SSMT resolution derives $(\emptyset^p, \mathcal{I})$ from an SSMT formula $\Phi = \mathcal{Q} : (A \wedge B)$, then $\mathcal{I}$ is a generalized Craig interpolant for (A, B) witnessing $Pr(\Phi) = p$.*

The previous corollary follows directly due to Def. 5.

Corollary 2 (Controlling strength of SSMT interpolants). *If $\mathcal{I} = true$ is used within each application of Rule GR.2, then $Pr(\mathcal{Q} : (A \wedge \neg \mathcal{I})) = 0$. If $\mathcal{I} = false$ is used within each application of Rule GR.2, then $Pr(\mathcal{Q} : (B \wedge \mathcal{I})) = 0$.*

Proof. The proof of this corollary follows the previous lemma. The complete proof is stated for the SSAT case in [1] and adapts easily to SSMT.

Example 1. In order to get the idea of computing the Craig interpolants for SSMT problems, let us consider the following formula: $\exists_{[1 \mapsto 0.2, 3 \mapsto 0.35, 5 \mapsto 0.45]}$ $x, \exists y \in \{2, 4\}$ $\exists_{[-1 \mapsto 0.5,\ 0 \mapsto 0.5]}$, z $\exists_{[0 \mapsto 0.15, 1 \mapsto 0.15, 2 \mapsto 0.7]} w : A \wedge B$ where $A = (z < -0.5) \wedge (x > 2.5 \vee y > 2.8)$ and $B = (y < 3) \wedge (z \geq 0 \vee w \leq 1.7)$. Fig. 2 shows formally how the generalized Craig interpolant is computed. DC stands for a *don't care* formula which can replaced by true or false, a.o. If we replace DC with *true*, then the interpolant becomes $z < -0.5 \vee y > 2$ which is implied by A. Likewise, if it is replaced by *false*, then the resulting interpolant $y > 2$ implies the negation of B as in Corollary 2.

5   Interpolation-Based Probabilistic Model Checking

In this section we demonstrate an application of generalized Craig interpolation to quantitative model-checking of probabilistic hybrid automata. Probabilistic hybrid automata (PHA) are Markov decision processes (MDPs) over infinite state space, with arithmetic-logical transition guards and actions. These permit a straightforward encoding by SSMT formulae as proposed in [2,1]. Let us consider that we are given some set T of target states in the PHA model, and we try to maximize the probability of reaching these states over all policies resolving the non-determinism in the PHA model. Applications would be that T represents bad (or good) states and that we are asked to assure that the maximum probability of reaching bad (good, resp.) states in the model does not violate a certain safety target (exceeds a desired service level, resp.).

The encoding of PHA into SSMT formulae pioneered in [2] directly applies to PHA capturing continuous dynamics by pre-post relations. For PHA containing ordinary differential equations, one has to add ICP for ODE, as suggested in [33] and integrated into SSMT solving in [9], or one has to resort to abstraction of ODE into pre-post relations by tools like PHAVer, as pursued in ProHVer [34,35]. For the thermostat case study presented in Fig. 3a, we use the latter approach, obtaining the abstraction depicted in Fig. 3b and taken from [34].

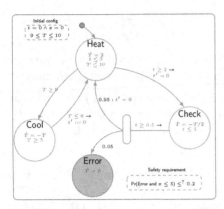
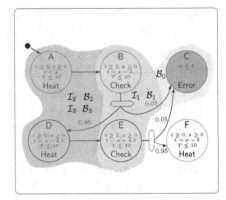

(a) PHA model of a thermostat involving ordinary differential equations

(b) Abstraction of the thermostat model using pre-post relations instead [34]

Fig. 3. Thermostat case-study discussed in [34,35]

5.1   Probabilistic Bounded Model-Checking (PBMC)

The idea of interpolation-based bounded model checking is to encode *the step-bounded reachability problem* as an SSMT formula. In each step, the transition relation, the non-deterministic choices, and the probabilistic choices are encoded, where the first one is achieved by an SMT formula, while the latter two require existential and randomized quantification respectively. Furthermore, the initial states and target states are encoded by predicates.

5.2   Interpolation-Based Unbounded Model-Checking

In order to use generalized interpolation in unbounded probabilistic model-checking, first one needs to *encode* the model's transiiton relation by a SMT representation. Then one generates a probabilistic bounded model-checking problem (PBMC) in SSMT [2] and determines whether the targets are reachable with probability exceeding the safety target within some step bound k. Should this not be the case, one can use generalized Craig interpolation to compute an *over-approximation of the states backward reachable* from the targets within that step bound. Technically, we interpolate between the initial state predicate and the k-fold iteration of the transition relation plus the target predicate, albeit under quantification. PBMC is iterated for increasingly larger k until either the safety property is falsified or the generalized Craig interpolant (CGI) stabilizes, i.e., a superset of all states backward reachable from the target has been computed.

Let us consider the PHA of Fig. 3(a) modelling a thermostat system. Using its safe abstraction Fig. 3(b), we want to verify whether *the maximum probability to reach the location* Error *within 5 time units is at most* $\frac{1}{5}$. Note that the property is expressed in terms of time units rather than computation steps. As there is no immediate correspondence between time units and computation steps, this verification problem cannot be solved by PBMC, but rather requires unbounded reachability computation by GCI.

In the abstract model, the probability to reach the error states within 5 time units is 0.0975, which is less than $\frac{1}{5}$ and thus acceptable. To determine this probability, we encode the abstraction of the thermostat as an SSMT formula and then compute overapproximations of the backward reachable states incrementally by GCI until it stabilizes. The target is C-Error which cannot be reached from the initial A-Heat via a single transition. In the first interpolation, the target C-Error together with a single transition relation represents the A part, while the initial state predicate A-Heat constitutes B. The first computed interpolant will thus equal all states except the initial one, providing a useless upper bound of 1 on the probability of eventually hitting the target. Successive interpolations for larger step numbers yield tighter approximations. In this model, the interpolant stabilizes after three iterations and yields a tight enough overapproximation of the backward reachable state set (cf. [22] for details).

Fig. 4 represents three results: the upper (red) curve represents the upper bound on the step-unbounded probability to reach location Error within 5 time units, as computed by GCI. The numbers on the horizontal axis here refer to the iteration (the number of steps), while the vertical axis refers to the computed probabilities. The middle (green) line represents the exact probability to reach location Error within 5 time units.

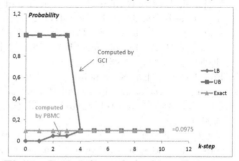

Fig. 4. Probability of reaching Error state within 5 time units with(out) interpolation

The lower (blue) curve represents the lower bound on the probability to reach an Error state within 5 time units, as computed by PBMC. One may observe that upper and lower bounds almost coincide after step $k = 4$. In fact, interpolation then tells us that the reachability probability is below 0.1, i.e., well below the safety target. All details of this example are shown in [22].

6   Conclusion and Future Work

We have successfully extended the concept of generalized Craig interpolation (CGI) from stochastic SAT to stochastic SAT modulo theory. We exposed a rule set suitable for automatically computing CGIs in non-polynomial arithmetic SSMT problems. An application of CGI on unbounded probabilistic model-checking problems was demonstrated, where the step-bounded probabilistic reachability of PHAs is encoded symbolically as an SSMT problem and interpolation serves as a means for generalizing the findings to the unbounded case. This approach can straightforwardly be extended to *probabilistic stability* problems [1]. In *future work* we will integrate the interpolation procedure into the SiSAT tool [4] for automatic quantitative analysis of PHA.

References

1. Teige, T., Fränzle, M.: Generalized Craig interpolation. Logical Methods in Computer Science 8(2) (2012)
2. Fränzle, M., Hermanns, H., Teige, T.: Stochastic satisfiability modulo theory: A novel technique for the analysis of probabilistic hybrid systems. In: Egerstedt, M., Mishra, B. (eds.) HSCC 2008. LNCS, vol. 4981, pp. 172–186. Springer, Heidelberg (2008)
3. Papadimitriou, C.H.: Games against nature. J. Comput. Syst. Sci. 31(2), 288–301 (1985)
4. Teige, T.: Stochastic Satisfiability Modulo Theories: A Symbolic Technique for the Analysis of Probabilistic Hybrid Systems. PhD thesis, Dpt. of Computing Science, Carl von Ossietzky Universität, Oldenburg, Germany (August 2012)
5. Majercik, S.M., Littman, M.L.: Maxplan: A new approach to probabilistic planning. In: Simmons, R.G., Veloso, M.M., Smith, S.F. (eds.) AIPS, pp. 86–93. AAAI (1998)
6. Majercik, S.M., Littman, M.L.: Contingent planning under uncertainty via stochastic satisfiability. Artif. Intell. 147(1-2), 119–162 (2003)
7. Bacchus, F., Dalmao, S., Pitassi, T.: DPLL with caching: A new algorithm for #sat and Bayesian inference. Electronic Colloquium on Computational Complexity (ECCC) 10(003) (2003)
8. Freudenthal, E., Karamcheti, V.: QTM: Trust management with quantified stochastic attributes. Technical Report NYU Computer Science Technical Report TR2003-848, Courant Institute of Mathematical Sciences, New York University (2003)
9. Teige, T., Eggers, A., Fränzle, M.: Constraint-based analysis of concurrent probabilistic hybrid systems: An application to networked automation systems. Nonlinear Analysis: Hybrid Systems 5(2), 343–366 (2011)
10. Mahdi, A., Fränzle, M.: Resolution for stochastic SAT modulo theories. Technical report, Dpt. of Computing Science, Carl von Ossietzky Universität Oldenburg, Germany (December 2013)
11. Benhamou, F., Granvilliers, L.: Combining local consistency, symbolic rewriting and interval methods. In: Pfalzgraf, J., Calmet, J., Campbell, J. (eds.) AISMC 1996. LNCS, vol. 1138, pp. 144–159. Springer, Heidelberg (1996)
12. Pudlák, P.: Lower bounds for resolution and cutting plane proofs and monotone computations. J. Symb. Log. 62(3), 981–998 (1997)
13. Kupferschmid, S., Becker, B.: Craig interpolation in the presence of non-linear constraints. In: Fahrenberg, U., Tripakis, S. (eds.) FORMATS 2011. LNCS, vol. 6919, pp. 240–255. Springer, Heidelberg (2011)
14. McMillan, K.L.: Interpolation and SAT-based model checking. In: Hunt Jr., W.A., Somenzi, F. (eds.) CAV 2003. LNCS, vol. 2725, pp. 1–13. Springer, Heidelberg (2003)
15. Christ, J., Hoenicke, J., Nutz, A.: Proof tree preserving interpolation. In: Piterman, N., Smolka, S.A. (eds.) TACAS 2013 (ETAPS 2013). LNCS, vol. 7795, pp. 124–138. Springer, Heidelberg (2013)
16. Brillout, A., Kroening, D., Wahl, T.: Craig interpolation for quantifier-free Presburger arithmetic. CoRR abs/0811.3521 (2008)
17. Griggio, A., Le, T.T.H., Sebastiani, R.: Efficient interpolant generation in satisfiability modulo linear integer arithmetic. In: Abdulla, P.A., Leino, K.R.M. (eds.) TACAS 2011. LNCS, vol. 6605, pp. 143–157. Springer, Heidelberg (2011)

18. Goel, A., Krstić, S., Tinelli, C.: Ground interpolation for combined theories. In: Schmidt, R.A. (ed.) CADE-22. LNCS, vol. 5663, pp. 183–198. Springer, Heidelberg (2009)
19. Cimatti, A., Griggio, A., Sebastiani, R.: Efficient generation of Craig interpolants in satisfiability modulo theories. ACM Trans. Comput. Log. 12(1), 7 (2010)
20. Lynch, C., Tang, Y.: Interpolants for linear arithmetic in SMT. In: Cha, S(S.), Choi, J.-Y., Kim, M., Lee, I., Viswanathan, M. (eds.) ATVA 2008. LNCS, vol. 5311, pp. 156–170. Springer, Heidelberg (2008)
21. Vizel, Y., Ryvchin, V., Nadel, A.: Efficient generation of small interpolants in CNF. In: Sharygina, N., Veith, H. (eds.) CAV 2013. LNCS, vol. 8044, pp. 330–346. Springer, Heidelberg (2013)
22. Mahdi, A., Fränzle, M.: Generalized Craig interpolation for SSMT. Technical report, Dpt. of Comuting Sceince, Carl von Ossietzky Universität, Oldenburg, Germany (2014)
23. Tseitin, G.S.: On the complexity of derivation in propositional calculus. In: Siekmann, J., Wrightson, G. (eds.) Automation of Reasoning 2: Classical Papers on Computational Logic 1967-1970, pp. 466–483. Springer, Heidelberg (1983)
24. Fränzle, M., Herde, C., Ratschan, S., Schubert, T., Teige, T.: Efficient solving of large non-linear arithmetic constraint systems with complex Boolean structure. Journal on Satisfiability, Boolean Modeling and Computation – Special Issue on SAT/CP Integration 1, 209–236 (2007)
25. Teige, T., Fränzle, M.: Resolution for stochastic boolean satisfiability. In: Fermüller, C.G., Voronkov, A. (eds.) LPAR-17. LNCS, vol. 6397, pp. 625–639. Springer, Heidelberg (2010)
26. Benhamou, F., McAllester, D.A., Van Hentenryck, P.: CLP(Intervals) revisited. In: ILPS, pp. 124–138. MIT Press (1994)
27. Craig, W.: Three uses of the Herbrand-Gentzen theorem in relating model theory and proof theory. J. Symb. Log. 22(3), 269–285 (1957)
28. Esparza, J., Kiefer, S., Schwoon, S.: Abstraction refinement with craig interpolation and symbolic pushdown systems. In: Hermanns, H., Palsberg, J. (eds.) TACAS 2006. LNCS, vol. 3920, pp. 489–503. Springer, Heidelberg (2006)
29. Cooper, D.C.: Theorem proving in arithmetic without multiplication. Machine Intelligence 7, 91–99 (1972)
30. Ferrante, J., Rackoff, C.: A decision procedure for the first order theory of real addition with order. SIAM J. Comput. 4(1), 69–76 (1975)
31. Tarski, A.: A decision method for elementary algebra and geometry. RAND Corporation, Santa Monica, Calif. (1948)
32. Davenport, J.H., Heintz, J.: Real quantifier elimination is doubly exponential. J. Symb. Comput. 5(1/2), 29–35 (1988)
33. Eggers, A., Fränzle, M., Herde, C.: SAT modulo ODE: A direct SAT approach to hybrid systems. In: Cha, S(S.), Choi, J.-Y., Kim, M., Lee, I., Viswanathan, M. (eds.) ATVA 2008. LNCS, vol. 5311, pp. 171–185. Springer, Heidelberg (2008)
34. Zhang, L., She, Z., Ratschan, S., Hermanns, H., Hahn, E.M.: Safety verification for probabilistic hybrid systems. In: Touili, T., Cook, B., Jackson, P. (eds.) CAV 2010. LNCS, vol. 6174, pp. 196–211. Springer, Heidelberg (2010)
35. Fränzle, M., Hahn, E.M., Hermanns, H., Wolovick, N., Zhang, L.: Measurability and safety verification for stochastic hybrid systems. In: HSCC, pp. 43–52. ACM (2011)

Transformations for Compositional Verification of Assumption-Commitment Properties*

Ahmed Mahdi[1], Bernd Westphal[2], and Martin Fränzle[1]

[1] Carl von Ossietzky Universität,
Ammerländer Heerstraße 114-118, 26111 Oldenburg, Germany
[2] Albert-Ludwigs-Universität Freiburg,
Georges-Köhler-Allee 52, 79110 Freiburg, Germany

Abstract. This paper presents a transformation-based compositional verification approach for verifying assumption-commitment properties. Our approach improves the verification process by pruning the state space of the model where the assumption is violated. This exclusion is performed by transformation functions which are defined based on a new notion of edges supporting a property. Our approach applies to all computational models where an automaton syntax with locations and edges induces a transition system semantics in a consistent way which is the case for hybrid, timed, Büchi, and finite automata. We have successfully applied our approach to Fischer's protocol.

1 Introduction

Many systems in real life are hybrid or real-time systems. Designing, developing, and verifying properties of these systems are becoming more and more complex. Hybrid and real-time systems are modelled by computational models such as *hybrid* and *timed automata*, respectively. This enables us to verify desired properties in these system models. The verification process is challenging because system models are increasingly complex and verification tools face the well-known space explosion problem.

We propose a new technique to improve the memory usage and time consumption of the verification process of *assumption-commitment* specifications. An assumption-commitment specification consists of an assumption and a commitment, which is required to hold if the assumption holds. For example, in the industrial field, *contracts* [7,8,19] consisting of assumptions and guarantees are used for component specifications. If the assumptions of a contract are fulfilled, then the guarantees have to hold. Consider, e.g., the avionics brake system [18]: if either the first or the second command units fail (no double failures), then the system has to guarantee that the brake system is safe.

Our approach is based on the new notion of edges *supporting* a specification. Intuitively, a specification is supported by an edge if there is a computation

---

* Partly supported by the German Research Council (DFG) as part of the Transregional Collaborative Research Center SFB/TR 14 AVACS (http://www.avacs.org).

J. Ouaknine, I. Potapov, and J. Worrell (Eds.): RP 2014, LNCS 8762, pp. 216–229, 2014.
© Springer International Publishing Switzerland 2014

path in the model's semantics which satisfies the specification and uses that edge. That is, if the edge is *reachable* by a computation path which satisfies the specification. Instead of verifying an assumption-commitment property on the model, we apply a source-to-source transformation to the model, where those edges which *do not support* the assumption are effectively disabled. This transformation excludes computation paths from the verification process which are irrelevant for the overall property because they violate the assumption. Thereby, our approach decreases complexity already before running a model checking tool. Furthermore, our approach is independent from particular model checking tools as we transform the model and leave the model checking procedure untouched. We develop our approach for a generalized notion of *automata* consisting of directed, action-labelled edges between locations in order to uniformly treat computational models such as finite and Büchi automata, timed and hybrid automata, and even programs. A necessary assumption of our approach is that the operational semantics by which an automaton induces a transition system is *consistent* for the syntactical transformations. This consistency assumption is typically satisfied by the standard semantics. Furthermore, our approach is particularly well-suited for systems which provide many functions and operation modes, e.g. a plane's brake system may offer landing and taxiing modes. For validation purposes, it is useful to have only a single system model including all features but verification may practically be infeasible on such a model. Given an assumption-commitment specification, where the assumption limits the focus to only some features, our approach allows to mechanically create a smaller verification model which is guaranteed to reflect the relevant behaviour of the original model. Thereby, there is no more need to create specially tailored verification models manually.

Related Work. There are many works [4,10,12,21] on excluding irrelevant computation paths from the verification process by abstracting the original model. Our work, in contrast, is a source-to-source transformation hence abstractions can still be applied. The exclusion of model behaviour by a source-to-source transformation proposed in [14] only considers networks of timed automata with disjoint activities. Slicing of timed automata [11] removes locations and clock and data variables on which a given property does not depend on, thus it also keeps variables on which an assumption depends while our approach may remove the corresponding behaviour. With partial model checking [2], verification problems are modularized by computing weakest context specifications through quotienting, which allows to successively remove components completely from the verification problem. We are instead trying to pragmatically reduce the size of components before composition by exploiting the specification. Both approaches could well go together. Static contract checking for functional programs [22] is dealing with a very different class of computational objects and relies heavily on assumptions local to the individual functions, while our approach is meant to also "massage" the global specification into the components.

The paper is structured as follows. Firstly, we motivate the idea of our approach using Fischer's protocol. Section 3 introduces generalized automata and

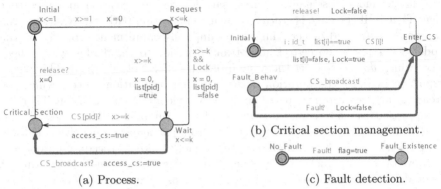

(a) Process.

(b) Critical section management.

(c) Fault detection.

Fig. 1. Uppaal model of the Fischer's protocol with direct fault detection

Section 4 defines the transformations 'edge removal' and 'edge redirection'. Section 5 introduces the concept of supporting edges and Section 6 shows how our approach is used in practice. Finally, we summarize the benefits of using our approach.

2   Motivating Example: Fischer's Protocol with Faults

Embedded systems are nowadays expected to provide increasingly many functions and different modes. One example are modes for fault detection and handling. In the real-world, faults cannot be avoided in general: wires may break, radio frequencies may continuously be blocked, and physical sensors and actors may fail. One way to deal with this situation is to detect and display faults in order to, e.g., inform users to take countermeasures against the fault. A system is then correct if and only if it delivers regular functionality *unless* a fault is displayed. One requirement is then that under the assumption of the absence of faults, the system functions properly.

As a simple example, consider a variant of the well-known Fischer's protocol [5]. Figure 1 shows the Uppaal [3] demo model of the Fischer's protocol which we extended with fault detection. If no fault occurs, processes (cf. Figure 1a) pose a request to enter their critical section by the shared variable list. The critical section manager (cf. Figure 1b) grants access to the critical section by a synchronisation on CS and expects notification of leaving the critical section on channel release. Our extensions are indicated by thick edges: if a fault occurs, processes may enter the critical section bypassing the manager and thereby violate the mutual exclusion property. For simplicity, we merged the environment model which triggers faults and fault detection in Figure 1c. Location Fault_Existence models the display of a fault occurrence. Table 1 shows results from attempts to verify mutual exclusion given no faults occur, formally, $(\Box p) \to (\Box q)$ with $p = \neg$Fault_Existence and $q = (\forall i \neq j : Process \bullet \neg(i.\mathsf{Crit\_Sec} \land j.\mathsf{Crit\_Sec}))$. Note that it is sufficient to check the Uppaal query $\mathsf{A}\Box(p \to q)$ for the considered model due to the immediate detection. In the original model as shown in

Table 1. Figures for verifying mutual exclusion[1]

#	original model query: $A\square(p \to q)$			non-supporting removed query: $A\square q$			non-supporting redirected query: $A\square(p \to q)$		
	seconds	MB	kStates	seconds	MB	kStates	seconds	MB	kStates
4	0.08	5.1	9.9	0.02	4.5	3.0	0.02	4.5	3.0
5	1.02	12.2	82.9	0.22	6.3	20.7	0.23	6.3	20.7
6	11.46	67.9	683.9	1.65	17.7	140.0	2.18	17.7	140.0
7	127.33	516.0	5,610.7	13.18	62.8	933.1	19.40	88.2	933.1
8	1,274.64	4,193.8	47,630.3	107.18	365.3	6,158.6	168.37	562.7	6,158.6
9	>2,000.00	–	–	894.83	2,297.0	40,310.8	1359.34	3,659.0	40,310.8

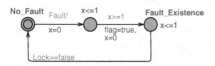

(a) Delayed fault detection.

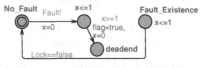

(b) Delayed fault detection redirected.

Fig. 2. Treating delayed detection

Figure 1, Uppaal does not succeed to verify a system with 9 processes in 2,000 seconds, a system with 8 processes takes about 20 min. to be successfully verified.

A clever verification engineer may observe that the verification is expensive because also all fault scenarios are explored – and found to violate the assumption that there are no faults. Faults are triggered by the edge in Figure 1c, thus if this edge is removed, all fault scenarios are excluded from the model. Column "non-supporting removed" of Table 1 shows results from the verification of the mutual exclusion property in the modified model. We observe savings in time and memory consumption of an order of magnitude for the larger instances and verification even scales better in the number of processes.

Note that Figure 1 is a special case, because fault detection is immediate (no delay between occurrence and detection) and persistent. For real-world systems, fault detection often needs time so there may be small durations of time, where the system cannot guarantee proper operation but where the fault is not yet displayed. An Uppaal model of delayed fault detection for Fischer's protocol is shown in Figure 2a. Here, the query stated above does not hold. Instead, we need to check the commitment "globally mutual exclusion" under the assumption "globally no fault". Still, we can effectively exclude fault scenarios from the verification procedure by *redirecting* the right edge to a fresh sink location deadend (cf. Figure 2b). Checking the overall property then reduces to checking that violations of mutual exclusion are always finally followed by fault display (results are provided in Section 6).

---

[1] All results: Linux x64, 16 Quad-Core Opteron 8378, 132 GB, Uppaal 4.1.18.

In the following, we develop a theory of redirecting and removing edges in order to prune the state space for assumption-commitment specifications. Our approach provides a formal justification of the removal applied *ad-hoc* above: if we prove that the edge in Figure 1c does *not* support the assumption, our results guarantee that we can conclude from a positive verification result for the transformed model to the original model. That is, we guarantee that no relevant scenarios are missed – a guarantee which cannot be given for manual ad-hoc transformations. We show that redirecting edges reflects all computation paths which satisfy the assumption. The redirection transformation is semantically optimal, if all edges which do not support the assumption, are redirected.

3   Compositional Verification of Assumption-Commitment Specifications for Generalized Automata

In the following, we consider a generalized notion of automata which allows us to treat, among others, timed and hybrid automata uniformly.

Definition 1 (Automaton). *An* automaton $\mathcal{A} = (Loc, Act, E, L_{ini})$ *consists of a finite set of* locations *Loc, a finite set of* actions *Act, a set* $E \subseteq Loc \times Act \times Loc$ *of directed* edges, *and a set of* initial locations $L_{ini} \subseteq Loc$. *Each edge* $(\ell, \alpha, \ell') \in E$ *has a* source location ℓ, *an* action α, *and a* destination location ℓ'.

Finite, Büchi, timed [1], and hybrid automata [9] can be represented as automata in the sense of Definition 1. For example, for timed automata, we can consider pairs of locations and invariants as locations, and triples consisting of synchronization, guard, and update vector as action. Thereby, the alphabet of a timed automaton is represented in the set of actions. Moreover, *programs* [15] are automata as follows: the nodes in the control flow graph (CFG) become automaton locations and the edges in the CFG become automaton edges labelled with statements.

In the following definition, we introduce an edge-centric notion of operational semantics for generalized automata, i.e. there is one transition relation per edge and one dedicated additional transition relation. This allows for a simple definition of *support* in Section 5. Later we will characterise those operational semantics for which our approach applies as *consistent* (cf. Section 4).

Definition 2 (Operational Semantics). *Let* V *be a set of* states *and Aut a set of automata. An* operational semantics *of Aut (over V) is a function $\mathcal{T}$ which assigns to each automaton $\mathcal{A} = (Loc, Act, E, L_{ini}) \in Aut$ a labelled transition system $\mathcal{T}(\mathcal{A}) = (Conf, \Lambda, \{\xrightarrow{\lambda} \mid \lambda \in \Lambda\}, C_{ini})$ where $Conf \subseteq Loc \times V$ is the set of* configurations, $\Lambda = E \cup \{\bot\}$, *where* $\bot \notin E$, *is the set of* labels, $\xrightarrow{\lambda} \subseteq Conf \times Conf$ *are transition relations, and $C_{ini} \subseteq (L_{ini} \times V) \cap Conf$ is the set of* initial configurations.

The standard operational semantics of hybrid and timed automata induce an operational semantics of the aforementioned generalized automata.

An operational semantics induces computation paths as usual. In addition, we distinguish computation paths based on the occurring labels.

Definition 3 (Computation Path). *A computation path of automaton $\mathcal{A} \in Aut$ under operational semantics $\mathcal{T}(\mathcal{A}) = (Conf, \Lambda, \{\overset{\lambda}{\rightarrow} \mid \lambda \in \Lambda\}, C_{ini})$ is an initial and consecutive, infinite or maximally finite sequence $c_0 \overset{\lambda_1}{\rightarrow} c_1 \overset{\lambda_2}{\rightarrow} \cdots$ where $c_0 \in C_{ini}$ (initiation) and for each $i \in \mathbb{N}_0$, $(c_i, c_{i+1}) \in \overset{\lambda_{i+1}}{\longrightarrow}$ (consecution).*

Let E be the set of edges of $\mathcal{A}$. We use $\Xi_\mathcal{T}(\mathcal{A}, F)$ to denote the set of computation paths of $\mathcal{A}$ where only label $\perp$ and labels from $F \subseteq E$ occur. $\Xi_\mathcal{T}(\mathcal{A}) := \Xi_\mathcal{T}(\mathcal{A}, E)$ denotes the set of all computation paths of $\mathcal{A}$ (under $\mathcal{T}$).

Our approach applies to so-called assumption-commitment specifications as defined in the following. Note that we use a *semantical* characterisation of specifications for simplicity. A specification is a set of sequences, i.e. we consider path specifications. Specifications can *syntactically* be described by, e.g., LTL [17].

Definition 4 (Assumption-Commitment Specification). *A specification over alphabet Σ is a set $S \subseteq \Sigma^* \cup \Sigma^\omega$ of finite or infinite sequences over Σ.*

A specification is called assumption-commitment *specification if there are specifications P and Q such that $S = \overline{P} \cup Q$, where $\overline{P}$ denotes the complement of P in $\Sigma^* \cup \Sigma^\omega$, i.e. the set $(\Sigma^* \cup \Sigma^\omega) \setminus P$. We write $P \rightarrow Q$ to denote the assumption-commitment specification $\overline{P} \cup Q$. A set $p \subseteq \Sigma$ is called atomic proposition, and the specification $\Box p := p^* \cup p^\omega$ is called an* invariant.

We establish the satisfaction relation between automata and specifications based on the observable behaviour of the automaton, i.e., the sequence of configurations obtained by disregarding the labelled transitions.

Definition 5 (Satisfying a Specification). *Let $\xi = c_0 \overset{\lambda_1}{\rightarrow} c_1 \overset{\lambda_2}{\rightarrow} \cdots \in \Xi_\mathcal{T}(\mathcal{A})$ be a computation path of automaton $\mathcal{A}$ under operational semantics $\mathcal{T}$. The observable behaviour of ξ is the sequence $\downarrow\xi = c_0, c_1, \ldots$ We use $\mathcal{O}_\mathcal{T}(\mathcal{A})$ to denote the set of observable behaviours of the computation paths of $\mathcal{A}$ under $\mathcal{T}$, i.e. $\mathcal{O}_\mathcal{T}(\mathcal{A}) = \{\downarrow\xi \mid \xi \in \Xi_\mathcal{T}(\mathcal{A})\}$. Automaton $\mathcal{A}$ is said to satisfy the specification S (under $\mathcal{T}$), denoted by $\mathcal{A} \models_\mathcal{T} S$, if and only if the set of observable behaviours of $\mathcal{A}$ (under $\mathcal{T}$) is a subset of S, i.e. if $\mathcal{O}_\mathcal{T}(\mathcal{A}) \subseteq S$.*

The following theorem states two observations for assumption-commitment specifications S of the form $P \rightarrow Q$. Firstly, whether an automaton satisfies S depends exactly on the observable behaviours satisfying P. That is, in order to check an automaton $\mathcal{A}_1$ against S, we may as well check $\mathcal{A}_2$ (even under a different operational semantics) as long as $\mathcal{A}_1$ and $\mathcal{A}_2$ (under the considered semantics) agree on the observable behaviours satisfying P. Secondly, it is possible to verify satisfaction of S by an automaton through checking only Q in an overapproximation of the automaton's observable behaviour.

Theorem 1 (Compositional Verification). *Let $\mathcal{A}_1 \in Aut_1$ and $\mathcal{A}_2 \in Aut_2$ be automata and $\mathcal{T}_1$ and $\mathcal{T}_2$ operational semantics for Aut_1 and Aut_2, respectively. Let $P \rightarrow Q$ be an assumption-commitment specification.*

1. *The* common-P-rule: *whenever the set of observable behaviours of $\mathcal{A}_1$ that satisfy P is equal to the set of observable behaviours of $\mathcal{A}_2$ that satisfy P, then $\mathcal{A}_1$ satisfies $P \rightarrow Q$ if and only if $\mathcal{A}_2$ satisfies $P \rightarrow Q$, i.e.,*

$$\mathcal{O}_{\mathcal{T}_1}(\mathcal{A}_1) \cap P = \mathcal{O}_{\mathcal{T}_2}(\mathcal{A}_2) \cap P \implies (\mathcal{A}_1 \models_{\mathcal{T}_1} P \to Q \iff \mathcal{A}_2 \models_{\mathcal{T}_2} P \to Q).$$

2. *The* over-approximating-*P*-rule: *whenever the set of observable behaviours of* $\mathcal{A}_1$ *that satisfy* P *is a subset of the set of observable behaviours of* $\mathcal{A}_2$, *then* $\mathcal{A}_1$ *satisfies* $P \to Q$ *if* $\mathcal{A}_2$ *satisfies* Q, *i.e.*,

$$\mathcal{O}_{\mathcal{T}_1}(\mathcal{A}_1) \cap P \subseteq \mathcal{O}_{\mathcal{T}_2}(\mathcal{A}_2) \implies (\mathcal{A}_2 \models_{\mathcal{T}_2} Q \implies \mathcal{A}_1 \models_{\mathcal{T}_1} P \to Q).$$

In general, the second implication does not hold in the other direction.

(Semi-)admissible transformation functions as introduced in the next section entail the premises of the over-approximating-*P*- and the common-*P*-rule.

4   Automata Transformations

In this section, we define a general concept of transformations for automata. We call transformations which preserve a specification *admissible* and those which over-approximate a specification *semi-admissible*. After that, we introduce the two transformations *redirecting edges* and *removing edges*.

Definition 6 (Transformation). *Let Aut be a set of automata. A transformation is a function* $\mathcal{F} : Aut \to Aut$ *which assigns to each original automaton* $\mathcal{A} \in Aut$ *a transformed automaton* $\mathcal{F}(\mathcal{A}) \in Aut$.

Definition 7 (Admissible Transformation). *Let* $\mathcal{T}$ *be an operational semantics of Aut and* S *a specification. Transformation* $\mathcal{F}$ *on Aut is called*

1. admissible *for* S *(under* $\mathcal{T}$*) if and only if for each automaton* $\mathcal{A} \in Aut$, *the observable behaviours of* $\mathcal{A}$ *and* $\mathcal{F}(\mathcal{A})$ *under* $\mathcal{T}$ *coincide on* S, *i.e. if*

$$\forall \mathcal{A} \in Aut \bullet \mathcal{O}_{\mathcal{T}}(\mathcal{F}(\mathcal{A})) \cap S = \mathcal{O}_{\mathcal{T}}(\mathcal{A}) \cap S.$$

2. semi-admissible *for* S *(under* $\mathcal{T}$*) if and only if for each automaton* $\mathcal{A} \in Aut$, *the observable behaviour of* $\mathcal{F}(\mathcal{A})$ *under* $\mathcal{T}$ *over-approximates the observable behaviour of* $\mathcal{A}$ *in* S, *i.e. if* $\forall \mathcal{A} \in Aut \bullet \mathcal{O}_{\mathcal{T}}(\mathcal{A}) \cap S \subseteq \mathcal{O}_{\mathcal{T}}(\mathcal{F}(\mathcal{A}))$.

The following lemma states the benefit of transformations which are (semi-) admissible for the assumption of assumption-commitment specifications: the original and the transformed automaton obtained by an admissible transformation satisfy the premise of the common-*P*-rule, for a semi-admissible transformation, the premise of the over-approximating-*P*-rule holds.

Lemma 1. *Let* $\mathcal{T}$ *be an operational semantics of Aut,* $S = P \to Q$ *an assumption-commitment specification, and* $\mathcal{F}$ *a transformation on Aut.*

1. *If* $\mathcal{F}$ *is admissible for* P, *then for* $\mathcal{A} \in Aut$, $\mathcal{F}(\mathcal{A}) \models S$ *if and only if* $\mathcal{A} \models S$.
2. *If* $\mathcal{F}$ *is semi-admissible for* P, *then for* $\mathcal{A} \in Aut$, $\mathcal{F}(\mathcal{A}) \models Q$ *implies* $\mathcal{A} \models S$.

Proof. Definition 7 and Theorem 1. $\square$

The first proposed transformation function *redirects* a set of edges in a given automaton to a *new location*. It is defined as follows.

Definition 8 (Redirecting Edges). *Let* $\mathcal{A} = (Loc, Act, E, L_{ini})$ *be an automaton,* $F \subseteq E$ *a set of edges, and* $\dashv \notin Loc$ *a fresh location. We use* $\mathcal{A}[F/\dashv]$ *to denote the automaton* $(Loc \cup \{\dashv\}, Act, E', L_{ini})$ *where*

$$E' = (E \setminus F) \cup \{(\ell, \alpha, \dashv) \mid (\ell, \alpha, \ell') \in F\}.$$

We say $\mathcal{A}[F/\dashv]$ *is obtained from* $\mathcal{A}$ *by* redirecting *the edges in* F *(to* $\dashv$*).*

A transformation is a *syntactical* operation, thus the observable behaviour of a transformed automaton may in general, given a sufficiently pathological operational semantics, not resemble the behaviour of the original automaton at all. The following definition of consistency states minimal sanity requirements on operational semantics which we need in order to effectively use the redirection transformation. These requirements are directly satisfied by the standard semantics of, e.g., timed automata.

Definition 9 (Consistent for Redirection). *An operational semantics* $\mathcal{T}$ *for Aut over states* V *is called* consistent *(for redirection) if and only if for each automaton* $\mathcal{A} = (Loc, Act, E, L_{ini}) \in Aut$, *there is a location* $\dashv$ *such that* $\mathcal{A}[F/\dashv] \in Aut$ *and* $\mathcal{T}(\mathcal{A}[F/\dashv]) = (Conf', \Lambda', \{\overset{\lambda}{\to}' \mid \lambda \in \Lambda'\}, C'_{ini})$ *where*

1. *the set of configurations over the old locations, and the transition relations for* $\perp$ *and the unchanged edges do not change, i.e.*

$$Conf' \cap (Loc \times V) = Conf, \quad \forall e \in E \setminus F \bullet \overset{e}{\to} = \overset{e}{\to}',$$
$$and \quad \overset{\perp}{\to}' \cap (Conf \times Conf) = \overset{\perp}{\to},$$

2. $\mathcal{T}(\mathcal{A}[F/\dashv])$ *simulates transitions induced by edges from* F *and vice versa, and the* $\perp$*-transition relation does not leave* $\dashv$*, i.e.*

$$\xrightarrow{(\ell,\alpha,\dashv)}' = \{(c, \langle \dashv, v' \rangle) \mid \exists e = (\ell, \alpha, \ell') \in F \bullet (c, \langle \ell', v' \rangle) \in \overset{e}{\to}\},$$
$$and \quad \forall v, v' \in V, \ell' \in Loc' \bullet ((\dashv, v), (\ell', v')) \in \overset{\perp}{\to}' \implies \ell' = \dashv$$

3. *the fresh location* $\dashv$ *is not initial, i.e.* $C'_{ini} = C_{ini}$.

The following lemma states that for consistent semantics, the redirection transformation affects only behaviours where redirected edges are used.

Lemma 2. *Let* $\mathcal{T}$ *be an operational semantics of Aut which is consistent for redirection. Let* $\mathcal{A} \in Aut$ *be an automaton with edges* E *and* $F \subseteq E$. *Then there is a location* $\dashv$ *such that* $\Xi_{\mathcal{T}}(\mathcal{A}[F/\dashv], E \setminus F) = \Xi_{\mathcal{T}}(\mathcal{A}, E \setminus F)$.

The following second transformation *removes* edges from an automaton.

Definition 10 (Removing edges). *Let* $\mathcal{A} = (Loc, Act, E, L_{ini})$ *be an automaton and* $F \subseteq E$ *a set of edges. We use* $\mathcal{A} \setminus F$ *to denote the automaton* $(Loc, Act, E \setminus F, L_{ini})$. *We say* $\mathcal{A} \setminus F$ *is obtained from* $\mathcal{A}$ *by removing* F.

As for redirection, we want that all computation paths of the original automaton that take only non-removed edges are preserved in the new automaton. A sufficient criterion is the following notion of consistency *for removal*.

Definition 11 (Consistent Operational Semantics for Removal). *An operational semantics $\mathcal{T}$ for Aut is called consistent (for removal) if and only if for each automaton $\mathcal{A} \in Aut$, $\mathcal{A} \setminus F \in Aut$ and*

$$\mathcal{T}(\mathcal{A} \setminus F) = (Conf, \Lambda \setminus F, \{\xrightarrow{\lambda} \mid \lambda \in \Lambda \setminus F\}, C_{ini}),$$

given $\mathcal{T}(\mathcal{A}) = (Conf, \Lambda, \{\xrightarrow{\lambda} \mid \lambda \in \Lambda\}, C_{ini})$. That is, if the operational semantics of $\mathcal{A} \setminus F$ is obtained from the operational semantics of $\mathcal{A}$ by removing some transition relations and leaving everything else unchanged.

Lemma 3. *Let $\mathcal{T}$ be an operational semantics of Aut which is consistent for removal. Let $\mathcal{A} = (Loc, Act, E, L_{ini}) \in Aut$ be an automaton and $F \subseteq E$ a set of edges. Then $\Xi_{\mathcal{T}}(\mathcal{A} \setminus F, E \setminus F) = \Xi_{\mathcal{T}}(\mathcal{A}, E \setminus F)$.*

5   Supporting Edges

In this section, we introduce the novel concept of supporting edges, based on *edge reachability*. This concept identifies a relation between a specification and edges. Informally, an edge supports a specification if and only if there is a computation path which satisfies the specification and where that edge is taken.

Definition 12 (Supporting Edges). *Let $\mathcal{T}$ be an operational semantics of Aut and $\mathcal{A} \in Aut$ an automaton with edges E. An edge $e \in E$*

1. *supports specification S (under $\mathcal{T}$) if and only if there is a computation path where label e occurs and whose observable behaviour is in S, i.e. if*

$$\exists \xi = c_0 \xrightarrow{\lambda_1} c_1 \xrightarrow{\lambda_2} \cdots \in \Xi_{\mathcal{T}}(\mathcal{A}) \; \exists i \in \mathbb{N} \bullet \lambda_i = e \wedge \downarrow\xi \in S.$$

2. *supports atomic proposition p (under $\mathcal{T}$) if and only if there is a computation path where label e occurs between two configurations that are in p, i.e. if*

$$\exists \xi = c_0 \xrightarrow{\lambda_1} c_1 \xrightarrow{\lambda_2} \cdots \in \Xi_{\mathcal{T}}(\mathcal{A}) \; \exists i \in \mathbb{N} \bullet \lambda_i = e \wedge \{c_{i-1}, c_i\} \subseteq p.$$

3. *potentially supports atomic proposition p (under $\mathcal{T}$) if and only if there are two configurations of $\mathcal{T}(\mathcal{A}) = (Conf, \Lambda, \{\xrightarrow{\lambda} \mid \lambda \in \Lambda\}, C_{ini})$ which are in p and in $\xrightarrow{e}$-relation, i.e. if $\exists c, c' \in Conf \cap p \bullet (c, c') \in \xrightarrow{e}$.*

Note that Definition 12.1 is the strongest and 12.3 the weakest notion of support as stated in the following lemma. For example, consider the timed automaton in Figure 3

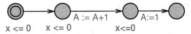

Fig. 3. Notions of support

where A is initially 0. If delays with duration 0 are not allowed, the leftmost edge supports the proposition $A = 0$, but not the specification $\square A = 0$. The middle edge potentially supports the proposition, but it does not support it. The rightmost edge does not even potentially support the proposition $A = 0$.

Lemma 4. *Let $\mathcal{A} \in Aut$ be an automaton and p an atomic proposition.*

1. *If an edge e of $\mathcal{A}$ supports the invariant $\Box p$ (under $\mathcal{T}$), then e supports the proposition p (under $\mathcal{T}$), but in general not vice versa.*
2. *If e supports p, then e potentially supports p, but in general not vice versa.*

Our main result shows that redirecting and removing edges which *do not support* a specification S are admissible and semi-admissible for S, respectively.

Theorem 2 (Admissibility). *Let $\mathcal{T}$ be an operational semantics of Aut with states V and let S be a specification over Σ. Let F be a set of edges of automaton $\mathcal{A} \in Aut$ which do not support S under $\mathcal{T}$.*

1. *$\mathcal{F}_{rd}^{F} : \mathcal{A} \mapsto \mathcal{A}[F/\dashv]$ is admissible for S if $\mathcal{T}$ is consistent for redirection and if S does not refer to the fresh location $\dashv$, i.e. if $(\{\dashv\} \times V) \cap \Sigma = \emptyset$.*
2. *$\mathcal{F}_{rm}^{F} : \mathcal{A} \mapsto \mathcal{A} \setminus F$ is semi-admissible for S if $\mathcal{T}$ is consistent for removal.*

To apply Theorem 2 we need a set of edges which do not support the given specification. In general, detecting edges which do not support a specification is as expensive as *reachability checking*. Though if the specification is an invariant, the contrapositions of the implications in Lemma 4 are particularly useful: if an edge does not potentially support a proposition, then it does not support the proposition, and if an edge does not support a proposition p, then it does not support the invariant $\Box p$. A sufficient criterion for an edge not (potentially) supporting a proposition p is to be a *cause* or a *witness*. An edge e is a *cause* of a violation of p if the p is always violated after taking this edge, e.g., if the action of e causes p not to hold. Similarly, an edge is a *witness* of a violation of p if p is necessarily violated when e is taken, e.g., if the guard of e implies $\neg p$. Removal of witnesses is even admissible. There are sufficient syntactical criteria to detect causes and witnesses. Furthermore, detection of potential support can be reduced to an SMT problem for the formula given by Definition 12.3 and attacked by SMT solvers like SMTInterpol [6]. For the special case of timed automata and bounded-integer propositions, a procedure based on the well-known reaching definitions static analysis detects all edges which support an atomic proposition [13]. Considering *all* edges which do not support a given specification is optimal in the sense that removing or redirecting any more edges breaks (semi-)admissibility. But it is not necessary to determine *all* non-supporting edges in order to obtain an optimal reduction of behavior. It is sufficient to determine all *points of no return* (PNR) for a given specification, i.e., edges which are the first on a computation path which do not support the specification. Causes and witnesses are often PNRs.

Networks of Automata. All previous discussions consider a single automaton. However, most practical models are networks of automata. In the following, we discuss briefly how our approach is applied to networks of automata and automata templates. For timed automata, each network has an equivalent timed automaton, the *parallel composition*. Edges in the parallel composition are constructed from internal transitions of automata in the network, or (with broadcast) from synchronisation edges of one or more automata in the network over a channel. An edge e in the network *supports a specification* if and only if there is an edge in the parallel composition which supports the specification and which is constructed from e. Edges not supporting a specification in this sense can safely be disabled by applying redirection or removal to the automata in the network. The same approach applies to hybrid automata and as neither redirection nor removal changes the set of actions, the sets of labels are preserved and thus no new computation paths emerge. In Uppaal, networks of automata are composed of automaton template instances. An edge in a template supports a specification if and only if there is an edge instance which supports the specification. That is, an edge can only be safely redirected or removed in the template, if all instances of this edge in the network do not support the specification.

Computation Paths vs. Runs The standard semantics of timed and hybrid automata distinguish between computation paths and *runs*, where the latter are computation paths with the *progress* property [16]. Interestingly, for timed automata, removing and redirecting edges have the same semantical effect if only *runs* are considered. However, in practice that will not give an obvious benefit, because verification tools typically check computation paths, not only runs.

6   Compositional Verification

In the previous sections, we have introduced a concept of transformation by either redirecting or removing edges and we introduced different notions of edges supporting a specification or an atomic proposition. This section proposes an approach to use the previous theory in practice with the Uppaal tool.

To use redirection and removal, we propose to apply the procedure shown in Figure 4 to all assumption-commitment properties $P \to Q$. The first step is to remove edges which don't support the assumption and check whether the resulting model satisfies the commitment Q. If Q is satisfied, we

Input: automaton $\mathcal{A}$ with edges E, specification $S = P \to Q$, $F \subseteq E$ not supporting P

if $\mathcal{A} \setminus F \models Q$ **return** *true*;
else return $\mathcal{A}[F/\dashv] \models S$;

Fig. 4. Verification procedure

deduce that the original model satisfies the property by the over-approximating-P-rule from Theorem 1. Otherwise, we need to redirect the edges that do not support P. Then checking whether the resulting model satisfies $P \to Q$ yields the final verification result by the common-P-rule from Theorem 1. The reason for using removal before redirection is that removing edges leads to a smaller state space than redirecting, and consequently less time and memory consumption. For an example, see Table 1, right-most and middle column.

Note that not all cases can be handled by removing, because we may remove edges which make a violation of the assumption observable. This is, e.g., the case for Fischer's protocol with delayed detection (cf. Section 2). In such cases, one has to use redirection to obtain a definite positive or negative answer. In order to alleviate *state-space explosion*, removing and redirecting is supposed to be performed locally at component level first. A *second sweep* can be done after the composition, but experiments show that the first, local one is the decisive.

Recall Fischer's protocol with immediate detection as introduced in Figure 1. According to our approach proposed above, we proceed as follows: the edges synchronizing on channel Fault in Figures 1c and 1b do not support the atomic proposition ¬Fault_Existence. As the automaton re-

Table 2. Fischer's protocol with delayed fault detection

#	original model query: $\neg q \rightsquigarrow \neg p$			non-supporting redirected query: $\neg q \rightsquigarrow \neg p$		
	seconds	MB	kStates	seconds	MB	kStates
3	0.10	3.9	6.0	0.07	3.9	2.7
4	5.90	29.7	109.6	0.87	5.1	37.0
5	788.20	130.1	2216.9	92.25	104.1	1250.0
6	>2,000.00	–	–	1037.24	228.7	3853.4
7	>2,000.00	–	–	>2,000.00	–	–

sulting from removing these edges satisfies the mutual exclusion property, we can conclude that the original model satisfies the assumption-commitment property by using Theorem 1.2. The verification results are stated in Table 1. If the fault detection is delayed as described in Section 2, then the automata model obtained from edge removal does not satisfy the mutual exclusion property (the commitment). So we can not conclude any beneficial results. Therefore we check whether the resulting automata model after redirecting satisfies the assumption-commitment property. Note that Tables 1 and 2 only report verification time. For the case study, identifying non-supporting edges using an SMT-solver takes less than one second and the time needed for the subsequent simple source-to-source transformation is negligible. Interestingly, using non-supporting edges enables us to reduce the LTL property $(\Box p) \rightarrow (\Box q)$, which is not directly supported by the TCTL fragment of Uppaal, to the leads-to query $\neg q \rightsquigarrow f$ where f is a fresh observer for non-supporting edges.

7 Conclusion

We presented a new technique of verifying assumption-commitment specifications in a large class of computational models, e.g., hybrid, timed, finite, and Büchi automata, and programs. The technique depends on transformations of automata by either redirecting or removing edges which do not support the assumption of the considered property. To this end, we introduced the new concept of "an edge supports a specification" which identifies a relation between specifications and edges in the automaton based on edge reachability. We showed for a model of Fischer's protocol that removing and redirecting edges significantly speeds up the verification process and improves the memory usage in comparison to verifying the same property in the original model without transformation.

Further work consists of an investigation of further uses of the notion of supporting edges, for example to indicate cut-points in a model where automata which over-approximate certain features of a multi-feature model can be inserted. Furthermore, there are methods to detect the supporting edges such as the *reaching definitions*-based approach in [13], but more powerful and efficient methods are needed. To this end, we will investigate syntactic criteria and significant extensions of the existing semantical methods.

References

1. Alur, R., Dill, D.L.: A theory of timed automata. TCS 126(2), 183–235 (1994)
2. Andersen, H.R.: Partial model checking (extended abstract). In: LICS, pp. 398–407. IEEE Computer Society (1995)
3. Behrmann, G., David, A., Larsen, K.G.: A tutorial on UPPAAL. In: Bernardo, M., Corradini, F. (eds.) SFM-RT 2004. LNCS, vol. 3185, pp. 200–236. Springer, Heidelberg (2004)
4. Benedetto, M.D.D., Gennaro, S.D., D'Innocenzo, A.: Verification of hybrid automata diagnosability by abstraction. IEEE TAC 56(9), 2050–2061 (2011)
5. Budkowski, S., Cavalli, A.R., Najm, E. (eds.): Formal Description Techniques and Protocol Specification, Testing and Verification, FORTE XI / PSTV XVIII 1998, IFIP Conference Proceedings, vol, vol. 135. Kluwer (1998)
6. Christ, J., Hoenicke, J., Nutz, A.: SMTinterpol: An interpolating SMT solver. In: Donaldson, A., Parker, D. (eds.) SPIN 2012. LNCS, vol. 7385, pp. 248–254. Springer, Heidelberg (2012)
7. Damm, W.: Contract-based analysis of automotive and avionics applications: The SPEEDS approach. In: Cofer, D., Fantechi, A. (eds.) FMICS 2008. LNCS, vol. 5596, pp. 3–3. Springer, Heidelberg (2009)
8. Damm, W., et al.: Using contract-based component specifications for virtual integration testing and architecture design. In: DATE, pp. 1023–1028. IEEE (2011)
9. Henzinger, T.A.: The theory of hybrid automata. In: LICS, pp. 278–292. IEEE (1996)
10. Herbreteau, F., et al.: Lazy abstractions for timed automata. In: Sharygina et al. [20], pp. 990–1005
11. Janowska, A., Janowski, P.: Slicing timed systems. FI 60(1-4), 187–210 (2004)
12. Laarman, A., Olesen, M.C., et al.: Multi-core emptiness checking of timed büchi automata using inclusion abstraction. In: Sharygina et al. [20], pp. 968–983
13. Mahdi, A.: Compositional verification of computation path dependent real-time system properties. Master's thesis, University of Freiburg (April 2012)
14. Muñiz, M., Westphal, B., Podelski, A.: Timed automata with disjoint activity. In: Jurdziński, M., Ničković, D. (eds.) FORMATS 2012. LNCS, vol. 7595, pp. 188–203. Springer, Heidelberg (2012)
15. Nielson, F., et al.: Principles of program analysis (2. corr. print). Springer (2005)
16. Olderog, E.R., Dierks, H.: Real-time systems. Cambridge University Press (2008)
17. Pnueli, A.: The temporal logic of programs. In: FOCS, pp. 46–57. IEEE (1977)

18. SAE Int.: ARP-4761. Tech. rep., Aerospace Recommended Practice (1996)
19. Sangiovanni-Vincentelli, A.L., Damm, W., et al.: Taming Dr. Frankenstein: Contract-based design for cyber-physical systems. EJC 18(3), 217–238 (2012)
20. Sharygina, N., Veith, H. (eds.): CAV 2013. LNCS, vol. 8044. Springer, Heidelberg (2013)
21. Sher, F., Katoen, J.P.: Compositional abstraction techniques for probabilistic automata. In: Baeten, J.C.M., Ball, T., de Boer, F.S. (eds.) TCS 2012. LNCS, vol. 7604, pp. 325–341. Springer, Heidelberg (2012)
22. Xu, D.N., Jones, S.L.P., Claessen, K.: Static contract checking for Haskell. In: Shao, Z., Pierce, B.C. (eds.) POPL, pp. 41–52. ACM (2009)

Compositional Reachability in Petri Nets

Julian Rathke, Paweł Sobociński, and Owen Stephens

ECS, University of Southampton, UK

Abstract. We introduce a divide-and-conquer algorithm for a modified version of the reachability/coverability problem in 1-bounded Petri nets that relies on the compositional algebra of nets with boundaries: we consider the algebraic decomposition of the net of interest as part of the input. We formally prove the correctness of the technique and contrast the performance of our implementation with state-of-the-art tools that exploit partial order reduction techniques on the global net.

Introduction

For finite-state Petri nets, the reachability problem—i.e. whether some target marking is reachable from the initial marking— is PSPACE-complete [4]. While compositional approaches to model checking were identified by the founders of the discipline [5] as a way of combating state-explosion, the large majority of model checkers work with the *global* statespace – which, in the case of Petri nets, means computing the *state graph*: a transition system where the states are markings and transitions reflect the firing of net-transitions. Of course, state graphs of large nets are prohibitively large to build naively; much of the research effort to date has focussed on taming the state explosion problem by exploiting symmetries and partial order reduction techniques [9, 12, 16, 18, 25].

Most real-life concurrent systems, however, are regular in their structure: they are naturally specified as a composition of relatively simple, often repeated, components. We contend that by allowing model checkers access to this high level information, we can exploit divide and conquer techniques to improve performance. The tool `Penrose`, described in this paper, exploits the high-level structure of a net, which is provided as input, to perform reachability checking. `Penrose` is written in Haskell and has not been optimised; despite this, it outperforms mature, state-of-the-art tools in a number of well-known examples.

Let us consider how a divide and conquer approach can help in checking reachability; consider a net, N, composed of two subnets, N_1 and N_2, with disjoint places. Any reachability question on N, stated as a desired marking, can be restated as a pair of desired markings on N_1 and N_2. Checking this pair of reachability questions independently is more efficient than directly checking reachability in N, since state graph size is exponential in the number of places of the corresponding net. However, such a naive approach is unsound: N_2's behaviour is constrained by its interactions with N_1, and vice versa. What is required is a representation of the behaviour of the subnet N_2, say, in which its dependency

J. Ouaknine, I. Potapov, and J. Worrell (Eds.): RP 2014, LNCS 8762, pp. 230–243, 2014.
© Springer International Publishing Switzerland 2014

and effect upon its environment (the rest of the system) is accounted for. The notion of a *Petri Net with Boundaries* provides such a representation.

Roughly speaking, a Petri Net with Boundaries [2] (PNB) represents a sub-net that is to be placed within a larger environment. The key feature of this model is a representation of how a net's transitions may connect with its environment, via "boundary ports". The state graph of a PNB is an automaton in which transition labels record interactions on these boundary ports. Using PNBs, reachability checking of a composed net, N, formed of N_1 and N_2, can be achieved by independently checking the pair of reachability problems on N_1 and N_2 using their labelled state graphs.

Once the state graph of a component PNB has been built, what remains important, in terms of checking reachability of the larger system is only its boundary interactions. This means that state graphs may be minimised with respect to behaviour that does not interact on a boundary. Moreover, these minimised graphs may be further minimised after composition. Our technique exploits this fact to keep the size of state graphs as small as possible. This may appear counter-intuitive as a means of obtaining efficiency, as minimisation is known to be expensive. Judicious use of memoisation comes to the fore here: we target our technique at a class of regular systems that feature many repeated component nets. As such, we expect many repeated reachability checks on the component nets and, crucially, many repeated compositions of such components.

Structure of the paper. In §1 we present the necessary background on Petri Nets with Boundaries, followed in §2 with definitions of the automata encoding reachability in PNBs. The details of our algorithm are given in §3 and in §4 we describe its implementation and detail our experimental results. Finally, we present a proof of correctness of the technique §5 and conclude in §6.

1   Background

In this paper, all Petri nets are assumed to be 1-bounded (a.k.a. *elementary net systems*): there is at most one token at each place. They are closely related to *1-safe nets*, indeed, any 1-safe net is 1-bounded. However, 1-bounded nets are not necessarily 1-safe: the semantics of 1-bounded nets simply prohibits the firing of a transition that would violate the restriction during any execution.

The compositional algebra of Petri nets with boundaries (PNB) is the theoretical workhorse that enables our approach. Here we only give a cursory overview: for formal details, the reader is referred to [2, 21].

A PNB is a Petri net with extra structure: two finite ordinals of *boundary ports*, to which net transitions can connect. Intuitively, transitions connected to a boundary port are not yet completely specified. The two sets of ports are drawn, from top to bottom, on the left and right hand sides of an enclosing box. An example is on the left in Fig. 1: here both boundaries consist of one port. We write $P : (1, 1)$ to mean that P is a PNB with both boundaries of size 1. Differently to [2, 21] we consider "vanilla" PNBs to be unmarked; in §2 we introduce a marked variant that contains both an initial and a target marking.

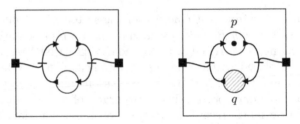

Fig. 1. An example PNB and marked PNB $(1, 1)$

There are two operations for composing PNBs: synchronisation on a common boundary (;) and a non-commutative, parallel composition that we call tensor ($\otimes$). The most interesting operation is synchronisation: we refer to [2] for the formalities, but the graphical intuition shown in Fig. 2 suffices for most examples. Note that the size of the right boundary of P agrees with the size of the left boundary of Q—nets can be composed iff they agree on the size of their intermediate boundary. Given $X : (k, l)$ and $Y : (l, m)$, the composition is written $X \; ; \; Y : (k, m)$. Transitions of the composed net—called *minimal synchronisations*—are, in general, sets of transitions of the two components. In Fig. 2, the transition $\{t, a\}$ results from synchronising t and a. Transition t can synchronise both with a and b; indeed, both choices are taken into account (b also synchronises with u). Transition c has no complementary transition to synchronise with and thus no composite transition results. Finally, v does not connect to any places, only to the fourth boundary port, and is thus synchronised with d.

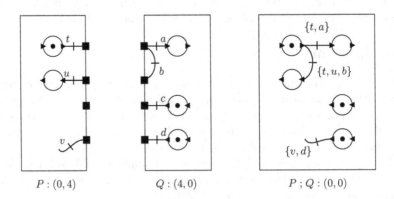

$$P : (0, 4) \qquad Q : (4, 0) \qquad P \; ; \; Q : (0, 0)$$

Fig. 2. Example synchronisation

The second PNB composition operation, tensor, is graphically represented by "stacking" one net on another; intuitively, it is a non-communicating parallel composition. Differently from synchronisation, any two nets can be tensored: given nets $X : (k, l)$ and $Y : (m, n)$, we have $X \otimes Y : (k + m, l + n)$. Both ';' and '$\otimes$' are associative up-to-isomorphism of PNBs, but neither is commutative.

2 From Marked Nets to Automata

A *marked* PNB consists of a PNB together with two subsets of net-places: the *initial* and *target marking*. Graphically, the places belonging to an initial marking are decorated with a token, whilst those belonging to the target marking are shaded. A place can be in both, only one, or neither the initial and a target marking. An example of a marked net is illustrated in the right part of Fig. 1.

Ordinary PNBs have a labelled transition system (LTS) semantics that captures the *step semantics* of the underlying net. The labels record the interactions on the boundaries, as we explain below with the aid of an example. Consider the LTS in the left part of Fig. 3 that corresponds to the left net in Fig. 1.

Let $\mathbb{B} = \{0, 1\}$ and consider a PNB $P : (k, l)$. The states of its LTS correspond to *markings* of P, the transitions to the firings of sets of independent, enabled transitions. Transition labels come from the set $\mathbb{B}^k \times \mathbb{B}^l$. Throughout the paper we write α/β for $(\alpha, \beta) \in \mathbb{B}^k \times \mathbb{B}^l$. A transition labelled with α/β indicates the firing of a set of transitions that is connected to ports on the left as indicated by the 1s in α, and on the right by the 1s in β. For example, in the LTS of Fig. 3, the rightmost transition firing in the PNB of Fig. 1 is represented by the transition labelled $0/1$ in the LTS.

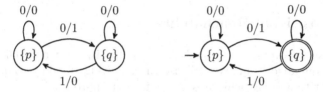

Fig. 3. LTS/NFA semantics of the PNB and marked PNB of Fig. 1

Just as a PNB gives rise to an LTS, a marked PNB gives rise to a non-deterministic finite automaton (NFA). The states and transitions are as described above; the initial state is the state representing the initial marking, while the final state is the state representing the target marking.

The NFAs that arise from PNBs can be composed using operations corresponding to PNB compositions; a specialised nomenclature is therefore useful:

Definition 1. *A non-deterministic finite automaton with boundaries (NFAB) $A : (k, l)$ is a non-deterministic finite automaton A with alphabet $\mathbb{B}^k \times \mathbb{B}^l$. Let $\mathcal{L}(A) \subseteq (\mathbb{B}^k \times \mathbb{B}^l)^*$ denote the language of A.*

Given a PNB $P : (k, l)$, we denote the resulting NFAB $[\![P]\!] : (k, l)$. Note that any ordinary marked net, N, can be regarded as a PNB, $N : (0, 0)$ with no boundaries. The resulting NFAB $[\![N]\!]$ has the alphabet $\mathbb{B}^0 \times \mathbb{B}^0$, which is the singleton—this is precisely the state graph of N w.r.t. step semantics. The following observation, which is central to our approach, is immediate.

Proposition 2. *Supposed that N is a marked net. Then the final marking is reachable from the initial marking iff $\mathcal{L}([\![N]\!]) \neq \varnothing$* □

Finally, we need to explain how NFABs are composed. If $A : (k, l)$, $B : (l, m)$ and $C : (n, o)$ are NFABs then both $A ; B : (k, m)$ and $A \otimes C : (k+n, l+o)$ have as states pairs (a, b) where a is a state of A and b is a state of B. Initial and final states are simply the product of the initial and final states of the component NFABs. The only difference is how the transition relations are defined:

$$\frac{a \xrightarrow{\alpha/\gamma} a' \quad b \xrightarrow{\gamma/\beta} b'}{(a, b) \xrightarrow{\alpha/\beta} (a', b')} \; (;) \qquad \frac{a \xrightarrow{\alpha/\beta} a' \quad b \xrightarrow{\gamma/\delta} b'}{(a, b) \xrightarrow{\alpha\gamma/\beta\delta} (a', b')} \; (\otimes)$$

The following is straightforward to show and builds on known compositionality properties of PNBs [2].

Proposition 3 (Compositionality). *Given PNBs P, Q, we have $[\![P ; Q]\!] \cong [\![P]\!] ; [\![Q]\!]$ and $[\![P \otimes Q]\!] \cong [\![P]\!] \otimes [\![Q]\!]$, where $\cong$ is isomorphism of automata, defined in the obvious way as bijective mappings on states and transitions.*

Of particular interest to our approach are NFA transitions witnessing the firing of net transitions that are not connected to any boundary ports. Thus we let $\tau_{k,l} \stackrel{\text{def}}{=} 0^k/0^l$. We will refer to $\tau_{k,l}$ as a τ-move or *silent move*.

3   Compositional Reachability

In this section we explain our technique for compositional reachability checking and present our algorithm. We will use the following running example, which features a net that is particularly suitable for our approach.

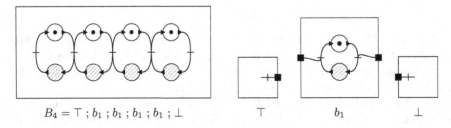

$$B_4 = \top ; b_1 ; b_1 ; b_1 ; b_1 ; \bot \qquad\qquad \top \qquad\qquad b_1 \qquad\qquad \bot$$

Fig. 4. The net B_4 as a composition of nets $\top$, b_1 and $\bot$.

Example 4. Consider the marked PNB, B_4, shown in Fig. 4 that models a 4 place buffer [9]. It enjoys a simple, regular structure, yet the number of transitions that need to be fired in order to reach the target marking is quadratic in the size of the buffer[1]. Using marked PNBs, we can express B_4 as:

$$\top ; (b_1 ; (b_1 ; (b_1 ; (b_1 ; \bot)))) \tag{1}$$

---

[1] Precisely, the length of the minimal firing sequence of B_i is the ith triangle number.

Our procedure takes a *decomposition* of a net as an input: roughly an expression akin to (1), expressing a net as a composition of simple components. We represent decompositions using *wiring expressions*; a wiring expression is the abstract syntax tree, t, of a PNB expression, where internal nodes are labelled with either ; or $\otimes$, and leaves are (possibly repeated) variables.

$$T ::= x \mid T ; T \mid T \otimes T$$

Now, a wiring expression together with an assignment map, $\mathcal{V}$, taking variables to marked PNBs, can be evaluated recursively to obtain a marked PNB, $[\![t]\!]_{\mathcal{V}}$:

$$[\![x]\!]_{\mathcal{V}} \stackrel{\text{def}}{=} \mathcal{V}(x) \qquad [\![t_1 ; t_2]\!]_{\mathcal{V}} \stackrel{\text{def}}{=} [\![t_1]\!]_{\mathcal{V}} ; [\![t_2]\!]_{\mathcal{V}} \qquad [\![t_1 \otimes t_2]\!]_{\mathcal{V}} \stackrel{\text{def}}{=} [\![t_1]\!]_{\mathcal{V}} \otimes [\![t_2]\!]_{\mathcal{V}}$$

We assume that variable assignments are compatible with t, in the sense that only nets with compatible boundaries are composed; in recent work, we used a simple type system to ensure this [24]. Given a net $N : (k, l)$, we say that $(t, \mathcal{V})$ is a *wiring decomposition* of N if $[\![t]\!]_{\mathcal{V}} \cong N$.

Example 5. The following are the wiring expression and variable assignment that correspond to (1):

$$t = x_1 ; (x_2 ; (x_2 ; (x_2 ; (x_2 ; x_3)))) \qquad \mathcal{V} = \{x_1 \mapsto \top, x_2 \mapsto b_1, x_3 \mapsto \bot\} \quad (2)$$

observe that $[\![t]\!]_{\mathcal{V}}$ is B_4, shown in the left side of Fig. 4; $(t, \mathcal{V})$ is therefore a wiring decomposition of B_4.

Consider any net N, together with corresponding initial and target markings. Given any ordinary PNB expression for N, notice that we can extend it into a wiring decomposition: first by translating the expression into a wiring expression, second by translating the initial and target markings of N component-wise into marked PNBs, that we bind to the variables. The *specification* of the reachability problem is thus naturally compositional.

The core idea of our algorithm is to convert a wiring decomposition $(t, \mathcal{V})$ of a net N to an—ideally small—NFAB that represents the "protocol" that N must adhere to w.r.t. its context (i.e. the nets connected to its boundaries), in order to reach its local target marking. The key property exploited by the algorithm is that *weak language equivalence is a congruence*[2] (Proposition 8): any weak language-preserving modifications can be made to a PNB's NFAB whilst ensuring a faithful representation of all interactions the PNB must perform to reach its target marking. Showing that weak language equivalence is a congruence is thus the key technical ingredient needed to show the correctness of our technique; this is the topic of §5.

Concretely, given an NFAB we perform *(i)* τ-closure, ignoring internal moves, and *(ii)* NFA minimisation to prune the statespace, preserving language equivalence. We leverage the structure of wiring decompositions by using memoisation to prevent repeated computation. Our algorithm maintains two maps:

---

[2] The adjective 'weak' refers to the forgetting of the τ-moves. See §5 for the formal definition.

1. knownNetNFAs, from component nets to their corresponding reduced NFABs,
2. knownNFAComps, from two NFABs and composition type, to reduced NFABs.

The second memoisation map is checked for membership up-to language-equivalence: $(n_1, n_2, Op) \in$ knownNFAComps is true if knownNFAComps contains an entry (n_1', n_2', Op) such that $n_1 \sim n_1'$ and $n_2 \sim n_2'$, where $\sim$ is language equivalence. The essence of this optimisation is that if we perform a (potentially expensive) composition and reduction on a pair of NFABs, we never repeat this computation for *any* pair of NFABs that are pairwise language equivalent.

The core algorithm is given in Fig. 5, and we briefly outline its steps here. The input wiring decomposition is traversed; each unique leaf (component net) is converted to its NFAB, which is then τ-closed and reduced, with memoisation (Line 3) preventing repeated performance of this conversion for equal components. On composition nodes, the procedure recurses on both child branches, to obtain a (reduced) NFAB for each; then, if the pair of NFABs is unique (up-to language-equivalence) they are composed using the appropriate operation on NFABs, before being τ-closed and reduced. Again, memoisation (Line 13) prevents unnecessary repeated computation.

Require: knownNetNFAs, knownNFAComps initially empty
1: **procedure** WDTONFA(t)
2:     **if** t is a PNB **then**
3:         **if** $t \in$ knownNetNFAs **then**
4:             **return** knownNetNFAs$[t]$
5:         **else**
6:             $n \leftarrow$ REDUCE(τ-CLOSE(NETTONFA(t)))
7:             knownNetNFAs$[t] := n$
8:             **return** n
9:         **end if**
10:     **else**   ▷ t is $(t_1, t_2, \mathtt{OP})$
11:         $n_1 \leftarrow$ WDTONFA(t_1)
12:         $n_2 \leftarrow$ WDTONFA(t_2)
13:         **if** $(n_1, n_2, \mathtt{OP}) \in$ knownNFAComps **then**   ▷ Up-to language equivalence
14:             **return** knownNFAComps$[(n_1, n_2, \mathtt{OP})]$
15:         **else**
16:             $n \leftarrow$ REDUCE(τ-CLOSE(n_1 OP n_2))
17:             knownNFAComps$[(n_1, n_2, \mathtt{OP})] := n$
18:             **return** n
19:         **end if**
20:     **end if**
21: **end procedure**

Fig. 5. Core Algorithm

Now since any ordinary net N can be considered as a PNB with no boundaries, running our algorithm on any wiring decomposition of N as input will construct an NFAB with the singleton alphabet $\{\tau_{0,0}\}$. Up to weak language equivalence there are only two such NFABs, both with one state that is either accepting (indicating a *reachable* desired marking) or non-accepting (indicating an *unreachable* desired marking). Therefore, running our core algorithm on a wiring decomposition of N decides the classical reachability problem for N.

It should be highlighted that our algorithm decides a modified version of the reachability problem: we take a wiring decomposition as input. When run on the trivial decomposition, the performance would typically be unsatisfactory since, for example, no partial order reduction techniques are employed when generating the state graph. The scalability of our algorithm thus depends on finding efficient decompositions. In our experience, finding suitable candidate decompositions is not difficult: concurrent and distributed systems are typically designed, and described, in a component-wise, rather than monolithic manner.

4   Implementation and Results

The core algorithm described in the previous section has been implemented in Haskell, as part of the `Penrose` tool. In the implementation we use current state-of-the-art algorithms for both: language-equivalence checking via bisimulation up-to techniques due to Bonchi and Pous [1], and NFA minimisation using forward and backwards variants of simulation of Clemente and Mayr [15].

Example 6. The running time of our implementation on the buffer nets of our running example is *linear* w.r.t. the size of the input net. Indeed, each additional component simply leads to another (successful) memoisation-map lookup, with constant cost. Contrast this with the fact that the minimum firing sequence is quadratic w.r.t. the size of the buffer, as described in Exm. 4. Checking reachability for buffer nets thus asymptotically outperforms approaches based on firing transitions in the global net: see the first five rows in the results Table 1.

As we have explained in §3, `Penrose` takes as input a wiring decomposition; Since problem descriptions in the literature are naturally described in terms of their constituent components, it is little work to arrive at high-level descriptions using the DSL recently introduced by the 2nd and 3rd authors [24]. The DSL programs evaluate to a wiring expression, that we have used as inputs to `Penrose`; alternatively, they can be evaluated to monolithic nets, which we have used as input to other tools for performance comparisons. Indeed, using `Penrose` it is possible to generate arbitrary instances of commonly used benchmarks.

The relative performance of `Penrose` was evaluated [3] by comparing it with the current state-of-the-art tools, all of which use unfolding-based approaches:

---

[3] All experiments were run on an Ubuntu Linux virtual machine (4-core 32-bit CPU, 8GB RAM) hosted on an Intel i7-2600 3.40GHz CPU, 16GB of RAM, running 64-bit Ubuntu Linux[4]. Tool performance was recorded using the standard Unix `time` command, measuring total (wall-clock) time and peak memory usage.

[4] Some tools required a 32-bit platform, hence the virtual machine.

1. LOLA [20], an established tool and winner of the reachability category of 2013 Petri Net model checking competition,
2. The PUNF[5] unfolder, which uses parallelisation techniques from [10] and CLP[6] checker, which uses linear-programming techniques from [14],
3. CUNF [19] unfolder, a recently-introduced tool[7], using the CNA checker.

In Table 1, T indicates a time-out (5 minutes), M denotes memory-exhaustion (8GB) and / marks an incorrect result; the best performance of each problem instance is highlighted.

As mentioned, **Penrose** directly computes using the particular wiring decomposition, $(t, \mathcal{V})$, that specifies each problem; all other tools were provided input that was generated by first computing $[\![t]\!]_{\mathcal{V}}$, and then converting into suitable format[8]. The time taken for this conversion was not included in the performance benchmarking—only the processing time of the individual tools was recorded.

The majority of problems in Table 1 are taken from Corbett's [6] benchmarks, except those marked with a ∗, which we briefly discuss here: *counter* is taken from [24], and models a distributed n-bit counter. It is an unsafe net, leading to incorrect results from CLP/CNA. *replicator* is taken from [22], modelling a sequence of components that can output an unbounded number of tokens at their right boundary after receiving a single token on their left boundary. Again, it is an unsafe net. Taken from [12], *iter-choice* models a sequence of transition choices. A

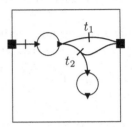

Fig. 6. iter-choice net

single component is illusrated in Fig. 6, the transition choice is between t_1 and t_2. Due to an exponentially-sized unfolding, the results show that moderately-sized instances[9] of iter-choice cannot be handled by the tested tools. **Penrose**, on the other hand, is able to handle very large instances quickly. Merged Processes [12] were designed to avoid such exponential unfoldings.

The time-vs-problem size results for **Penrose** are plotted in Fig. 7. There is a clear distinction between the scalable examples, and those that are (much) less scalable. The causes of the poor performance include increase in (language inequivalent) NFA sizes, as the wiring decomposition is traversed: each new NFA grows the memoisation map, and larger NFAs take longer to check for language (in)equivalence. The examples with good performance (e.g. Exm. 4) quickly reach fixed-points w.r.t. composition, in that no new NFAs are ever generated after a certain point; indeed, the buffer reaches a fixed point at $n = 1$.

Statespace growth is unavoidable in systems such as the counter; it is an inherent problem with the compositional approach. In this case, avoiding the

---

[5] http://homepages.cs.ncl.ac.uk/victor.khomenko/tools/punf/

[6] http://homepages.cs.ncl.ac.uk/victor.khomenko/tools/clp/

[7] http://code.google.com/p/cunf/

[8] Either LL_NET format or LOLA's input format.

[9] Checking for an alternating taken/not-taken marking.

Table 1. Time and Memory results

Problem		Time (s)				Max Resident (MB)			
name	size	LOLA	CLP	CNA	Penrose	LOLA	CLP	CNA	Penrose
buffer	8	**0.001**	0.003	0.017	**0.001**	**7.51**	33.30	38.45	14.36
buffer	32	**0.001**	0.013	0.824	**0.001**	**7.51**	34.49	48.09	14.35
buffer	512	0.058	*T*	*M*	**0.001**	83.44	*T*	*M*	**14.40**
buffer	4096	*T*	*T*	*M*	**0.002**	*T*	*T*	*M*	**14.70**
buffer	32768	*T*	*T*	*M*	**0.005**	*T*	*T*	*M*	**16.07**
over	8	31.039	0.008	1.071	**0.003**	3812.00	37.63	141.85	**16.53**
over	32	*M*	*T*	*M*	**0.003**	*M*	*T*	*M*	**16.52**
over	512	*M*	*T*	*M*	**0.003**	*M*	*T*	*M*	**16.52**
over	4096	*M*	*T*	*M*	**0.003**	*M*	*T*	*M*	**16.53**
over	32768	*M*	*T*	*M*	**0.004**	*M*	*T*	*M*	**17.85**
dac	8	**0.001**	0.003	0.017	**0.001**	**7.51**	33.28	38.85	15.37
dac	32	**0.001**	0.005	0.028	**0.001**	**7.50**	34.50	49.45	15.34
dac	512	0.005	*T*	255.847	**0.001**	20.62	*T*	6012.00	**15.36**
dac	4096	2.462	*T*	*M*	**0.002**	166.07	*T*	*M*	**15.62**
dac	32768	*T*	*T*	*M*	**0.009**	*T*	*T*	*M*	**16.91**
philo	8	**0.002**	0.003	0.016	0.004	**8.86**	33.22	38.54	16.98
philo	32	*M*	**0.003**	0.017	0.004	*M*	33.53	40.87	**16.97**
philo	512	*M*	0.020	0.086	**0.004**	*M*	41.69	290.77	**16.90**
philo	4096	*M*	7.853	*M*	**0.004**	*M*	172.76	*M*	**17.13**
philo	32768	*M*	*T*	*M*	**0.005**	*M*	*T*	*M*	**18.32**
hartstone	8	**0.000**	0.002	/	0.002	**7.51**	33.05	/	15.48
hartstone	32	**0.001**	0.002	/	0.002	**7.52**	33.22	/	15.48
hartstone	512	0.002	0.005	/	**0.001**	17.82	36.38	/	**15.49**
hartstone	4096	0.044	0.029	/	**0.002**	96.27	58.15	/	**15.74**
hartstone	32768	56.050	3.008	*M*	**0.003**	727.63	278.23	*M*	**17.10**
iter-choice*	8	0.006	5.025	19.062	**0.002**	36.37	465.17	1570.64	**15.34**
iter-choice*	32	*M*	*T*	*T*	**0.002**	*M*	*T*	*T*	**15.34**
iter-choice*	512	*M*	*T*	*T*	**0.002**	*M*	*T*	*T*	**15.38**
iter-choice*	4096	*M*	*T*	*T*	**0.002**	*M*	*T*	*T*	**15.56**
iter-choice*	32768	*M*	*T*	*T*	**0.003**	*M*	*T*	*T*	**16.95**
replicator*	8	**0.001**	/	0.016	**0.001**	**7.51**	/	38.15	15.39
replicator*	32	**0.001**	/	0.017	**0.001**	**7.51**	/	39.41	15.40
replicator*	512	0.002	/	1.023	**0.001**	**14.72**	/	77.87	15.41
replicator*	4096	0.062	/	64.046	**0.002**	86.85	/	3256.00	**15.56**
replicator*	32768	91.646	/	*M*	**0.006**	1524.50	/	*M*	**16.97**
counter*	8	**0.001**	/	/	0.050	**7.51**	/	/	20.61
counter*	16	**0.000**	/	/	4.056	**7.51**	/	/	22.52
counter*	32	**0.001**	/	/	46.027	**7.51**	/	/	39.66
counter*	64	**0.001**	/	/	*T*	**8.60**	/	/	*T*
token-ring	8	**0.001**	0.007	0.071	1.024	**7.51**	39.96	89.81	20.74
token-ring	16	**1.824**	*T*	*T*	12.034	318.08	*T*	*T*	**24.77**
token-ring	32	*M*	*T*	*T*	**133.636**	*M*	*T*	*T*	**39.65**
token-ring	64	*M*	*T*	*T*	*T*	*M*	*T*	*T*	*T*

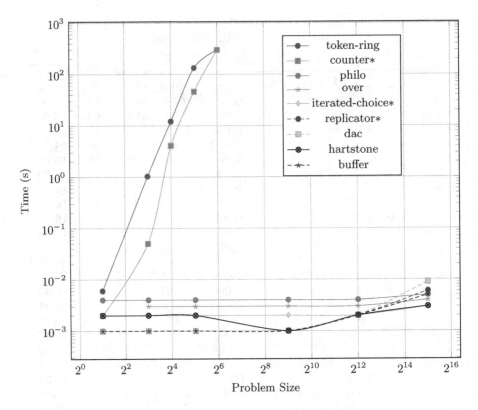

Fig. 7. Time vs Problem size for `Penrose`

slowdown could be achieved by observing a monotone increase in state size and abandoning the component-wise approach, falling back to other techniques.

It could be argued that the playing field is unfair: `Penrose` uses a formal description of the decomposition of a problem at hand into smaller components while other tools take a global, monolithic net as input. This is, however, precisely our point: there is no reason for model checkers not to take advantage of compositional descriptions–it is how *real* systems are designed and described.

5   Proof of Correctness

In this section we outline a proof that the algorithm presented in Fig. 5 is correct. Given NFABs $A, B : (k, l)$, A and B are said to be *(strong) language equivalent*, written $A \sim B$, if $\mathcal{L}(A) = \mathcal{L}(B)$. The following result is simple to show, using the definitions of ; and $\otimes$ on NFABs.

Proposition 7 (Strong language equivalence is a congruence). *Suppose that A and A' are NFABs and $A \sim A'$. Then the following hold, where in each point below, B ranges over those NFAB where the composition is defined.*

$(i)\ A\ ;\ B \sim A'\ ;\ B$ $\qquad\qquad$ $(ii)\ B\ ;\ A \sim B\ ;\ A'$

$(iii)\ A \otimes B \sim A' \otimes B$ $\qquad$ $(iv)\ B \otimes A \sim B \otimes A'$ $\quad\square$

Now let $\hat{-} : (\mathbb{B}^k \times \mathbb{B}^l)^* \to (\mathbb{B}^k \times \mathbb{B}^l - \{\tau_{k,l}\})^*$ be the unique monoid homomorphism where, on elements x of $\mathbb{B}^k \times \mathbb{B}^l$, $\hat{x} = \epsilon$ if $x = \tau_{k,l}$ and x otherwise. Intuitively, $\hat{x}$ results from stripping the silent moves from $\mathbf{x}$. Given a NFAB $A : (k,l)$ we define $\mathcal{L}^\tau(A) \stackrel{\text{def}}{=} \{\hat{\mathbf{x}} \mid \mathbf{x} \in \mathcal{L}(A)\}$. NFABs $A, B : (k,l)$ are said to be *weak language equivalent*, written $A \approx B$, when $\mathcal{L}^\tau(A) = \mathcal{L}^\tau(B)$.

An NFAB $A : (k,l)$ is said to be *reflexive* if for all states $a \in A$ we have a loop transition $a \xrightarrow{\tau_{k,l}} a$. When we restrict our attention to reflexive NFABs, also weak language equivalence is a congruence.

Proposition 8. *Suppose that A and A' are reflexive NFABs and $A \approx A'$. Then the following hold, where at each point below B ranges those over reflexive NFABs where the composition is defined.*

$(i)\ A\ ;\ B \approx A'\ ;\ B$ $\qquad\qquad$ $(ii)\ B\ ;\ A \approx B\ ;\ A'$

$(iii)\ A \otimes B \approx A' \otimes B$ $\qquad$ $(iv)\ B \otimes A \approx B \otimes A'$ $\quad\square$

Any NFAB that results from a marked PNB is reflexive, since the empty set of transitions can fire at any marking, yielding a τ-move in the underlying NFAB. The reductions performed in Fig. 5 replace reflexive NFABs with smaller, weak language equivalent automata. Correctness is a straightforward consequence.

Theorem 9. *The algorithm in Fig. 5 is correct: the computed NFAB is weak language equivalent to the semantics of the corresponding global net.* $\quad\square$

6 Related Work and Discussion

We introduced a technique for checking reachability that takes a decomposition of a net as input and relies on the use of weak language equivalence to discard local state. The compositional approach was briefly discussed in [22] and in the technical report [23], where further examples are described in detail. Initial efforts were based on determinisation, which was considerably more expensive than our current use of NFA minimisation [15] and language equivalence checking [1].

The algebra of automata with boundaries used in this paper is an instance of the algebra of Span(Graph) [11]. The goal of the more recent work [2, 3, 21] was to lift this algebra to the level of nets in a compositional way and explore connections with process algebra: our approach ignores local state and focusses only on external interactions: here we were inspired by the ideas of Milner [17].

The tools that we have used in order to compare our performance are based on the unfolding approach pioneered by McMillan [16]. The algorithm to compute finite complete prefix was improved in [9, 13]. Unfoldings carry more information about the computations of nets than merely reachability, for instance, allowing LTL model checking [7]. For an overview of the extensive field see [8].

References

1. Bonchi, F., Pous, D.: Checking NFA Equivalence with Bisimulations up to Congruence. In: PoPL (2013)
2. Bruni, R., Melgratti, H., Montanari, U., Sobociński, P.: Connector algebras for C/E and P/T nets' Interactions. Logical Methods in Computer Science 9(3) (2013)
3. Bruni, R., Melgratti, H., Montanari, U.: A connector algebra for P/T nets interactions. In: Katoen, J.-P., König, B. (eds.) CONCUR 2011. LNCS, vol. 6901, pp. 312–326. Springer, Heidelberg (2011)
4. Cheng, A., Esparza, J., Palsberg, J.: Complexity results for 1-safe nets. In: Shyamasundar, R.K. (ed.) FSTTCS 1993. LNCS, vol. 761, pp. 326–337. Springer, Heidelberg (1993)
5. Clarke, E.M., Long, D., McMillan, K.: Compositional model checking. In: LiCS 1989, pp. 352–362 (1989)
6. Corbett, J.C.: Evaluating Deadlock Detection Methods for Concurrent Software. IEEE Transactions on Software Engineering 22(3), 161–180 (1996)
7. Esparza, J., Heljanko, K.: Implementing LTL model checking with net unfoldings. In: Dwyer, M.B. (ed.) SPIN 2001. LNCS, vol. 2057, pp. 37–56. Springer, Heidelberg (2001)
8. Esparza, J., Heljanko, K.: Unfoldings: a partial-order approach to model checking. Springer (2008)
9. Esparza, J., Römer, S., Vogler, W.: An improvement of McMillan's unfolding algorithm. Form Method Syst Des 30(3), 285–310 (2002)
10. Heljanko, K., Khomenko, V., Koutny, M.: Parallelisation of the Petri Net Unfolding Algorithm. In: Katoen, J.-P., Stevens, P. (eds.) TACAS 2002. LNCS, vol. 2280, pp. 371–385. Springer, Heidelberg (2002)
11. Katis, P., Sabadini, N., Walters, R.F.C.: Span(Graph): A categorical algebra of transition systems. In: Johnson, M. (ed.) AMAST 1997. LNCS, vol. 1349, pp. 307–321. Springer, Heidelberg (1997)
12. Khomenko, V., Kondratyev, A., Koutny, M., Vogler, W.: Merged Processes — A New Condensed Representation of Petri Net Behaviour. In: Abadi, M., de Alfaro, L. (eds.) CONCUR 2005. LNCS, vol. 3653, pp. 338–352. Springer, Heidelberg (2005)
13. Khomenko, V., Koutny, M., Vogler, W.: Canonical prefixes of Petri net unfoldings. Acta Inform. 40(2), 95–118 (2003)
14. Koutny, M., Khomenko, V.: Linear Programming Deadlock Checking Using Partial Order Dependencies. Technical report, Newcastle University (2000)
15. Mayr, R., Clemente, L.: Advanced Automata Minimization. In: POPL (2013)
16. McMillan, K.: A technique of a state space search based on unfolding. Form. Method Syst. Des. 6(1), 45–65 (1995)
17. Milner, R.: A Calculus of Communicating Systems. Prentice Hall (1989)
18. Nielsen, M., Plotkin, G., Winskel, G.: Petri Nets, Event Structures and Domains, Part I. Theoretical Computer Science 13(1), 85–108 (1981)
19. Rodríguez, C., Schwoon, S.: Cunf: A Tool for Unfolding and Verifying Petri Nets with Read Arcs. In: Van Hung, D., Ogawa, M. (eds.) ATVA 2013. LNCS, vol. 8172, pp. 492–495. Springer, Heidelberg (2013)
20. Schmidt, K.: LoLA A Low Level Analyser. In: Nielsen, M., Simpson, D. (eds.) ICATPN 2000. LNCS, vol. 1825, pp. 465–474. Springer, Heidelberg (2000)
21. Sobociński, P.: Representations of petri net interactions. In: Gastin, P., Laroussinie, F. (eds.) CONCUR 2010. LNCS, vol. 6269, pp. 554–568. Springer, Heidelberg (2010)

22. Sobociński, P., Stephens, O.: **Penrose**: Putting Compositionality to Work for Petri Net Reachability. In: Heckel, R., Milius, S. (eds.) CALCO 2013. LNCS, vol. 8089, pp. 346–352. Springer, Heidelberg (2013)
23. Sobociński, P., Stephens, O.: Reachability via compositionality in Petri nets. arXiv:1303.1399v1 (2013)
24. Sobociński, P., Stephens, O.: A Programming Language for Spatial Distribution of Net Systems. In: Ciardo, G., Kindler, E. (eds.) PETRI NETS 2014. LNCS, vol. 8489, pp. 150–169. Springer, Heidelberg (2014)
25. Starke, P.: Reachability analysis of Petri nets using symmetries. Systems Analysis Modelling Simulation 5, 292–303 (1991)

Author Index